Einarr Skúlason's *Geisli*

A CRITICAL EDITION

Geisli is the earliest Nordic Christian drápa (long stanzaic poem) known to exist. Written by Einarr Skúlason, the twelfth century's premier Icelandic poet, *Geisli* marked a stylistic shift in Old Norse poetry brought about by Christianity and European learning. Einarr Skúlason was a priest as well as a skald, and his writing demonstrates that he was as familiar with the traditions of Latin liturgy and hagiography as with the conventions of skaldic poetry.

Geisli is a very important source for the modern scholar studying Old Norse hagiography and the history of Christianity in Iceland and Norway. This new critical edition features a version in normalized orthography, as well as a version in prose word order, a translation into English, a complete glossary, an introduction that situates the poem in its context, and substantial explanatory notes. Editor Martin Chase uses the famous *Flateyjarbók* manuscript as a base text, but takes into account all known manuscripts of the poem. Long needed by scholars, this new edition will be extremely valuable to anyone with an interest in Old Norse as well as medievalists in other disciplines.

(Toronto Old Norse and Icelandic Studies)

MARTIN CHASE is a professor in the Department of English and the Center for Medieval Studies at Fordham University

Einarr Skúlason's *Geisli*

A CRITICAL EDITION

Edited by Martin Chase

UNIVERSITY OF TORONTO PRESS
Toronto Buffalo London

© University of Toronto Press Incorporated 2005
Toronto Buffalo London
Printed in Canada

ISBN 0-8020-3826-3 (cloth)
ISBN 0-8020-3822-0 (paper)

Printed on acid-free paper

Library and Archives Canada Cataloguing in Publication

Einarr Skúlason, prestr, 1090 (ca.) – 1165.
  Einarr Skúlason's Geisli : a critical edition / edited by Martin Chase.

  (Toronto Old Norse and Icelandic studies)
  Includes bibliographical references and index.
  ISBN 0-8020-3826-3 (bound). – ISBN 0-8020-3822-0 (pbk.)

  1. Einarr Skúlason, prestr, 1090 (ca.) – 1165. Geisli.   2. Einarr
Skúlason, prestr, 1090 (ca.) – 1165 – Translations into English.   I. Chase,
Martin, 1953–   II. Title.   III. Series.

PT7328.E47G4 2005   839′.61   C2005-902243-4

University of Toronto Press acknowledges the financial assistance to its publishing
program of the Canada Council for the Arts and the Ontario Arts Council.

University of Toronto Press acknowledges the financial support for its publishing
activities of the Government of Canada through the Book Publishing Industry
Development Program (BPIDP).

Contents

Acknowledgments

This project has been underway long enough for me to incur many debts. Roberta Frank introduced me to skaldic poetry and guided the edition through its first incarnation as my doctoral dissertation at the University of Toronto. George Tate suggested that I take on *Geisli*, and his edition of *Líknarbraut* served as a model and an inspiration. Angus Cameron, Denton Fox, Frances Nims, and Ursula Dronke also gave helpful advice in the early stages. A Fulbright grant provided funds for a year of manuscript research in Denmark and Iceland, and grants from the American Council of Learned Societies and the Pontifical Institute of Mediaeval Studies made possible a postdoctoral year. Funds for summer visits to libraries abroad came from the American Philosophical Society. Peter Springborg, Jonna Louis-Jensen, and Rolf Stavnem offered gracious hospitality and good advice at Det Arnamagnæanske Institut in Copenhagen on more than one occasion, as did Vésteinn Ólason, Sverrir Tómasson, Guðrún Nordal, and Valgerður Erna Þorvaldsdóttir at Stofnun Árnamagnússonar á Íslandi and the University of Iceland. I am especially grateful to Valgerður for reviewing the prose versions of the stanzas with an eye to improving the Icelandic syntax. Ian McDougall valiantly read the entire manuscript and offered many helpful suggestions, and I am likewise thankful for the detailed comments of the readers of the University of Toronto Press. Michael Agnew, Susan Boynton, Giuseppe Gerbino, Marlene Villalobos Hennessy, David McDougall, Margaret Pappano, and Jens Ulff-Møller all read parts of the manuscript and made comments, and my colleagues at Fordham, Mary Erler, Thelma Fenster, Maryanne Kowaleski, and Jocelyn Wogan-Browne, shared their wisdom and encouragement as I worked to complete the project. Charlotte Labbe and Christine Campbell of the Interlibrary Loan Department of the Walsh Library at Fordham never failed to provide. The assistance of Barbara Porter and Allyson N. May of the University of Toronto Press lies hidden on almost every page. Finally, I am grateful to Dr John Hollwitz and the Office of Academic Affairs at Fordham University for generous financial support of the publication of this book, and to my parents and my Jesuit brothers for that which cannot be quantified.

Einarr Skúlason's *Geisli*

A CRITICAL EDITION

Introduction

Manuscripts of *Geisli*

Complete texts of *Geisli* are found in two medieval manuscripts, both from the late fourteenth century: GKS 1005, fol., or *Flateyjarbók*, and Holm perg. fol. nr. 1, or *Bergsbók*. Both of these manuscripts are considerably younger than the *drápa* itself and represent different textual traditions. Unfortunately, nothing is known of how the *drápa* survived, more or less intact from its composition in 1153 until it was recorded in *Flateyjarbók*. In view of the circumstances surrounding its origin, it seems likely that the text would have been committed to parchment immediately,[1] but no manuscript evidence attests to this.

In addition to the texts in *Flateyjarbók* and *Bergsbók*, individual stanzas (*vísur* or *helmingar*) are quoted in three important works: the *Snorra Edda*, *Heimskringla*, and the saga of St Óláfr known as *Den store saga* or the Great Saga. Parts of *Geisli* are found in all five of the primary manuscripts of *Snorra Edda*: AM 748 I, 4to (*A*); GKS 2367, 4to, or *Codex Regius* (*R*); Utrecht manuscript 1374, or *Codex Trajectinus* (*T*); DG 11, 4to, or *Codex Upsaliensis* (*U*); and AM 242, fol., or *Codex Wormianus* (*W*). Five *Heimskringla* manuscripts contain stanzas from *Geisli*: AM 47, fol., or *Eirspennill* (*E*); AM 66, fol., or *Hulda* (*H*); GKS 1010, fol., or *Hrokkinskinna* (*Hr*); AM 63, fol., a transcript of the lost *Kringla* manuscript (*K*); and AM 39, fol. (*O*). *Flateyjarbók* (*F*) and *Bergsbók* (*B*) contain texts of the late, encyclopedic 'Great Saga' (*Den store saga*), and in this edition the portions of *Geisli* quoted in the Óláfs saga texts of these manuscripts are designated *Fx* and *Bx* to distinguish them from citations of the complete texts found elsewhere in the manuscripts. Other manuscripts of *Den store saga* that contain parts of *Geisli* include AM 73a, fol., a transcript of the lost *Bæjarbók* (*P*); GKS 1008, fol., or *Thomasskinna* (*Tm*); Holm perg. 4to nr. 2 (*Y*); and Holm perg. 4to nr. 4 (*Z*).

Finally, *Geisli* is preserved in eleven seventeenth- and eighteenth-century manuscripts: AM 1009, 4to; AM 72, fol.; Copenhagen KB Thott 1498, 4to; Oslo UB 262, fol.; Trondheim DKNVSB 3, 4to; Oxford Boreales 102; Reykjavík Lbs. 444, 4to; Reykjavík JS 260, 4to; Reykjavík JS 406, 4to; Edinburgh Advocates' 21.2.9; and Edinburgh Advocates' 21.8.14. All of these manuscripts are transcripts of *Flateyjarbók*, and although I have examined them (with the exception of the Edinburgh and Trondheim manuscripts, where I used photographs), they were not used in the preparation of this edition.

Flateyjarbók is the largest of the surviving Icelandic parchment manuscripts. It consists of 225 leaves, each measuring 42.5   29 cm. Since the eighteenth century the manuscript has been bound in two volumes. It contains the following texts: *Geisli, Óláfsrima Haraldssonar, Hyndluljóð, Ór Kristnisǫgu meistara Adams, Þáttr frá Sigurði konungi slefu, Hversu Nóregr bygðizt, Ættartǫlur, Eiríks saga víðfǫrla, Óláfs saga Tryggvasonar, Óláfs saga hins helga, Sverris saga, Hákonar saga Hákonarsonar, Viðbætir við Óláfs saga hins helga, Magnúss saga hins góða ok Haralds saga harðráða, Hemings Þáttr Áslákssonar, Auðunar Þáttr vestfirzka, Sneglu-Halla Þáttr, Halldórs Þáttr Snorrasonar, Þórsteins Þáttr tjaldstæðings, Blóðegils Þáttr, Helga Þáttr ok Úlfs, Eðvarðar saga hins helga, Annálar.*[2]

Bergsbók is a large codex, its parchment leaves measuring 32   24 cm. The contents of the manuscript are a collection of texts associated with Óláfr Tryggvason and St Óláfr Haraldsson: *Óláfs saga Tryggvasonar, Rekstefja, Óláfs drápa Tryggvasonar, Lilja, Geisli, The Great Saga of St Óláfr.*[3]

This edition is in the form of a corrected base text, with variant readings from the other manuscripts. Neither of the two manuscripts of the complete text has clear advantages over the other: three stanzas are missing from *F*, but the arrangement of the stanzas in that manuscript is better than in *B*. Both manuscripts are highly corrupt, but the language and orthography of *F* are more regular, and for these reasons I have chosen it over *B* as the base manuscript. My editorial principle has been to attempt to make sense of the *F* text as it stands and to avoid emendation wherever possible, but where *F* is hopelessly corrupt I have emended (usually supplying a reading from one of the other manuscripts) rather than abandon the line as a *locus desperandus*. All emendations should be regarded only as suggestions: the reader is encouraged to use the information provided in the apparatus and consider other possible solutions.

Each stanza is also presented in a version of the text with the spellings in the classical forms used in ON lexicography, and the primary purpose of this normalized orthography is to facilitate reference to dictionaries and grammars. The punctuation, which attempts to designate sentences and parenthetic phrases, represents my understanding of the syntax and is normally explained in the notes that follow. Again this is not meant to be definitive, but rather an illustration of my own reading of the stanza. Often the syntax can (and probably should) be construed in a variety of ways, and the reader is urged to refer primarily to the unpunctuated text and avoid constraining his or her imagination.

Manuscript Distribution of Individual Stanzas

A	stanzas 1.1–4, 16.5–8
B	stanzas 1–71
Bx	stanza 37
E	stanza 37
F	stanzas 1–30, 34–71
Fx	stanza 37
H	stanzas 28, 30
Hr	stanzas 28, 29, 30.1–4
K	stanza 37
O	stanza 37
P	stanza 37
R	stanza 16.5–8
T	stanza 16.5–8
Tm	stanza 37
U	stanzas 16.5–8
W	stanzas 1.1–4, 16.5–8, 59.5–8
Y	stanza 37
Z	stanza 37

Editions of *Geisli*

Gerhardus Schöning, ed. *Heimskringla eðr Noregs Konunga Sögur*. 3 vols. Copenhagen, 1777–1826, 3: 461–80.

A text of *Geisli* is appended to Schöning's early edition of *Heimskringla*. It is based entirely on *Flateyjarbók*, and is accompanied by parallel translations into Danish and Latin. Schöning emends frequently, for reasons of both metre and sense, and his emendations are surprisingly sane and judicious even though they are not based on manuscript evidence. He does not supply *bragarmál*, or elision of vowels for the sake of the metre, and he preserves the *Flateyjarbók* orthography with a few exceptions: the long vowels *é* and *á*, which are often written 'ee' and 'aa' in the manuscript, are rendered as 'é' and 'á,' and all other long vowels are similarly marked with acute accents. The vowel *ǫ*, usually written 'o' in the manuscript, is rendered 'ö,' and consonantal *i* is rendered as 'j.' Manuscript 'k,' when not in initial position, is rendered 'c,' and middle verb forms are normalized, for example, 'kalladiz' for manuscript 'kalladizst' (2.4). The only punctuation is a full stop at the end of each stanza.

[C.C. Rafn, et al., eds.] *Fornmannasögur eptir gömlum handritum*. 12 vols. Copenhagen, 1925–37, 5: 349–70.

This text is based on *Flateyjarbók*, but the editors made heavy use of Schöning's edition: many of his emendations are incorporated into the text, as well as a few of his errors in transcription (e.g., 'gunnöfligr' for manuscript 'gunnoflugr' in stanza 1.6). Vowels are normalized after the manner of Schöning's text, and *ð*, which the manuscript always gives as 'd,' is rendered 'ð.' Middle verbs are normalized with the cluster 'st,' for example, 'kallaðist' for manuscript 'kalladizst' (2.4) and 'berast' for manuscript 'berazst' (2.6). A semicolon is printed at the end of the fourth line of each stanza, and a full stop at the end of the eighth.

G. Vigfússon and C.R. Unger, eds. *Flateyjarbók*. Christiania, 1860–8, 1: 1–7.

Vigfússon and Unger's text is a diplomatic transcription of the manuscript, without annotation or textual apparatus. The verses are printed in the conventional eight-line form, with a full stop at the end of each. The manuscript reading 'æzstann' (71.5) is emended without comment to 'ytum,' but otherwise the editors have attempted to reproduce the manuscript text as exactly as possible. There are a few errors in transcription (or unmarked emendations): 'miskunnar' for manuscript 'miskunar' (1.6), 'hrokkinseids' for 'hrockuiseids' (16.2), 'þat er' for 'þvi at' (18.1), 'Gutthormr' for 'Gutthorm' (34.3), 'finnr' for 'fremr' (45.1), and 'iorfa' for 'i orfa' (54.5).

G. Cederschiöld, ed. *Geisli eða Óláfs Drápa ens Helga er Einarr orti Skúlason. Eftir 'Bergsboken' Utgifven*. Lunds Universitets Årsskrift, 10. Lund, 1873.

Cederschiöld was the first to produce a critical edition of *Geisli*. His edition is based entirely on *Bergsbók*, and in addition to the text it contains a brief introduction with comments on the historical setting of the poem, the metre, and the orthography of the *Bergsbók* text. The text itself is heavily emended, usually by conjecture, in an attempt to achieve uniformity of metre and to solve all difficulties involving syntax and meaning. Spelling and orthography are normalized (although *bragarmál* is not supplied) and the resulting reconstructed form of the language is quite different from that of the manuscript. Punctuation is lavishly supplied. Cederschiöld appends to the text a version of the poem in prose word order, with translations into Swedish of the more difficult stanzas, and lists of 'okend heiti,' 'kenningar,' 'viðkenningar,' and 'sannkenningar.'

Lars Wennberg, ed. *Geisli. Einarr Skúlason orti. Öfversätning med Anmärkningar*. Diss. Lund, 1874.

Wennberg's dissertation is an annotated translation of the poem into Swedish. It is based primarily on the *Fornmanna sögur* text, but variants from the other editions of the *Flateyjarbók* version are occasionally interpolated without notice. He supplies his own punctuation in the Old Norse text, which is often bizarre, as are the resulting translations. The work, which has no introduction, consists of the Old Norse text of the poem with Wennberg's rather free metrical translation on facing pages. The 'anmärkningar' are prose versions of the stanzas in Old Norse accompanied by literal translations into Swedish and explanatory notes.

G. Vigfússon and F. York Powell, eds. *Corpus Poeticum Boreale*. 2 vols. Oxford, 1883, 2 [*Court Poetry*]: 283–94.

This is the first edition of *Geisli* for which more than one manuscript was consulted. Vigfússon and York Powell use *Bergsbók* as a base manuscript, but attempt to correct the text with readings from *Flayeyjarbók*. The text is heavily emended, with normalized spelling and orthography and a great deal of punctuation. All emendations are made without notice, although there are a few notes calling attention to readings from *Flateyjarbók* and Cederschiöld's edition which the editors propose as possible alternatives to their version. There is no commentary apart from an English translation. This is occasionally helpful, but its ornate language and strange syntax often make it as obscure as the Old Norse text.

Theodor Wisén, ed. *Carmina Norrœnæ. Ex Reliquiis Vetustioris Norrœnæ Poësis. Selecta, Regognita, Commentariis et Glossario Instructa* 1 [texts and commentary] – 2 [glossary]. Lund, 1886–9, 1: 52–62.

Wisén produced his text without reference to the manuscripts: he used Cederschiöld's edition as a base text, interpolating some variants from the *Fornmanna sögur* edition of *Flateyjarbók* text as well as a number of conjectural emendations. In addition to *bragarmál* he supplied his own punctuation, but the absence of annotation often makes it difficult to know what interpretation is intended. The only commentary is a brief note on the metre. The second volume of the anthology is an Old Norse–Latin glossary of the most frequently recurring words in the poems of vol. 1.

Finnur Jónsson, ed. *Den norsk-islandske skjaldedigtning A: Tekst efter håndskrifterne.* I–II. *B: Rettet Tekst.* Copenhagen. 1912–15. IA: 459–73, IB: 427–45.

Finnur Jónsson's A-text is transcribed from *Flateyjarbók*, with stanzas 31–3 supplied from *Bergsbók*. The transcription is strictly diplomatic and attempts to reproduce every detail of manuscript orthography. There are errors in the transcription: accents are misplaced as often as they are given correctly, and minimal attention seems to have been given to word division. The following words are transcribed (or printed) incorrectly: 'segdi' for manuscript 'sagdi' (15.1), 'sniollum' for 'sniallum' (16.8), 'huiliz' for 'huilir' (26.1), 'guthormr' for 'guthorm' (34.3), 'messu' for 'messo' (35.3), 'greiddra' for 'greiddur' (40.4), 'vr' for 'or' (40.6), 'ser' for 'ler' (57.7), 'asande' for 'i sande' (59.1), and 'blezan' for 'blezon' (69.8). Finnur cites variants from all manuscripts, although not consistently, as well as a few editorial variants from Cederschiöld, Konráð Gíslason's *Njála*, and the 1852 *Edda Snorra Sturlusonar*.

Ernst A. Kock, ed. *Den norsk isländska skaldediktningen.* 2 vols. Lund, 1946–9. 1: 211–19.

This edition is useful chiefly as a guide to Kock's *Notationes norrœnæ.* The text is a reworking of Finnur Jónsson's in an attempt to be more true to the manuscripts, and it often succeeds. Kock's conviction that the poetry should fall into a 'natural' word order sometimes leads to drastic emendation and oversimplification. The language is normalized; punctuation and *bragarmál* are supplied. There is no annotation in the edition itself, but references are given to the articles dealing with *Geisli* in *Notationes norrœnæ.*

Author and Date

There is no reason to doubt that Einarr Skúlason is the author of *Geisli*: all of the manuscripts containing the poem, some of them little more than a half-century younger than the text, ascribe it to him. Einarr was probably the most prolific skald of the twelfth century. He was a favourite of Snorri Sturluson, who in the *Snorra Edda* and *Heimskringla* quotes twice as many stanzas from Einarr as from any other skald, and in the surviving corpus of skaldic poetry Einarr's stanzas are outnumbered only by those of Sigvatr Þórðarson. *Geisli* is almost certainly the earliest of the great Christian *drápur*, and its influence can be seen in all the others.[4]

Little is known of Einarr's life. He was a member of the Kveld-Úlfr family and, as a descendant of Skalla-Grímr,[5] a kinsman of Egill Skallagrímsson, Snorri, and Óláfr Þórðarson. The date and place of his birth are obscure, but he was probably born in the last decade of the eleventh century in the area around Borgarfjörður. By 1114 he was in Norway with King Sigurðr *Jórsala-fari*: *Þingasaga* reports that he was used as a messenger in a series of disputes between the king and Sigurðr Hranason which occurred between 1112 and 1114.[6] *Morkinskinna* reports another anecdote concerning Einarr and Sigurðr *Jórsalafari* which took place when Sigurðr was awaiting the arrival of Haraldr *Gilli* in Norway, ca. 1124,[7] although Finnur Jónsson suggests that this is an interpolation in the saga.[8] We know that Einarr was with Haraldr *Gilli* sometime during his reign (1130–6), because he composed two poems in honor of Haraldr,[9] and *Skáldatal* reports that he composed a poem (now lost) for Magnús *blindi*, who shared the rule with Haraldr from 1130–5.[10] By 1143 he was back in Iceland: his name appears in a list of priests in the west country which was compiled in that year.[11] The position of his name in the list suggests that he lived in the Borgarfjörður district, probably at Borg. It is not clear where Einarr received his clerical education. The schools at Skálholt, Haukadalr, and Oddi in Iceland were well established by his time, but he may have followed the example of the many learned Icelanders and Norwegians who studied in Germany and France.[12]

Sometime during the joint reign of the Haraldssons Einarr returned to Norway. He composed poems for all three kings, as well as a 'Haralds-sonakvæði,'[13] but his principal patron and great friend was Eysteinn, who according to *Morkinskinna* made Einarr his *stallari*.[14] As stanzas 8 and 71 of *Geisli* make clear, it was Eysteinn who commissioned the *drápa*, which Einarr recited in the Trondheim cathedral in the presence of an assembly including the three kings, the archbishop, and a large group of retainers (cf. stanzas 8–11). The event is described in *Morkinskinna*, which reports that St Óláfr himself gave a sign of approval:

Einar S. s. var með þeim brøðrom S. oc Eysteini. oc var Eysteinn konvngr mikill vin hans. oc Eysteinn konvngr bað han til at yrkia Olafs drapo. oc hann orti. oc førþi norþr iþrandheime iKristz kirkio sialfri oc varþ þat með miclom iartegnom.

oc kom dyrligr ilmr ikirkiona. oc þat segia menn at þer amiɴingar vrþo af konvn-
giom sialfum. at honom virþiz vel qveþit.[15]

This meeting probably took place in 1153, and certainly not later than 1154.
The see of Trondheim had already been raised to an archbishopric (cf. *Geisli*
65), which points to a *terminus ante quem* of spring 1153, when Cardinal
Nicholas Breakspear consecrated the first archbishop, Jón Birgisson, and
began his return journey to Rome.[16] King Ingi killed his brother Sigurðr in the
summer of 1155, and since all three brothers were assembled peaceably at the
time of *Geisli*'s composition (cf. stanza 8), we have a *terminus post quem*. The
character of the *drápa* suggests that it was composed for a celebration of St
Óláfr's feast, 29 July, and if this is true, the summer of 1153 is a much more
likely date than the following year, because the brothers seem to have been at
odds for some time before Sigurðr was killed. Another reason for favouring
1153 is that the *drápa* has the spirit one might expect in the aftermath of Car-
dinal Breakspear's visitation. The establishment of an independent see had
long been sought by the Norwegian church, and this official recognition by
Rome of both their church and their national saint led to a new spirit of nation-
alism which was reflected in a wave of literary activity under the patronage of
Archbishop Eysteinn.[17]

Einarr probably remained with King Eysteinn until Eysteinn's death in
1157, and then he may have left Norway to travel through Denmark and Swe-
den. *Skáldatal* reports that he composed *drápur* for King Sǫrkvir of Sweden
and his son Jón, and for King Sveinn of Denmark, although none of these
poems survives. At some time he returned to Norway and was with King Ingi
and Grégóríús Dagsson: his poem *Elfarvísur*[18] was composed for Grégóríús
sometime between the battle of Elfi (1159) and the fall of Ingi and Grégóríús
in 1161. It is not known whether Einarr then went back to Iceland or remained
in Norway, but he would have been an old man and cannot have lived long
after.

Sources and Analogues

The life and miracles of St Óláfr were the subject of many literary works, in the
vernacular as well as in Latin, produced in medieval Scandinavia and Iceland.
While it is clear that written accounts of the legend were in circulation well
before the composition of *Geisli*, none survives, and it is impossible to deter-
mine what, if any, literary sources Einarr used. There are two known hagio-
graphical skaldic poems on St Óláfr which antedate *Geisli*. The earlier of the

two, *Glælognskviða*,[19] was composed by the skald Þórarinn *loftunga* shortly after Óláfr's death, probably in the year 1032. The poem is a memorial of Óláfr addressed to Sveinn Knútsson, Óláfr's successor as king of Norway, and it shows that in the years immediately following his death Óláfr was already believed to be a saint. Þórarinn tells that Óláfr's body is beautiful and incorrupt, and that his hair and nails continue to grow. He also reports that the bells above the shrine ring themselves, and the blind and the dumb are healed by the virtue of the 'holy king.' At the conclusion of the poem Þórarinn boldly urges Sveinn to pray to Óláfr and ask for permission to rule Norway. The skald refers to Óláfr as *Guðs maðr* ('God's man'), and claims that the saint obtains prosperity and peace for all people from God himself. About ten years later[20] Sigvatr Þórðarson composed an *Erfidrápa*[21] in memory of St Óláfr. Only fragments of this poem survive, but Óláfr's sanctity seems to have been a principal theme. Sigvatr describes the miracle of the solar eclipse at Óláfr's death, and reports that Óláfr's hair continues to grow as his body lies in the shrine. He praises Óláfr's holiness, saying that he was free of sin and is now with God, who gives him the power to work miracles: many blind men have been cured at the shrine. Finally, Sigvatr urges that Óláfr's feast day be observed.

All of the surviving prose versions of the legend are contemporary with or younger than *Geisli*, but there must have been texts, now lost, from the time of *Glælognskviða* and the *Erfidrápa*. In his *Historia de Antiquitate Regum Norwagiensium*, written ca. 1177–80, Theodoricus Monachus remarks ambiguously of Óláfr's translation and miracles,

> It has been related by several how almighty God soon made known the merits of his martyr Óláfr, by restoring sight to the blind and bestowing manifold comforts on the infirm; and how, after a year and five days, Bishop Grímkell (who was the nephew of Bishop Sigeweard, whom Óláfr Tryggvason had brought with him from England) had Óláfr's body exhumed and laid in a fitly adorned place in the metropolitan city of Niðaróss, where it had been conveyed immediately after the battle was finished. But because all these things have been recorded [*tradita sunt*] by several, I regard it as unnecessary to dwell on matters which are already known.[22]

Gustav Storm understood the phrase 'hæc omnia a nonnullis memoriæ tradita sunt' to be a reference to a now-lost work, which he called **Translatio Sancti Olavi*, and many subsequent scholars have followed him in this assumption.[23] According to nearly all versions of the legend, a series of miracles began to occur from the time, one year after Óláfr's death, when his body was exhumed and translated to a proper shrine. It was the standard practice for the ecclesiastical authorities in charge of a shrine to keep a detailed chronicle of miracles wrought on the premises, and this is the type of work to which Storm thought Theodoricus was referring. The lack of any evidence of such a text, however, has led an increasing number of scholars to doubt this theory. There has been a renewal of interest in the development and transmission of the Óláfr-legend in recent years, and while many questions remain unanswered, scholars have refined and modified Storm's ground-breaking work.[24] While there is literary evidence of a cult of St Óláfr in England in the mid-eleventh century (perhaps the accomplishment of Óláfr's friend the English bishop Grímkell),[25] the absence of any mention of Óláfr in Norwegian sources until a hundred years later makes the *Translatio* theory unlikely.[26] The verb *trado* in Theodoricus's text need not refer to writing: the phrase 'omnia mihi tradita sunt' appears in the gospels in reference to the relationship between Jesus and God the Father,[27] and in theological writings it often refers to tradition in the broad sense. Eyolf Østrem is probably right in arguing that to assume that Theodoricus is referring to a specific text is to read too much into the passage, and that his remark is simply an acknowledgment that the events have been described by other authors (e.g., chroniclers and skalds) and that they are generally known.[28] The eleventh-century English sources include numerous references to churches dedicated to Óláfr,[29] the mention of Óláfr in three litanies used at Exeter,[30] and most significantly, three prayers for a mass of St Óláfr in The Red Book of Darley[31] and an office for the feast of St Óláfr in The Leofric Collectar.[32]

St Óláfr took on a new significance in Norway as *rex perpetuus* and national patron after the establishment of the archdiocese of Trondheim in 1152. *Geisli* is the earliest known of the many vernacular and Latin texts which appeared in the second half of the twelfth century and bear witness to this. A manuscript fragment in the Arnamagnæan collection, AM 325, 4to, fragm. IV, contains an early vernacular account of Óláfr's miracles.[33] The text mentions Cardinal Nicholas Breakspear's visit to Trondheim,[34] so it cannot be older than *Geisli*. Jonna Louis-Jensen suggests that it was composed ca. 1155–65, although it may be a redaction of an older text.[35] The manuscript is Icelandic, dating from the middle of the thirteenth century, but it is likely that the original version was written in Norway.[36] This text records the translation of Óláfr's remains and gives accounts of six miracles, five of which are found in *Geisli*: Guthormr's victory at Anglesey, the battle of Pézínavellir, the cure of Kolbeinn, the cure of the man mutilated by the Wends, and the cure of the priest Ríkarðr. The additional miracle reported here is the cure of a cripple in London.

The saga of St Óláfr known as the Legendary Saga,[37] dating from the middle of the thirteenth century, is descended from the fragmentary text through one or more lost vernacular versions. This saga, written in the Trondish dialect of Old Norse, is hagiographical in style and places a strong emphasis on Óláfr's miracles and on the conformity of his life to Christ's. Of the miracles related in *Geisli*, it includes Óláfr's dream of the ladder, the solar eclipse, the cure of the blind man with blood washed from Óláfr's body, the rising of Óláfr's coffin, Guthormr's victory at Anglesey, the bread turned to stone, the cures of Kolbeinn and the man injured by the Wends, the battle of Pézínavellir, and the cure of Ríkarðr.

In this same legendary tradition there is a Latin *vita et miracula* written by Archbishop Eysteinn of Trondheim. The final redaction of this text probably written near the end of Eysteinn's life (he died in 1188), has been edited by F. Metcalfe from a thirteenth-century English manuscript and published under the title *Passio et Miracula Beati Olaui*.[38] This text circulated in earlier versions throughout Eysteinn's reign (1161–88), and its history is not yet fully understood. Gustav Storm pieced together a version from liturgical fragments which he published as *Acta Sancti Olavi*,[39] and the discovery of new manuscripts has led to detailed studies by scholars such as Inger Ekrem[40] and Lars Boje Mortensen.[41] Mortensen speaks for most when he says that an early version of the *Passio Olaui* is thought to have existed by ca. 1150, but his claim that the similarity of this text to *Geisli* is evidence of this[42] does not necessarily follow: it relies on the assumption that the similarity between the texts indicates that Einarr Skúlason must have used a version of the *Passio Olaui* as a source for *Geisli*, while the influence could just as well have been the other way around. The complex relationship between the vernacular and Latin texts of this period is just beginning to be studied seriously,[43] but as Mortensen points out elsewhere, 'the model of two distinct literary spheres – a written, Latin, ecclesiastical one and an oral, lay, vernacular one – is not tenable.'[44] Given that *Geisli* and the *Passio Olaui* are not only similar but equally sophisticated, it is impossible to know whether they were composed independently at about the same time and using existing materials, or whether one influenced the other. What is becoming increasingly clear is that they come from the same milieu. With some alterations, the *Passio Olaui* was translated into Old Norse and is included in the twelfth-century Norwegian Homily Book under the title 'In die sancti Olaui Regis et martiris.'[45] The *Acta*, the *Passio Olaui*, and the homily contain seven of the miracles found in *Geisli*: Óláfr's dream, Guthormr's battle victory, the bread turned to stone, the cures of Kolbeinn and the man hurt by the Wends, the victory at Pézínavellir, and the cure of Ríkarðr.

Less closely associated with the legendary tradition are a number of early historical works dealing with Óláfr's life. The *Ágrip*,[46] a history of the kings of Norway beginning with Haraldr *hárfagri*, is a vernacular Norwegian work written in the twelfth century. It contains an account of the battle of Hlýrskógsheiðr. The *Ágrip* is the ancestor of an early historical saga known as the Oldest Saga, or First Saga, of St Óláfr, although it dates from the end of the twelfth century and is probably younger than the text in AM 325 IV.[47] This saga exists in six fragments of an Oslo manuscript (NRA 52), which have been edited by Gustav Storm.[48] The Arnamagnæan fragment 325 IV was for many years thought to be a part of this saga, but careful examination has shown that we are dealing with two texts, one with a hagiographical and the other with a historical emphasis.[49]

The legendary and historical traditions were combined by the saga writers of the thirteenth and fourteenth centuries. In the 1220s the Icelander Styrmir Kárason wrote a saga of St Óláfr which was an important source for Snorri Sturluson and the later Icelandic writers. This saga no longer survives as a separate work, but Sigurður Nordal has demonstrated that it was part of a literary tradition incorporating both legendary and historical vernacular works.[50] Shortly after Styrmir wrote his saga, Snorri wrote a saga about Óláfr, which he later made a part of his *Heimskringla*. Snorri's *Óláfs saga helga*[51] contains the miracles associated with Óláfr's martyrdom and translation, and the later sagas of *Heimskringla*[52] record all the miracles *Geisli* ascribes to Óláfr after the translation, with the exception of Magnús's victory at Hlýrskógsheiðr. A proliferation of Óláfs sagas followed Snorri's, and many dating from the late-thirteenth and fourteenth centuries have survived. These works are usually called the encyclopedic sagas of St Óláfr, because they incorporate a wide variety of literary and oral sources. A scholarly edition using all the known manuscripts has been produced by O.A. Johnsen and Jón Helgason.[53] The miracles from *Geisli* found in these sagas are the same as those found in *Heimskringla*.

Three of *Geisli's* miracles are recorded in chronicles and other historical works. The *Gesta Hammaburgensis Ecclesiae Pontificum* written by Adam of Bremen[54] at the end of the eleventh century describes Óláfr's vision of the ladder, as does the *Historia de Antiquitate Regum Norwagiensium* of Theodricus.[55] Magnús's victory at Hlýrskógsheiðr is also found in the *Historia*, as well as in the twelfth-century *Gesta Danorum* of Saxo Grammaticus,[56] and an account of the battle of Pézínavellir is given in the Byzantine chronicle written by John Kinnamos ca. 1180.[57] Finally, the influence of Latin saints' Lives must be acknowledged. Several of the miracles in *Geisli* have roots in the continental hagiographical tradition, but it is difficult to determine the point at which they came into the Óláfr legend. Einarr Skúlason would have been familiar with such stories of the saints, presumably in both oral and literary versions. While it is possible that Einarr himself introduced miracles associated with other saints into the legend of St Óláfr (*Geisli* is the earliest surviving literary record of many of the miracles associated with Óláfr), it is equally possible, and perhaps more likely, that the miracles had been incorporated into lost liturgical works and the early vernacular versions of the legend, and were known to Einarr either through these literary works or from an oral tradition arising from them.

While it is impossible to ascertain the literary relationships between *Geisli* and the other versions of the legend, it is clear that Einarr's poem was influenced by texts existing at the time of its composition, and in turn was a source for subsequent works. In the explanatory notes to the text I have pointed out the possibility of influence wherever it was apparent to me, but owing to a number of factors (the great number of lost texts, uncertainty concerning date and provenance of surviving texts, the flourishing oral tradition connected with the legend), these observations must remain hypotheses.

Einarr's borrowing from literary sources is not limited to the *materia* of *Geisli*, but extends to the diction of the poem. The debt to the skaldic tradition is obvious, especially in the accounts of battles, where Einarr's style is more reminiscent of the extended mythological kennings and tortuous syntax of the tenth-century skalds than of his more restrained and prosaic predecessors in the century following the conversion of Iceland. In the stanzas dealing with Christian themes Einarr had to work out his own diction: as the first skald to compose a *drápa* on a Christian subject, he had no established system of skaldic rhetoric on which to draw. The Bible (especially the book of Psalms) and Latin hymns are the primary sources of the Christian imagery and vocabulary of *Geisli*. Einarr knew more than a little theology, and much of the imagery of the *drápa* has parallels in the homilies and treatises of the Church Fathers and medieval theologians. While we can only speculate, it seems likely that the Liturgy of the Hours was a primary contributor to the Christian diction of *Geisli*. Einarr's education as a cleric, however rudimentary, would have been in a monastic house or cathedral school where the Divine Office was recited every day, and the regular repetition of the Psalms, hymns, passages from Scripture and the Church Fathers, not to mention the many hagiographical texts, would have secured phrases and images in his memory.[58] It is also possible that as a priest, Einarr continued to recite the Office, in which case its language would have been continually fresh in his mind. Indeed, the very form of *Geisli*, with its series of miracle accounts punctuated by the recurring *stef*, is not so different from the office of matins for a saint's day, in which the *lectiones* are separated and framed by an antiphon. I have identified in the notes a number of borrowings, although it is not always possible to be specific, and many more must remain to be discovered.[59]

The Poetics of *Geisli*

Geisli is a *drápa*,[60] and quite possibly the oldest *drápa* to have survived as a coherent work. The many earlier poems referred to by skalds and scribes as *drápur* now exist only as isolated stanzas cited in prose texts. It is unlikely that all the stanzas of any of these poems have been preserved, and attempts to reconstruct a semblance of their original forms must rely on descriptions of the *drápa* in poetic manuals and what we can learn from later *drápur* like *Geisli*. The distinguishing characteristic of the *drápa* is the *stef*, a refrain of two or four lines incorporated as the conclusion of an eight-line *dróttkvætt* stanza and recurring at regular intervals – often every three stanzas, as it does in *Geisli*. Most scholars now accept Sigurður Nordal's theory that the word *drápa* means *kvæði drepit stefjum*, 'a poem set with stefs.'[61]

Drápur normally consisted of three parts: an introduction, a central section, in which the *stef* appears, and a conclusion. The skaldic terms for the central section and the conclusion were *stefjamél* and *slœmr*. The skalds appear not to have had a term for the introduction, but modern scholars sometimes call it the *upphaf* or *inngangr*. In some of the *drápur* that have survived intact, the introduction and *slœmr* are of equal length, but there is too little evidence to know if this was the norm. *Geisli*, at least in the version that has come down to us, is irregular, with seventeen stanzas in the introduction, twenty-eight in the *stefjamél* and twenty-six in the *slœmr*. The structure of *Geisli* may have been tighter in its original form. It is not inconceivable that Einarr considered stanza 18, which introduces the *stef*, a part of the introduction, or at least a transition stanza that can be reckoned with the introduction, rather than as belonging to the *stefjamél*.[62] Viewed in this way, the introduction is composed of three thematically linked groups of six stanzas and the *stefjamél* of twenty-seven, which is likewise a multiple of three. The *slœmr* begins with three 'new' miracles, each dealt with in a group of six stanzas. Stanza 63, the last of these, recapitulates the theme of the poem, while stanzas 64–8 form a loose, discrete sequence, and stanzas 69–71 are an appended, as it were, bid for a reward.[63] Is it possible that *Geisli* originally ended at stanza 63? If so, it would have had a balanced structure with two congruent sections of three groups of six stanzas framing a central section of twenty-seven.

The three-stanza units of the *stefjamél* follow a consistent pattern. Each unit treats one of Óláfr's posthumous miracles, naming the need for healing or assistance in the first stanza, reporting the result of Óláfr's intervention in the second, and praising the saint in the final, *stef*-stanza. Despite this repetition of self-contained units, *Geisli* is not a static display of Óláfr's various achievements in the manner of earlier shield-poems or, say, a Romanesque altar frontal. There is movement forward, which is achieved both by Einarr's clearly chronological organization of his material (as in the list of miracles appended to a typical saint's Life) and by his syntactic joining of *helmingar* and stanzas with conjunctions, a technique that first appears in *Geisli* and is imitated in the Christian *drápur* that follow it.[64] Einarr also uses alliterative concatenation to link stanzas. In the most precise form of this technique the *stuðlar*, or required alliterating syllables, of the first line of a stanza alliterate with the *hǫfuðstafr*, or initial alliterating syllable of the last line of the previous stanza:

> **d**agbols konungr stoli (5.8)
> Veitti **d**yrdar **d**rottin (6.1)

> **H**aurda gramr af iordu (15.8)
> Ok **h**agliga **h**udgiz (16.1)

There are also numerous instances of concatenation where the catchword is a word other than the *hofuðstafr* of line 8:

> hans **b**rogd I grof logdu (22.8)
> Kom þar **b**lindr en ek **b**yria (23.1)

or even of stanzas linked by double alliteration:

> Olafr af **g**ram **s**olar (27.8)
> **G**eck **s**inum bur **s**ueckuir (29.1).[65]

While the general metrical norms of the *dróttkvætt* stanza are clear (eight six-syllable lines in trochaic rhythm), the variations employed by skalds are subtle and complex. Several excellent theoretical studies of *dróttkvætt* metre have appeared in recent years,[66] and what now remains to be done is the analysis and comparison of the verses that make up the *dróttkvætt* corpus in light of the principles they have identified. Diana Whaley has done this for the poetry of Arnórr *jarlaskáld*,[67] and since he was the leading skald of the eleventh century much as Einarr Skúlason was of the twelfth, her study offers a good point of comparison with *Geisli*. Various systems of describing the metre of the *dróttkvætt* line have been proposed over the years, and while none is entirely satisfactory, the one developed by Eduard Sievers over a century ago is still the norm.[68] Since *dróttkvætt* requires each line to end in a stress-unstress or trochee (´ x), the various patterns apply to the first four syllables of a line. Scansion of some lines is debatable, but by my calculation the frequency of occurrence of Sievers types and subtypes in *Geisli* is as follows:[69]

A	´ x | ´ x	209 lines[70]
Ah	(A with a heavy unstress)	16 lines[71]
A2k	´ ` | ˇ x	78 lines[72]
B	x ´ | x ´	8 lines[73]
C1	x ´ | ´ x	8 lines[74]
C3	x ´ | ˇ x	4 lines[75]
D1	´ | ´ ` x	47 lines[76]
D2	´ | ´ ˇ x	53 lines[77]
D4	´ | ´ x `	42 lines[78]
E	´ ` x | ´	66 lines[79]

Counting the four-line *stef* only once, *Geisli* has 532 lines. As might be expected, the majority of these (303, or 57 per cent), are Sievers type A. The proportion of A lines is somewhat lower than in the poetry or Arnórr, where 65 per cent of the lines are type A. Just 3 per cent of *Geisli*'s lines, as opposed to 15 per cent of Arnórr's, are the anomalous and less desirable type Ah, which may reflect Einarr's greater technical proficiency and regard for norms. *Geisli* has a small percentage of B and C lines (1.5 and 3 per cent, respectively), as does Arnórr's poetry (3 per cent). When it comes to D and E lines, however, the difference is striking. Over 27 per cent of the lines in *Geisli* are type D, fairly evenly divided between types D1 (9 per cent), D2 (10 per cent), and D4 (8 per cent), while only 5 per cent of Arnórr's lines are type D. An explanation of this is beyond the scope of this study, but comparative analysis of the entire skaldic corpus will someday reveal whether the phenomenon reflects merely the taste of these two skalds or a broader change in what was considered desirable. In contrast to its high proportion of type D lines, *Geisli* contains a dramatically lower percentage of type E lines (12 per cent) than Arnórr's poetry (25 per cent).

Some patterns appear to emerge in the distribution of the Sievers types in *Geisli*, although it is not always possible to know whether (or why) they may have been intended. As is customary in skaldic poetry, type A (and type Ah) lines occur predominately in odd-numbered lines: of the 225 total, 162 (78 per cent) of type A lines and a corresponding 75 per cent (12 out of 16) type Ah lines are in the odd-numbered position, and 65 per cent of all odd-numbered lines are type A or Ah. As in Arnórr's poetry[80] (and in skaldic poetry in general,)[81] however, there is a sharp distinction between the use of types A and Ah on the one hand, and type A2k on the other. While 162 (78 per cent) of type A lines and a corresponding 75 per cent (12) of type Ah lines are odd-numbered, 90 per cent of A2k lines are even-numbered. According to Kari Ellen Gade, type A2k is the most frequently found pattern in even *dróttkvætt* lines.[82] This is true of *Geisli*, where the breakdown is type A2k: 70 even lines (26 per cent), E1: 50 (19 per cent), A: 47 (18 per cent), D2: 40 (15 per cent), D1: 32 (12 per cent), D4: 24 (9 per cent), and Ah: 4 (1.5 per cent).

Einarr's use of rising-metre B and C lines is somewhat more generous than Arnórr's, but it is still minimal. Since even-numbered lines must begin with a stressed alliterating syllable, these types can occur only in odd-numbered lines, and in *Geisli* 3 per cent of odd-numbered lines are type B and 4.5 per cent type C, compared with 2.7 per cent and 2.2 per cent in Arnórr's poetry.[83] Einarr does appear to have had a favoured position for B and C lines: 16 out of 20 (80 per cent) occur in line 5, the beginning of the second *helmingr*. Einarr deviates somewhat more freely from the normative type A at the beginning of the second *helmingr* than of the first: there are fourteen occurrences (20 per cent) of non-type A in line 1, and twenty-five (39 per cent) in line 5. *Geisli* has sixteen long runs of three or more type A lines[84] and, conversely, twelve runs of non-type A lines.[85] It is difficult to see more than coincidence in the runs of A lines, but the occurrence of very long runs of non-A lines in the first two stanzas suggests that Einarr considered the metrical variation an added beauty rather than an awkward necessity.

Einarr's diction is treated in detail in the commentary to the text. His use of kennings is skilful and ample, more reminiscent of the early skalds than of Arnórr and the skalds of the eleventh century, and this is characteristic of the skalds who followed him in the two centuries after.[86] It has often been noted that Einarr is sparing in his use of kennings associated with pre-Christian religion. While he avoids direct references to important gods like Óðinn or Týr, he does use kennings based on Huginn, Óðinn's raven (13.2, 29.4, 41.6); Hǫrn, which may be a name for the goddess Freyja (37.1); the sea-king Reifnir (49.3, 54.7); and Njǫrðr (55.3). A surprisingly large number of *Geisli*'s kennings are associated with the Vǫlsung-Niflung legends (e.g., 16.2, 3, 4; 23.7, 8; 28.1, 2; 32.1, 2, 4; 38.7; 41.4; 48.2, 3; 52.7; 53.4; 56, 6, 7), and these tend to be the most elaborate and extended kennings in the poem. About half of the kennings in *Geisli* are somewhat conventional kennings for warriors and battle. Traditional kennings for the retainer who enjoys the material generosity of his lord are used in a new context to represent those who are granted favours by God through Óláfr's intercession. As we might expect given the imagery of *Geisli*, there are many kennings for heaven, the home of God, Óláfr, and light. There are kennings for poetry and the 'tools of speech' (8.1; 19.8; 26.3; 40.7, 8; 67.4) as well as the eyes (23.5; 59.7, 8). Kennings associated with poetry and with the body began to appear in skaldic poetry in the twelfth century, perhaps reflecting the emerging interest in poetic theory and Neoplatonic cosmology as contact with the schools of Europe increased.[87] Einarr's kennings for God, Christ, heaven, and other Christian concepts are original and were widely imitated in later Christian skaldic poetry. Some of these are analogous to earlier kenning types (e.g., God-kennings similar to traditional king-kennings), but many are more closely related to the metaphors of Scripture and Christian liturgical texts, especially hymns. Noteworthy among these new kennings are those based on abstract nouns ('lif allre fyrda iardar' 3.6, 7, 8; 'vmgeypnandi allz heims' 16.7, 8; 'valld foldar' 28.3).

Appreciation

Geisli begins with an elaborately constructed introduction, or *upphaf*, consisting of three sections of six stanzas each. The first is a religious *invocatio*, the second is a traditional skaldic bid for a hearing, and the third is a historical preface. Stanzas 1–6 are a remarkable theological and poetic *tour de force*, filled with complex imagery and learned allusions. Its theme and structure are a key to understanding the theme and structure of the *drápa* as a whole. After a brief invocation of the Trinity and a dedication to St Óláfr in stanza 1 Einarr turns to his primary theme, the identification of St Óláfr with Christ. He introduces the idea symbolically with the image of the *geisli* (ray of sunlight), a figure that has roots in Scriptural passages like Hebrews 1:1–3: 'God, who, at sundry times and in divers manners, spoke in times past to the fathers by the prophets, last of all, in these days hath spoken to us by his Son, whom he hath appointed heir of all things, by whom also he made the world. Who being *the brightness of his glory, and the figure of his substance*, and upholding all things by the word of his power, making purgation of sins, sitteth on the right hand of the majesty on high.'[1]

The *Glossa Ordinaria* commentary on this famous passage, which since the earliest days of the church has been the epistle for the morning Mass of Christmas, explicates the metaphor: 'The Father is glory; the Son is one with him, and made man, makes him known, just as the sunbeam makes known the sun.'[2] The analogy that God the Father is to the Son as the sun is to its rays gained wide circulation through the writings of John Scotus Eriugena, who used it to explain the diffusion of divine grace in the world. His *Expositiones in Ierarchium Coelestem*, which became a handbook of light imagery for medieval writers, says:

> And as I seek to understand, nothing seems more likely than that the Word of God the Father, like a ray from the inaccessible and invisible sun (i.e. the Father),

is poured out into the universe of the sensible and intelligible creature; especially into human and angelic intellects, filling everything, perfecting the imperfect, penetrating secrets, illuminating mysteries, forming visions in the interior senses of theologians, opening the minds of those desiring to seek and understand those visions, and manifesting himself to all attempting to know him, according to his relationship to every single individual.[3]

He states the idea more succinctly further on in the text: 'He makes of them divine representations or images, and bright and clean mirrors in whose faces divine glory shines; and they receive the principal light, which is the Father, and his divine ray, who is the Son, and the Spirit of both.'[4] The metaphor also appears in dozens of Latin hymns, perhaps the earliest and most familiar being the Ambrosian *Splendor paternæ gloriæ*:

> Splendor paternæ gloriæ,
> De luce lucem proferens,
> Lux lucis et fons luminis,
> Diem dies illuminans,
>
> Verusque sol, illabere
> Micans nitore perpeti
> Iubarque sancti spiritus
> Infunde nostris sensibus ...
>
> Aurora cursus provehit,
> Aurora totus prodeat,
> In patre totus filius
> Et totus in verbo pater.[5]

[Radiance of the Father's glory, bringing forth light from light, light of light and fountain of light, day illumining day; and true sun, shining with perpetual brightness, flow in and pour into our senses the light of the Holy Spirit ... The dawn draws its course, may dawn come forth fully: the Son is entirely in the Father, and the Father entirely in the Word.]

The sun : sunbeam figure had a wide currency in homiletic literature as an exemplum of God's grace communicated through Christ. It occurs, for example, in homilies by Bede[6] and Ælfric,[7] as well as in the Old Norse homily collections.[8]

As a variation of this theme the sun is sometimes used as a symbol for the

Trinity or Christ, and its light as symbolic of the saints. The popular *sol iustitiæ* (son of righteousness) image was often used in reference to Christ, but equally frequently we find the sun used more generally as a symbol for the Godhead without signifying a particular member of the Trinity. In skaldic poetry, however, with its preference for concrete visual images, almost every mention of 'God' seems to refer to the incarnate Christ. The definitions in the *Distinctiones* of Alan of Lille give an indication of the variety of meanings the terms for sun and light had in the twelfth century. In this theological dictionary Alan defines *lux* as Christ ('I am the light of the world'), preachers and apostles ('you are the light of the world'), and as the divine nature ('who dwells in inaccessible light').[9] Alan says that the 'proper meaning' of *lumen* is 'the predication of Christ, and the cognition of the Father and the Holy Spirit, whence "For with thee is the fountain of life, and in thy light we shall see light"'; but the term also denotes the saint, 'who is illumined by Christ.'[10] In theological discourse, the term *predicatio* is commonly used to express the idea that Christ, as the uttered and incarnate Word of God, is a 'making known' of God the Father. *Sol* can mean Christ ('as in the hymn, "Aurora totus prodeat"'), the saint ('as in the Book of Wisdom, "the just will shine like the sun"'), or Christ's divine nature, 'which illumines his human nature.'[11]

A number of literary examples of the shift of the sun : sunbeam symbol from God : Christ to Christ : saint survive, some of which Einarr may have known. Rimbert's Life of St. Ansgar describes a vision experienced by Ansgar in terms reminiscent of Pseudo-Dionysius and Eriugena: 'In that place in the east there was a wonderful brightness, light utterly inaccessible and of immense clarity ... I believed that therein was he [or "I believed it to be Jesus"] of whom Peter said "on whom the angels desire to look." And immense brilliance came from him, by which the length and breadth of the saints was illumined. And in a certain way he was in all of them, and they in him; he surrounded them exteriorly, he governed them interiorly by entirely filling them; he protected them from above, he supported them from below.'[12] Ansgar's vision explains the mutual indwelling of God and the saints: the holy person, filled with God, somehow participates in the eternal while living in the world, and likewise God's virtue acts in the temporal through the saint.

A homily of Gregory the Great carries the analogy a step further and sees in the saints a revelation of God, a manifestation of the Divine in a human form that humans can comprehend:

> Although we cannot see God, there is something we can do whereby the eye of our understanding can journey to him. Certainly we can in no way see him in himself, but we can see him in his servants. When we see them perform mira-

cles it is evident to us that God dwells in their minds. By means of the corpo-
real we are drawn into the incorporeal. No one staring into the face of the rising
sun can see it clearly, because the strained eyes fight against its rays; but we
look at the mountains lighted by the sun, and we see that the sun has risen.
Therefore, we are not able to see the sun of righteousness in itself, but we can
look at the mountains illumined by its brightness, namely, the holy apostles who
shine with virtues and gleam with miracles. The brightness of the risen sun has
filled them, and although it may be invisible in itself it shows itself to us
through them, as if reflected on the sunlit mountains. The power of the Divinity
is in itself like the sun in the heavens; the power of the Divinity in human
beings is like the sun on earth.[13]

All of this lies behind Einarr's *geisli*-metaphor. By naming Óláfr the beam
of the Sun of Righteousness, he suggests that the saint is filled with the Divine
in a way analogous to the way in which Christ was, and that Óláfr manifests
the power of Christ in the world just as the human Christ showed the power of
the Father. Like Christ, St Óláfr is both an example of godliness for edifica-
tion and emulation, and God's agent, actually effecting his will in the world.
The association of the saints with light is common in hagiography: the Scrip-
tural antiphon 'Fulgebunt justi sicut sol in regno Patris eorum' (The just shine
like the sun in the kingdom of their Father) (Matthew 13:43) appears in the
common of saints in nearly every medieval liturgical usage,[14] and missionary
saints were often depicted as bearers of light to the nations waiting in the dark-
ness of sin and error. But Einarr's use of the sunbeam as a metaphor for a saint
is rare as a poetic motif. Fredrik Paasche has noted a Carolingian parallel in
Radbod's *Carmen Allegoricum* on St Switbert, the apostle to the Frisians, but
Radbod does not use the metaphor of the *radius*.[15] Rather, Switbert, filled
with the light of faith which comes from Christ the sun, illumines the Franks
and the Angles with 'new light.'[16] Einarr may have created the *geisli*-meta-
phor himself, drawing on his knowledge of theological and liturgical literature
for allusions which surely would have been recognized.[17]

The relationship between St Óláfr and Christ, as Einarr develops it in
Geisli, is figural or typological. Many hagiographers worked from the point of
view that the life of Christ is at the centre of history: just as all of the works
that God performed for the benefit of his people in Old Testament times antic-
ipate and prefigure the life of Christ, his life is post-figured, as it were, by the
works of the saints in subsequent ages. The *mirabilia* of the Old Testament
and those of the saints point to (and are fulfilled in) the life of Christ in pre-
cisely the same way – simply from different perspectives. The various events
typified in the Old Law are really different expressions or descriptions of the

one event of salvation through Christ, and the lives of the saints are one mani-
festation, under various guises, of his life. Thus Gregory of Tours could say
that it is better to speak of the 'life' rather than the 'lives' of the Fathers, since
despite the diversity of their merits and strengths, a single life (Christ's) sus-
tained them all in the world.[18]

Einarr Skúlason was not the first or only hagiographer to produce a typo-
logical saint's Life: the form developed in England and Scandinavia during
the eleventh and twelfth centuries to the point of becoming a subgenre.[19] It
was used almost exclusively for kings who, like Óláfr, died in battle against
pagan enemies. In these Lives, the deaths or 'passions' of the saints are made
to conform as closely as possible to Christ's, with every conceivable corre-
spondence, however remote, carefully noted. The saint is often called *christus
Domini*,[20] and there is a great emphasis on posthumous miracles, because like
Christ, the innocent saint must first be sacrificed in order to bring grace to his
people. The holy kings are depicted as bringers of light to 'those who sit in
darkness and in the shadow of death'; their evil betrayers are those who 'loved
darkness rather than light.' The hagiographical works conforming to this
model included Bishop Eysteinn's *Passio et Miracula Beati Olaui*,[21] the *His-
toria de Antiquitate Regum Norwagiensum* of Theodoricus,[22] the anonymous
Passio Sancti Kanuti regis et martyris,[23] Aelnoth's *Passio gloriosissimi
Canuti regis et martyris*,[24] the *Tabula Othiniensis*,[25] the *Epitaphium S.
Canuti*,[26] Abbo's *Passio Sancti Eadmundi*,[27] the *Liber de Miraculis Sancti
Eadmundi* of Herman the Archdeacon,[28] the Life of Edward in the anonymous
Vita Oswaldi,[29] the Lives of Ethelbert by Giraldus Cambrensis and Osbert,[30]
the *Vita Sancti Thomæ Cantuariensis* by John of Salisbury,[31] and the *Vita
Sancti Erici Regis et Martyris*.[32]

The cult of St Óláfr developed slowly and in the usual manner during the
hundred years following his death. It acquired its strong figural character,
probably under English and Danish influence, during its period of rapid
growth in the twelfth century, and thenceforth Óláfr was intimately and some-
times even inextricably associated with Christ. This can be partly attributed to
a lack of understanding: the newly converted and poorly catechized Norsemen
at times may have confused Christ and Óláfr in the same way they sometimes
confused Christ and God the Father. But works like *Geisli* leave no doubt that
there were those who understood the distinction clearly and saw the advantage
in fostering this comparison. In iconography the attributes of Christ and Óláfr
became so closely associated that at times art historians can determine which
of them a sculpture or painting represents only by means of an inscription or
other contextual evidence.[33] The theme found literary representation in the
vernacular sagas of St Óláfr (including *Heimskringla*) and in Latin hagio-

graphical and liturgical writings. A pair of skaldic stanzas found side by side in the Fourth Grammatical Treatise makes the point succinctly and strikingly:

Hverr fell horða stiller
hvar þar er karlfolk barðiz
hvenær hneíg at noní
hver var sok ofvnd voknvð.
hverr váá kalfr hellt daʀri
hverer bendv sliks þrændir
hvat nytr heilsa botnvt
hvat sytir fira lyti. [34]

[Who fell? The king of the Hordar. Where? There where the farmers fought. When? He fell at nones (3:00 p.m.). What was the cause? Awakened enmity. Who was to blame? Kálfr held the spear. Who wanted such a thing? The Tronds. What did it achieve? Improvement and healing. What grieves? Human sin.]

Hverr deyr. hiarðar styrir
hvi. firi sauða lifí
hversv. hekk a krossi
hvar. þar er lazarus iarðaz
hvenær. helldz at noní
hverir knvðv að ivðar.
hver nytr. heiðní botnuð
hvat gelldr diofuls velldí.[35]

[Who dies? The leader of the flock. Why? For the life of the sheep. How? He hung on a cross. Where? There where Lazarus is buried. When? About nones. Who wanted it? The Jews. What did it achieve? It healed the heathens. What pays? The devil's power.]

The tradition of identifying Óláfr and Christ came to a climax in the late Middle Ages in texts like the Life of Óláfr from the version of the Golden Legend printed in Leuven in 1485.[36] The text describes how Óláfr experiences in his own life, sometimes literally, sometimes mystically, the miracles and passion (including crucifixion) of Christ. There is a striking iconographic counterpart to this text in the late-fifteenth-century altarpiece from Andenes in Norway. When open, the three-part altarpiece, consisting of a central panel and two wings, shows Jesus at prayer in the Garden of Gethsemane, his flagellation, the crowning with thorns, and his bearing of the cross. When the altarpiece is

closed, the four scenes painted on the reverse of the wings show Óláfr simi-
larly being whipped, crowned with thorns, mocked, and crucified.[37]

The typological context of *Geisli* is the key to understanding the introduc-
tory *upphaf* and its place in the structure of the *drápa*. On an obvious level the
summary of the life of Christ is juxtaposed against the saint's Life so that the
hearer will compare the two and note the similarities. It is an example of what
the rhetoricians of Einarr's time called *icon*, the 'inexpressed' comparison of
similars without directly stating the relationship.[38] But this introduction is an
icon of the body of the poem in a deeper sense of the word. If we accept Ein-
arr's view that Christ and Óláfr share the same life, then what we have here is
not so much a comparison of two similars as two ways of stating the same
truth. The life of the individual saint is the means by which the (one) supernat-
ural life of Christ and all the saints enters into history, just as, according to the
geisli-metaphor, the sunbeam is the means by which the sun itself warms and
enlightens the world. The deeds ascribed to Óláfr are thus the deeds of Christ,
made manifest in history by the saint, and the body of the *drápa* may be
regarded as a logical expansion of the first six stanzas.

The Latin rhetorical tradition suggests another way of looking at this. The
Rhetorica ad Herennium, echoed by the poetic manuals of the twelfth century,
recommends that the poet make his hearers receptive by including in the *exor-
dium* a brief outline of the main points he proposes to discuss, a summary that
encapsulates the meaning of the whole poem.[39] This is also the model we see
in the Gospel of John, which opens with a highly compressed poetic prologue
(John 1:1–18) that encapsulates the meaning of the text that follows. Indeed,
the verbal and thematic echoes of John's prologue (word, life, light/darkness,
the Incarnation as an enlightening making-present of the invisible God) sug-
gest that Einarr intended an allusion to the Gospel, and John's words are
worth recalling and keeping in mind while reading *Geisli*:

> In the beginning was the Word, and the Word was with God, and the Word was
> God. The same was in the beginning with God. All things were made by him: and
> without him was made nothing that was made. In him was life, and the life was
> the light of men. And the light shineth in darkness, and the darkness did not com-
> prehend it ... That was the true light, which enlighteneth every man that cometh
> into this world. He was in the world, and the world was made by him, and the
> world knew him not. He came unto his own, and his own received him not. But as
> many as received him, he gave them power to be made the sons of God, to them
> that believe in his name ... And the Word was made flesh, and dwelt among us,
> (and we saw his glory, the glory as it were of the only begotten of the Father,) full
> of grace and truth ... And of his fulness we all have received, and grace for grace

... No man hath seen God at any time: the only begotten Son who is in the bosom
of the Father, he hath declared him.

Too few *drápur* remain intact to warrant generalization, but the beginning
of a *drápa* with a compressed summary of the whole appears to have been a
skaldic technique, as well. In several of the surviving examples (cf. Markús
Skeggjason's *Eiríksdrápa* 4, *Leiðarvísan* 5, and *Lilja* 5) the skald concludes
his introduction with a stanza outlining the subject matter of the *drápa* and the
themes he intends to develop. Einarr's introduction may be an extended form
of such a summary. Understood in this way it becomes a microcosm of the
drápa, and Óláfr's life and miracles become an explication of the Gospel his-
tory, a new and living commentary on the principal themes of salvation. The
life of the individual saint is the means by which the supernatural life of Christ
and all the saints breaks into time. The deeds ascribed to Óláfr are the deeds of
Christ, given a particular form in history through the mediation, as it were, of
the saint. The body of the *drápa* then becomes an unfolding or an expansion
of the exemplum of the *upphaf*. There is an obvious and familiar analogue to
this technique in *Beowulf*, where the mysterious arrival and departure across
the waves of the archetypal figure Scyld Scefing are emblematic of Beowulf's
arrival from and return to Geatland. The story of Scyld Scefing in the pro-
logue encapsulates the entire poem, giving it a point of reference and focus
from the very beginning.[40]

Einarr Skúlason likewise compresses an epitome of *Geisli* into its opening
stanzas, and the story of Óláfr's life and miracles that follows becomes an
explication, a filling-out, of the synopsis of the life of Christ presented in the
exordium. Painted altar frontals found in Scandinavia and Catalonia provide
an analogy in twelfth-century visual art. Typically, these Romanesque altars
depict either a mandalic medallion of Christ in majesty superimposed on six
panels showing Gospel scenes, or a medallion of a saint with scenes of his or
her life. But there are a few which have a central medallion of Christ against
background panels illustrating a saint's life, thus mirroring Einarr's attempt to
represent the identity of Christ and saint by juxtaposition.[41]

After bringing the theologically complex *invocatio* to a close, Einarr shifts
the focus from Christ to Óláfr in stanza 7. Lest there be any confusion, he
briefly restates what he has already said: the *drápa* honours Óláfr, the sun-
beam, who brings light to the world in the form of miracles which are to be
related shortly. Then, with the phrase 'menn nemi mæl min sem ek inni' (let
men accept my speech as I report it), he introduces a favourite skaldic topos,
the bid for a hearing (stanzas 8–11). The bid for a hearing as a topic of the
exordium did not originate with the skalds: it was a principle of Roman rheto-

ric and became a commonplace in medieval Latin prose and poetry. According to the *Rhetorica ad Herennium*, 'The beginning is when we dispose the mind of the listener to give us a good hearing. The object is to make the hearers attentive, receptive, and benevolent ... They will be attentive if we promise to speak about important, new, or unusual matters, or about matters which pertain to the public, or to the listeners themselves, or to the religion of the immortal gods; and if we ask them to listen attentively.[42]

Whether the skalds learned this technique or developed it independently of their European counterparts, the first and last poems in *Skjaldedigtning* (*Ragnarsdrápa* and *Gyðingsvísur*) bear witness that it was a feature of their poetry through all five centuries of skaldic composition. The topic is as prevalent in Christian skaldic poetry as in the earlier *drápur*, but in the Christian poems it comes in second place, preceded by an *invocatio* of the kind we find in *Geisli*. The stylized skaldic beginning typically consists of three elements: a vocative, a verb, and a word for poetry as an object.[43] In stanza 8, addressed to three kings, we have the formula in triplicate: twice in standard form (lines 1–2, 3–4) and once in a slight variation (line 5). Einarr addresses his listeners in hierarchical order: first the joint monarchs, beginning with his patron Eysteinn, then the archbishop, and finally the clerics, retainers, and all others. The grandiose apostrophe to 'Þrændir ok nordmenn allir' (Trondheimers and all Norsemen) in stanza 11 is atypical of skaldic poetry (it was customary to address only those actually within hearing range), and suggests that Einarr expected the *drápa* to be published and circulated after the initial delivery.

Stanza 12 concludes the bid for a hearing and makes a transition into the final subsection of the three-part introduction. Einarr announces that while other skalds have composed *drápur* celebrating Óláfr as a warrior king, he will be the first to celebrate Óláfr the saint. The theme of his *drápa* will not be Óláfr's mortal accomplishments and exploits, but rather the miracles he has worked by virtue of the participation in divine power he has achieved through his participation in the suffering and death of Christ. Nonetheless, Einarr prefaces his discussion of Óláfr's heavenly life with a brief summary of his life on earth in stanzas 13–18. In stanza 13 he rather apologetically asserts that although Óláfr's actions may not have appeared exemplary from a Christian point of view, Óláfr led a hidden, saintly life known only to God, a mystical life in spiritual conformity to Christ's. Bjarne Fidjestøl has observed that Einarr's allusion to the poetry of Sigvatr and Óttarr is an innovation in the skaldic tradition. He suggests that the self-conscious reference is a means by which the poet places himself in a literary-historical context. It is related to the 'Quellenberufung' typical of twelfth-century European poetry, whereby the poet shows his knowledge of the subject by referring to other authors and texts. But Einarr does not cite his predecessors as authorities or sources. Rather, he mentions their poems to distance himself from them and to point out that he is doing something new.[44] Stanza 14 tells that Óláfr was king for fifteen years before his death, providing a transition to the account of his 'martyrdom,' which is in a sense the beginning of his supernatural life.

The prose Lives of the martyr kings are normally in the form of *Vita et Miracula*, and this is the structure Einarr follows in *Geisli*. In *Geisli*, as in the prose Lives, the *miracula* section is proportionally much larger than the *vita*. Óláfr's military and political exploits are not to be disparaged or ignored, but as Einarr states in stanza 12, they have been sufficiently proclaimed by Óláfr's skalds Sigvatr and Óttarr; his own purpose is to celebrate Óláfr the holy king, the miracle worker. The instigation of a martyr's cult in veneration of its fallen leader was a way in which a deposed royal family or political faction could associate itself with God in the popular mind and thereby foster its return to power. By the twelfth century this pattern had occurred enough times in England and Scandinavia that people would have been aware of the possibility of manipulation. This may have been part of Einarr's reason for insisting on Óláfr's hidden life of sanctity during his career as king: he was not transformed from a Viking into a saint the instant he died, rather, his previously secret virtue could now become apparent. Einarr may also be making a comparison between Óláfr and Christ, who was careful to conceal his divinity during his life and death as a man, permitting it to become known only after his resurrection. The order of stanzas 13 and 14 is reversed in *Bergsbók*, but *Flateyjarbók* clearly has the proper scheme. Stanza 13 deals with Óláfr's career as king, while stanza 14 follows chronologically and ends with the report of his death.

Stanzas 15–17 deal with Óláfr's vision on the eve of his final battle followed by his fall at Stiklarstaðir. The ladder vision was regarded as the first of Óláfr's miracles, and thus Einarr follows the prose versions and reports it after the account of Óláfr's death: even though it occurred before he died, it belongs to the *miracula* rather than to the *vita*. Just as the ladder itself symbolically links the earthly and heavenly realms, the story of Óláfr's vision in the *vita et miracula* forms a link upon which his mortal life as a Viking king and his eternal life as a saint hinge. The vision is not found in the early vernacular accounts of Óláfr's miracles, and it is clearly a learned borrowing rather than a popular addition to the legend. The earliest surviving Old Norse version of the miracle is in the Legendary Saga of St Óláfr:

Þat er sact ifra Olave kononge, at litlu aðr en barezt være at hanum þyngdi litt þat, oc þa hæyrðu þæir gnyenn af liði boandanna. Þa gecc Finnr Arnasun til konongsens oc vakte hann, oc mællte þa konongrenn. 'Ec sa stiga standa til himna oc himna upp lukazt. Oc var ek komenn a œpsta stiget, er þu vakter mec.' Oc var þat auðsynt, sagðe sa er ritaðe saguna af þesse vitran, at sia hinn hælgi guðs dyrlingr hævir aðr længi veret a þæiri himirikis gatu, er þa var at ænda komet. Oc hanum var þa ambun ætlað firir sitt ærveðe af almatkom guði.[45]

[It is said of King Óláfr that a short while before the battle he nodded off for a little while. And then they heard the din of the farmers' army. Then Finnr Árnason went to the king and woke him, and the king said, 'I saw a ladder reach up to the heavens. And I saw the heavens open up, and I had come to the uppermost rung of the ladder when you woke me.' And it was apparent, said he who wrote the report of this vision, that the holy man, beloved of God, had long been on the path to heaven, and then had reached its end. And that was then intended as a reward to him from Almighty God for his suffering.]

Adam of Bremen gives a similar account in his Latin chronicle:

It is said that Óláfr, sleeping in his tent, had a dream. And when the enemy drew near to the sleeping king, Finnr, the leader of his army, woke him. At that Óláfr sighed, 'O! What have you done? It seemed as though I was climbing a ladder which reached to the stars. Alas! I had just reached the top and was about to enter heaven, which was opened before me, but you called me back by waking me.' After the king saw the vision he was attacked by his own men, and unable to repel them, he was killed and crowned with martyrdom.[46]

Bernhard Schmeidler ascribes the passage to Adam himself, which would mean that it was written no later than 1085.[47] The mention by name of Óláfr's marshal Finnr Árnason is a likely indication that the German chronicler was quoting a Norwegian source.

The symbolism of the vision is complex. Like the sunbeam, the ladder is a bridge between heaven and earth, a point at which the material and the transcendent come together. Mircea Eliade has studied the image in a variety of contexts, and he observes that 'the ascents, the climbing of mountains or stairs ... always signify a transcending of the human and a penetration into higher cosmic levels.'[48] The vision is more than a promise to Óláfr of his heavenly reward: it is a sign to all that he is entering a liminal state between the world he is leaving and that which he is about to enter. Anticipatory revelations of this sort are a hagiographical commonplace, but the motif of the ladder occurs in only a few other saints' Lives. It first appears in the *Passio* of St Perpetua, who died at Carthage in the persecution of Septimus Severus. During her imprisonment she had a vision of a ladder hung with instruments of torture, which reached over a fierce dragon and into heaven. She ascended, and at the top met a shepherd who fed her a mouthful of cheese. Upon awakening, Perpetua understood the dream's meaning: 'I described the dream to my brother immediately, and we understood that it was to be a passion, and from that time we ceased to have any hope in the world.'[49] The association of Perpetua and the ladder was probably best known in the Middle Ages from the sequence *Scalam ad caelos subrectam*, used for the feasts of virgins and attributed to Notker. The sequence explains that 'The love of Christ made this ladder accessible to the women, who overcame the dragon and escaped the Ethiopian's sword; they conquered every kind of torture and reached the summit of heaven, where they received the golden crown from the hand of the comforting king.'[50]

The Merovingian saints Pardulf and Balthild died in bed, but their visions are analogous. Pardulf saw the archangel Michael, who led him up a ladder into heaven and showed him where God was waiting: 'Behold the Lord God, whom you love, standing at the top of the ladder, holding in his hands the crown he intends to place on your head, and a scepter for ruling his people, so that you may teach the way of salvation to the pursuers of good works.'[51] The account of Balthild's vision is similar: she ascended a ladder into heaven where it seemed to her that she had the angels as her companions. The author of the Vita gives an interesting commentary on its significance: 'Behold the ladder to heaven which she built during her life! Behold the kindred angels, whose friendship she acquired by adhering to good works in the world! It can be clearly understood from this revelation that her virtues were to lead her to the height of the eternal king and the swift conferment of a crown of reward. The holy mother knew from the vision she had received that she was to depart from her body very soon.'[52]

For Óláfr, as for Perpetua, Pardulf, and Balthild, the vision signifies transcendence and the ladder symbolizes the means of it. The glimpse of heaven is not so much a warning of impending death as a promise of a new mode of life. Whether the ladder represents martyrdom or a life of self-sacrifice, the way is arduous and fraught with peril; it is a rite for passing from the profane to the sacred, from the passing and illusory to reality and eternity, from man to God.[53]

Understood in a typological sense the ladder has still deeper meaning: it is not merely a sign of liminality or a means of transcendence: it is the way of Christ, the way of the cross.[54] Jacob's ladder (Genesis 28:11–22) was commonly interpreted as a type of the cross,[55] and in Einarr's system of reverse typology Óláfr's ladder has an analogous relationship to the passion of Christ.

The Old Norse translation of Genesis 28 quotes Peter Comestor's explanation of the correspondence:

Ok er Jacob uaknaði af suefninum. sagdi hann sua. Senniliga er drottin i þersum stað. ok uissa þat eigi. Ok enn talaði hann sua sem af nockurum otta eðr rædzlu sua segiandi. Hardla hræðiligr er þersi stadr. her biðr ecki nôckut annat nema her er guds hus ok himinrikiss port. *scolastica hystoria.* J þersum ordum spaadi hann fyrir af þeim .iii. lutum. sem aa þersu sama landi komu longu sidarr fram. þat uar af eptirkomanda lôgmaali. af guds musteri ok af piningu Jesu Kristi. Þiat lôgmælit er hræðiligt ok ottaligt. guds hus er musterit. enn pining Jesu Kristi er himinrikis port ok upplokning. [56]

[And when Jacob awoke from his dream he said, 'Truly the Lord is in this place, and I did not know it. And he spoke in fear or dread, saying, 'this place is exceedingly terrible. Here there is to be found nothing else but the house of God and the gate of heaven.' With these words he made a threefold prophecy of things which came to pass in that place later on: the Law that was to come, the Temple of God, and the passion of Jesus Christ. Because the Law is fearful and to be dreaded, the house of God is the Temple, and the suffering of Jesus Christ is the gate and opening of heaven.]

The cross was seen as a ladder to paradise (hymns call it 'scala peccatorum'[57] and 'scala novæ legis'),[58] the 'gate of heaven' through which Christ draws all things to himself.[59] There are a few instances where the relationship between cross and ladder is made even clearer and the two are symbolically conflated. The Merovingian saint Emmeram [Haimhrammus], for example, was crucified on a ladder,[60] and the *Meditationes vitæ Christi* reports that Christ ascended the cross by means of a small ladder.[61] The Life of Óláfr in the 1470 Leuven Golden Legend, according to which Óláfr is literally crucified, explicitly relates the dream to his death:

The day before his martyrdom the Lord Jesus appeared to him at night and said, 'Óláfr, open your eyes and look up.' When he looked above he saw a beautiful ladder extending from heaven down to the earth, and angels were descending and singing a beautiful song, carrying a red crown of roses. They said, 'With these roses our king and fellow-citizen Óláfr will be crowned.' And Christ said, 'Beloved Óláfr, tomorrow at the ninth hour you will ascend this ladder crowned with the roses of martyrdom and praised with angelic song, as my blessed mother and all my elect await you.'[62]

The St Olav altar frontal (ca. 1300) in the Trondheim cathedral similarly associates the dream of the ladder with Óláfr's death: the upper left panel depicts the dream, while the corresponding lower right panel shows his death. The composition of the two panels is almost identical: Óláfr is supine, surrounded by warriors. The faces and postures of all the figures are the same, as is the background. The only difference is that in the depiction of the dream, an angel extends a ladder to Óláfr, while in the 'martyrdom' panel, a spear (in exactly the same position as the ladder) pierces Óláfr's breast, and a sword and an axe lie beside him. Einarr's approach in *Geisli* is more moderate than this extreme development of the Óláfr/Christ typology, and it at least purports to be grounded in fact. Óláfr was not actually crucified, but the account of the ladder vision, in *Geisli*, as elsewhere, formally associates him with the cross: his death is viewed as an echoing or re-presentation of the passion of Christ, a perceptible manifestation of it to the medieval Scandinavians.

Here and throughout the *drápa* Einarr's account is sparse in comparison with the prose versions (with the exception of Adam of Bremen, whose style is similar to Einarr's). His paratactical juxtaposition of stanzas 15–16 (the dream) and stanza 17 (Óláfr's death) leaves the audience to draw the connection between the two. The effect is not unlike the visual effect of the Trondheim altarpiece. The account of the battle of Stiklarstaðir (17.1–4) is in the old skaldic style. Óláfr is a worthy and powerful leader who fought well before falling: the *heiti* and kennings used to designate him ('vidlendr almreyrlitudr' [widely landed arrow-reddener], 'gram' [king], 'branddrif' [sword-driver]) refer only to his aspect as a warrior king. But in the second *helmingr*, which deals with Óláfr's death, Einarr departs from tradition. The skalds normally reported battles from an impartial, historical point of view, but here Einarr passes moral judgment on the men who killed Óláfr: 'þeir drygdu bol' (they committed evil).

Stanza 18, which introduces the *stef*, or refrain, again compares Óláfr the earthly king with Óláfr the saint. The verse is transitional: the first *helmingr* uses the past tense to sum up the treatment of Óláfr's mortal career (he was a great king and accomplished much), while in the second the *stef* shifts to the present in reference to Óláfr, the holy *rex perpetuus*. The *stef* expresses the theme of a *versus ad responsorium* for matins in the Office of St Óláfr: 'Felici commercio pro celesti regnum commutans terrenum: regem rex videt in decore suo et in salutari regis magna gloria regis' (Happy exchange, to trade an earthly kingdom for a heavenly one; the king sees the king in his own honor, and the great glory of the king is in the salvation of the king).[63] Like Christ, Óláfr trades the earthly for the heavenly: Christ sees himself in the saintly Óláfr, and Óláfr's glory is his participation in the salvation of Christ. The *stef*, in its first appearance, marks precisely the point where the *commer-*

cium takes place, where Óláfr exchanges one kingdom for another. It likewise presents Óláfr as a point of overlap between the Divine and humanity. God grants Óláfr's every desire, and the saint uses this favour to relieve the afflictions of people in the world.

Stanzas 19–21 deal with Óláfr's death and the miracles associated with it. The solar eclipse as a sign of divine displeasure has been a literary motif since ancient times. It appears in the writings of the Hebrew prophets,[64] and Roman historians associated an eclipse of the sun with the death of Julius Caesar. The synoptic gospels report an eclipse at the crucifixion of Jesus,[65] and the theme of stanza 19 is the figural relationship between that event and an eclipse which took place at the death of Óláfr. The style of the stanza is paratactical. The first *helmingr* tells that an eclipse occurred when Óláfr died; the second, that an eclipse occurred at the death of Christ. The poet makes no attempt to explicate the relationship between these events, but by juxtaposing them he suggests their typological relationship: Óláfr's death post-figures the crucifixion of Christ. The imagery recalls the opening stanzas of *Geisli* where the sun signifies God the Father and the sunbeam, Christ. Here, by analogy, Christ is the sun and Óláfr, the beam, as Einarr develops further the complex symbolism introduced in stanza 3. Just as it was necessary for the Crucifixion to obscure the light of Christ's earthly life to make way for the better light of the Resurrection, the darkness at Stiklarstaðir marks Óláfr's transition from earthly king to heavenly intercessor.

The eclipse motif is rare in hagiography, but there are analogues in the two twelfth-century Latin Lives of Ethelbert, king of East Anglia.[66] According to the Ethelbert legend, which heavily emphasizes a typological relationship between the saint and Christ, the darkness of an eclipse engulfed the martyr and his companions shortly before he was ambushed and beheaded. Giraldus Cambrensis comments, 'No wonder that the signs which appeared at the death of Christ also appeared before the death of this limb of Christ, and that they presaged the death of his beloved ... The darkened sun averted its face as if it did not want to see.'[67] The Legendary Saga of St Óláfr has a similar statement: 'Nu let Olafr konongr þar lif sitt. Þa varð sva mikil ogn, at solen fal gæisla sinn oc gerðe myrct, – en aðr var fagrt veðr – æftir þui sem þa var, er sialfr skaparenn for af verolldenne' (Now King Óláfr gave up his life. Then there was such dismay that the sun withdrew its rays and grew dark, though the weather had been fair before, just as it did when the Creator himself departed from the world).[68] The Life of Ethelbert attributed to Osbert of Clare further interprets the signs, saying that the eclipse prefigures 'the glorious king martyred for the name of Christ, taken from the light of this world and crowned with heavenly glory.'[69]

The only early account of Óláfr's death to mention the eclipse is Sigvatr's *Erfidrápa Óláfs helga*.[70] Among the other sources of the legend it is found only in the Legendary Saga,[71] *Heimskringla*,[72] and *Den store saga*.[73] There is no record of it in the contemporary chronicles or histories, and to complicate the matter further, modern calculations show that there could not have been a solar eclipse at Trondheim on 29 July 1030, but that an eclipse did in fact occur there a month later on 31 August. It is possible that the battle of Stiklarstaðir took place on that day, but the traditional date of 29 July is attested by liturgical manuscripts dating from the decades immediately following Óláfr's death,[74] and there is no indication that the commemoration was shifted from the August date. If we did not have the evidence of the *Erfidrápa*, it would be easy to say that the eclipse was a late addition to the legend reflecting the twelfth-century enthusiasm for typological saints' Lives. It may be, as Knut Liestøl suggests, that the 31 August eclipse went unnoticed because of overcast skies and that the whole thing is a literary invention unrelated to fact,[75] or that the July death and August eclipse became linked in popular memory within a few years after the events. We must remember that Sigvatr was not reporting from first-hand experience – he was away on pilgrimage at the time of the battle – but if his *drápa* was composed only ten years later, as Finnur Jónsson suggests, there surely would have been eyewitnesses in the audience. The *Erfidrápa* differs in style from Sigvatr's other poetry (its elaborate diction and liberal use of kennings are more typical of the twelfth-century skalds), and perhaps its dating and authorship need to be reexamined.

The light that shone around Óláfr's body, as Einarr reports in stanza 20, refers both to an actual miracle on the battlefield and, more symbolically, to the series of posthumous miracles that made his sanctity evident. In Germanic hagiography it is common for a supernatural light to illuminate the body of a saint (e.g., in the legends of the Anglo-Saxon martyrs Ethelbert and Ethelred,[76] Kenelm,[77] Wigstan,[78] Oswald,[79] Ethelbert of Hereford,[80] Edward,[81] Edmund,[82] Ælfwold,[83] and Wulflad and Rufinus),[84] but there is also a tradition, dating from the earliest days of hagiographical writing, of a bright light marking the passage of a saint's soul to the other world. The Legendary Saga applies the latter interpretation:

En þa er Olafr konongr var fallenn, þa lauk guð upp augu Þores hunz, oc sa hann, hvar ænglar guðs foro með salo hanns upp til himna með miklu liose. Hanum syndizt, sem hon være skrydd með hinum dyrlegsta purpura. Anlet hans syndizt hanum huitt sem snior.[85]

[And when King Óláfr had fallen, God opened the eyes of Þórir the dog and he saw how angels of God took his soul up to heaven with a great light. It seemed to him that he was adorned with the costliest purple. His face seemed to him to be white as snow.]

In *Geisli*, Einarr may be attributing both miracles to Óláfr: his use of the word *lík* specifically associates the miracle with Óláfr's body, but the account of the ascent of his soul in the last three lines of the stanza suggests that both images are intended. The miracle is not reported in any other version of the legend, so whatever conclusions we draw must come from these two accounts.

The symbolic meaning of the light – the holiness of Óláfr that shines in his miracles – provides a link with stanza 21, which discusses the dissemination of Óláfr's fame. Again, there is a typological association: as with Christ, those who killed Óláfr thought they could extinguish the light of his good works. But just as the light of the sun can be eclipsed only temporarily, the saint's power is not hindered by his physical death. One might compare Ælnoth's comments on the death of Óláfr's Danish contemporary, Knútr, in his twelfth-century *Historia*: 'Just as it is better to place a lamp in a high place where its light can shine forth than to hide it away in darkness, the wisdom of the most noble leader is widely disseminated by the report of his virtue and steadfastness.'[86]

The first *helmingr* of stanza 21 is a reminder that although these miracles serve to increase Óláfr's fame in the world, the saint acts as God's agent and not through any power of his own. It is God who is 'grædari allz,' the supreme 'healer of all' who chooses to glorify his friend by working miracles through him. The eleventh-century account of St Edward's martyrdom makes the same point. When Edward's uncorrupt body was discovered, says the author, 'All seeing this were amazed, rejoicing in this sign from the Lord, who alone works wonders in the world.'[87] Although we later see Óláfr working miracles through active intercession and intervention, his role is passive in the marvels that occur at his death and immediately thereafter. The posthumous miracles are arranged, to the best of Einarr's knowledge, in chronological order. Stanzas 22–4 tell the story of Óláfr's first miraculous cure: when the king's corpse is washed in preparation for burial, a blind man accidentally smears some of the bloody water on his eyes and regains his sight. This miracle has often been compared with the legend of Longinus, the blind soldier who pierced the side of the crucified Christ with his spear and was healed by the water and blood which sprang from the wound. Because this was traditionally the first miracle to occur after Christ's death, it would be an apt parallel with Óláfr's miracle.

But the story of Longinus's cure is late: the earliest written source is a commentary on the gospels by Peter Comestor,[88] a contemporary of Einarr Skúlason, and we cannot be certain that Einarr knew the legend. The Legendary Saga gives two versions,[89] and other early works which include it are the *Acta Sancti Olavi*,[90] the *Passio Olaui*,[91] and the Norwegian Homily Book.[92] The motif appears in other eleventh- and twelfth-century vitae: the Life of Ethelbert talks of a blind man who was healed by touching the martyr's bloody severed head,[93] and the Lives of Oswald[94] and Agilus[95] describe similar cures worked by the water with which their relics were washed. Analogous stories are common and go back at least as far as the *Libri Miraculorum* of Gregory of Tours.[96]

The translation of Óláfr's body from its original burial place to a shrine in the church of St Clement in Niðaróss (Trondheim) was an important event in the development of his cult. The availability of relics for public veneration greatly increased the possibility of miracles, which led to the recognition of Óláfr as a saint and the establishment of Trondheim as a major pilgrimage destination. Stanza 25 corresponds to the accounts of the translation in the Legendary Saga and *Den store saga*: after Óláfr's body had been buried for a year and five days it rose to the surface. It was reburied, but nine days later it rose again. This time it was decided that God did not wish Óláfr's remains to lie in the ground, and translation to the shrine followed.[97] The healing of a man whose tongue had been cut out is the first of the miracles at the newly established shrine to be described in *Geisli* (stanza 26). There are no analogues in the twelfth-century prose versions of the Óláfr-legend, but *Heimskringla* and *Den store saga* report that at a celebration of Óláfr's feast the relics were carried out into the churchyard, and there a man who had long been mute regained his speech. This is supposed to have happened during the reign of Óláfr *kyrri*, two summers after the dedication of the new church of the Holy Trinity, the predecessor of the Trondheim cathedral.[98] Miracles of healing the dumb, ultimately derived from the Gospels, are common in medieval hagiography, and for some reason they were inordinately popular in twelfth-century Scandinavia. The three such cures reported in *Geisli* (stanzas 26, 37–8, and 40–1) are paralleled in *Vitae Sanctorum Danorum*, where seven healings of mutes are ascribed to the Danish saints Ketillus (Kjeld), Wilhelmus, and Nicolaus.[99]

The miracle associated with the battle of Hlýrskógsheiðr (stanzas 28–30) is part of a historical rather than a legendary tradition. Its early literary analogues are not in liturgical and hagiographical texts but in twelfth-century historical writings: the *Historia de Antiquitate Regum Norwagiensium* of Theodoricus,[100] Saxo's *Gesta Danorum*,[101] and the anonymous vernacular

Ágrip.[102] According to these sources Óláfr appeared to his son Magnús in a dream the night before the battle, told him how to arrange his ranks, and promised him victory on the following day. The details of the battle are obscure, but it is clear that Magnús won an important victory over the invading Wends on Hlýrskógsheiðr (a broad plain in southern Jutland, west of Slesvik) ca. 1043. Adam of Bremen gives an extensive account of the battle (without mentioning the dream),[103] and it is recorded in several Icelandic annals.[104] But hagiographical influence is also a possibility. The histories including the dream were all written more than a century after the event, and the authors may have seized the opportunity to use a military victory as material for an exemplum. Inspiration for such embellishment was at hand in the *Vita Ambrosii* of Paulinus, one of the models of Western hagiography. Among the posthumous miracles of Ambrose are recounted two occasions when he appeared on the eve of a battle, gave instructions, and granted victory in the morning.[105] There is also an analogue, possibly derived from the Óláfr-legend, in the thirteenth-century *Knýtlinga saga*, in which Knútr *lávarðr* promises victory over Sveinn to his son Valdimarr.[106]

Stanzas 31–4 tell of a victory achieved by Óláfr's nephew Guthormr after he prayed to the saint for assistance. Guthormr is not documented as a historical figure, but the incident at Anglesey is recorded in early versions of the Óláfr-legend.[107] According to these sources Guthormr, a Viking, was the son of Óláfr's sister Gunnhildr.[108] He and Margaðr (Eachmargach) Rǫgnvaldsson,[109] who ruled Dublin 1035–8 and 1046–52, travelled together for a time on Viking expeditions in the British Isles. After a raid on Anglesey a quarrel arose concerning the division of spoils, and they agreed to settle the matter with a battle. Guthormr was by far the weaker, but he prayed to Óláfr on the eve of the battle (which took place on Óláfr's feast day) and won a resounding victory. In gratitude he contributed a silver cross to Óláfr's shrine at Trondheim.

The miracle described in stanzas 35–6, like the preceding story of Guthormr, comments on objects that were visible in the cathedral as Einarr declaimed his *drápa*. The Guthormr-legend explained the history of the silver cross, and now the legend of the petrified loaves refers to the three rocks which were kept at the shrine until the Protestant Reformation and which were a favourite emblem of Óláfr.[110] The story, as found in ecclesiastical sources of Óláfr's legend, tells of an evil Danish count who commanded his Norwegian maidservant to bake bread on Óláfr's feast day. She protested, but was forced to give in to her master's threats. When she prayed to St Óláfr for revenge, the count was struck blind and the bread in the oven turned to stone. This miracle, according to the legend, inspired the Danish people to keep St Óláfr's day as a major feast.[111]

Punishment for working on a saint's feast is a familiar motif in hagiography:[112] on major feasts, as on Sundays, the church forbade unnecessary labour (the eleventh-century *Ældre Borgarthings-Christenret* specifically forbids baking bread on holy days).[113] But the exemplum of the petrified loaves is unusual.[114] Other saints' Lives tell of loaves turned to stone in punishment for refusal to share them with the needy,[115] but the only direct analogue I have found is in an account of the miracles of St Zoilus (Zoyl) written by the monk Rodulfo ca. 1136. Little is known of Zoilus, who was martyred in Cordova during the persecution of Diocletian, but after his body was discovered and translated to the Benedictine monastery of Carrion ca. 1083 an active cult sprang up around the place. The last miracle in Rodulfo's treatise tells of an inhabitant of Carrion who disregarded the celebration of Zoilus's feast and set about baking bread, only to find that although his finished loaves had beautiful crusts, the insides were like ashes and dung. The man repented and led a great crowd to the saint's tomb where they sang a *Te Deum*.[116] Zoilus is not found in Scandinavian liturgical calendars, but his feast was observed in various places in Europe and England[117] and his legend may be a source for Óláfr's miracle. The miracle is an inversion of Christ's refusal to accept the devil's challenge to change stone to bread, but the moral is the same: spiritual nourishment is more important than biological food.[118]

The wicked woman who abused her servant (stanzas 37–9) is presumably Þóra Guthormsdóttir, the mother of King Sigurðr *munnr*. According to the prose versions, Þóra had become enraged when a servant named Kolbeinn ate a morsel from her plate, and she commanded that his tongue be cut out. He subsequently made a pilgrimage to Óláfr's shrine and fell asleep during the singing of vespers. While he slept St Óláfr appeared to him, took hold of the stump of his tongue, and pulled. The pain woke Kolbeinn and he found himself suddenly healed.[119] Einarr was bold to imply so obvious a criticism of Þóra's behaviour: he refrains from mentioning her name but the evidence of the prose accounts suggests that his audience knew the story and would have recognized the allusion. It must have been an embarrassing moment for Sigurðr, who was present when Einarr performed the poem in Trondheim. Einarr's patron was Eysteinn, Sigurðr's rival, and there may have been a political motive for humiliating him.

The miracle described in stanzas 40–2 is told in all of the prose versions, but the details remain obscure.[120] We are told only that a group of Wends (*Sclavi* in the Latin versions) took a man named Halldórr and cut his tongue. Halldórr went to the shrine on Óláfr's feast, which fell just a few weeks later, and was cured. The account in AM 325 IV, 4to gives the additional information that this happened while Cardinal Nicholas Breakspear was in Norway (the year preceding the composition of *Geisli*) and that the cures of both Halldórr and Kolbeinn were witnessed by a monk named Hallr.

The story of the sword Hneitir, spread out through eight stanzas (stanzas 43–50), is the longest miracle account in *Geisli*. It is not found in any of the earlier versions of the legend, and it is likely that Einarr knew of the incident (which must have occurred not long before the completion of his *drápa*) only from an oral tradition. The style of his account suggests that he did not expect his audience to be familiar with the story: his version is detailed and prosaic, designed more to present the facts in a logical and comprehensible manner than to evoke a new perception of something already known. The story is found elsewhere only in *Heimskringla*[121] and *Den store saga*,[122] and Snorri acknowledges that his *Heimskringla* account is derived from *Geisli*: 'Eindriði ungi var þá í Miklagarði, er þessir atburðir gerðusk. Sagði hann þessa sǫgu í Nóreg, svá sem Einarr Skúlason váttar í drápu þeiri, er hann orti um Óláf konung inn helga, ok er þar kveðit um þenna atburð' (Eindriði the Young was in Miklagarðr when this incident occurred. He told about it in Norway, as Einarr Skúlason bears witness in the *drápa* which he composed about King Óláfr the holy, in which he relates the story).[123] Eindriði is otherwise known from *Orkneyinga Saga* and *Heimskringla*.[124] He was probably a Norwegian nobleman, possibly from the family of Einarr *þambarskelfir*, who served for many years as a mercenary soldier in Byzantium. He appears to have been in Norway on a visit to King Ingi in Bergen in 1148, when he would have had the opportunity to meet Einarr Skúlason. Einarr uncharacteristically names him in stanza 45 as the source for his story.

The miracle itself is unspectacular. It does not come out of the hagiographical tradition, and the phenomenon Einarr describes could easily be explained without resorting to the supernatural. Stanzas 43–5 provide the setting for the story: Einarr tells that Óláfr's sword, named Hneitir ('Stinger'), was picked up after the battle of Stiklarstaðir by a Swedish soldier, and was handed down through the generations of his family until it eventually came into the possession of a member of the Varangian Guard, the Norse mercenaries in Constantinople. Stanza 45 is the last of the nine three-stanza units that conclude with the *stef*. It is surprising that the *stefju-bálkr* (main section) of the *drápa* should conclude here, in the middle of a narrative. Einarr alludes to the shift in his compositional style in a self-conscious aside at the beginning of stanza 46: 'Mer er ... of stilli styrkann vant at yrkia' (It is difficult for me to compose about the strong prince). The 'difficulty' of narrating this event is reflected in the structure of the section: Einarr uses eight stanzas to tell the story, making it the only miracle story in the *drápa* that is not told in three or a multiple of three stanzas. The closing of the middle section of the *drápa* here may reflect the transition from already-known miracles to new, previously unheard mate-rial – the skald goes on to remind his hearers that the case for Óláfr's sanctity becomes increasingly strong as new miracles continue to come to light. The device of spilling the final three miracle stories over the section boundary gives an impression of abundance – Óláfr's miracles, as they continue to occur, are too numerous to be contained by the poetic form. The break also coincides with a geographical shift: the setting of the miracles moves from the familiar locale of northwestern Europe to the exotic shores of Byzantium.

Einarr resumes the story of the sword, now in the possession of a soldier 'in the army of the Greeks,' and relates that one night the man was sleeping out under the stars, with the sword under his head as was the custom. When he awoke he was surprised to find the sword lying in the ground some distance away from him. This happened three nights in succession and caused a stir among his comrades, and when word reached the Byzantine king he pur-chased the sword for a high price and hung it over the altar as a relic to be ven-erated in a church the Varangians had dedicated to Óláfr. This is presumably the church mentioned in *Den store saga*, built by the Varangians in Constanti-nople after the battle of Beroë (see below) and dedicated to 'the Holy Virgin Mary and the Blessed King Óláfr.'[125] Benedikt S. Benedikz and Sigfús Blön-dal cite Byzantine records attesting to the existence of a Varangian church near Hagia Sophia and dedicated to the Blessed Virgin Mary,[126] and it is not inconceivable that 'Óláfr's sword' was displayed there. The sword as an archetypal symbol tends to represent an extension, literally as well as figur-ally, of the power of its owner. The story of Hneitir in Byzantium shows that Óláfr's dominance prevails wherever 'his men' might find themselves, and sets the stage for the account of the miraculous victory at Pézínavellir.

Stanza 51 makes a transition to this story, also associated with the Varan-gians in Byzantium. Unlike the Hneitir-miracle, the victory at Pézínavellir (stanzas 51–6) is well documented by other versions of the legend.[127] The cir-cumstances of this miracle, too, are rather ordinary. The Varangians, in the service of a Greek king, were losing a battle and decided to pray to Óláfr. After vowing to build a church in his honour if they should defeat their ene-mies, they were victorious. This is almost certainly a reference to the Varan-gian church mentioned above. The passage has been thought to describe the historically documented encounter between the Byzantine king Johannes II Komnenos (the son of Kirjalax) and the Petchenegs[128] in the winter of 1121–2 near Beroë (Stara Zagora) in Bulgaria. There is an account of the event in the Byzantine chronicle of Kinnamos (ca. 1180), but although Kinnamos gives the Varangians credit for the victory, he does not mention Óláfr's supernatural intervention.[129] The author of the Chronicle of Nicetas Choniates (ca. 1206), who does not appear to have known the work of Kinnamos, reports that the emperor knelt in tears to pray before the icon of the Blessed Virgin, who then granted victory over the enemy.[130] It is conceivable that all prayed, the Varangians to Óláfr and the Byzantines to Mary, and attributed the results of the battle accordingly. More recently, Odd Sandaaker has argued convincingly that the story has its origin much earlier, in the experience of Óláfr's half-brother Haraldr *harðráði* and the Norwegian mercenaries who fought on the side of the Byzantine emperor in the Bulgarian revolt incited by Peter Delianos in 1040. He suggests that the battle actually took place on the plain of the Pčinja River in Macedonia, and was later conflated with stories of the battle of Stara Zagora. It shows the influence of the Byzantine tradition of warrior saints like St George and St Demetrios.[131]

The final miracle, narrated in stanzas 57–62, is found in all the prose sources of Óláfr's legend.[132] Einarr tactfully refrains from using proper names, but we know from the other accounts that this is another incident linked to King Sigurðr *munnr* (cf. stanzas 37–8). The story concerns Sigurðr's maternal uncles Einarr and Andréás, sons of Guthormr *grábarðr*. An English priest named Ríkarðr was staying with the brothers at their farm in Uppland, and unpleasant rumours about Ríkarðr and their flirtatious sister (Gutthormr's mother Þóra again?) began to circulate. They decided to seek vengeance on the priest, and under a pretext persuaded Ríkarðr to accompany them on a short journey to another district. En route, the brothers and their servant attacked the man with an axe, smashing his leg and knocking both of his eyes out of their sockets. They did not kill him, but they cut out his tongue to insure that he would never testify against them. After the beating, Ríkarðr was found by a peasant woman and her daughter, who took him into their house. That night as he lay in bed the man prayed to Óláfr ('mállauss með hugrenningum ok sútfullu hjarta' [mutely, with searching thoughts and a mournful heart], according to Snorri),[133] and the saint appeared to him in a dream and cured him of all his afflictions. Einarr introduces the story by implying that the man was innocent and that the brothers were at fault for believing the rumours and acting so rashly. Stanza 58 is a homiletic aside that explains the exemplum: rumours and lies are evil and have the power to corrupt good men, and blame for the crime rests not only on the two brothers, but also on those who perpetrated the rumours.

Stanzas 63–8 form the proper conclusion of the *drápa*. In stanza 63 Einarr refers once more to Óláfr's earthly life. This is the theme he used to introduce the account of miracles that makes up the body of the poem, and the return to it here at the conclusion of the miracle section contributes to the symmetry of the *drápa*. Einarr uses this juxtaposition of Óláfr the king and Óláfr the saint to comment on the relationship between the two: that is, not only was Óláfr *amicus Dei* because he was saintly, but more mysteriously he was saintly because he was God's friend. Like Christ, he answered a summons from God to conform his life to a divine plan, the reward for which was the establishment of his reputation as a wonder-worker. The theology of this pattern of sanctity stems from St Paul: 'And we know that to them that love God, all things work together unto good, to such as, according to his purpose, are called to be saints. For whom he foreknew, he also predestinated to be made conformable to the image of his son; that he might be the firstborn among many brethren. And whom he predestinated, them he also called. And whom he called, them he also justified. And whom he justified, them he also glorified.'[134] Einarr reminds us that Óláfr, always 'the Savior's friend' (lausnara langvinr),[135] kept himself from sin and passed the severe test of martyrdom that God reserves for most of his friends before raising them to glory ('allz mest vini flesta Gud reynir sva sina' [in such wise God usually tests most of his friends]).[136] We find St Paul's idea echoed in other twelfth-century *vitæ* that portray the saint as *alter Christus*: Saints Edward,[137] Knútr,[138] and Thomas Becket[139] are all described as predestined and chosen companions of Christ in their martyrdom and glorification.

These final stanzas of *Geisli* have little thematic content. Narration gives way to high rhetoric and grandiose conclusion. Einarr draws on a variety of poetic traditions: the topics of inexpressibility in stanzas 64, 66, and 67 have their roots in classical literature, and they became a standard element of medieval saints' Lives. There is also a close parallel in the final verse of the Gospel of John ('there are also many other things which Jesus did; which, if they were written every one, the world itself, I think, would not be able to contain the books that should be written').[140] This calls to mind the echoes of John in the opening stanzas of *Geisli*, and again suggests that the Gospel of John and its themes were a significant model for Einarr. The final prayer in stanzas 67–8, corresponding to the invocation at the beginning of the *drápa*, reminds us that the ostensible purpose of the literary saint's Life is to stir up faith, and Einarr expresses the hope typical of the hagiographer that his poetry and the inspiration of Óláfr's miracles will lead those who hear it to the love of Christ. This concluding and framing device, like the invocation at the beginning of the poem, shows the influence of continental Christian literature. But the *drápa* does not end here. Einarr Skúlason was first of all a skald, and the skaldic tradition wins over piety for the last word: the final three stanzas are what we would expect in any *drápa*: a proud claim that the skald has brilliantly executed the work commissioned by his patron and a justified request for praise and reward.

Headnotes to the Text

The orthography of the *Flateyjarbók* text has been faithfully preserved, with the exception that manuscript *r*-rotunda [ɹ] has been replaced with *r*. Capitalization has been normalized in accordance with modern practice. All proper names and the beginnings of sentences are capitalized, as well as the words *Guð* and *Kristr*. Manuscript punctuation has been somewhat normalized. The manuscript generally has a full stop [.] at the end of each *helmingr*; where the second *helmingr* of a stanza begins with a conjunction I have omitted punctuation, and likewise, in places where a full stop is required (at the end of a stanza or *helmingr*) but does not appear in the manuscript, I have supplied it. I have not reproduced the accent mark [´] which is used in the manuscript to distinguish lowercase *i* from other minims, but in the few instances where accents are used with *o* or *a* to indicate vowel quantity, they are retained. All words or letters that do not appear in *Flateyjarbók* but have been supplied or produced by emendation are enclosed in pointed brackets < >. Words or letters that are only partly legible in the manuscript but are almost certainly correct readings are in square brackets [ ].

The apparatus is divided into four sections. The first contains textual notes on the basic manuscript. All words in brackets are discussed here, as well as peculiarities of the manuscript that may affect the text. Where the text of the manuscript has been emended, the readings from *Flateyjarbók* and all other manuscripts are recorded here. The second section lists all lexical variants, including variants affecting sense or grammar, words or sequences of words differing from those of the basic manuscript, and differences in case, number, person, tense, and mood. But where *Flateyjarbók* has been emended, all variants are recorded in the textual notes and are not repeated here or in phonological and spelling variants. The third group of notes records phonological and spelling variants from other manuscripts. Spellings involving *i/j* and *u/v* are reproduced as they stand in the manuscripts but are not themselves cited as variants. Variants involving *d/ð*, however, are always indicated. Capitalization and orthography are otherwise in accordance with the practice of the main text. The last section includes lexical variants from previous editions of the poem. These variants may be the result of a different reading of the manuscript, but more often they represent emendations. Variants involving punctuation, capitalization, orthography, and spelling (including *d/ð* variation) are not recorded. Since here, as elsewhere, all notes refer to the edited text, readings from other editions which are in accordance with the manuscript but not with the present edition are listed as variants.

The following abbreviations are used in the notes:

Manuscripts

A	AM 748 I, 4to
B	Holm perg. fol. nr. 1 (*Bergsbók*)
Bx	(the *Bergsbók* text of Óláfs saga)
E	AM 47, fol. (*Eirspennill*)
F	GKS 1005, fol. (*Flateyjarbók*)
Fx	(the *Flateyjarbók* text of Óláfs saga)
H	AM 66, fol. (*Hulda*)
Hr	GKS 1010, fol. (*Hrokkinskinna*)
K	AM 63, fol. ([*Kringla*])
O	AM 39, fol.
P	AM 73a, fol. ([*Bœjarbók*])
R	GKS 2367, 4to (*Codex Regius* of *Snorra Edda*)
T	Utrecht 1374 (*Codex Trajectinus*)
Tm	GKS 1008, fol. (*Thomasskinna*)
U	DG 11, 4to (*Codex Upsaliensis*)
W	AM 242, fol. (*Codex Wormianus*)
Y	Holm perg. 4to nr. 2
Z	Holm perg. 4to nr. 4

Editions

AF	Faulkes, Anthony, ed. *Snorri Sturluson Edda: Skáldskaparmál*. 2 vols. London, 1998.

C   Cederschiöld, G., ed. *Geisli eða Óláfs Drápa ens Helga er Einarr orti Skúlason. Eftir 'Bergsboken' Utgifven*. Lunds Universitets Årsskrift, 10. Lund, 1873.

CN   Wisén, Theodor, ed. *Carmina Norræna*, 1. Lund, 1886.

CPB   Vigfússon, G., and F. York Powell, eds. *Corpus Poeticum Boreale*, 2. Oxford, 1883.

EAK   Kock, Ernst A., ed. *Den norsk-isländska skaldediktningen*, 1. Lund, 1946.

FL   Vigfússon, G., and C.R. Unger, eds. *Flateyjarbók*, 1. Christiania, 1860.

FMS   [Rafn, C.C., et al., eds.] *Fornmanna Sögur eptir gömlum handritum*, 5. Copenhagen, 1830.

Hkr   Snorri Sturluson. *Heimskringla*, ed. 3. ÍF, 28. Bjarni Aðalbjarnarson. 1941–51, 2nd ed. Reykjavík, 1979.

S   Schöning, Gerhardus, ed. *Heimskringla*, vol. 3. Copenhagen, 1783.

Skj   Finnur Jónsson, ed. *Den norsk-islandske skjaldedigtning*, IB. Copenhagen, 1912.

W   Wennberg, Lars, ed. *Geisli. Einarr Skúlason orti. Öfversat med Anmærkninger*. Diss. Lund, 1874.

Geisli

— *1* —

1	Eins ma ord ok bænir	[Eins má orð ok bœnir
2	allz rædanda hins snialla	(alls ráðanda hins snjalla
3	vel er frodr sa er getr goda	vel er fróðr sá er getr góða)
4	Guds þrenning mer kenna.	Guðs þrenning mér kenna.
5	Gofugt lios bodar geisli	Gǫfugt ljós boðar geisli
6	gunnoflugr miskunar	gunnǫflugr miskunnar
7	agætan byd ek itrum	(ágætan býð ek ítrum
8	Olæfi brag solar.	Óláfi brag) sólar.]

Prose syntax:
Þrenning eins Guðs má kenna mér orð ok bœnir; sá er getr góða alls ráðanda er vél fróðr. Gunnǫflugr geisli sólar miskunnar boðar gǫfugt ljós; ek býð ítrum Óláfi ágætan brag. [May the Trinity of one God teach me words and prayers; he who gets the good-will of the eloquent ruler of all is indeed wise. The battle-strong beam of the sun of mercy proclaims a splendid light; I offer the excellent poem to glorious Óláfr.]

Textual notes:
A rubric at the head of the column reads Geisli er Einarr Skulason quad vm Olaf Haraldsson. *The text of the poem begins with a large initial* E, *three lines high*.

Lexical variants:
1 ord] oð *AB*. 2 rædanda] valdanda *B*, kiosanda *AW*. hins] ens *B*. snialla] liosa *AW*. 3 vel] miok *B*, mi[ok] *W*, miǫk *A*. goda] greiða *B*.

Phonological and spelling variants:
1 Eins] Æins *A*. ord] orð *W*. 3 frodr] froðr *B*, [froðr] *W*, froðe *A*. er] ær *A*. getr] gætr *A*. goda] goða *W*. 4 Guds] Gvðs *ABW*. þrenning] þrening *B*. 5 Gofugt] Gavfvkt *B*. 7 byd] býð *B*. 8 Olæfi] Olafi *B*.

Editorial variants:
1 ord] óð *Skj, EAK, CN, CPB, C*. 2 rædanda] valdanda *CN, CPB, C, S*. hins] ens *Skj, EAK, CN, CPB, C*. 3 vel er] mjǫk's *Skj, EAK, CN*; mjǫk er *CPB, C*. sa er] sás *Skj, EAK, CN*. goda] greiða *EAK, CN, CPB, C*. 7 byd ek] býðk *Skj, EAK*.

— *2* —

1	Þeirrar er heims i heimi	[Þeirar er heims í heimi
2	heims myrkrum bra þeima	heims myrkrum brá þeima
3	ok lios medan var visi	ok ljós meðan var vísi
4	vedr kalladizst hallar.	veðr- kallaðisk -hallar.
5	Sa leet bert fra biartri	Sá lét bert frá bjartri
6	berazst madr vnd skyiadri	berask maðr und skýjaðri
7	frægr stod af þui flædar	frægr stóð af því flœðar
8	faurnudr raudull stiornu.	fǫrnuðr rǫðull stjǫrnu.]

Prose syntax:
Þeirar er brá heims myrkrum, ok var vísi veðr-hallar meðan kallaðisk ljós heims í heimi. Sá rǫðull bert lét berask maðr frá bjartri stjǫrnu flœðar und skýjaðri; frægr fǫrnuðr stóð af því. [of that sun which destroyed the darkness of the world, and was the prince of the wind-hall while in the world he called himself the light of the world. That sun clearly caused himself to be born a man under heaven from the bright star of the sea; widely renowned prosperity proceeded from that.]

Lexical variants:
5 bert] biartr *B*. 6 skyiadri] skyranne *B*. 8 stiornu] stiornur *B*.

Phonological and spelling variants:
1 Þeirrar er] Þêirar *B*. heimi] heime *B*. 3 medan] meþan *B*. 4 vedr] veðr *B*. kalladizst] kallaðizt *B*. 5 leet] lett *B*. 6 berazst] berazt *B*. madr] mann *B*. vnd] vnð *B*. 7 stod] stoð *B*. 8 faurnudr] faurnoðr *B*. raudull] ravðvll *B*.

Editorial variants:
1 Þeirrar er] Þeirar's *Skj, EAK, CN*. 2 heims] húms *EAK, C, W, FMS, S*. 4 vedr] veðrs *Skj, EAK, CN*. 5 bert] bjartr *Skj, EAK, CN, CPB, C*. 6 skyiadri] skýranni *Skj, EAK, CN, CPB, C*.

— *3* —

1	Sidar heilags bra solar	[Síðar heilags brá sólar
2	setrs var þat fyrir betra	setrs var þat fyr betra
3	audfinnendum annars	auðfinnǫndum annars
4	omiors roduls <liosi>.	ómjós rǫðuls ljósi.
5	Æzstr þrifnudr reed efnázst	Œztr þrifnuðr réð efnask
6	oss þa er lif a krossi	oss þá er líf á krossi
7	iardar allra fyrda	jarðar allra fyrða
8	onaudigr tok dauda.	ónauðigr tók dauða.]

Prose syntax:
Síðar brá sólar ljósi. Þat var auðfinnǫndum fyr betra heilags setrs annars ómjós rǫðuls. Œztr þrifnuðr réð efnask oss, þá er líf allra jarðar fyrða tók ónauðigr dauða á krossi. [Later, the light of the sun was destroyed. For finders of riches, that preceded the better [light] of the holy abode of another not-small sun. Then the best prosperity decided to bring itself to us, when the life of all the men of earth willingly accepted death on a cross.]

Textual notes:
4 liosi] F *reads* lorsi, *altered to* liorsi *with the insertion of a superscript* i. B *reads* liosi.

Lexical variants:
2 setrs] setr B. 5 reed] nam B.

Phonological and spelling variants:
1 heilags] heilgs[.] B. 2 fyrir] fir B. 3 audfinnendum] avðfinnandum B. 4 omiors] vmioss B. roduls] ravðvls B. 5 Æzstr] Æstr B. þrifnudr] þrifnoðr B. efnazst] efnazt B. 6 krossi] krosse B. 8 onaudigr] vnavðigr B. dauda] davða B.

Editorial variants:
1 Sidar] Síz CN. 2 setrs] setr EAK, CN, CPB, C. omiors] ómjós Skj, EAK, CN, C, W, FMS, S. liosi] lorsi FL. 5 reed] nam EAK, CN, CPB, C. 6 þa er] þás Skj, EAK, CN.

— *4* —

1	Upp rann allrar skepnu	[Upp rann allrar skepnu
2	iduandr á dag þridia	iðvandr á dag þriðja
3	Cristr med krapti hæstum	Kristr með krapti hæstum
4	kunnr rettlætis sunnu.	kunnr réttlætis sunnu.
5	Veit ek at milldr fra molldu	Veit ek at mildr frá moldu
6	meginfioldi reis holda	meginfjǫlði reis hǫlða
7	ifláust ma þat efla	(iflaust má þat efla
8	ossa væn med hænum.	ossa ván) með hánum.]

Prose syntax:
Iðvandr Kristr, kunnr allrar skepnu, rann upp með hæstum krapti réttlætis sunnu á þriðja dag. Ek veit, at meginfjǫlði hǫlða reis frá moldu med hánum; iflaust má þat efla ossa ván. [Carefully acting Christ, known to all creation, rose up with the very great strength of the sun of righteousness on the third day. I know that a worthy multitude of men rose from the earth with him; may that strengthen our hope beyond doubt.]

Lexical variants:
1 allrar] engla *B*. 2 á] vf *B*. 3 med] rædr *B*. 4 sunnu] sunna *B*.

Phonological and spelling variants:
1 skepnu] skeppnv *B*. 2 iduandr] iðvanðr *B*. þridia] þriðia *B*. 3 Cristr] Kristr *B*. 4 kunnr] kvnn *B*. rettlætis] retlætis *B*. 5 molldu] mollǫv *B*. 6 fioldi] fiolði *B*. holda] holða *B*. 8 væn] ván *B*. hænum] hanum *B*.

Editorial variants:
1 allrar] engla *Skj, EAK, CN, CPB, C*. 2 á] of *Skj, EAK, CN, CPB, C*. 3 med] ræðr *Skj, EAK, CN, CPB, C*. 4 kunnr] kunn *Skj, EAK, CN, CPB, C*. sunnu] sunna *Skj, EAK, CN, CPB, C*. 5 Veit ek] Veitk *Skj, EAK, CN*.

— 5 —

1	Sonr ste vpp med yndi	[Sonr sté upp með ynði
2	audar milldr fra haudri	auðar mildr frá hauðri
3	iofra bezstr til æzstrar	jǫfra beztr til œztrar
4	allz rædanda hallar.	alls ráðanda hallar.
5	Lofadr sitr englum efri	Lofaðr sitr englum efri
6	audlinga hnigr þingat	(ǫðlinga hnigr þingat
7	dǫglings hird a <dyrum>	dǫglings hirð) á dýrum
8	dagbols konungr stoli.	dagbóls konungr stóli.]

Prose syntax:
Auðar mildr sonr alls ráðanda, beztr jǫfra, sté upp með ynði frá hauðri til œztrar hallar. Lofaðr konungr dagbóls sitr efri englum á dýrum stóli; hirð dǫglings ǫðlinga hnigr þingat. [The son of the ruler of all, generous with riches, the best of princes, ascended with ease from earth to the best hall. The praised king of the sun-home sits above angels on the precious throne; the cohort of the prince of princes bows down there.]

Textual notes:
7 dyrum] dyran *F*, dyrdar *B*.

Lexical variants:
5 englum] ollvm *B*.

Phonological and spelling variants:
1 med] meðr *B*. yndi] ynði *B*. 2 milldr] millðr *B*. 3 bezstr] bestr *B*. æzstrar] æstrar *B*. 4 rædanda] raðanða *B*. 5 Lofadr] Lofaðr *B*. sitr] situr *B*. 7 dǫglings] davglings *B*. hird] hirð *B*. 8 kunungr] kongr *B*. stoli] stole *B*.

Editorial variants:
5 englum] ǫllum *CN*, *CPB*, *C*. 7 dyrum] dyran *FL*; dýrðar *Skj*, *EAK*, *CN*, *CPB*, *C*.

56   *Geisli*

— *6* —

1	Veitti dyrdar drottin	[Veitti dýrðar dróttinn
2	dæduandr giafir anda	dáðvandr gjafar anda
3	mæl kynazst þau monnum	mǫl kynnask þau mǫnnum
4	mattigs framir vætta.	máttigs framir vátta.
5	Þa reis vpp su er einum	Þá reis upp sú er einum
6	alþyd Gudi hlydir	alþýð Guði hlýðir
7	hæstr skiolldungr bydr haulldum	(hæstr skjǫldungr býðr hauldum
8	himinvistar til kristni.	himinvistar til) kristni.]

Prose syntax:
Dáðvandr dýrðar dróttinn veitti mǫnnum gjafar máttigs anda. Framir kynnask mǫl vátta. Þá kristni alþýð, sú er hlýðir einum Guði, reis upp; hæstr skjǫldungr býðr hauldum til himinvistar. [The carefully acting lord of glory gave the gifts of the mighty spirit to men; excellent men study the sayings of witnesses. Then Christianity, common to all men who obey one God, rose up; the highest prince invites men to dwell in heaven.]

Lexical variants:
3 kynazst] sanna *B*. 4 vætta] vottar *B*. 5 þa] þaðan *B*.

Phonological and spelling variants:
1 dyrdar] dyrðar *B*. 2 dæduandr] ðaðvandr *B*. anda] anða *B*. 3 mæl] mal *B*. 6 alþyd] alþið *B*. 7 skiolldungr] skiolldvnghr *B*. bydr] byðr *B*. haulldum] havlðum *B*. 8 himinvistar] himinsvistar *B*.

Editorial variants:
2 giafir] gjafar *Skj, EAK, CN, CPB, C*. 3 kynazst] sanna *Skj, EAK, CN, CPB, C*. 4 vætta] váttar *Skj, EAK, CN, CPB, C*. 5 þa] þaðan *Skj, EAK, CN, CPB, C*. su er] sús *Skj, EAK, CN*. 8 himinvistar] himins vistar *Skj, EAK, CN, C*.

— 7 —

1	Nu skulum gofgann geisla	[Nú skulum gǫfgan geisla
2	Guds hallar ver allir	Guðs hallar vér allir
3	itr þann er Olafr heitir	(ítr þann er Óláfr heitir
4	alstyrkann vel dyrka.	alstyrkan) vel dyrka.
5	Þiod veit hann vnd heida	Þjóð veit hann und heiða
6	hridblæsnum sal vida	hríðblásnum sal víða
7	menn nemi mæl sem ek inni	(menn nemi mál sem ek inni
8	min iarteignum skina.	mín) jarteignum skína.]

Prose syntax:
Nú skulum vér allir dyrka vel gǫfgan geisla Guðs hallar, þann alstyrkan, er heitir ítr Óláfr. Þjóð veit, hann skína jarteignum víða und hríðblásnum sal heiða; menn nemi mál mín sem ek inni. [Now we all should honour well the splendid beam of God's hall, that all-strong one named glorious Óláfr. People know that he shines with miracles widely under the storm-blown hall of the heath; may men accept my speech as I report it.]

Lexical variants:
4 vel] val *B*.

Phonological and spelling variants:
1 gofgann] gavfgan *B*. 2 guds] gvðs *B*. ver] vær *B*. 5 vnd] vnðh *B*. heida] heiða *B*. 6 hridblæsnum] hridblasnum *B*. vida] viða *B*. 7 nemi] neme *B*. mæl] mal *B*.

Editorial variants:
3 þann er] þann's *Skj, EAK, CN*. 4 vel] val *C*. 7 ek inni] innik *Skj, EAK, CN*.

— *8* —

1	Heyr du til afreks orda	[Heyr þu til afreks orða
2	Eysteinn konungr beinna	Eysteinn konungr beinna.
3	Sigurdr hygg at þui snoggum	Sigurðr hygg at því snøggum
4	soknsterkr hue ek fer verka.	sóknsterkr hvé ek ferr verka.
5	Dreingr berr od fir Ingá	Drengr berr óð fyr Inga
6	yduart bid ek magnit	(yðvart bið ek magnit
	<styrkna>	styrkna)
7	mærd þa er myklu vardar	mærð þá er miklu varðar
8	mætig hofud attar.	(máttig hǫfuð áttar.)]

Prose syntax:

Heyr þu, Eysteinn konungr, til beinna afreks orða! Sóknsterkr Sigurðr, hygg at því, hvé ek ferr snøggum verka! Drengr berr óð, þá mærð er miklu varðar, fyr Inga. Yðvart magnit bið ek styrkna, máttig hǫfuð áttar. [King Eysteinn, listen to smooth words of great deeds! Battle-strong Sigurðr, consider this – how I deliver the quick work! The man bears poetry, that praise which is of great value, before Ingi; I desire that your power be strengthened, mighty heads of the nation.]

Textual notes:

6 magnit styrkna] magnit styrkua *F*, stydia *B*.

Lexical variants:

4 fer] fór *B*. 7 þa] þat *B*. 8 mætig] maktvgt *B*.

Phonological and spelling variants:

1 du] þv *B*. afreks] afregs *B*. orda] orða *B*.
3 at] ath *B*. snoggum] snæggium *B*. 4 soknsterkr] sognsterkr *B*. 5 berr] ber *B*. od] oð *B*.
6 bid] bið *B*. 7 mærd] mærð *B*. myklu] miclu *B*. vardar] varðar *B*. 8 hofud] hofvð *B*.

Editorial variants:

1 Heyr du] Heyr *Skj*, *EAK*. 3 hygg] bygg *S*. 6 yduart] yðvarrar *Skj*, *CN*, *CPB*, *C*. bid ek] bið*k Skj*, *EAK*, *CN*. magnit styrkna] magnit styrkva *W*, *FL*, *FMS*, *S*; magn styðja *EAK*; styðja *Skj*, *CN*, *CPB*, *C*.

___ *9* ___

1	Yfirmanni byd ek vnnin	[Yfirmanni býð ek (unnin
2	vpp er mærd borin lærdra	upp er mærð borin) lærðra
3	Jon kollum sva allrar	(Jón kǫllum svá) allrar
4	alþydu brag hlyda.	alþýðu brag hlýða.
5	Hefium hendr enn leyfá	Hefjum hendr en leyfa
6	hygg ek vin roduls tiggia	hygg ek vin rǫðuls tyggja
7	stols vex hæd þar er huilir	(stóls vex hæð þar er hvílir
8	heilagr konungr fagran.	heilagr konungr) fagran.]

Prose syntax:
Ek býð yfirmanni allrar alþyðu lærðra, Jón kǫllum svá, hlýða brag; unnin mærð er borin upp. Hefjum hendr, en ek hygg leyfa fagran vin rǫðuls tyggja; hæð stóls vex, þar er heilagr konungr hvílir. [I ask the superior of the whole multitude of learned men (we call him Jon) to listen to the poetry; the finished poem is offered up. We lift up our hands, and I intend to praise the beautiful friend of the king of the sun; the value of the [bishop's] seat increases, there where the holy king rests.]

Lexical variants:
2 borin] kominn *B.* lærdra] lærdrar *B.* 3 kollum] kalla *B.* sva] ek *B.* 5 Hefium] Hofum *B.* hendr] hrodr *B.* 7 vex] vegs *B.*

Phonological and spelling variants:
1 Yfirmanni] Yfirmanne *B.* vnnin] vnninn *B.* 4 hlyda] hlyða *B.* 6 roduls] ravðvls *B.* 7 hæd] hæð *B.* huilir] hylir *B.*

Editorial variants:
1 byd ek] býðk *Skj, EAK, CN.* 2 vpp er] upp's *Skj, EAK, CN.* lærdra] lærðrar *CN, CPB, C.* 3 kollum] kalla *CN, CPB, C.* sva] ek *CN, CPB, C.* allrar] allra *EAK.* 5 Hefium] Hófum *CN, CPB, C.* hendr] hróðr *Skj, EAK, CN, CPB.* 6 hygg ek] hygg *Skj, EAK, CN.* 7 þar er] þars *Skj, EAK, CN.*

—— *10* ——

1	Aulld samir Olafs gillda	[Qld samir Óláfs gilda
2	ordgnottar bid ek drottinn	(orðgnóttar bið ek dróttin)
3	oss at odgerd þessi	oss at óðgerð þessi
4	itrgeds lofi kuedia.	ítrgeðs lofi kveðja.
5	Fánn ek alldri uál villdra	Fann ek aldri val vildra
6	vallriodanda allra	(vallrjóðanda allra
7	ráun samir rett i einu	raun samir) rétt í einu
8	ranni fremdar manna.	ranni fremdar manna.]

Prose syntax:
Samir oss kveðja gilda ǫld at þessi óðgerð, lofi ítrgeðs Óláfs; ek bið dróttin orðgnóttar. Ek fann aldri vildra val fremdar manna rétt í einu ranni; samir raun allra vallrjóðanda. [It is fitting for us to summon able men to this poetry-making, the praise of high-minded Óláfr; I ask the Lord for word-wealth. I never found a more agreeable selection of men of accomplishment right in one house; it befits the experience of all field-reddeners.]

Lexical variants:
1 Aulld] Oss *B*. Olafs] enn at *B*. gillda] þessv *B*. 3 oss at] alldar *B*. odgerd] Olæfs *B*. þessi] gillða *B*. 7 samir] dygir *B*.

Phonological and spelling variants:
2 ordgnottar] orðgnóttar *B*. bid] bið *B*. 4 geds] geðs *B*. 6 vallriodanda] vallrioðanda *B*. 8 ranni] ranne *B*.

Editorial variants:
1 Aulld] Oss *CN*, *CPB*, *C*. Olafs] enn at *CN*, *CPB*, *C*. gillda] þessu *CN*, *CPB*, *C*. 2 bid ek] biðk *Skj*, *EAK*, *CN*. 3 oss at] aldar *CN*, *CPB*, *C*. odgerd] Óláfs *CN*, *CPB*, *C*. þessi] gilda *CN*, *CPB*, *C*. 5 Fann ek] Fank *Skj*, *EAK*, *CN*. 6 riodanda] rjóðandi *CPB*. 7 samir] dugir *Skj*, *EAK*, *CN*, *CPB*, *C*.

— *11* —

1	Þreklyndz skulu Þrændir	[Þreklynds skulu Þrœndir
2	þegns prydibrag hlyda	þegns prýðibrag hlýða
3	Kristz lifir hann i hæstri	Krists (lifir hann í hæstri
4	hall ok nordmenn allir.	hall) ok norðmenn allir.
5	Dyrd er ægæt ordin	Dýrð er ágæt orðinn
6	elianhress i þessum	eljanhress í þessum
7	þiod ne þeingill fædizst	þjóð- né þengill fœðisk
8	þuilikr i konungs riki.	þvílíkr í -konungs ríki.]

Prose syntax:
Þrœndir ok allir norðmenn skulu hlýða prýðibrag þreklynds þegns Krists; han lifir í hæstri hall. Dýrð eljanhress þjóð-konungs er orðinn ágæt í þessum; né fœðisk þvílíkr þengill i ríki. [Trondheimers and all Norsemen should listen to the splendid poem of the strong-minded thane of Christ; he lives in the highest hall. The fame of the brave people-king has become renowned among these [people]; such a prince will not be born [again] in the realm.]

Lexical variants:
2 þegns prydibrag] þegn prydes brag *B*. 3 Kristz] Krist *B*. 6 þessum] þessv *B*. 8 þuilikr i] þvilikr *B*. konungs] konvngh *B*.

Phonological and spelling variants:
1 Þreklyndz] Þreklynz *B*. skulu] skulo *B*. Þrændir] Þrendir *B*. 4 nordmenn] norðmenn *B*. 5 Dyrd] Ðyrd *B*. ægæt] agæt *B*. 6 elianhress] elivnhress *B*. 7 fædizst] fædizt *B*.

Editorial variants:
2 þegns prydibrag] þegnprýðis brag *Skj*, *EAK*, *CN*, *CPB*, *C*. 3 Kristz] Krist *C*. 6 þessum] þessu *Skj*, *EAK*, *CN*, *CPB*, *C*, *W*, *S*. 8 þuilikr i] þvílikr *Skj*, *EAK*, *CN*, *CPB*, *C*.

—— *12* ——

1	Sighuatr fra ek át segdi	[Sigvatr frá ek at segði
2	<soknbrads> konungs dædir	sóknbráðs konungs dáðir
3	spurt hefir aulld at orti	spurt hefir ǫld at orti
4	Ottar vm gram drottar.	Óttarr um gram dróttar.
5	Þeir hafa þeingil Mæra	Þeir hafa þengil Mœra
6	þvi er syst frama lystánn	(því er sýst) frama lýstan
7	helgum lyt ek er hetu	helgum lýt ek er hétu
8	hofudskælld fira iofri.	hǫfuðskáld fira jǫfri.]

Prose syntax:
Ek frá, at Sigvatr segði dáðir sóknbráðs konungs; ǫld hefir spurt, at Óttarr orti um gram dróttar. Þeir, er hétu hǫfuðskáld, hafa lýstan frama þengill Mœra; því er sýst. Ek lýt helgum jǫfri fira. [I heard that Sigvat told the deeds of the battle-quick king; man has learned that Óttarr composed poetry about the king of the *drótt*. They who are called the best skalds have proclaimed the brave king of Møre; that has been done. I do homage to the holy king of men.]

Textual notes:
2 soknbrads] soknbradr *F*, soknbrads *B*.

Lexical variants:
2 konungs] jofurs *B*. 4 vm] of *B*. 5 þeingil] þeingils *B*.

Phonological and spelling variants:
1 Sighuatr] Sigvatr *B*. 2 dædir] dadir *B*. 3 aulld] olld *B*. 6 lystann] lystan *B*. 8 hofud-skælld] hofudskalld *B*. iofri] jofre *B*.

Editorial variants:
1 fra ek] frák *Skj, EAK, CN*. 2 soknbradr] sóknbráðs *Skj, EAK, CN, C*. konungs] jǫfurs *Skj, EAK, CN, CPB, C*. 3 spurt] frétt *CPB*. hefir] hefr *Skj, EAK, CN, CPB, C*. 6 þvi er] því's *Skj, EAK, CN*. 7 lyt ek] lýtk *Skj, EAK, CN*. 8 fira] firar *Skj, EAK, W, S*.

—— *13* ——

1	Modr vann margar dædir	[Móðr vann margar dáðir
2	munnriodr Hugins gunna	munnrjóðr Hugins gunna
3	satt var at siklingr bætti	satt var at siklingr bœtti
4	sin mein Gudi einum.	sín mein Guði einum.
5	Leyndi lofdung[r] Þrænda	Leyndi lofðungr Þrænda
6	lidgegn snara þegna	liðgegn snara þegna
7	fær gramr hefir frægri	(fár gramr hefir frægri
8	fæz hæleitri gæzsku.	fœðisk) háleitri gœzku.]

Prose syntax:
Móðr munnrjóðr Hugins vann margar dáðir gunna; satt var, at siklingr bœtti sín mein Guði einum. Liðgegn lofðungr Þrænda leyndi snara þegna háleitri gœzku. Fár gramr hefir fœðisk frægri. [The brave mouth-reddener of Huginn accomplished many deeds of battle; it is true that the king made atonement to God alone for his wrongdoing. The prince of the Trondheimers, fair with men, concealed sublime goodness from able thanes; not many a more celebrated king has been born.]

Textual notes:
The order of this stanza and the following one is reversed in B.
5 lofdungr] F *reads* lofdung *corrected to* lofdungr *with the addition of a superscript* r, *apparently by the original scribe.* B *reads* lofdvngr.

Lexical variants:
1 Modr] Moðs *B.* 2 gunna] kvnnan *B.* 7 fær] fæstr *B.* frægri] fremre *B.*

Phonological and spelling variants:
1 dædir] dadir *B.* 2 munnriodr] munnrioðr *B.* 4 Gudi] Gvði *B.* 5 Þrænda] Þrenða *B.*
8 fæz] fest *B.* hæleitri] haleitri *B.* gæzsku] gæskv *B.*

Editorial variants:
1 Modr] Móðs *CN, C.* dædir] dáðar *C.* 2 gunna] kunnar *Skj, EAK, CN, CPB, C.* 7 fær]
fæstr *CN, CPB, C.* frægri] fremri *Skj, EAK, CN, CPB, C.*

— 14 —

1	Red vm tolf sa er trudi	[Réð um tolf sá er trúði
2	tiirbrædr a Gud lædi	tírbráðr á Guð láði
3	þiod muna þegnar fæda	þjóð- muna þegnar fœða
4	þria vetr konung betra	þría vetr -konung betra,
5	ædr fullhugadr felli	áðr fullhugaðr felli
6	folkualldr i dyn skiallda	folkvaldr í dyn skjalda
7	hann speni oss fir innan	hann speni oss fyr innan
8	Aulfishaug fra baulfi.	Ǫlvishaug frá bǫlvi.]

Prose syntax:
Sá tírbráðr, er trúði á Guð, réð láði þría vetr um tolf (þegnar muna fœða betra þjóð-konung), áðr fullhugaðr folkvaldr felli í dyn skjalda fyr innan Ǫlvishaug. Hann speni oss frá bǫlvi. [He who believed in God, eager for praise, ruled the land for three winters beyond twelve (thanes will not engender a better people-king); before the very wise ruler of the nation fell in the din of shields near Olvishaug. May he guide us away from evil.]

Lexical variants:
1 vm] ok *B*. 3 þegnar] þeingil *B*. fæda] biðia *B*.

Phonological and spelling variants:
1 tolf] xij *B*. 2 tiirbrædr] tirbradr *B*. lædi] ladi *B*. 4 konung] konungh *B*. 5 ædr] adr *B*. 7 speni] spenne *B*. innan] innann *B*. 8 Aulfishaug] Avlvishaug *B*.

Editorial variants:
1 vm] ok *EAK, CN, CPB, C*. sa er] sás *Skj, EAK, CN*. 3 þegnar] þengill *Skj, EAK, CN, CPB, C*. fæda] bíða *Skj, EAK, CN, CPB, C*. 4 konung] konungs *CN, C*.

— *15* —

1 Fregit hef ek satt at sagdi	[Fregit hef ek satt at sagði
2 sniallri ferd ædr \<bardizst\>	snjallri ferð áðr barðisk
3 drott nytr doglings mættar	(drótt nýtr dǫglings máttar)
4 draum sinn konungr Rauma.	draum sinn konungr Rauma.
5 Stiga sa standa fagran	Stiga sá standa fagran
6 stiornar fimr til himna	stjórnar fimr til himna
7 rausn dugir hans at hrosa	(rausn dugir hans at hrósa)
8 Haurda gramr af iordu.	Hǫrða gramr af jǫrðu.]

Prose syntax:
Fregit hef ek satt, at konungr Rauma sagði snjallri ferð draum sinn áðr barðisk (drótt nýtr dǫglings máttar). Hǫrða gramr, stjórnar fimr, sá fagran stiga standa af jǫrðu til himna (dugir at hrósa hans rausn). [I have heard truly that the king of the Raumar told the clever band his dream before they fought (the *drótt* enjoys the prince's might). The king of the Hordar, accustomed to leadership, saw a beautiful ladder ascending from earth to heaven (it is fitting to praise his greatness).]

Textual notes:
2 bardizst] berdizst *F*, bardizt *B*.

Lexical variants:
5 sa] kvad *B*. 6 stiornar] styriar *B*.

Phonological and spelling variants:
1 sagdi] segdi *B*. 2 ædr] adr *B*. 3 doglings] davglings *B*. mættar] mattar *B*. 5 standa] stanða *B*.

Editorial variants:
1 hef ek] hefk *Skj, EAK, CN*. sagdi] segði *Skj, EAK, CN, CPB, C*. 5 sa] kvað *CN, CPB, C*. 6 stiornar] styjar *Skj, EAK, CN, CPB, C*. 8 af] frá *CPB*.

— *16* —

1	Ok <hagliga> hugdiz	[Ok hagliga hugðisk
2	hrockuiseids hins dockua	hrøkkviseiðs hins døkkva
3	lyngs i lopt vpp ganga	lyngs í lopt upp ganga
4	lætrs stridandi siþan.	látrs stríðandi síðan.
5	Leit sa er <landzfolk gætir>	Lét sá er landsfolk gætir
6	liknframr himinriki	líknframr himinríki
7	vmgeypnandi opnaz	umgeypnandi opnask
8	allz heims fir gram sniallum.	alls heims fyr gram snjǫllum.]

Prose syntax:
Ok stríðandi látrs hins døkkva lyngs hrøkkviseiðs hugðisk síðan ganga hagliga upp í lopt. Líknframr umgeypnandi alls heims, sá er gætir landsfolk, lét himinríki opnask fyr snjǫllum gram. [And then the enemy of the lair of the dark coiling fish of the heather thought that he went easily up into the air. The outstandingly merciful one, who watches over the people of the land, holding all the world in his hands, caused the kingdom of heaven to open before the clever king.]

Lexical variants:
1 hagliga] huerlofadr *F*, hagliga *B*. 2 hrockuiseids] hravkkvibavgs *B*. hins] ens *B*. 4 lætrs] latr *B*. 5 landsfolk gætir] landz folkgætir *F*, landfolks gætir *ABRW*, landfolks getir *U* land folcs getir *T*. 6 liknframr] liknsamr *AB*, liknbiartr *U*, likbiartr *RW*, licbiartr *T*. 7 vmgeypnandi] vmgeupnanda *T*. opnaz] opna *ABRTUW*. fir] firir *W*, fyrir *U*, firi *T*.

Phonological and spelling variants:
1 hugdiz] hvgdizt *B*. 2 dockua] davcka *B*. 4 siþan] sidan *B*. 5 Leit] Let *BRTUW*, Læt *A*. 6 Himinriki] himinnriki *B*. 7 vmgeypnandi] vmgæypnandi *A*, umgæypn[a]ndi *W*. 8 heims] hæims *A*. sniallum] snjǫllum *AW*.

Editorial variants:
1 hagliga] huerlofadr] *FL*, *FMS*; hvarlofaðr *W*, *S*. 2 hrockuiseids] hrøkkvibaugs *CN*, *CPB*, *C*; hrokkinseids *FL*, *FMS*, *S*. hins] ens *Skj*, *EAK*, *CN*, *CPB*, *S*. 5 sa er] sás *Skj*, *EAK*, *CN*. landzfolk gætir] landfolks gætir *AF*, *Skj*, *EAK*, *CN*, *CPB*, *C*; lands folkgætir *W*, *FMS*, *S*. 6 liknframr] líknsamr *CN*, *C*; líksamr *S*. 7 opnaz] opna *AF*, *CN*, *CPB*, *C*.

— 17 —

1 Vakit fra ek vig a Stikla	[Vakit frá ek víg á Stikla-
2 vidlendr stodum siþan	víðlendr -stǫðum síðan
3 Innþrændum leet vndir	Innþrœndum lét undir
4 almreyrlitudr dreyra.	almreyrlituðr dreyra.
5 Heims þessa fra ek huassann	Heims þessa frá ek hvassan
6 huatir felldu gram skatnar	(hvatir felldu gram skatnar)
7 þeir drygdu bol brigdu	(þeir drýgðu bǫl) brigðu
8 branddrif numin lifi.	branddríf numinn lífi.]

Prose syntax:
Síðan frá ek vakit víg á Stikla-stǫðum, víðlendr almreyrlituðr lét Innþrœndum dreyra undir. Frá ek hvassan branddríf numinn brigðu lífi þessa heims. Hvatir skatnar felldu gram; þeir drýgðu bǫl. [I heard that a battle then broke out at Stiklarstaðir; the widely landed arrow-reddener caused the Trondheimers to bleed from wounds. I heard that the brave sword-driver was taken from the transitory life of this world. Rash men killed the king; they committed evil.]

Lexical variants:
4 almreyrlitudr] almreys litvdur *B*. 8 branddrif] bavgdrif *B*.

Phonological and spelling variants:
2 siþan] sidan *B*. 3 Innþrændum] Innþrendum *B*. leet] let *B*. 7 drygdu] dryvgdv *B*. bol] bavl *B*. 8 numin] nvminn *B*.

Editorial variants:
1 fra ek] frák *Skj, EAK, CN*. Stikla] Stiklar *Skj, EAK*. 4 almreyrlitudr] almreyrs lituðr *Skj, EAK, CN, CPB, C*; almreyrlundr *W, FMS, S*. 5 fra ek] frák *Skj, EAK, CN*. 8 branddrif] baugdrif *CN, CPB, C*.

— 18 —

1	Fuss er ek þvi at vann visir	[Fúss em ek því at vann vísir
2	var hann mestr konungr	(var hann mestr konungr
	flestra	flestra)
3	drott nemi mærd ef ek	(drótt nemi mærð) ef ek
	mætta	mætta
4	manndyrdir stef vanda.	manndýrðir stef vanda.
5	Greitt mæ gumnum letta	Greitt má gumnum létta
6	Guds <ridari> stridum	Guðs ríðari stríðum
7	rauskr þiggr allt sem æskir	rǫskr þiggr alt sem œskir
8	Olafr af gram solar.	Óláfr af gram sólar.]

Prose syntax:
Fúss em ek vanda stef, ef ek mætta, því at vísir vann manndýrðir (hann var mestr konungr flestra); drótt nemi mærð. Guðs ríðari má greitt létta gumnum stríðum; rǫskr Óláfr þiggr alt sem œskir af gram sólar. [I am eager to make a *stef*, if I can, because the prince accomplished man-ornaments (he was a great king over many); may the *drótt* accept praise. God's knight can easily alleviate the afflictions of men; brave Óláfr gets all he desires from the king of the sun.]

Textual notes:
6 ridari] ridadri *F*, ridari *B*.

Lexical variants:
1 er] em *B*. visir] visi *B*. 2 flestra] flestar *B*. 7 rauskr] hravstr *B*. æskir] æstir *B*.

Phonological and spelling variants:
1 Fuss] Fvs *B*. þvi at] þvit *B*. 4 vanda] vannða *B*. 5 mæ] ma *B*. 6 guds] gðs *B*. stridum] striðvm *B*.

Editorial variants:
1 þvi at] þvít *Skj*, *EAK*, *CN*; þat er *FL*. visir] vísi *Skj*, *EAK*, *CN*, *CPB*, *C*. 2 flestra] flestrar *Skj*, *EAK*, *CN*, *CPB*, *C*. 3 ef ek mætta] ef mættak *Skj*, *EAK*, *CN*. 7 rauskr] hraustr *Skj*, *EAK*, *CN*, *CPB*, *C*. æskir] æstir *Skj*, *EAK*, *CN*, *CPB*, *C*.

— 19 —

1	\<Nædit\> biartr þa er beidir	[Náðit bjartr þá er beiðir
2	baugskiallda lauk alldri	baugskjalda lauk aldri
3	syndi saluordr grundar	(sýndi salvǫrðr grundar
4	sin takn rodull skina.	sín tákn) rǫðull skína.
5	Fyrr var hitt at harra	Fyr var hitt at harra
6	haudrtiallda \<bra\> dauda	hauðrtjalda brá dauða
7	happ nytaz mer mætt[u]	happ- nýtask mér -mætu
8	mæltol \<skini\> solar.	máltól skini sólar.]

Prose syntax:
Bjartr rǫðull náðit skína, þá er beiðir baugskjalda lauk aldri; salvǫrðr grundar sýndi sín tákn. Hitt var fyr, at happ-mætu skini sólar brá dauða harra hauðrtjalda; máltól nýtask mér. [The bright sun was not permitted to shine then, when the desirer of the ring-shield lost his life; the guardian of the hall of earth showed his signs. It was previously that the blessing-rich shining of the sun ceased at the death of the king of earth's roof; speech-tools are of use to me.]

Textual notes:
1 Nædit] Nædiz *F*, Naðit *B*. 6 bra] bar *F*, bra *B*. 7 mættu] *The last letter of the word is smudged in* F; *it could be either* u *or* a, *but* u *is almost certainly the correct reading.* B *reads* mætv. 8 skini] skinu *F*, skine *B*.

Lexical variants:
2 baugskiallda] bavgs skialldar *B*. 5 at] er *B*. 6 dauda] alldri *B*. 7 happ] hept *B*.

Phonological and spelling variants:
3 syndi] synði *B*. 4 rodull] dauðvll *B*. skina] skinæ *B*. 8 mæltol] maltol *B*.

Editorial variants:
1 Nædit] Nædiz *FL*, *S*. þa er] þás *Skj*, *EAK*, *CN*. 2 baugskiallda] baugskjaldar *Skj*, *EAK*, *CN*, *CPB*, *C*. 6 dauda] aldri *EAK*, *CN*, *CPB*, *C*. 7 happ] hept *EAK*, *CN*, *CPB*, *C*. mættu] mætti *CN*, *CPB*, *C*; mætta *W*, *FMS*, *S*. 8 skini] skinu *W*, *FL*, *FMS*, *S*.

— *20* —

1	Gerdiz bratt þa er bardiz	[Gerðusk brátt þá er barðisk
2	broddriodr vid kyn þiodar	broddrjóðr við kyn þjóðar
3	gramr <vandit> sæ syndum	(gramr vanðit sá synðum
4	sik iarteignir <miklar>.	sik) jarteignir miklar.
5	Lios bran liki visa	Ljós brann líki vísa
6	logskids yfir siþan	lǫgskíðs yfir síðan
7	þa er aund med ser sendiz	þá er ǫnd með sér sendis
8	samdægrs Gud framdi.	samdægris Guð framði.]

Prose syntax:
Miklar jarteignir gerðusk brátt, þá er broddrjóðr barðisk við kyn þjóðar; sá gramr vanðit sik synðum. Ljós brann síðan yfir líki vísa, þá er Guð framði samdægris ǫnd sendis lǫgskíðs með sér. [Great miracles were immediately wrought then, when the point-reddener fought with the family of peoples; that king did not accustom himself to sin. Light burned over the body of the prince then, when God raised the soul of the sender of sea-skis to himself that same day.]

Textual notes:
3 vandit] vandiz *F*, firde *B*. 4 miklar] milar *F*, miclar *B*.

Lexical variants:
1 þa] þar *B*. 5 visa] ræsis *B*. 7 þa er] þvit *B*. sendiz] synðizt *B*.

Phonological and spelling variants:
1 Gerdiz] Giordizt *B*. bardiz] bardizt *B*. 2 vid] við *B*. 3 sæ] sa *B*. 6 logskids] laugskids *B*. siþan] sidan *B*. 7 aund] ǫnð *B*. 8 samdægrs] samdægurs *B*. Gud] Gvð *B*.

Editorial variants:
1 þa er] þars *Skj*, *EAK*, *CN*. 3 gramr] framr *EAK*. vandit] vandiz *FL*. 5 visa] ræsis *CN*, *CPB*, *C*. 7 þa er] þvít *Skj*, *CN*, *CPB*, *C*. sendiz] sýndisk *CN*, *C*; syndis *CPB*; senda *S*. 8 samdægrs] samdægris *Skj*, *EAK*, *CN*, *CPB*, *C*, *W*, *FMS*, *S*.

— *21* —

1	Dyrd lætr \<drottins\> Horda	[Dýrð lætr dróttins Hǫrða
2	dragizst mærd þannig	(dragisk mærð þannig)
	hrærda	hrœrða
3	itr munat odlingr betri	ítr munat ǫðlingr betri
4	allz grædari fædaz.	alls grœðari fœðask.
5	Greitt \<mæa gumnum letta	Greitt má gumnum létta
6	Guds ridari stridum	Guðs ríðari stríðum
7	rauskr þiggr allt sem æskir	rǫskr þiggr alt sem œskir
8	Olafr af gram solar.\>	Óláfr af gram sólar.]

***Prose syntax*:**
Ítr grœðari alls lætr dýrð dróttins Hǫrða hrœrða; mærð dragisk þannig. Betri ǫðlingr munat fœðask. Guðs ríðari má greitt létta gumnum stríðum; rǫskr Óláfr þiggr alt sem œskir af gram sólar. [The glorious healer of all causes the fame of the lord of the Hordar to be disseminated; the poem turns itself thither. A better prince will not be born. God's knight can easily alleviate the afflictions of men; brave Óláfr gets all he desires from the king of the sun.]

***Textual notes*:**
The full text of the stef appears only twice in F, *in stanzas 18 and 30, and the two versions differ slightly. I have printed the version from stanza 18 each time the stef is abbreviated in the MS.* 1 drottins] drottin *F*, davgling *B*.

***Lexical variants*:**
2 dragizst mærd þannig hrærda] dvlęzt menn við þat gleðia *B*.

***Phonological and spelling variants*:**
1 Horda] Havrda *B*. 3 odlingr] avdlingr *B*. 4 grædari] greðari *B*. fædaz] fædazt *B*.

***Editorial variants*:**
1 drottins] drottin *FL*; drottinn *FMS*; dǫgling *CN, CPB, C*. 2 dragizst mærd þannig hrærda] dyljat meðr þess gleðia *CN*; dyljask meðr við þat gleðja *CPB, C*.

—— *22* ——

1	Drott þo dyrann sueita	[Drótt þó dýran sveita
2	doglings riks af liki	dǫglings ríks af líki
3	vǫn gledr hug med hreinu	ván gleðr hug með hreinu
4	hans batnadar vatni.	hans batnaðar vatni.
5	Satt var at Sygna drottins	Satt var at Sygna dróttins
6	særendr Gudi kærann	særendr Guði kæran
7	hrings megu heyra dreingir	hrings megu heyra drengir
8	hans brogd i grof logdu.	hans brǫgð í grǫf lǫgðu.]

Prose syntax:
Drótt þó dýran sveita af líki ríks dǫglings með hreinu vatni; ván hans batnaðar gleðr hug. Satt var, at særendr hrings lǫgðu kæran Guði í grǫf; megu Sygna dróttins drengir heyra hans brǫgð. [The *drótt* washed precious blood from the body of the powerful prince with pure water; anticipation of his improvement gladdens the mind. It was true that wounders of the ring laid God's dear one in the grave; may the men of the lord of Sogn hear his deeds.]

Lexical variants:
4 hans] hars *B*. 5 var] er *B*. drottins] drottinn *B*. 7 megu] skulo *B*.

Phonological and spelling variants:
1 þo] þvo *B*. 2 doglings] davglings *B*. 3 vǫn] van *B*. 4 batnadar] battnadar *B*. 5 Sygna] Sygnæ *B*. 6 kærann] kæran *B*. 8 brogd] bravgd *B*. grof] gravf *B*. logdu] logðu *B*.

Editorial variants:
4 hans] hǫs *Skj*, *EAK*, *CN*, *C*. 5 Satt var] Satt's *Skj*, *EAK*, *CN*; Satt er *CPB*, *C*. drottins] dróttin *Skj*, *EAK*, *CN*, *CPB*, *C*, *W*, *FMS*. 7 megu] skulu *CN*, *CPB*, *C*. 8 grof] róf *W*, *S*.

— *23* —

1	Kom þar blindr enn ek byria	[Kom þar blindr (en ek byrja
2	blid verk muné sidar	blíð verk) muni síðar
3	audar niotr er ytar	auðar njótr er ýtar
4	iofurs bein þuegit hofdu.	jǫfurs bein þvegit hǫfðu.
5	Sionbrautir þó sinar	Sjónbrautir þó sínar
6	seggium kunnz i brunni	seggjum kunns í brunni
7	ær þeim er Olafs dreyra	árr þeim er Óláfs dreyra
8	orms landa var blandinn.	orms landa var blandinn.]

Prose syntax:
Blindr auðar njótr kom þar muni síðar, er ýtar hǫfðu þvegit jǫfurs bein; en ek byrja blíð verk. Árr orms landa þó sjónbrautir sínar í brunni, þeim er Óláfs dreyra, seggjum kunns, var blandinn. [A blind enjoyer of wealth came there later, where men had washed the prince's bones; and I put the happy work into motion. The messenger of the serpent's lands washed his sight-paths in the liquid which was blended with the blood of Óláfr, known to men.]

Lexical variants:
1 Kom þar] Þar kom *B*. 5 þó] stravk *B*.

Phonological and spelling variants:
1 blindr] blinðr *B*. 2 muné] mvni *B*. 4 hofdu] hǫfðv *B*. 6 brunni] brune *B*. 7 ær] ávr *B*. 8 landa] lanða *B*. blandinn] blandin *B*.

Editorial variants:
1 Kom þar] Þar kom *Skj, EAK, CN, CPB, C*. enn ek byria] en byrjak *Skj, EAK, CN*. 5 þó] strauk *Skj, EAK, CN, CPB, C*. 6 kunnz] kunnr *EAK*. 7 þeim er] þeim's *Skj, EAK, CN*.

— *24* —

1	Sion feck seggr af hreinu	[Sjón fekk seggr af hreinu
2	su dyrd munat fyrdum	sú dyrð munat fyrðum
3	fôrnudr mun þat fyrnaz	fǫrnuðr mun þat fyrnask
4	fiolgodr konungs blodi.	fjǫlgóðr konungs blóði.
5	Greitt <mæa gumnum letta	Greitt má gumnum létta
6	Guds ridari stridum	Guðs ríðari stríðum
7	rauskr þiggr allt sem æskir	rǫskr þiggr alt sem œskir
8	Olafr af gram solar.>	Óláfr af gram sólar.]

Prose syntax:
Seggr fekk sjón af hreinu blóði konungs (þat mun fjǫlgóðr fǫrnuðr); sú dyrð munat fyrnask fyrðum. Guðs ríðari má greitt létta gumnum stríðum; rǫskr Óláfr þiggr alt sem œskir af gram sólar. [The man got his sight from the pure blood of the king (that will be good fortune); the fame [of it] will not be forgotten by men. God's knight can easily alleviate the afflictions of men; brave Óláfr gets all he desires from the king of the sun.]

Lexical variants:
2 munat] muna *B*. 3 mun] var *B*.

Phonological and spelling variants:
3 fôrnudr] favrnvdr *B*. fyrnaz] fyrnazt *B*.

Editorial variants:
3 mun] vas *Skj*, *EAK*, *CN*, *CPB*, *C*. 4 fiolgodr] fjǫlgóðs *CPB*.

— *25* —

1	Tolf mænudr var tynir	[Tolf mánuðr var týnir
2	<tandrauds> hulidr sandi	tandrauðs huliðr sandi
3	fremdar lystr ok fasta	fremðar lystr ok fasta
4	fimm nætr vala strætis	fimm nætr vala strætis,
5	aadr enn vpp or vidu	áðr en upp ór víðu
6	vlfs nistanda kistu	ulfs nistanda kistu
7	dyrr lætr drottinn harra	dýrr lætr dróttinn harra
8	dædmilldz koma lædi.	dáðmilds koma láði.]

Prose syntax:
Fremðar lystr týnir tandrauðs fasta vala strætis var huliðr sandi tolf mánuðr ok fimm nætr, áðr en dýrr dróttinn harra lætr kistu dáðmilds ulfs nistanda koma upp ór víðu láði. [The destroyer of the flame-red fire of the street of hawks, desirous of fame, was covered with sand twelve months and five nights, before the dear lord of princes causes the coffin of the good-doing feeder of the wolf to come up out of the wide land.]

Textual notes:
2 tandrauds] tandraudr *F*, tandravds *B*.

Lexical variants:
6 vlfs nistanda] vlfnistanda *B*. 7 lætr] let *B*.

Phonological and spelling variants:
1 mænudr] manvdr *B*. tynir] tinir *B*. 2 hulidr] hvlidur *B*. sandi] sanði *B*. 4 strætis] stretis *B*. 5 aadr] adr *B*. vidu] viðv *B*. 7 harra] harræ *B*. 8 dædmilldz] daðmilldz *B*. lædi] laði *B*.

Editorial variants:
1 mænudr] mánuði *W*, *FMS*, *S*. 2 tandraudr] tandrauðs *Skj*, *EAK*, *CN*, *CPB*, *C*, *W*; tandranðr *FMS*; tandra *S*. 3 ok] auk *EAK*. 6 vlfs nistanda] úlfnistanda *CN*, *CPB*, *C*. 7 lætr] lét *Skj*, *EAK*, *CN*, *CPB*, *C*.

— *26* —

1	Mæl feck madr þar er huilir	[Mál fekk maðr þar er hvílir
2	margfridr iofurr sidan	margfríðr jǫfurr síðan
3	adr sa er orda hlyru	áðr sá er orða hlýru
4	<afskurdi> <farit> hafdi.	afskurði farit hafði.
5	Frægd ridr fylkis Egda	Frægð ríðr fylkis Egða
6	folksterks af þvi verki	folksterks af því verki
7	iofrs snilli fremz alla	jǫfurs snilli fremask alla
8	vngs a danska tungu.	ungs á danska tungu.]

Prose syntax:
Síðan fekk maðr mál, sá er áðr hafði farit afskurði hlýru orða, þar er margfríðr jǫfurr hvílir. Frægð folksterks fylkis Egða ríðr af því verki; snilli ungs jǫfurs fremask á alla danska tungu. [Then a man, the one who previously had forfeited a cut-off piece of his ship-bow of words, gained speech there where the very beautiful king rests. The fame of the people-strong leader of Agdir travels because of this deed; the honour of the young king is advanced wherever Norse is spoken.]

Textual notes:
4 afskurdi] afskurdr *F*, af skyfdur *B*. farit] fariz *F*, farizt *B*.

Lexical variants:
1 þar er] er *B*. 3 hlyru] hlyðu *B*. 5 ridr] vinr *B*. 6 folksterks] folks sterks *B*. 7 fremz] þreifst *B*.

Phonological and spelling variants:
1 Mæl] Mal *B*. feck] fekk *B*. 2 margfridr] margfriðr *B*. iofurr] jofur *B*. 3 adr] aðr *B*. 5 Frægd] Frêgð *B*. 7 iofrs] jofurs *B*.

Editorial variants:
1 þar er] þars *Skj*, *EAK*; er *CN*, *CPB*, *C*. huiliz] hvílir *Skj*, *EAK*, *CN*, *CPB*, *C*, *W*, *FMS*, *S*. 3 sa er] sás *Skj*, *EAK*, *CN*. hlyru] hlýðu *Skj*, *EAK*, *CN*, *CPB*, *C*, *W*. 4 afskurdi] afskurðr *Skj*, *W*, *FL*, *FMS*; af skýfðr *EAK*, *CN*, *CPB*, *C*. farit] fariz *CPB*, *FL*. 5 ridr] vinnr *CN*, *CPB*, *C*. 6 folksterks] folks sterks *C*. 7 fremz] þreifsk *CN*, *CPB*, *C*.

—— *27* ——

1	Faudr skulum fulltings bidia	[Fǫður skulum fultings biðja
2	fremdarþiod ens goda	fremdarþjóð ens góða
3	mædir mart æ lædi	mœðir mart á láði
4	Magnus huatir bragnar.	Magnúss hvatir bragnar.
5	Greitt <mæa gumnum letta	Greitt má gumnum létta
6	Guds ridari stridum	Guðs ríðari stríðum
7	rauskr þiggr allt sem æskir	rǫskr þiggr alt sem œskir
8	Olafr af gram solar.>	Óláfr af gram sólar.]

Prose syntax:

Hvatir bragnar skulum biðja fǫður Magnúss ens góða fultings; mart mœðir frem-
darþjóð á láði. Guðs ríðari má greitt létta gumnum stríðum; rǫskr Óláfr þiggr alt sem
œskir af gram sólar. [We brave men should pray to the father of Magnus the Good for
help; much afflicts the valiant people in the land. God's knight can easily alleviate the
afflictions of men; brave Óláfr gets all he desires from the king of the sun.]

Textual notes:

1 Faudr] *A contraction of* faðir. 4 Magnus] *Genitive of* Magnús.

Lexical variants:

1 skulum] skul[u] *B.* 2 ens] enn *B.*

Phonological and spelling variants:

1 Faudr] Favdur *B.* bidia] biðia *B.* 3 æ] a *B.* lædi] laði *B.*

Editorial variants:

1 skulum] skulu *Skj, EAK, CN, CPB, C.* 2 ens] enn *Skj, EAK, CN, CPB, C.* frem-
darþiod] fremðar þjóð *Skj, CPB, C, W, FL, FMS, S.*

— 28 —

1	Geck sinum bur sueckuir	[Gekk sínum bur søkkvir
2	solar straums i drauma	sólar straums í drauma:
3	valld letz fylgia folldar	vald lézk fylgja foldar
4	framlyndum gram myndu	framlyndum gram mundu,
5	adr a Hlyrskogsheidi	áðr á Hlýrskógsheiði
6	hardgedr konungr bardiz	harðgeðr konungr barðisk
7	gods eldis naut gyldir	(góðs eldis naut gylðir
8	gnott vid heidnar drottir.	gnótt) við heiðnar dróttir.]

Prose syntax:
Søkkvir straums sólar gekk sínum bur í drauma (foldar vald lézk mundu fylgja fram-
lyndum gram), áðr harðgeðr konungr barðisk við heiðnar dróttir á Hlýrskógsheiði;
gylðir naut gnótt góðs eldis. [The enemy of the sun of the stream went to his son in a
dream (the strength of the land said he would help the forward-striving prince) before
the hard-minded king fought against the heathen *drótt* at Hlýrskógsheiðr; the wolf got
an abundance of good food.]

Lexical variants:
3 valld] valldr *BHHr*. letz] kvæzt *B*, quedz *Hr*, kvaðz *H*. 6 hardgedr] hardfeingr *B*,
harðfeingr *H*, hardlyndr *Hr*. konungr] jofur *B*, iǫfurr *H*, gramr *Hr*. 7 gods] god *Hr*.
naut] feck *BH*, fieck *Hr*.

Phonological and spelling variants:
4 framlyndum] framlundum *B*, frammlyndum *H*. myndu] mundu *BHr*. 5 adr] aðr *H*,
adur *Hr*. a] æ *Hr*. Hlyrskogsheidi] Hlyskogsheidi *Hr*, Hlyrskógsheiði *H*. 6 bardiz]
bardizt *B*. 7 gods] godz *B*, goðs *H*. eldis] elldis *B*. gyldir] gylldir *B*. 8 heidnar] heiðnar
Hr.

Editorial variants:
3 valld] valdr *Skj, EAK, CN, CPB, C, W, S*. letz] kvazk *CN, CPB, C*. 6 hardgedr]
harðfengr *Skj, EAK, CN, CPB, C*. konungr] jǫfurr *Skj, EAK, CN, CPB, C*. 7 naut] fekk
Skj, EAK, CN, CPB, C; hlaut *W, S*.

—— 29 ——

1	Let <iarplidan> ætu	[Lét jarplitan átu
2	arnar iods enn godi	arnar jóðs enn góði
3	munn raud mælmþings	munn rauð malmþings
	kennir	kennir
4	Magnus Hugins fagna.	Magnús Hugins fagna.
5	Hrætt vard folk a flotta	Hrætt varð folk á flótta
6	fran beit egg at leggia	frǫn beit egg at leggja
7	sorg bidu vif enn vargar	sorg biðu víf en vargar
8	Vindversk of hræ gindu.	Vinðversk of hræ ginðu.]

Prose syntax:
Magnús enn góði lét jarplitan fagna Hugins átu. Malmþings kennir rauð munn arnar
jóðs. Hrætt folk varð at leggja á flótta; frǫn egg beit, Vinðversk víf biðu sorg, en vargar
ginðu of hræ. [Magnus the Good made the brown-coloured one glad with the food of
Hugin; the prover of the weapon-meeting reddened the mouth of the eagle's offspring.
The frightened army fled, the sharp blade bit, the Wendish women experienced sorrow,
and wolves gaped over the corpses.]

Textual notes:
1 iarplidan] iarplidr *F*, jarplitan *B*, jarpleitan *Hr*. ætu] ætu ætu *F*.

Lexical variants:
2 enn] hin *Hr*. 3 mælmþings] milldingr *B*, milldingur *Hr*. kennir] innann *B*, innan *Hr*.
4 hugins] hvginn *B*, hugan *Hr*. 5 vard] var *Hr*. 6 beit] leit *B*. at] æ *Hr*. leggia] leggi *Hr*.
7 bidu] hlvtv *BHr*. 8 of] vm *Hr*.

Phonological and spelling variants:
1 Let] Liet *Hr*. ætu] átu *B*, ato *Hr*. 2 godi] goði *B*. 6 leggia] legia *B*. 8 Vindversk] Vind-
vesk *BHr*.

Editorial variants:
1 iarplidan] iarplidr *FL*, jarplitaðs *Skj*, *CN*; jarplitan *EAK*, *CPB*, *C*; jarplits *W*, *FMS*, *S*.
3 mælmþings] mildingr *CN*, *CPB*, *C*. kennir] innan *CN*, *CPB*, *C*. 4 hugins] hugin *Skj*,
EAK, *CN*, *CPB*, *C*, *W*, *S*. 7 bidu] hlutu *CN*, *CPB*, *C*.

— 30 —

1	Raun er at sigr gaf sinum	[Raun er at sigr gaf sínum
2	sniallr lausnára spialli	snjallr lausnara spjalli
3	hrosa ek verkum visa	(hrósa ek verkum vísa
4	vigdiarfs fromum arfa.	vígdjarfs) frǫmum arfa.
5	Greitt ma gumnum letta	Greitt má gumnum létta
6	Gods ridari i stridum	Guðs ríðari stríðum
7	rauskr þiggr allt þat er æskir	rǫskr þiggr alt þat er œskir
8	Olaf[r] af gram solar.	Óláfr af gram sólar.]

***Prose syntax*:**
Raun er, at snjallr spjalli lausnara gaf frǫmum arfa sínum sigr; ek hrósa verkum víg-djarfs vísa. Guðs ríðari má greitt létta gumnum stríðum; rǫskr Óláfr þiggr alt þat er œskir af gram sólar. [It is a matter of experience that the brave confidant of the Saviour gave victory to his distinguished son; I praise the deeds of the battle-bold prince. God's knight can easily alleviate the afflictions of men; brave Óláfr gets all he desires from the king of the sun.]

***Textual notes*:**
8 Olafr] *The* r *is written above the line.*

***Phonological and spelling variants*:**
1 sigr] sigur *Hr*. 2 sniallr] sniallur *Hr*. 3 lausnara] lavnsara *B*. spialli] pialli *B*. 4 vig-diarfs] vighdiarfs *Hr*. fromum] fraumum *Hr*.

***Editorial variants*:**
1 Raun er] raun's *Skj, EAK, CN*. 3 hrosa ek] hrósak *Skj, EAK, CN*. 6 ridari i stridum] ríðari stríðum *Skj, EAK, CN, CPB, C*. 7 rauskr] hraustr *Skj, EAK, CN, CPB, C*. þat er] sem *Skj, EAK, CN, CPB, C, S*.

— *31* —

1	<Reynði Gutthormr grundar	[Reyndi Gutthormr grundar
2	gat hann rett við þravm	(gat hann rétt) við þrǫm
	slettan	slettan
3	adr hvat Olafs tedu	áðr hvat Óláfs téðu
4	alkæns við Gvð bænir.	alkœns við Guð bœnir.
5	Dag let sinn med sigri	Dag lét sinn með sigri
6	soknþydr jofur prydazt	sóknþýðr jǫfurr prýðask
7	þa er j Avngvlseyiar	þá er í Ǫngulseyjar-
8	vnðreyr bitv svnde.>	undreyr bitu -sundi.]

Prose syntax:
Gutthormr reyndi við slettan þrǫm grundar, hvat bœnir alkœns Óláfs téðu áðr við Guð; hann gat rétt. Sóknþýðr jǫfurr lét sinn dag prýðask með sigri, þá er undreyr bitu í Ǫngulseyjar-sundi. [On the flat coast of the land Guthormr proved how previously the prayers of much-skilled Óláfr prevailed with God; he knew well. The battle-happy king caused his day to be adorned with victory then, when the wound-reeds bit in Ongulseyjarsund.]

Textual notes:
The text of this stanza is found only in B.

Editorial variants:
7 þa er] þás *Skj, EAK, CN.*

— 32 —

1	<Vist hafdi lid lestir	[Víst hafði lið lestir
2	li[nnz] þrimr lvtum minna	linns þrimr hlutum minna
3	heiptar milldr at hialldri	heiptar mildr at hjaldri
4	hardr fvndr var sæa grundar.	(harðr fundr var sá) grundar.
5	Þo red hann at hvorv	Þó réð hann at hvǫru
6	honum tioði vel moðir	honum tjóði vel móðir-
7	harr fekst af þvi hlyre	hár fekst af því -hlýri
8	hagnadr or styr gagne.>	hagnaðr ór styr gagni.]

Prose syntax:
Víst hafði heiptar mildr lestir linns grundar þrimr hlutum minna lið at hjaldri; sá fundr
var harðr. Þó at hvǫru réð hann gagni ór styr; af því fekst hár hagnaðr; móðir-hlýri tjóði
honum vel. [Clearly the generous-with-hate breaker of the land of the snake had three
times fewer men at the battle; it was a hard meeting. Nevertheless, he won victory in
the battle; from that he got a great advantage for himself; the brother of his mother
helped him well.]

Textual notes:
The text of this stanza is found only in B. 2 linnz] *The MS is unclear; it apparently
reads* linz, *altered to* linnz *by the original scribe.*

Editorial variants:
6 moðir] móður *Skj, EAK, CN, CPB, C.*

— *33* —

1	<Avlld hefir opt enn milldi	[Ǫld hefir opt enn mildi
2	aunnar bliks fra <miclum>	unnar bliks frá miklum
3	Krist mære ek <linan> leysta	(Krist mæri ek linan) leysta
4	litravðs konungr navdum.	litrauðs konungr nauðum.
5	Greitt ma gumnum letta.>	Greitt má gumnum létta
6	<Guds ridari stridum	Guðs ríðari stríðum
7	rauskr þiggr allt sem æskir	rǫskr þiggr alt sem œskir
8	Olafr af gram solar.>	Óláfr af gram sólar.]

***Prose syntax*:**
Enn mildi litrauðs unnar bliks konungr hefir opt leysta ǫld frá miklum nauðum; ek mæri linan Krist. Guðs ríðari má greitt létta gumnum stríðum; rǫskr Óláfr þiggr alt sem œskir af gram sólar. [The king, generous with the red-colored light of the waves, has often rescued men from great need; I praise merciful Christ. God's knight can easily alleviate the afflictions of men; brave Óláfr gets all he desires from the king of the sun.]

***Textual notes*:**
This stanza is found only in B; *lines 6–8 are supplied from* F. 2 miclum] miclu *B*. 3 linan] lin *B*.

***Editorial variants*:**
1 hefir] hefr *Skj, EAK, CN*. 2 aunnar] unnar *Skj, EAK, CN, CPB, C*. 3 Krist] Krists *Skj, EAK, CN, CPB, C*. mære ek] mærik *Skj, EAK, CN*. linan] lim *Skj, EAK, CN, CPB, C*. 4 litrauðs] lætrauðr *CN*.

— *34* —

1	Satt var at silfri skreytta	[Satt var at silfri skreytta
2	seggium hollr ok gulli	seggjum hollr ok gulli
3	her let Guthorm g[er]fa	hér lét Gutthormr gerva
4	[grams hrodr v]ar þat [ro]du.	grams hróðr var þat róðu.
5	Þat hafa menn at minnum	Þat hafa menn at minnum
6	meirr iarteigna þeira	meir jarteigna þeira
7	mark stendr Cristz i kirkiu	mark stendr Krists í kirkju
8	konungs <nidr> g[a]f [þat	(konungs niðr gaf þat)
	m]id[ri].	miðri.]

Prose syntax:

Satt var, at Gutthormr, seggjum hollr, lét hér gerva róðu, skreytta silfri ok gulli; þat var grams hróðr. Þat hafa menn meir at minnum – mark þeira jarteigna stendr í miðri Krists kirkju; konungs niðr gaf þat. [It was true that Gutthormr, friendly to men, had a cross made here, ornamented with silver and gold. That was praise for the king. Men have that as all the more a reminder: the mark of those miracles still stands in the middle of Christ's church; the king's descendant gave that.]

Textual notes:

This stanza begins col. 2 in F. *There is a discoloured area at the top of col. 2, and the ends of 11.1–4 are illegible. The readings here are based on evidence from the early editions and from* B.

Lexical variants:

1 var] er *B*. 2 hollr] hollz *B*. ok] af *B*. 3 Guthorm] Gutthormr *B*. 4 var] er *B*. 5 Þat] Slikt *B*.

Phonological and spelling variants:

2 seggium] segium *B*. gulli] golli *B*. 3 gerfa] giorfa *B*. 4 rodu] roðv *B*. 6 meirr] meir *B*. iarteigna] jartegna *B*. 7 stendr] stenðr *B*. Cristz] Kristz *B*.

Editorial variants:

1 Satt var] Satt's *Skj, EAK, CN*; satt er *CPB, C*. 2 hollr] holls *Skj, EAK, CN, CPB, C*. ok] af *C*. 3 Guthorm] Gutthormr *Skj, EAK, CN, CPB, C, W, FL, FMS, S*. 4 var] er *Skj, EAK, CN, CPB, C*. 5 þat] Slíkt *Skj, EAK, CN, CPB, C*. 8 nidr gaf þat] vidr gaf þat *FL*; friðgafar *W, FMS, S*.

— *35* —

1	Menn hafa sagt at suanni	[Menn hafa sagt at svanni
2	sunnr Skanungum kunnir	sunnr Skánungum kunnir
3	oss vm Olafs messo	oss um Óláfs messu
4	almilldz baka villdi	almilds baka vildi,
5	enn þa er brudr at braudi	en þá er brúðr at brauði
6	brennheitu tok leita	brennheitu tók leita
7	þa vard grion at granu	þá varð grjón at grónu
8	grioti danskrar [s]n[otar].	grjóti danskrar snótar.]

Prose syntax:
Menn, kunnir Skánungum, hafa sagt oss, at svanni sunnr vildi baka um almilds Óláfs messu; en þá er brúðr tók leita at brennheitu brauði, þá varð grjón danskrar snótar at grónu grjóti. [Men known to the Scanians have told us that a woman in the south wanted to bake on the feast of all-mild Óláfr, but when the woman went to seek the burning-hot bread, the meal of the Danish woman had become a grey stone.]

Textual notes:
8 snotar] *see textual notes to stanza 34.*

Lexical variants:
2 Skanungum] Skaneyium *B.* 3 vm] ath. *B.* 4 almilldz] omilldr *B.*

Phonological and spelling variants:
1 suanni] svanne *B.* 2 sunnr] svdr *B.* 4 baka] bacha *B.* 5 brudr] bruðr *B.* 7 granu] grænv *B.* 8 danskrar] danskar *B.*

Editorial variants:
2 Skanungum] Skáneyjum *CN, CPB, C.* 3 vm] at *Skj, EAK, CN, CPB, C.* 4 almilldz] ómildr *CN, CPB, C.* 5 þa er] þás *Skj, EAK, CN.* 7 þa] þat *CPB.* 8 snotar] snótu *FMS, S.*

— *36* —

1	Hilldings hefir halldin	[Hildings hefir haldin
2	hætid verit siþan	hátíð verit síðan
3	sannspurt er þat sunnan	(sannspurt er þat) sunnan
4	sniallz vm Danmork alla.	snjalls um Danmǫrk alla.
5	Greitt <mæa gumnum letta	Greitt má gumnum létta
6	Gods ridari stridum	Guðs ríðari stríðum
7	rauskr þiggr allt þat er æskir	rǫskr þiggr alt sem œskir
8	Olafr af gram solar.>	Óláfr af gram sólar.]

Prose syntax:
Síðan hefir hátíð snjalls Hildings verit haldin sunnan um alla Danmǫrk – þat er sannspurt. Guðs ríðari má greitt létta gumnum stríðum; rǫskr Óláfr þiggr alt sem œskir af gram sólar. [Since then the feast of the clever warrior has been observed from the south throughout all Denmark; that is truly learned. God's knight can easily alleviate the afflictions of men; brave Óláfr gets all he desires from the king of the sun.]

Lexical variants:
1 Hilldings] Milldings *B*. 4 vm] of *B*.

Phonological and spelling variants:
2 hætid] hatid *B*. verit] verid *B*. siþan] sidan *B*. 4 sniallz] snialls *B*.

Editorial variants:
1 Hilldings] Mildings *Skj*, *CN*, *C*. 4 vm] of *Skj*, *EAK*, *CN*, *CPB*, *C*, *S*.

— *37* —

1	Gaufug red Horn or <hofdi>	[Gǫfug réð Hǫrn ór hǫfði
2	huitings vm sok litla	hvítings um sǫk lítla
3	audar aumum beidi	auðar aumum beiði
4	ungs mannz sker[a] t[un]gu.	ungs manns skera tungu.
5	Þann sæm ver er uorum	Þann sǫm vér er vǫrum
6	vælaust numin mæli	válaust numinn máli
7	hodda niot þar er heitir	hodda njót þar er heitir
8	Hlid fæm viku[m si]dan.	Hlíð fǫm vikum síðan.]

Prose syntax:
Gǫfug hvítings Hǫrn réð skera tungu ór hǫfði aumum auðar beiði, um lítla sǫk ungs manns. Þann hodda njót sǫm vér, válaust numinn máli, er vǫrum fǫm vikum síðan þar er heitir Hlíð. [A noble Hǫrn of the drinking-horn decided to cut the tongue out of the head of a poor seeker of riches, for little fault of the young man. We saw that user of treasure, without a doubt deprived of speech, a few weeks later when we were there at the place called Hlid.]

Textual notes:
4, 8 *cf. textual notes to stanza 34.* 1 hofdi] hofi *F*, hofði *BOY*, hofde *Bx*, hofþe *K*, hôfði *P*, hǫfðe *E*, haᷓde *Z*, haufði *Tm*.

Lexical variants:
1 red] skar *B*, scar *Y*, let *EKOTmZ*, liet *P*, lot *Bx*. 2 huitings] hiorrungs *Tm*. vm] of *BEFx*, fyrir *Bx*, fir *Tm*. 3 aumum] aumir *Tm*. beidi] beida *Tm*. 4 ungs] vngr *BY*, ungur *Tm*. mannz] maðr *BY*. skera] skerda *Tm*, var sa *BY*. 5 sæm] sann *Tm*, sa *EKO*. ver er] ver þa er *Bx*, ver þar *B*, er er *P*. 7 hodda niot] hodda briot *BOYZ*, hôððа briot *P*, hoða briot *E*, hoddbriot *K*, hoddv briost *Bx*, hodda briotr *Fx*, odda nioth *Tm*. er] or *Bx*. 8 sidan] sidar *BFxTm*, siðar *Bx*, siþar *O*, siðarr *EKPY*.

Phonological and spelling variants:
1 Gaufug] Gaᷓ[f]g *B*, Gaufog *O*, Gofug *EKZ*, Gófaᷓg *Fx*, Gǫfug *BxP*, Gofûg *K*. Horn] Havrn *B*, Hau[rn] *Tm*, Haᷓrn *O*, Hôrn *P*, Hôrnn *Fx*, Hǫrn *E*, Hęyrn *Y*. or] vr *Tm*, ôr *P*. 2 vm] ûm *K*. sok] sôk *BxP*, soc *KO*, sauk *ETm*, sauc *Y*. 3 audar] avðar *BEPY*, aᷓdar *OZ*, aᷓðar *K*. aumum] aumon *Y*, aᷓmom *O*, aᷓmum *Bx*, aᷓmûm *K*. beidi] beiði *Y*, 4 ungs] unngs *Z*. tungu] tunngv *BTm*, tungû *EK*, tungo *OY*. 5 sæm] sáám *P*, sám *B*, sam *FxYZ*, saᷓm *Bx*. ver] vér *E*, várom *K*, varom *Y*. 6 vælaust] valaust *BFxTmY*, válaust *EP*, válaᷓst *K*, valaᷓst *BxOZ*. numin] numinn *BxFxEKOPYZ*, nymin *B*. 8 Hlid] Hlið *EKOPY*. fæm] fám *K*, fam *BEOTmYZ*. vikum] vicum *Y*, vicom *EO*, vikom *K*. sidan] siþan *KZ*.

Editorial variants:
1 ór] úr *S*. red] lét *Hkr, Skj, CN, S*; skar *EAK, CPB, C*. 2 vm] of *Hkr, Skj, EAK, CN, CPB, C, W, FMS, S*. 4 ungs mannz skera] ungr maðr vas sa *EAK, CN, C*. 5 er] þás *CN*; þa er *CPB, C*. 7 niot] brjót *Hkr, Skj, EAK, CN, CPB, C, S*. þar er] þars *Hkr, Skj, EAK, CN*. 8 síðan] síðar *Hkr, Skj, EAK, CN, CPB, C*.

— 38 —

1	Frett hef ek at sæ sotti	[Frétt hef ek at sá sótti
2	sidan mælma stridir	síðan malma stríðir
3	heim þann er hialp gefr	heim þann er hjǫlp gefr
	aumum	aumum
4	\<harm\>skerdanda ferdum.	harmskerðanda ferðum.
5	Her feck hann enn byria	Hér fekk hann (en byrja
6	hætt kuædi skal ek bædi	hátt kvæði skal ek bæði
7	snæka vangs of slongui	snáka vangs of slǫngvi
8	slungin mal ok [tungu].	slungin mál ok tungu.]

Prose syntax:
Frétt hef ek, at sá malma stríðir sótti síðan harmskerðanda heim, þann er gefr hjǫlp aumum ferðum. Hér fekk hann bæði slungin mál ok tungu of slǫngvi snáka vangs; en ek skál byrja hátt kvæði. [I have heard that that enemy of weapons then sought the home of the harm-diminisher, the one who gives help to wretched men. Here he received both lost speech and tongue from the distributor of the field of the snake; and I shall put high poetry into motion.]

Textual notes:
4 harmskerdanda] harskerdand[a] *F*, harmskerdanda *B*. 8 tungu] *The MS is badly worn here (col. 2, line 9) but the letters are faintly legible.*

Lexical variants:
7 of] ok *B*. 8 slungin] slvngins *B*.

Phonological and spelling variants:
1 sæ] sa *B*. 2 mælma] malma *B*. 6 hætt] hatt *B*. kuædi] kvæði *B*. 7 snæka] snaka *B*. slongui] slaunge *B*. 8 tungu] tvnngv *B*.

Editorial variants:
1 hef ek] hefk *Skj, EAK, CN.* 3 þann er] þann's *Skj, EAK, CN.* 4 harmskerdanda] harmskerðaranda *EAK*; hár skerðandi *W, FL.* 6 skal ek] skalk *Skj, EAK, CN.* 8 slungin] slungins *Skj, EAK, CN, CPB, C.*

— *39* —

1	Dyrd er agæt ordin	[Dýrð er ágæt orðinn
2	audlings riks af sliku	ǫðlings ríks af slíku
3	mærd ridr milldings Horda	mærð ríðr mildings Hǫrða
4	mest vm heims bydg flest[a].	mest um heims bygð flesta.
5	Greitt <mæa gumnum letta	Greitt má gumnum létta
6	Guds ridari stridum	Guðs ríðari stríðum
7	rauskr þiggr allt sem æskir	rǫskr þiggr alt sem œskir
8	Olafr af gram solar.>	Óláfr af gram sólar.]

Prose syntax:
Dýrð ríks ǫðlings er orðinn ágæt af slíku; mest mærð Hǫrða mildings ríðr um flesta heims bygð. Guðs ríðari má greitt létta gumnum stríðum; rǫskr Óláfr þiggr alt sem œskir af gram sólar. [The fame of the powerful nobleman has become renowned from such things; the very great praise of the king of the Hordar travels over the whole dwelling of the world. God's knight can easily alleviate the afflictions of men; brave Óláfr gets all he desires from the king of the sun.]

Textual notes: 4 flesta] *The line is badly worn in the MS, and the last letter of the word is illegible.* B *reads* flesta.

Lexical variants:
3 ridr] nemi *B*. 4 vm] of *B*.

Phonological and spelling variants:
1 Dyrd] Dyrð *B*. ordin] orðin *B*. 3 Horda] Haurða *B*.

Editorial variants:
3 ridr] nemi *CN, CPB, C*. 4 vm] of *Skj, EAK, CN, CPB, C, S*.

—— 40 ——

1	Veit ek at Vindr fir skauti	[Veit ek at Vinðr fyr skauti
2	verdr bragr enn þeir skerdu	verðr bragr en þeir skerðu
3	gialfrs nidranda grundar	gjalfrs níðranda grundar
4	greiddur sarliga [meiddu]	greiddr sárliga meiddu,
5	ok endr fir tru <tyndir>	ok endr fyr trú tyndir
6	tirar sterks or kuerkum	tírar sterks ór kverkum
7	audskyfanda odar	auðskýfanda óðar
8	ær grimliga skæru.	ár grimmliga skáru.]

Prose syntax:
Veit ek, at Vinðr meiddu fyr níðranda skauti gjalfrs grundar, en þeir skerðu sárliga – bragr verðr greiddr; ok endr fyr trú tyndir skáru grimmliga óðar ár ór kverkum tírar sterks auðskýfanda. [I know that the Wends mutilated the twig of the land of noise on the riverbank, and they cut it painfully. Poetry is made; and men lost from the faith long ago horribly cut the oar of poetry from the throat of the most honourable distributor of riches.]

Textual notes:
4 meiddu] *The word is partly worn away in the MS (col. 2, 1.11), but still legible.*
5 tyndir] tyndri *F*, tindir *B*.

Lexical variants:
2 enn] af *B*. þeir] þvi *B*. skerdu] skerdi *B*. 5 fir] fra *B*.

Phonological and spelling variants:
1 Veit] Veitt *B*. Vindr] Vinðr *B*. 3 nidranda] niðranda *B*. gialfrs] gialfurs *B*. 4 greiddur] greidur *B*. 6 vr] or *B*. 8 ær] ár *B*. grimliga] grimmliga *B*. skæru] skarv *B*.

Editorial variants:
1 Veit ek] Veitk *Skj*, *EAK*, *CN*. fir] fer *S*. 2 enn þeir skerdu] af því skerði *Skj*, *EAK*, *CN*, *CPB*, *C*. 3 nidranda] niðbranda *Skj*, *EAK*, *CN*, *CPB*, *C*; *ríðanda W*, *S*. grundar] grindar *W*, *S*. 4 fir] frá *Skj*, *EAK*, *CN*, *CPB*, *C*; ferr *W*, *FMS*. 5 tyndir] tyndri *W*, *FL*, *FMS*, *S*.

— *41* —

1	Sotti skrin et skreytta	[Sótti skrín et skreytta
2	skidrennandi siþan	skíðrennandi síðan
3	ord finnaz mer vnnar	(orð finnask mér) unnar
4	Olæfs d[re]ka boli	Óláfs dreka bóli,
5	ok þeim er vel vakti	ok þeim er vel vakti
6	veit ek saunn Hugins teiti	veit ek sǫnn Hugins teiti
7	mæls feck hilmir heilsu	máls fekk hilmir heilsu
8	heilagr a þvi deili.	heilagr á því deili.]

Prose syntax:
Skíðrennandi unnar sótti síðan Óláfs skrín, et skreytta dreka bóli (orð finnask mér); ok heilagr hilmir, er vel vakti Hugins teiti, fekk þeim heilsu máls; ek veit sǫnn deili á því. [The ski-runner of the waves then sought Óláfr's shrine, ornamented with the dwelling-place of the dragon (words come to me); and the holy prince, who had well aroused the gladness of the raven, got for that man health of speech; I know true proof of that.]

Textual notes:
4 dreka] *The word is partly worn away in the MS (col. 2, 1.13).* B *reads* dreka.

Lexical variants:
5 vel] val *B*. 8 deili] deilir *B*.

Phonological and spelling variants:
1 et] eð *B*. 2 skidrennandi] skiðrennandi *B*. siþan] *B*. 3 finnaz] finnazt *B*. 4 Olæfs] Olafs *B*. boli] bole *B*. 5 vakti] vakte *B*. 6 saunn] sonn *B*. hugins] hvgens *B*. 7 mæls] mals *B*.

Editorial variants:
5 vel] val *C*. 6 veit ek] veitk *Skj, EAK, CN*.

— *42* —

1	Hærs lætr helgann ræsi	[Hás lætr helgan ræsi
2	heims <domari> soma	heims dómari sóma
3	fyllir framlyndr stillir	(fyllir framlyndr stillir
4	ferd himneska <verdan>.	ferð himneska) verðan.
5	Greitt <mæ gumnum letta	Greitt má gumnum létta
6	Guds ridari stridum	Guðs ríðari stríðum
7	rauskr þiggr allt sem æskir	rǫskr þiggr alt sem œskir
8	Olafr af gram solar.>	Óláfr af gram sólar.]

Prose syntax:
Heims dómari lætr helgan ræsi verðan hás sóma; framlyndr stillir fyllir himneska ferð. Guðs ríðari má greitt létta gumnum stríðum; rǫskr Óláfr þiggr alt sem œskir af gram sólar. [The judge of the world causes the holy king to be worthy of high honour; the forward-striving king fulfils the heavenly band. God's knight can easily alleviate the afflictions of men; brave Óláfr gets all he desires from the king of the sun.]

Textual notes:
2 domari] domara domara *F*, domare *B*. 4 verdan] verda *F*, verdan *B*.

Phonological and spelling variants:
1 Hærs] Hars *B*. lætr] lętr *B*. helgann] helgan *B*. 3 framlyndr] framlynðr *B*.

Editorial variants:
2 domari] domara *FL*, *FMS*, *S*. 4 verdan] verda *FL*, *FMS*, *S*.

—— *43* ——

1 Hneitir fra ek at heti	[Hneitir frá ek at héti
2 hialldrs at vopna galldri	hjaldrs at vápna galdri
3 Olafs hiorr þess er orra	Óláfs hjorr þess er orra
4 ilbleikum gáf \<steikar>.	ilbleikum gaf steikar.
5 Þeim klauf þengill Rauma	Þeim klauf þengill Rauma
6 þunn vaxinn sky gunnar	þunn vaxin ský gunnar
7 rekin bitu stæl a \<Stikla>	(rekin bitu stól) á Stikla-
8 staudum valbastar raudli.	stǫðum valbastar rǫðli.]

Prose syntax:
Frá ek, at Óláfs hjorr, þess er gaf ilbleikum orra hjaldrs steikar at vápna galdri, héti Hneitir. Þeim valbastar rǫðli klauf þengill Rauma þunn vaxin ský gunnar á Stikla-stǫðum; rekin stól bitu. [I heard that Óláfr's sword, that gave meat to the pale-footed heathcock of battle at the song of weapons, was called Hneitir. With that sun of the sword-hilt the king of the Raumar clove the clouds of battle, grown thin, at Stik-larstaðir; driven steel bit.]

Textual notes:
4 steikar] stikar *F*, steikar *B*. 7 Stikla] Stika *F*, Stiklar *B*.

Lexical variants:
2 at] af *B*. 3 Olafs] avdlings *B*. 6 vaxinn] vaxins *B*.

Phonological and spelling variants:
2 hialldrs] hialldurs *B*. 5 þengill] þeingill *B*. 7 stæl] stal *B*. 8 staudum] stodvm *B*. raudli] raudle *B*.

Editorial variants:
1 fra ek] frák *Skj*, *EAK*, *CN*. 2 at] af *CN*. 3 Olafs] ǫðlings *Skj*, *EAK*, *CN*, *C*. þess er] þess's *Skj*, *EAK*, *CN*. 4 steikar] stikar *FL*. 7 Stikla] Stika *FL*; Stiklar *Skj*, *EAK*.

—— *44* ——

1 Tok þa er fell [e]nn frækni	[Tók þá er fell enn frœkni
2 fylkis kundr til grundar	fylkis kundr til grundar
3 suerd er sok[n] var ordin	sverð er sókn var orðinn
4 suænskr madr af gram	svænskr maðr af gram
þrænskum.	þrænskum.
5 Sa hefir hiorr [ens] hafá	Sá hefir hjǫrr ens háfa
6 hrings <stridanda> siþan	hrings stríðanda síðan
7 gulli merktr i Girkia	gulli merktr í Girkja
8 gunndiárfs lidi fundiz.	gunndjarfs liði fundizk.]

Prose syntax:
Svænskr maðr tók sverð af þrænskum gram, er sókn var orðinn, þá er enn frœkni fylkis kundr fell til grundar. Sá gulli merktr hjǫrr ens háfa gunndjarfs hrings stríðanda hefir síðan fundizk í Girkja liði. [A Swedish man took the sword from the Trondish king, when the brave descendant of the king fell to the ground, when the battle was over. That sword of the high, battle-eager enemy of the ring, marked with gold, later has been found in the army of the Greeks.]

Textual notes:
1; 5 *A discoloured area in col. 2, 11.18–19 makes the bracketed letters illegible.*
3 sokn] *the* n *is written above the line.* 6 stridanda] stridandi *F*, stridandæ *B*.

Lexical variants:
3 er] hinn er *B*. sokn var] sækia *B*. ordin] þordi *B*. 5 hefir] var *B*. 6 hrings] harm *B*. 8 fundiz] funndinn *B*.

Phonological and spelling variants:
1 frækni] frækne *B*. 2 kundr] kunðr *B*. 4 þrænskum] þrenskum *B*. 5 sa] sæ *B*. ens] enns *B*. hafa] háfa *B*. 6 siþan] sidan *B*. 8 lidi] liði *B*.

Editorial variants:
1 þa er] þás *Skj, EAK, CN*. 3 er sokn var ordin] hinn er sœkja þorði *CN, CPB, C*. 6 hrings] harm *C*. stridanda] stridandi *C, FL, FMS*. 8 fundiz] fundinn *Skj, EAK, CN, CPB, C*.

— *45* —

1	Nv fremr sa er gaf gumnum	[Nú fremr sá er gaf gumnum
2	gaufug dyrd iofur fyrdá	gǫfug dyrð jǫfur fyrða
3	slaung Eindridi vngi	slǫng Eindriði ungi
4	armglædur i brag rædu.	armglœðr í brag rœðu.
5	Greitt <mæa gumnum letta	Greitt má gumnum létta
6	Guds ridari stridum	Guðs ríðari stríðum
7	rauskr þiggr allt sem æskir	rǫskr þiggr alt sem œskir
8	Olafr af gram solar.>	Óláfr af gram sólar.]

Prose syntax:
Nú fremr gǫfug dyrð jǫfur fyrða, sá er gaf gumnum armglœðr; Eindriði ungi slǫng rœðu í brag. Guðs ríðari má greitt létta gumnum stríðum; rǫskr Óláfr þiggr alt sem œskir af gram sólar. [Now excellent fame promotes the prince of men; he who gave men the fire of the arm, Eindridi the young, cast this story into the poem. God's knight can easily alleviate the afflictions of men; brave Óláfr gets all he desires from the king of the sun.]

Lexical variants:
1 sa] þann *B*. 2 iofur] konungr *B*.

Phonological and spelling variants:
2 gaufug] gǫfvg *B*. dyrd] dyrþ *B*. 3 slaung] slavngh *B*. Eindridi] Einriðe *B*. 4 armglæ-dur] armglæðr *B*.

Editorial variants:
1 fremr] finnr *W*, *FL*, *FMS*, *S*. sa] þann *C*, *CN*, *CPB*, *EAK*, *Skj*.

— *46* —

1	Mer er þvi mærd skal skyrá	[Mér er (því mærð skal skýra
2	milldings þess er gaf ringa	mildings þess er gaf hringa
3	styriar <sniallz> of stilli	styrjar snjalls) of stilli
4	styrkann vant at yrkia	styrkan vant at yrkja,
5	þvi at takn þess er lid læknar	því at tǫkn þess er lið læknar
6	lofdungs himintunglá	lofðungs himintungla
7	lios kemr raun vm ræsi	(ljós kemr raun um ræsi)
8	rannz ferr huert a annat.	ranns ferr hvert á annat.]

Prose syntax:
Mér er vant at yrkja of styrkan stilli; því skal skýra mærð styrjar snjalls mildings, þess er gaf hringa; því at tǫkn himintungla ranns lofðungs, þess er lið læknar, ferr hvert á annat – ljós raun kemr um ræsi. [It is difficult for me to make poetry about a strong prince; with this I shall make clear the praise of the clever-of-battle prince, he who gave rings; because the signs of the prince of the house of stars, he who heals men, go one after another; the proof about the king comes to light.]

Textual notes:
3 sniallz] snallz *F*, sniallz *B*.

Lexical variants:
1 þvi] en *B*. skyra] stæra *B*. 5 þvi at] þvit *B*. læknar] læknir *B*. 6 himintungla] vinar tungla *B*. 7 kemr] verdr *B*. vm] of *B*.

Phonological and spelling variants:
1 mærd] mærð *B*. 2 milldings] millðings *B*. ringa] hringa *B*. 4 styrkann] styrkian *B*. vant] vannt *B*. 5 lid] lið *B*. 7 ræsi] ræse *B*.

Editorial variants:
1 Mer er] Mér's *Skj, EAK, CN*. þvi] en *Skj, EAK, CN, CPB, C*. skyra] stœra *Skj, EAK, CN, CPB, C*. 2 þess er] þess's *Skj, EAK, CN*. 3 sniallz] valðs *W*; valls *FMS, S*. 4 styrkann] styrkjan *Skj, EAK, CN, CPB, C*. 5 þvi at] þvít *Skj, EAK, CN*. læknar] læknir *Skj, EAK, CN, CPB, C*. 6 himintungla] vinar tungla *Skj, EAK, CN, CPB, C*. 7 kemr] verðr *Skj, EAK, CN, CPB, C*. vm] of *Skj, EAK, CN, CPB, C*.

— *47* —

1	Gerdiz hæla herdum	[Gerðisk hála herðum
2	helldr sidallá a kuelldi	heldr síðarla á kveldi
3	glaumkennandi gunnar	glaumkennandi gunnar
4	gladr vetþryma nadri.	glaðr véttrima naðri.
5	Dreingr red dyrr a vangi	Drengr réð dýrr á vangi
6	dagr rofnadiz sofna	(dagr rofnaðisk) sofna
7	itrs landreka vndir	ítrs landreka undir
8	<ognfimr> berum himni.	ormfimr berum himni.]

Prose syntax:
Glaðr glaumkennandi gunnar gerðisk hála herðum véttrima naðri heldr síðarla á kveldi. Dýrr ógnfimr drengr ítrs landreka réð sofna á vangi undir berum himni; dagr rofnaðisk. [The happy noise-experiencer of battle prepared himself with the well-hardened snake of the *véttrim* rather late in the evening. The valuable, battle-clever soldier of the splendid land-ruler decided to sleep on a field under the bare heaven; the day was waning.]

Lexical variants:
1 Gerdiz] Gyrdest *B*. 2 sidalla] naliga *B*. a] at *B*. 3 glaumkennandi] glaum vekiandr *B*. gunnar] grimo *B*. 4 vetþryma] vettrimar *B*. 5 red] nam *B*. 8 ognfimr] ormfimr *F*.

Phonological and spelling variants:
1 hæla] hǫla *B*. 4 gladr] glaðr *B*. 5 vangi] vange *B*. 6 rofnadiz] rofnaðast *B*. 8 himni] himne *B*.

Editorial variants:
2 sidalla] síðarla *Skj*, *EAK*; naliga *CN*, *CPB*, *C*. 3 glaumkennandi] glaum vekjandi *CN*, *CPB*, *C*; Glann kennandi *W*, *FMS*, *S*. 4 vetþryma] véttrimar *Skj*, *EAK*, *CN*, *CPB*, *C*; vetrima *S*. 5 red] nam *CN*, *CPB*, *C*. a] at *FMS*, *S*. 6 rofnadiz] rofnaði *Skj*, *EAK*. 8 ognfimr] orðfimr *W*, *FMS*, *S*.

— *48* —

1	Misti madr er lysti	[Misti maðr er lýsti
2	morginn var þa borgar	(morginn var þá) borgar
3	styrks mundrida <steindrar>	styrks mundriða steindrar
4	styrs bradr Regins væda.	styrs bráðr Regins váða.
5	Nytr gat sed a slettri	Nýtr gat séð á sléttri
6	seimþiggiandi liggia	seimþiggjandi liggja
7	grundu gylldis kindar	grundu gylðis kindar
8	gomsparra ser fiarri.	gómsparra sér fjarri.]

Prose syntax:
Styrs bráðr maðr misti styrks mundriða steindra borgar Regins váða er lýsti – morginn var þá. Nýtr seimþiggjandi gat séð gómsparra gylðis kindar liggja fjarri sér á sléttri grundu. [The quick-of-battle man missed his strong *mundriði* of the painted fortress of Regin's peril when it grew light; it was morning then. The useful gold-receiver had the sight of his gum-spar of the wolf's offspring lying far from him on the flat ground.]

Lexical variants:
3 steindrar] steindra *F*. 4 styrs bradr] styrsniallr *B*. Regins] rodins *B*. væda] galla *B*.
5 nytr gat sed] þatti sinn *B*. 6 seimþiggiandi] seimþiggiandr *B*.

Phonological and spelling variants:
2 morginn] morgenn *B*. 3 mundrida] mundriða *B*. 5 a] á *B*. 7 gylldis] gylþes *B*.

Editorial variants:
3 steindrar] steindra *W, FMS, S*. 4 styrs bradr] styrsnjallr *Skj, EAK, CN, CPB, C*.
Regins] roðins *Skj, EAK, CN, CPB, C*. væda] galla *Skj, EAK, CN, CPB, C*. 5 nytr gat
sed] þátti sin *Skj, EAK, CN, CPB, C*. 7 kindar] kundar *W, FMS, S*.

—— *49* ——

1	Þriar <grimur> vann þeima	[Þríar grímur vann þeima
2	þiodnytr Haralldz <brodir>	þjóðnýtr Haralds bróðir
3	rauckstefnanda Reifnis	rauknstefnanda Reifnis
4	rikr bendingar slikár	ríkr bendingar slíkar,
5	aadr þrifhuassir þessir	áðr þrifhvassir þessir
6	þingdiarfs firar jnga	þingdjarfs firar inga
7	biort e[r]u bauga snyrtis	(bjǫrt eru bauga snyrtis
8	brogd iárteignir sogdu.	brǫgð) jarteignir sǫgðu.]

Prose syntax:
Ríkr, þjóðnýtr bróðir Haralds vann slíkar bendingar þeima rauknstefnanda Reifnis þríar grímur, áðr þessir þrifhvassir firar sǫgðu jarteignir þingdjarfs inga; brǫgð bauga snyrtis eru bjǫrt. [The powerful, useful-to-people brother of Haraldr gave such signs to that horse-driver of Reifnir three nights, before these very lucky men told the miracles of the battle-brave king; the deeds of the polisher of rings are bright.]

Textual notes:
1 grimur] grimar *F*, grimur *B*. 2 brodir] brodur *F*, brodir *B*. 7 eru] *The* r *is written above the line.*

Lexical variants:
5 þrifhuassir] þrekhva/ssum *B*. þessir] þessar *B*. 6 jnga] yngva *B*.

Phonological and spelling variants:
2 þiodnytr] þioðnytr *B*. Haralldz] Haraldz *B*. 3 rauckstefnanda] rauknstefnanða *B*. Reifnis] Reifnes *B*. 5 aadr] aðr *B*. 7 eru] ero *B*. snyrtis] snytris *B*. 8 brogd] bravgd *B*. iarteignir] jartegnir *B*. sogdu] sogðv *B*.

Editorial variants:
2 brodir] brodur *FL*. 3 rauckstefnanda] rauknstefnandi *CPB*; röknstefnanda *W, S*. 5 þrifhuassir] þrekhvǫssum *Skj, EAK, CN, CPB, C*. þessir] þessar *Skj, EAK, CN, CPB, W, FMS, S*.

— *50* —

1	Mæs let iardar eisu	[Más lét jarðar eisu
2	allualldz fir hior giallda	allvalds fyr hjǫr gjalda
3	slettig od þann er ætti	sléttik óð þann er átti
4	Olæfr bragar tolum.	Óláfr bragar tólum.
5	Yfirskiolldungr let iofra	Yfirskjǫldungr lét jǫfra
6	oddhridar þar siþan	oddhríðar þar síðan
7	gardz af gulli vordu	garðs af gulli vǫrðu
8	grand alltari standa.	grand altári standa.]

Prose syntax:
Lét gjalda eisu más jarðar fyr allvalds hjǫr, þann er Óláfr átti; sléttik óð bragar tólum. Yfirskjǫldungr jǫfra lét síðan grand garðs oddhríðar standa þar af altári vǫrðu gulli. [[Kirjalax] had the sword of the all-ruler, the one which Óláfr owned, paid for with the fire of the gull's land (I smooth my poem with the tools of poetry). The over-king of princes then caused the harm of the yard of the point-shower to stand there over the altar adorned with gold.]

Lexical variants:
1 Mæs] Meiðs *B*. let] fra ek *B*. 2 allualldz] allzvalld *B*. 7 af] a *B*.

Phonological and spelling variants:
1 eisu] eiso *B*. 2 giallda] giallða *B*. 3 slettig] sletti ek *B*. od] oð *B*. 4 Olæfr] Olafr *B*. 6 oddhridar] oððhriðar *B*. siþan] sidan *B*. 7 vordu] va⁄rdv *B*. 8 alltari] altare *B*.

Editorial variants:
1 let] frák *Skj*, *EAK*, *CN*; frá ek *CPB*, *C*. 2 allualldz] allvald *Skj*, *EAK*, *CPB*; allsvald *CN*, *C*; alvaldr *W*, *FMS*, *S*. 3 slettig] slétti ek *CPB*. þann er] þann's *Skj*, *EAK*, *CN*. 7 af] a *CN*, *CPB*, *C*.

— *51* —

1	Tækn e[r]u biort þau er	[Tǫkn eru bjǫrt þau er
	birtazst	birtask
2	brandel a Girklandi	brandél á Girklandi
3	mæl finnz vm þat monnum	mál finnsk um þat mǫnnum
4	\<margþarfr\> Haralldz arfi.	margþarfr Haralds arfi.
5	Fregn ek at allt ne \<ognar\>	Fregn ek at alt né ógnar
6	innenndr megud finna	innendr megut finna
7	dyrd Olafs ridr dælá	dýrð Óláfs ríðr dála
8	dagræfrs konung hæfra.	dagræfrs konung hæfra.]

Prose syntax:
Tǫkn þau er birtask um þat brandél á Girklandi eru bjǫrt. Haralds margþarfr arfi finnsk mál mǫnnum. Fregn ek, at Óláfs dýrð ríðr alt dála dagræfrs, né megut innendr ógnar finna hæfra konung. [The signs that make themselves clear concerning that battle in Greece are bright. Haraldr's very useful heir is found to be [a topic of] conversation for men. I hear that Óláfr's fame rides all across the whole heaven; you doers of battle will not find a more worthy king.]

Textual notes:
1 eru] *The* r *is written above the line*. 4 margþarfr] margþæþr *F*, mannþarfr *B*. 5 ognar] aungir *F*, ognar *B*.

Lexical variants:
1 eru] gerir *B*. birtazst] birta *B*. 3 mæl] mærd *B*. vm] of *B*. 5 at allt] allz *B*. 7 ridr] vidur *B*.

Phonological and spelling variants:
1 Tækn] Takn *B*. 2 Girklandi] Gircklandi *B*. 3 finnz] finnzt *B*. 4 Haralldz] Haraldz *B*. 6 innenndr] innendr *B*. megud] meguð *B*. 7 dæla] dala *B*. 8 dagræfrs] dagræfurs *B*.

Editorial variants:
1 eru] gerir *Skj, EAK, CN, CPB, C*. þau er] þau's *Skj, EAK, CN*. birtazst] birta *Skj, EAK, CN, CPB, C*. 3 mæl] mærð *CPB, C*. vm] of *Skj, EAK, CN, CPB, C*. 4 margþarfr] mannþarfr *CN, C*. 5 fregn ek] fregnk *Skj, EAK*. at allt] allt *CPB, C, S*. ognar] aungir *W, FL, FMS, S*. 6 megud] *Skj, EAK, CN, S*. 7 dæla] ála *W*. 8 dagræfrs] dagræfr *Skj*.

— *52* —

1	Hadiz hialldr æ vidum	[Háðisk hjaldr á víðum
2	hunngr slǫkte vel þunngan	(hungr sløkði vel þungan
3	gunnar mær j geira	gunnar már í geira
4	gaull Pecinavǫllum.	gǫll) Pézínavǫllum,
5	Þar er svo ath þiod fyrir	þar er svá at þjóð fyr
	hiorfue	hjǫrvi
6	þushunndum fell vnndan	þúsundum fell undan
7	hrid <ox> Hamdis klęda	(hríð óx Hamðis klæða)
8	hialmskęd Grikkir flędu.	hjalmskœð Girkir flœðu.]

Prose syntax:

Háðisk hjaldr á víðum Pézínavǫllum; gunnar már sløkði vel þungan hungr í geira gǫll, svá at Girkir flœðu undan þar, er þjóð fell þúsundum fyr hjǫrvi; hjalmskœð hríð Hamðis klæða óx. [A battle was held on wide Pezinavoll (the gull of battle slaked well its heavy hunger in the noise of spears); so that the Greeks fled away, there where people fell by the thousands before the sword; the storm of Hamdir's clothing, dangerous to helmets, increased.]

Textual notes:

This stanza and the following one are written in a different hand. 7 ox] ǫr *F*, óx *B*.

Lexical variants:

1 hialldr] hilldr *B*. 5 Þar er] Þar *B*. 6 fell] lavt *B*.

Phonological and spelling variants:

1 Hadiz] Hadizt *B*. æ] a *B*. vidum] vidjum *B*. 2 hunngr] hvngr *B*. slǫkte] slokte *B*. 3 mær] mær *B*. 4 Pecinavǫllum] Peízímavollom *B*. 5 ath] at *B*. þiod] þioð *B*. fyrir] fir *B*. hiorfue] hiorfe *B*. 6 þushunndum] þusvndum *B*. vnndan] vndan *B*. 7 hrid] hrið *B*. Hamdis] Hanðis *B*. klęda] klæda *B*. 8 hialmskęd] hialmskæð *B*. Grikkir] Girckir *B*. flędu] flæðv *B*.

Editorial variants:

1 hialldr] hilldr *Skj, EAK, CN, CPB, C.* 5 Þar er] Þar *Skj, EAK, CN, CPB, C.* svo ath] svát *Skj, EAK, CN.* 6 fell] laut *Skj, EAK, CN, CPB, C.*

—— *53* ——

1	Munndi mest vnnd fiǫnndum	[Myndi mest und fjǫndum
2	Miklagarðr ok iardir	Miklagarðr ok jarðir
3	hrygs dugde lid liggia	hryggs (dugði lið) liggja
4	lagar elldbrota vellde	lagar eldbrota veldi,
5	nema raunnd j byr brannda	nema rǫnd í byr branda
6	<bardraugns> <fæir> harda	barðraukns fáir harða
7	rauduls bliku vopn j vedre	rǫðuls bliku vǫpn í veðri
8	Vęrinngiar fram bęre.	Væringjar fram bæri.]

Prose syntax:
Mest veldi hryggs eldbrota lagar, Miklagarðr ok jarðir, myndi liggja und fjǫndum –
dugði lið – nema harða fáir Væringjar bæri rǫnd fram í byr branda; vǫpn bliku í veðri
barðrauks rǫðuls. [Most of the kingdom of the sorrowful flame-breaker of the sea,
Constantinople and the lands, would have lain under the enemy (the army did its best),
except that a very few Varangians pushed their shields forward in the fair breeze of
swords; weapons gleamed in the storm of the sun of the prow-ox.]

Textual notes:
cf. *textual notes to stanza 52*. 6 bardraugns] barraugn *F*, bardravgns *B*. fæir] fæit *F*,
faeir *B*.

Lexical variants:
3 dugde] dugðit *B*.

Phonological and spelling variants:
1 Munndi] Mvnði *B*. vnnd] vnd *B*. fionndum] fiondum *B*. 2 Miklagarðr] Miclagards *B*.
iardir] jardar *B*. 4 vellde] velldi *B*. 5 raunnd] ravnd *B*. brannda] branda *B*. 7 vedre] vedri
B. 8 Vęrinngiar] Væringiar *B*. bęre] bære *B*.

Editorial variants:
2 Miklagardr] Miklagarðs *EAK, CN, CPB, C, W, FMS, S*. iardir] jarðar *C*. 3 dugde]
dugðit *Skj, EAK, CN, CPB, C*. 6 bardraugns] barðraukn *W, FMS, S*; barraugn *FL*. fæir]
fæit *FL*; fáin *W, S*.

— *54* —

1	Hetu bart a itran	[Hétu hart á ítran
2	hraustir menn af trausti	hraustir menn af trausti
3	strid <svall> ognar eydis	(stríð svall ógnar eyðis)
4	<Olæf> i gny stæla.	Óláf í gný stála.
5	Þar er of <einn> i orfa	Þar er of einn í ǫrva
6	<vndbærum> flug væru	undbǫrum flug vǫru
7	<rodin> <klofnudu> Reifnis	roðin klofnuðu Reifnis
8	rann <sex tigir> manna.	rǫnn sex tigir manna.]

Prose syntax:
Hraustir menn hétu af trausti hart á ítran Óláf í gný stála; stríð ógnar eyðis svall. Þar klofnuðu Reifnis rann, roðin undbǫrum, er sex tigir manna vǫru of einn í ǫrva flug. [Strong men called hard on bright Óláfr with confidence in the noise of steel; the strife of the destroyer of fear increased. There Reifnir's houses (i.e., shields), reddened with wound-waves, were cloven, where six tens of men were against one in the flight of arrows.]

Textual notes:
3 svall] stall *F*, svall *B*. 4 Olæf] Olæfr *F*, Olaf *B*. 6 vndbærum] vndbær æ *F*, vndbarv *B*. 7 rodin] rofin *F*, rodin *B*. klofnudu] klofnadi *F*, klofnvðv *B*. 8 sex tigir] lx *F*, *B*.

Lexical variants:
3 ognar] ogn þa er *B*. eydis] oðuzt *B*. 5 einn] einum *F*, einn *B*.

Phonological and spelling variants:
4 stæla] stala *B*. 5 orfa] aurfa *B*. 6 væru] varv *B*. 7 Reifnis] Refinz *B*.

Editorial variants:
3 svall] stall *FL*; stóð *W*, *FMS*, *S*. ognar] ógn þás *Skj*, *EAK*, *CN*; ógn þá er *CPB*, *C*. eydis] óðusk *Skj*, *EAK*, *CN*, *CPB*, *C*. 5 einn] einum *W*, *FL*, *FMS*, *S*; i orfa] iorfa *FL*, *FMS*, *S*. 6 vndbærum] undbǫru *Skj*, *EAK*, *CN*, *CPB*, *C*, *W*, *FMS*, *S*; vndbær æ *FL*. 7 rodin] rofin *FL*, *FMS*. klofnudu] klofnaði *W*, *FL*, *FMS*, *S*.

— *55* —

1	Þa er rauk af riki	[Þá er rauk af ríki
2	regn dreif <stæls> æ þegna	regn dreif stáls á þegna
3	hialmniordungum harda	hjalmnjǫrðungum harða
4	heidingia lid gingi.	heiðingja lið gingi.
5	Hælft fimta vann heimtann	Halft fimta vann heimtan
6	<hundrad> <brimis> sunda	hundrað brimis sunda
7	nyzstann tir þar er <nærra>	nýztan tír þar er næra
8	nordmanna val þordu.	norðmanna val þorðu.]

Prose syntax:
Þá rauk, er lið heiðingja gingi af ríki, stáls regn dreif hjalmnjǫrðungum harða á þegna. Halft fimta hundrað norðmanna vann heimtan nýztan tír þar, er þorðu næra val brimis sunda. [Then the air was dense with smoke, when the army of heathens came forth powerfully; the rain of weapons drove helmet-men hard against the thanes. Half of the fifth hundred of Norsemen, those who dared to feed the falcon of the sound of the sword, went home with very useful honour.]

Textual notes:
2 stæls] stæl *F*, stals *B*. 6 brimis] brimils *F*, brimirs *B*. hundrad] C *F*, hundrad *B*. 7 nærra] nærri *F*, næra *B*.

Lexical variants:
1 Þa] Var *B*. er] sem *B*. rauk] reyk *B*. 2 æ] j *B*. þegna] gegnum *B*. 3 hialmniordungum] hialmniordunar *B*. harda] hardan *B*. 7 þar] þat *B*. 8 þordu] þorðe *B*.

Phonological and spelling variants:
4 lid] lið *B*. 5 hælft] halft *B*. 6 sunda] svnða *B*. 7 nyzstann] nystan *B*. 8 nordmanna] norðmanna *B*.

Editorial variants:
1 Þa er rauk] Var sem reyk *Skj*, *EAK*, *CN*, *CPB*, *C*. 2 stæls] stæl *W*, *FL*, *FMS*, *S*. æ þegna] í gegnum *Skj*, *EAK*, *CN*, *CPB*, *C*. harda] harðan *Skj*, *EAK*, *CN*, *CPB*, *C*. 4 lid] liðs *W*, *S*. 6 brimis] brimils *FL*, *FMS*. sunda] sundi *S*; fundi *W*. 7 þar er] þat er *CPB*, *C*; þat's *Skj*, *EAK*; þaz *CN*. nærra] nærri *W*, *FL*, *FMS*, *S*. 8 þordu] þorði *Skj*, *EAK*, *CN*, *CPB*, *C*.

—— *56* ——

1	Ruddu gumnar gladdir	[Ruddu gumnar gladdir
2	gaufugr þeingill barg	(gǫfugr þengill barg
	dreingium	drengjum)
3	vagna borg þar er vargar	vagna borg þar er vargar
4	vopnsundrat hræ fundu.	vápnsundrat hræ fundu.
5	Nennir aulld at inna	Nennir ǫld at inna
6	vngr brimloga slunginns	ungr brimloga slungins
7	doglings verk þau er dyrka	dǫglings verk þau er dýrka
8	dædsniallz verolld allá.	dáðsnjalls verǫld alla.]

Prose syntax:
Gladdir gumnar ruddu vagna borg, þar er vargar fundu vápnsundrat hræ; gǫfugr þengill barg drengjum. Ungr nennir at inna ǫld verk dáðsnjalls dǫglings slungins brimloga, þau er dýrka alla verǫld. [The happy warriors cleared the fortress of wagons there, where wolves found the weapon-torn corpse; the noble king saved men. The young man strives to tell men the works of the quickly acting prince of scattered river-fire, those which glorify the whole world.]

Lexical variants:
1 Ruddu] Eyddv *B*. 4 vopnsundrat] vopnsundurd *B*. 5 aulld] oll *B*. 6 vngr] eingur *B*. slunginns] slavngir *B*. 7 þau] þess *B*. dyrka] dyrkar *B*.

Phonological and spelling variants:
2 gaufugr] gavfurgr *B*. 4 hræ] hre *B*. 7 doglings] davglings *B*. 8 dædsniallz] ðaðsnialls *B*. verolld] veroll *B*.

Editorial variants:
1 Ruddu] Eyddu *Skj*, *EAK*, *CN*, *CPB*, *C*. 3 þar er] þars *Skj*, *EAK*, *CN*. 5 aulld] ǫll *Skj*, *EAK*, *CN*, *CPB*, *C*. 6 vngr] ǫngr *Skj*, *EAK*, *CN*, *CPB*, *C*; ungs *W*, *S*. slunginns] slǫngvir *Skj*, *EAK*, *CN*, *CPB*, *C*; slungin *S*. 7 þau er] þess's *Skj*, *EAK*, *CN*; þess er *CPB*, *C*. dyrka] dýrkar *Skj*, *EAK*, *CN*, *CPB*, *C*.

— *57* —

1	Nu er þau er vann visir	[Nú er þau er vann vísir
2	verk fir þiod at merkia	verk fyr þjóð at merkja
3	naudr i nyium odi	nauðr í nýjum óði
4	næst ridrat þat smæstu.	næst (ríðrat þat smæstu).
5	Krapt skulum Guds þess er	Krapt skulum Guðs þess er
	giftu	giptu
6	gunnstyrks lofi dyrka	gunnstyrks lofi dyrka
7	ler halldfromum harar	lér haldfrǫmum hárar
8	heims læknis gram þeima.	heims læknis gram þeima.]

Prose syntax:
Nú er nauðr at merkja fyr þjóð í nýjum óði þau verk, er vísir vann næst; ríðrat þat smæstu. Skulum lofi dyrka krapt gunnstyrks Guðs, þess heims læknis, er lér hárar giptu þeima haldfrǫmum gram. [Now it is necessary to make known to people, in new poetry, the deeds which the king accomplished next; that is not least important. We should honour with praise the strength of battle-strong God, the healer of the world who gives high gifts to the strong king.]

Lexical variants:
1 er þau] er oss þav *B*. visir] vise *B*. 4 ridrat] ridr a *B*. smæstu] smæstum *B*. 5 þess er] enn *B*. 6 gunnstyrks] gedstyrks *B*. 7 halldfromum] hialldrfromum *B*. 8 læknis] læknir *B*.

Phonological and spelling variants:
1 vann] van *B*. 3 nyium] nygium *B*. odi] oði *B*. 5 skulum] skulom *B*. giftu] giptu *B*. 7 harar] harrar *B*.

Editorial variants:
1 Nu er] Nús *Skj*, *EAK*, *CN*. þau er] oss þau's *Skj*, *EAK*, *CN*; oss þau er *CPB*, *C*. visir] vísi *Skj*, *EAK*, *CN*, *CPB*, *C*. 4 ridrat smæstu] ríðra þat smæstum *CN*, *CPB*, *C*. 5 þess er] enn *Skj*, *EAK*, *CN*, *CPB*, *C*. 6 gunnstyrks] geðstyrks *Skj*, *EAK*, *CN*, *CPB*, *C*. 7 halldfromum] hjaldrfrǫmum *Skj*, *EAK*, *CN*, *C*. 8 læknis] læknir *Skj*, *EAK*, *CN*, *CPB*, *C*.

— *58* —

1	Angrs <fylldra> vard alldar	[Angrs fylldra varð aldar
2	illr geriz hugr áf villu	illr gerisk hugr af villu
3	milldings þionn fir manna	mildings þjónn fyr manna
4	margfalldr ofund kalldri.	margfaldr ǫfund kaldri.
5	Lygi hefir b[ra]gna brugdit	Lygi hefir bragna brugðit
6	brytr stundum frid nytra	brýtr stundum frið nýtra
7	hermdar kraptr til heiftar	hermðar kraptr til heiptar
8	hialldrstrid skapi blidu.	hjaldrstríð skapi blíðu.]

Prose syntax:

Þjónn aldar mildings varð fyr kaldri ǫfund manna angrs fylldra; margfaldr hugr gerisk illr af villu. Hjaldrstríð lygi hefir brugðit blíðu skapi nýtra bragna til heiptar; hermðar kraptr stundum brýtr frið. [The servant of the king of mankind was up against the cold hatred of men full of sin; the many-sided mind becomes evil from delusion. Battle-strong lying has turned the happy mind of useful men to hatred; the power of anger sometimes breaks the peace.]

Textual notes:

1 fylldra] fylldir *F*, fylldrar *B*. 5 bragna] *F reads* bgna. *The expansion symbol is illegible, but presumably it is* a *for* ra. *B reads* bragna.

Lexical variants:

1 Angrs] Ængur *B*. 7 heiftar] heipta *B*. 8 hialldrstrid] hialldstridr *B*.

Phonological and spelling variants:

1 vard] varð *B*. 2 geriz] gerizt *B*. 6 frid] frið *B*.

Editorial variants:

1 Angrs fylldra] Angrfyldrar *Skj, EAK, CN, CPB, C*. 4 margfalldr] margfaldri *EAK*. 5 Lygi] Lygd *S*. hefir] hefr *Skj, EAK, CN*. 7 heiftar] heipta *Skj, EAK, CN, CPB, C*. 8 hialldrstrid] hjaldrstríðr *Skj, EAK, CN, CPB, C*.

— *59* —

1	Lustu i sundr i sande	[Lustu í sundr í sandi
2	sex <marglitendr> eggia	seggs marglitendr eggja
3	hord greri fion med fyrdá	hǫrð greri fjón með fyrða
4	fot alldrtrega rotum	fót aldrtrega rótum,
5	ok prest þeir er <log lestu>	ok prests þeir er lǫg lestu
6	<liknar> krofd or hofdi	líknar krǫfð ór hǫfði
7	hætt mæl var þat heila	(hætt mál var þat) heila
8	himintungl firar stungu.	himintungl firar stungu.]

Prose syntax:
Marglitendr eggja lustu seggs fót í sundr í sandi. Fjón greri hǫrð með rótum aldrtrega fyrða, ok firar, þeir er leystu lǫg, krǫfð líknar, stungu himintungl heila ór hǫfði prest; þat var hætt mál. [The frequent-stainers of blades broke apart the man's leg in the sand. Hatred grows hard with the disturbances of the unceasing strife of men, and men, those who broke the law, the demand of mercy, stung the heavenly bodies of the brain from the priest's head; that was a dangerous undertaking.]

Textual notes:
2 sex] A g *is written above the* x *in a second hand.* marglitendr] marglitudr *F*, margli-tendur *B*. 3 hord] hord hord *F*. 5 log] lim *F*, log *B*, lóg *W*. 6 liknar] feyfdar *F*, leygðar *W*, liknar *B*.

Lexical variants:
1 i sundr] sunndr *B*. i sande] a sannði *B*. 2 eggia] eggi *B*. 3 greri] grerr *B*. med] af *B*. 5 prest] fyrst *W*. lestu] leystv *F*. 6 krofd] krǫf *W*. 8 firar] þegar *W*.

Phonological and spelling variants:
3 hord] haurð *B*. fyrdá] fyrda *B*. 4 alldrtrega] alldur trega *B*. 6 hofdi] hofði *B*, hǫfði *W*. 7 hætt] hett *B*. mæl] mal *B*. 8 himintungl] himinntvnngl *B*.

Editorial variants:
1 i sundr] sundr *Skj, EAK, CN, CPB, C, S*. i sande] á sandi *Skj, EAK, CN, CPB, C*. 2 sex] seggir *W, FMS, S*. marglitendr] marglitudr *FL, FMS*; marglituðs *W, S*. 3 greri] grœr *Skj, EAK, CN, CPB, C*. med] af *Skj, EAK, CN, CPB, C*. fyrda] fyrðum] *W*. 5 prest] prests *Skj, EAK*. þeir er] þeir's *Skj, EAK, CN*. log] lim *W, FL, FMS, S*. 6 liknar] leyfðar *W, FMS, S*; feyfdar *FL*. 8 firar] þegar *CN, CPB, C*.

— 60 —

1	Tungan var med tangar	[Tungan var með tangar
2	tirkunnz lokin munni	tírkunns lokinn munni
3	vara sem vænst ok þrysuar	vara sem vænst ok þrysvar
4	vidrlif skorin knifi.	viðrlíf skorinn knífi.
5	Audskiptir læ eftir	Auðskiptir lá eptir
6	aund lætr madr a strondu	ǫnd lætr maðr á strǫndu
7	margr of minni sorgir	margr of minni sorgir
8	meinsamliga hamladr.	meinsamliga hamlaðr.]

Prose syntax:
Tungan tírkunns var lokinn með tangar munni ok þrysvar skorinn knífi; vara sem vænst viðrlíf. Auðskiptir lá eptir á strǫndu meinsamliga hamlaðr. Margr maðr lætr ǫnd of minni sorgir. [The tongue of the man accustomed to praise was grasped by the mouth of tongs and cut three times with a knife; that was not a very hopeful treatment. Afterward, the distributor of riches lay on the strand dangerously mangled. Many a man gives up the ghost for fewer afflictions.]

Lexical variants:
1 Tungan] Tvnnga *B*. 2 tirkunnz] tirkunn *B*. lokin] nvmin *B*. 5 Audskiptir] Avrskiptir *B*.

Phonological and spelling variants:
2 munni] mvnne *B*. 3 vara] vasa *B*. vænst] vænnst *B*. þrysuar] tysvar *B*. 4 skorin] skorinn *B*. 5 eftir] eptir *B*. 6 strondu] stronðv *B*. 7 minni] minne *B*. 8 hamladr] hamlaðr *B*.

Editorial variants:
1 Tungan] Tu̅ga *Skj, EAK, CN, CPB, C*. 2 tirkunnz] tírkunn *Skj, CN, CPB, C*. lokin] numin *Skj, EAK, CN, CPB, C*. 3 þrysuar] tysvar *CN, CPB, C*. 5 Audskiptir] Ǫrskiptir *CN, CPB, C*.

— *61* —

1	Leyfdr er sa er let of	[Leyfðr er sá er lét of
	<styfdrar>	stýfðrar
2	lamins fotar gram niota	lamins fótar gramr njóta
3	itran þegn <sem> augna	ítran þegn sem augna
4	ut stunginna ok tungu.	út stunginna ok tungu.
5	Hond Olafs vann heilann	Hǫnd Óláfs vann heilan
6	hreins giorfallra meina	hreins gjǫrvallra meina
7	ger munu giolld þeim er	gǫr munu gjǫld þeim er
	byriar	byrjar
8	Guds þræl ofugmæli.	Guðs þræl ofugmæli.]

Prose syntax:
Leyfðr er sá, er lét gram njóta lamins fótar, sem ítran þegn of-stýfðrar tungu ok út-stunginna augna. Hǫnd hreins Óláfs vann Guðs þræl heilan gjǫrvallra meina; gǫr munu gjǫld þeim, er byrjar ofugmæli. [Praised is he who granted the man the use of his lame leg, the excellent thane likewise of his cut-off tongue and stung-out eyes. The hand of pure Óláfr won for God's thrall health of all his injuries; payment will be exacted from the one who commits slander.]

Textual notes:
1 styfdrar] styfdar *FB*. 2 gram] gramr *B*.

Lexical variants:
1 of] ok *B*. 2 lamins] lamiþs *B*. 3 itran] vngann *B*. sem] til *F*, sem *B*. 4 ok tungu] tungu *B*. 6 giorfallra] grimligra *B*. 7 byriar] byria *B*.

Phonological and spelling variants:
1 Leyfdr] Leyfðr *B*. sa] sæ *B*. 5 heilann] heilan *B*. 7 ger] gior *B*. giolld] giǫllð *B*. 8 Guds] Gvðs *B*. þræl] þrel *B*. ofugmæli] avfogmæli *B*.

Editorial variants:
1 Leyfdr er] Leyfðr's *Skj, EAK, CN*. sa er] sás *Skj, EAK, CN*. of styfdrar] ok stýfðrar *Skj, EAK, CN, CPB, C*; of stýfðar *FL, FMS, S*; stýfðar *W*. 2 lamins] lamiðs *Skj, EAK, CN, CPB, C*. gram] gramr *Skj, EAK, CN, CPB, C*. 3 itran] ungan *CN, CPB, C*. sem] til *FL, FMS, S*. 4 stunginna ok tungu] stunginna tungu *Skj, EAK, CN, CPB, C*. 6 giorfallra] grimligra *CN, CPB, C*; giǫrvastra *S*. 7 þeim er byriar] þeim's byrja *Skj, EAK, CN*; þeim er byria *CPB, C*; þeim byriar *S*.

— *62* —

1	Bidr allzkonar ædri	[Bíðr allskonar œðri
2	orugt mæl ek þat sælu	(øruggt mæl ek þat) sælu
3	dyrdar vottr med drottni	dýrðar váttr með dróttni
4	dyggri enn þiod of hyggi	dyggri en þjóð of hyggi,
5	[þvi at] lausnara leysi	því at lausnara leysi
6	lids valldr numin alldri	liðs valdr numinn aldri
7	langvinr firdi sik syndum	langvinr firði sik syndum
8	slik verk a iardriki.	slík verk á jarðríki.]

Prose syntax:
Dyggri dýrðar váttr bíðr með dróttni allskonar sælu, œðri en þjóð of hyggi (øruggt mæl ek þat), því at langvinr lausnara, numinn aldri, leysi slík verk á jarðríki; liðs valdr firði sik syndum. [The exceedingly valiant witness of glory gets from the Lord all kinds of blessedness, higher than men can imagine; I say that fearlessly; because the old friend of the Saviour, taken from life, can perform such works in the earthly kingdom; the ruler of men kept himself from sin.]

Textual notes:
1 þvi at] *The MS (col. 2, 1.59) is badly discoloured, but the words are legible.*

Lexical variants:
2 mæl] mæli *B*. 4 dyggri] dyggr *B*. 5 þvi at] ef *B*. leysi] lysir *B*. 7 langvinr] vinr *B*.

Phonological and spelling variants:
1 allzkonar] allz skonar *B*. ædri] æðri *B*. 2 orugt] avrogt *B*. 3 drottni] drottne *B*. 6 lids] liðs *B*. numin] nvminn *B*. 7 firdi] firde *B*. sik] sic *B*. 8 iardriki] jarðrike *B*.

Editorial variants:
2 mæl ek] mælik *Skj, EAK, CN*. 4 dyggri] dyggr *Skj, EAK, CN, CPB, C*; dyggvi *W, FMS, S*. enn] an *Skj, EAK, CPB*. hyggi] hyggvi *W, FMS, S*. 5 þvi at] þvít *Skj, EAK*; ef *CN, CPB, C*; sérat *W, FMS*; sier at *S*. leysi] lysir *Skj, EAK, CN, CPB, C*. 7 langvinr] vinr *Skj, EAK, CN, CPB, C*. firdi] friði *W, FMS, S*.

— *63* —

1	Hedann var vngr fra angri	[Heðan var ungr frá angri
2	allz mest <vini> <flesta>	(alls mest vini flesta
3	Gud reynir sva sina	Guð reynir svá sína)
4	siklingr numin miklu.	siklingr numinn miklu.
5	Nu lifir hraustr af hæstri	Nú lifir hraustr af hæstri
6	himna valldz þar er alldri	himna valds þar er aldri
7	færskerdandi fyrda	fárskerðandi fyrða
8	fridarsyn gledi tyniz.	friðarsýn gleði týnisk.]

Prose syntax:
Siklingr var ungr numinn heðan frá miklu angri (Guð reynir svá alls mest flesta vini sína). Nú lifir hraustr fárskerðandi fyrða af himna valds hæstri friðarsýn þar er gleði aldri týnisk. [The king was taken young from here, from great affliction; in such wise God usually tests most of his friends. Now the strong fortune-diminisher of men lives in the heavenly ruler's highest vision of peace, where joy never ceases.]

Textual notes:
This stanza begins col. 3 in F. 2 vini] vinir *F*, vini *B*. flesta] flestir *F*, flesta *B*.

Lexical variants:
5 af] j *B*.

Phonological and spelling variants:
1 Hedann] Hedan *B*. angri] avgri *B*. 4 numin] nvminn *B*. miklu] miclv *B*. 6 valldz] vallz *B*. 7 færskerdandi] farskerdanði *B*. 8 tyniz] tynist *B*.

Editorial variants:
2 vini] vinir *FL*. flesta] flestir *FL, FMS*. 5 af] í *EAK, CN, CPB, C*. 6 þar er] þars *Skj, EAK, CN*.

— 64 —

1	Hu[er] er sva hoskr at hyriar	[Hverr er svá hoskr at hyrjar
2	hans \<vegs\> megi of segiá	hans vegs megi of segja
3	lioss i lifi þessu	ljóss í lífi þessu
4	lofdungs giafar tunga.	lofðungs gjafar tunga?
5	Þar e[r] hreggsalar hyggium	Þar er hreggsalar hyggjum
6	heitfastr iofur veit[ir]	heitfastr jǫfurr veitir
7	skreytt megu skatnar lita	skreytt megu skatnar líta
8	skrin dyrdar vin sinum.	skrín dýrðar vin sínum.]

Prose syntax:
Hverr er svá hoskr, at tunga hans megi segja of gjafar lofðungs ljóss hyrjar vegs í lífi þessu? Hyggjum þar, er heitfastr jǫfurr hreggsalar veitir dýrðar vin sínum; megu skatnar líta skreytt skrín. [Who is so wise that his tongue can tell the gifts of the prince of the bright path of fire in this life? There, where we believe the oath-keeping king of the storm-hall assists his glorious friend, men can see the ornamented shrine.]

Textual notes:
1, 5 *The MS (col. 3, 11.3–4) is badly discoloured but the words are faintly legible.*
2 vegs] veg *F*, vegs *B*. 6 veitir] *F reads* veit, *with a dot above the* t; *B reads* veitir.

Lexical variants:
1 hyriar] byriar *B*. 2 hans] háss *B*. megi of segia] megi segia *B*. 4 tunga] tungna *B*. 5 Þar] Þær *B*. hreggsalar hyggium] hims ok himna *B*. 7 megu] er of *B*. skatnar] skatna *B*. lita] drottinn *B*. 8 sinum] þinum *B*.

Phonological and spelling variants:
3 lioss] lios *B*. lifi] life *B*. 7 skreytt] skreyt *B*.

Editorial variants:
1 Huer er] Hverr's *Skj, EAK, CN*. hoskr] horskr *Skj, EAK, CPB*; horsk *CN, C*. hyriar] byrjar *Skj, EAK, CN, CPB, C*. 2 hans] hǫs *EAK, CN, CPB, C*. vegs] veg *W, FL, FMS, S*. megi of] megi *CN, CPB, C*. 4 giafar] grafar *W, S*. tunga] tungla *CPB*. 5 Þar] Þær *Skj, EAK, CN, CPB, C*; Þann *W*. hreggsalar hyggium] heims ok himna *Skj, EAK, CN, CPB, C*. 6 iofur] iofra *FMS*. 7 skreytt megu] skreytt's of *Skj, EAK, CN*; skreytt er of *CPB, C*. skatnar lita] skatna dróttin *Skj, EAK, EN, CPB, C*. 8 sinum] þínum *CN, C*.

— *65* —

1	Heims hygg ek hingat kuomu	[Heims hygg ek hingat kómu
2	\<hofudsmenn\> i stad þenna	hǫfuðsmenn í stað þenna
3	snarr tiggi bergr seggium	(snarr tyggi bergr seggjum
4	solar \<erchistoli.\>	sólar) erchistóli.
5	Her er af himna geruis	Hér er af himna gervis
6	heilagr vid[r] sem bidium	heilagr viðr (sem biðjum
7	yfirskiolldungr biarg þu alldar	yfirskjǫldungr bjarg þú aldar
8	oss piningarcrossi.	oss) píningar krossi.]

Prose syntax:
Ek hygg hǫfuðsmenn heims kvómu erchistóli hingat í stað þenna (snarr tyggi sólar bergr seggjum). Hér er heilagr viðr af píningar krossi himna gervis (yfirskjǫldungr aldar, bjarg þú oss sem biðjum). [I know that the rulers of the world brought an archbishopric here to this place; the quick prince of the sun saves men. There is holy wood here from the torture-cross of the maker of heaven; supreme king of the ages, protect us as we pray.]

Textual notes:
4 erchistoli] erchistolar *F*, erkistole *B*. 6 vidr] *The MS (col. 3, line 6) is discoloured and the* r *is only partly legible.*

Lexical variants:
2 hofuds menn] hofud mannz *F*, hofuds menn *B*. 3 snarr] snart *B*. 7 þu alldar] biargh alldar *B*.

Phonological and spelling variants:
5 gervis] giorfers *B*. 7 biarg] biargh *B*. 8 piningarcrossi] piningarkrosse *B*.

Editorial variants:
1 hygg ek] hykk *Skj, EAK, CN.* kuomu] kvǫmu *Skj, EAK*; kvámu *CN, C*; kómo *CPB*; komu *W, FMS, S.* 2 hofuds menn] höfuðmenn *W, FMS, S.* 4 erchistoli] erchistolar *W, FMS, S.* 5 her er] hér's *Skj, EAK, CN.* 7 þu alldar] aldar *Skj, EAK, CN, CPB, C.*

— *66* —

1	Aulld nytr Olafs milldi	[Qld nýtr Óláfs mildi
2	iofurs dyrd hofum skyrda	jǫfurs dýrð hǫfum skýrða
3	þrotnar hars fra þessum	þrotnar hárs frá þessum
4	þingsniallz verolld alla.	þingsnjalls verǫld alla.
5	Luti landzfolk itrum	Lúti landsfolk ítrum
6	lim <sals> <konungs> himna	lim sals konungs himna;
7	sæll er huerr er hollan	sæll er hverr er hollan
8	hann gerir ser manna.	hann gerir sér manna.]

Prose syntax:
Qld nýtr hárs Óláfs mildi; hǫfum skýrða alla dýrð þingsnjalls jǫfurs; verǫld þrotnar frá þessum. Landsfolk lúti ítrum lim himna sals konungs; sæll er hverr manna, er hann gerir hollan sér. [People avail themselves of high Óláfr's mercy; we have made clear all the fame of the battle-brave king; the world dwindles from these things. The people of the land should bow before the bright limb of the king of the hall of heaven; blessed is every man who makes him his friend.]

Textual notes:
6 sals] salmls *F*, sal *B*. konungs] konungi *F*, konunguns *B*.

Lexical variants:
3 þrotnar] þrottar *B*. hars] hvass *B*. fra] af *B*. 4 þingsniallz] þreksnioll *B*. verolld] frama *B*. alla] ollvm *B*. 7 hollann] hyllan *B*.

Phonological and spelling variants:
5 luti] loti *B*. landzfolk] lanðfolk *B*. 7 sæll] sêll *B*.

Editorial variants:
3 þrotnar] þróttar *Skj*, *EAK*, *CN*, *CPB*, *C*. hars fra] hvass at *Skj*, *EAK*, *CN*, *CPB*, *C*. 4 þingsniallz verolld alla] þreksnjǫll frama ǫllum *Skj*, *EAK*, *CN*, *CPB*, *C*. 6 lim sals konungs] limsalmls konungi *FL*; lim salkonungs *Skj*, *EAK*, *CN*, *CPB*, *C*; lima síns konungi *FMS*, *S*.

— 67 —

1	Talda ek fætt i fiolda	[Talða ek fátt í fjǫlða
2	fridgegns af iartegnum	friðgegns af jarteignum
3	ber koma ord af orum	ber koma orð af órum
4	Olæfs bragar stoli.	Óláfs bragar stóli.
5	Bæls fai seggr huerr er solar	Bóls fái seggr hverr er sólar
6	siklings hefir mikla	siklings hefir mikla
7	hilmis æst ens hæsta	hilmis ást ens hæsta
8	heidbiartr er lof reidir.	heiðbjartr er lof reiðir.]

Prose syntax:
Talða ek fátt í fjǫlða af jarteignum friðgegns Óláfs; ber orð koma af órum bragar stóli. Fái hverr heiðbjartr seggr, er hefir lof siklings sólar bóls, ást ens hæsta hilmis, er reiðir mikla. [I have told few of all-peaceful Óláfr's many miracles; clear words come from our seat of poetry. May every heaven-bright man who raises the praise of the king of the sun's home receive the love of the highest king, who influences much.]

Lexical variants:
1 i] or *B*. 3 af] fra *B*. 5 fai] taki *B*. 6 hefir] þess er Gvð *B*. mikla] miclar *B*. 7 hilmis] hilmir *B*. 8 heidbiartr] heidbiartrar *B*. er lof] lof *B*. reidir] greiðir *B*.

Phonological and spelling variants:
1 fætt] fatt *B*. fiolda] fiolða *B*. 4 Olæfs] Olafs *B*. 5 bæls] bols *B*. 7 æst] ast *B*. ens] enns *B*.

Editorial variants:
1 Talda ek] Talðak *Skj, EAK, CN*. i] ór *Skj, EAK, CN, CPB, C*. 3 af] fra *Skj, EAK, CN, CPB, C*. 5 fai] taki *Skj, CN, CPB, C*. huerr er] hverr's *Skj, CN*; hverr *EAK, W, FMS, S*. 6 siklings] siklingr *EAK*. hefir mikla] þess's Guð miklar *Skj, CN*; þess er Goð miklar *CPB, C*. 8 heidbiartr er] heiðbjartrar *Skj, CN, CPB, C*; heiðbjarts *EAK, W, S*. reidir] greiðir *CN, CPB, C*.

— *68* —

1	Sua at lausnara leysi	[Svá at lausnara leysi
2	<langvinr> fra kuol strangri	langvinr frá kvǫl strangri
3	nyta þiod or naudum	nýta þjóð ór nauðum
4	nafnkudr vid tru iafnan	nafnkuðr við trú jafnan,
5	viga skys þeir er visa	víga skýs þeir er vísa
6	velendr framan telia	veljendr framan telja
7	auflugs Cristz af astum	ǫflugs Krists af ǫstum
8	<alnenins> brag þenna.	alnennins brag þenna.]

Prose syntax:
Svá at nafnkuðr langvinr lausnara leysi jafnan nýta þjóð frá strangri kvǫl ór nauðum við trú, þeir veljendr víga skýs, er telja framan þenna brag alnennins vísa af ǫstum ǫflugs Krists. [So that the well-known old friend of the Saviour can immediately release the able people from great torment, out of need with respect to the faith, those choosers of the cloud of battle who tell forth this, the extremely effective prince's poem about the love of mighty Christ.]

Textual notes:
2 langvinr] langvinn *F*, langvinr *B*. 8 brag þenna] *The words are written in a space at the end of col. 3, line 11, two lines above their proper place in the text. The scribe has drawn a line to point the way.*

Lexical variants:
3 or] ok *B*. 4 nafnkudr] naglkvaddr *B*. iafnan] stadda *B*. 5 þeir] þar *B*. 6 framan] gladir *B*. 7 Cristz] Krist *B*. 8 alnenins] almenins *F*, alnenens *B*.

Phonological and spelling variants:
1 Sua] Svo *B*. 3 þiod] þioð *B*. 6 velendr] velivndr *B*.

Editorial and spelling variants:
1 Sua at] Svát *Skj*, *EAK*, *CN*. 2 langvinr] langvin *FL*. 3 or] ok *Skj*, *EAK*, *CN*, *CPB*, *C*. 4 nafnkudr] naglskadds *CN*, *CPB*, *C*. iafnan] stadda *CN*, *CPB*, *C*. 5 þeir er] þar's *Skj*, *EAK*, *CN*; þar er *CPB*, *C*. alnenins] alnennins *Skj*, *EAK*; allnennins *CN*, almennins *FL*, *FMS*, *S*.

— *69* —

1	Olafs hofum iofri	[Óláfs hǫfum jǫfri
2	ordhags kyni sagdar	orðhags kyni sagðar
3	fylgir hugr ens helga	fylgir hugr ens helga
4	hapsdædir þvi rædi	happsdáðir því ráði.
5	Laun fæum holl <ef> hanum	Laun fǫm holl af hánum
6	hresiks þrimu likar	hræsiks þrimu líkar
7	gofugs odar hialp <gædi>	gǫfugs óðar hjalp gæði
8	Guds blezon lofs þessa.	Guðs blezan lofs þessa.]

Prose syntax:
Hǫfum sagðar jǫfri happsdáðir orðhags Óláfs ens helga; hugr fylgir því ráði kyni. Fǫm holl laun þessa lofs ef hánum líkar; Guðs blezan gǫfugs óðar hjalp gæði hræsiks þrimu. [We have told the king the blessed deeds of eloquent Óláfr the holy; the mind follows this counsel to the family. We will receive a friendly reward for this poem, if it pleases him; may God's blessing of the noble poem help the increaser of the storm of the corpse-salmon.]

Textual notes:
The order of this stanza and the following one is reversed in B.

Lexical variants:
1 iofri] iofra *B*. 3 fylgir] fylgði *B*. 4 hapsdædir] hapsdada *B*. 5 fæum] fæ ek *B*. ef] af *F*, eff *B*. hænum] hreinum *B*. 7 hialp] let *B*. gædi] gædum *F*, gædir *B*. 8 lofs] lids *B*.

Phonological and spelling variants:
3 ens] enns *B*. 4 rædi] raði *B*. 6 hresiks] hræsiks *B*. 7 gofugs] gavfvgs *B*. 8 blezon] blezsvn *B*.

Editorial variants:
1 iofri] jǫfra *Skj, EAK, CN, CPB, C*. 2 kyni] liði *CPB*. 3 fylgir] fylgði *Skj, EAK, CN, CPB, C*. 5 ef] af *W, FL, FMS, S*. 6 hresiks] hræsik *FMS, S*. 7 hialp] létt *Skj, CN, C*; lát *EAK*, lér *CPB*. gædi] gædum *EAK, W, FL, FMS, S*; gæðir *CPB*. 8 lofs] lof *Skj*; liðs *CN, CPB, C*.

— *70* —

1	Mundi bragr ens <brondum>	[Myndi bragr ens brǫndum
2	baug <ness> vera þessi	baugness vera þessi
3	kann ek rausnarskap ræsis	(kann ek rausnarskap ræsis)
4	raundyrliga launadr	raundýrliga launaðr,
5	ef lofda gramr lifdi	ef lofða gramr lifði
6	leikmilldr Sigurdr hilldar	leikmildr Sigurðr hildar
7	þess lysek veg visa	(þess lýsek veg vísa)
8	vellum grimr enn ellri.	vellum grimr enn ellri.]

Prose syntax:
Bragr þessi myndi vera raundýrliga launaðr brǫndum ens baugness (ek kann raus-
narskap ræsis), ef Sigurðr enn ellri, vellum grimr lofða gramr, leikmildr hildar, lifði
(lýsek veg þess vísa). [This poem would be rewarded magnificently with the flames of
the bracelet-ness (I know the generosity of the king), if Sigurðr the elder, king of men,
eager for the play of battle, grim to gold, were alive (I praise the honour of this king).]

Lexical variants:
1 Mundi bragr] Bragr mundi *B*. ens] nu *B*. brondum] brenda *F*, grondv *B*. 2 ness] huers
F, ness *B*. 3 kann] man *B*. 4 launadr] lavnat *B*. 7 lysek] hrosa ek *B*. 8 grimr] grims *B*.

Phonological and spelling variants:
3 rausnarskap] rausnirskap *B*. ræsis] resis *B*. 5 ef] eff *B*. lifdi] lifði *B*.

Editorial variants:
1 Mundi bragr] Bragr myndi *Skj, EAK, CN, CPB, C*. ens] nú *Skj, EAK, CN, CPB, C*.
brǫndum] brenda *W, FL, FMS, S*. 2 baug ness] baugness *Skj, EAK, CN, CPB, C*. þessi]
þersi *W, FMS, S*. 3 kann ek] mank *Skj, EAK, CN*; man ek *CPB, C*. 7 lysek] hrosa ek
CN, CPB, C. 8 grimr] grimms *Skj, EAK, CN, CPB, C*.

— *71* —

1	Bæn hef ek þengill þina	[Bœn hef ek þengill þína
2	þrekrammr stodat framla	þrekrammr stoðat framla
3	iflaust hafum iofri	iflaust hǫfum jǫfri
4	vnnit mærd sem kunnum.	unnit mærð sem kunnum.
5	Agætr segir æzstann	Ágætr segir œztan
6	<Eysteinn> hue ek brag	Eysteinn hvé ek brag
	leysta	leysta
7	hæs elskig veg visa	(hás elskik veg vísa
8	vagnræfrs en ek þagna.	vagnræfrs) en ek þagna.]

Prose syntax:

Þrekrammr þengill, bœn þína hef ek framla stoðat; iflaust hǫfum unnit jǫfri mærð, sem kunnum. Ágætr Eysteinn segir, hvé ek brag œztan leysta (elskik veg vísa hás vagnræfrs), en ek þagna. [Strong prince, I have excellently fulfilled your request; without a doubt we have made praise of the king, as we are able. Excellent Eysteinn will say how I delivered the best poem (may I love the way of the king of the high wagon-roof); and I fall silent.]

Textual notes:

6 Eysteinn hue ek] Hue ek *F*, Eysteinn hve *B*.

Lexical variants:

5 segir] segit *B*. æzstann] jtrann *B*. 6 leysta] leystek *B*. 7 elskig] elskit *B*.

Phonological and spelling variants:

1 hef] heff *B*. þengill] þeingill *B*. 2 stodat] stoðat *B*. 3 hafum] hofum *B*. 7 hæs] hæss *B*. 8 vagnræfrs] vagnræfurs *B*. þagna] þagnna *B*.

Editorial variants:

1 hef ek] hefk *Skj*, *EAK*, *CN*; hefir *FMS*. 5 segir æzstann] segið ítran *Skj*, *EAK*, *CN*, *CPB*, *C*; segir ytum *FL*, *FMS*; segi ytum *W*, *S*. 6 Eysteinn] Æzstann *W*, *FL*, *FMS*, *S*. hue ek] hvé *Skj*, *EAK*, *CN*, *CPB*, *C*. leysta] leystak *Skj*, *EAK*, *CN*; leysta ek *CPB*, *C*. 7 elskig] elskið *Skj*, *EAK*, *CN*, *CPB*, *C*.

Commentary

1.1–4. *Geisli* opens with an invocation of the Trinity. According to the traditional theory of skaldic composition, every aspect of poetic creation was regarded as the personal achievement of the skald, and Einarr broke a tradition of three centuries by beginning in the manner of medieval Latin poetry with a prayer for inspiration. As the continental influence grew stronger the *invocatio* became more common in skaldic poetry: among the *drápur* of the century following the composition of *Geisli* it appears in *Harmsól* (*Skj* IA: 562), *Óláfs drápa Tryggvasonar* (IA: 573), *Leiðarvísan* (IA: 618), and *Líknarbraut* (IIA: 150).

1.1. *ord.* This has the sense not only of 'words,' but of words of poetry, or poetry. Cf. the alternative reading 'oð' in *A* and *W*. For a similar use of *orð* see Egill's Lausavísa 41 (*Skj* IA: 58).

1.2. *allz rædanda.* Cf. 5.4. This name for God (cf. Old English *eallwealdend, eallwealda*) also appears in Abbot Arngrimr's *Guðmundar kvæði byskups* 46.7 (*Skj* IIA: 357). The image of lord or ruler of all was one of the earliest kenning formulas for God to be used in skaldic poetry: it first appears in the eleventh-century *Knútsdrápa* of Hallvarðr háreksblesi ('allz drotni' 8.2 [*Skj* IA: 318]). Other versions include 'allz styrande' (Markús Skeggjason, *Eiríksdrápa* 31.2 [*Skj* IA: 451]) and 'allz kannande' (*Líknarbraut* 5.6 [*Skj* IIA: 151]), as well as the *Geisli* variants 'allz valdanda' and 'allz kiosanda.'

1.2. *snjalla.* The proper meaning of *snjallr* is 'swift,' but it also came to mean 'quick with words,' translating Latin *eloquens*. This meaning is well attested in prose; for an instance in poetry see *Óláfs drápa Tryggvasonar* 2.3 (*Skj* IA: 574).

1.3. *frodr, goda.* The use of *aðalhending* in the third line of the *helmingr* breaks the rhyming laws of the *dróttkvætt* metre; the blame is due more likely to textual transmission than to the poet. The variant reading 'greiða' in *B* offers another possibility. If we take 'greiða' as the noun *greiði* (ordering, dis-entanglement, arrangement) we can translate 'very wise is he who gets order-ing [of his words] from the eloquent ruler of all.' For alternative readings see Cederschiöld, *Geisli*, 11, and *NN* § 924.

1.4. *þrenning.* This is the only instance of the word in poetry; its earliest appearance in prose is in *GNH*, roughly contemporary with *Geisli*.

1.3–6. Lines 5–6 echo the alliteration scheme of lines 3–4 ('getr'/'goda'/ 'Guds'; 'gofugt'/'geisli'/'gunnoflugr'), reinforcing the link between the *helmingar*.

1.5–8. The second *helmingr* of the verse, a dedication to St Óláfr, likewise imi-tates continental style. It is the only instance of a formal dedication ('ek byd itrum Olæfs agætan brag') in skaldic poetry. In the encomiastic *drápur* the skalds often begin by naming the prince who is the object of praise, but always in the form of a declaration ('I now praise ____'), using such words as *leyfa*, *segja*, and *kveðja*. Einarr's use of *bjóða* has no counterpart in skaldic poetry.

The syntax of the *helmingr* is ambiguous. The parenthetical dedication to Óláfr is clear enough, but the main clause can be construed in a variety of ways:

The battle-strong beam of the sun of mercy proclaims a splendid light.
The battle-strong beam proclaims the splendid light of the sun of mercy.
The battle-strong beam of mercy proclaims the splendid light of the sun.
The battle-strong beam of the sun proclaims the splendid light of mercy.

The same idea lies behind all these possibilities. The sun symbolizes Christ, and the sunbeam Óláfr. This imagery introduces the theme of the *drápa*, the typological relationship between the saint and Christ. The first suggested reading (which is the one adopted by all previous editors) and the second have essentially the same meaning. The kenning for Christ, 'miskunar solar,' is unusual; it may be a play on the Biblical *sol iustitiae* (Malachi 4:2). The third and fourth readings are at least as convincing. The image of Óláfr as 'beam of mercy' or the one who proclaims the 'light of mercy' is appropriate in a poem that portrays him as a miracle worker, a transmitter of Christ's mercy to the world. There is a verbal parallel in the Norwegian Nativity homily: 'ſkin þvi gnoglegar lios guðſ miſkunnar yfir þæim' (the abundant light of God's mercy shone over them) (*GNH*, 39). The image may be derived from Bede's Nativity homily (*CCSL*, 122:46), which quotes Psalm 111:4: 'to the righteous a light is risen up in darkness: he is merciful, and compassionate and just.' 'Sun' is ade-quate as a metaphor for Christ; it is common in Latin hymns, and Einarr uses it again in *Geisli* 3.1 (cf. also 'raudull' 2.8).

1.6. *gunnoflugr*. The epithet may seem more appropriate for a Viking king than for a sunbeam radiating God's mercy, but here it implies that Óláfr is a strong ally in the battle against darkness and evil.

2.1–4. This emphasizes the doctrine that Christ's eternal kingship remained intact during his life as a man (see, e.g., St Thomas Aquinas, *Summa Theologiae* 3a, 17, 2). For another interpretation see Finnur Jónsson, *Skj* IB: 427, and *NN* § 2051. Cf. John 1:5: 'et lux in tenebris lucet et tenebrae eam non conprehenderunt' (and the light shineth in darkness, and the darkness did not comprehend it').

2.1. *Peirrar*. The pronoun refers to 'solar' 1.8. This is the only instance in skaldic poetry of a stanza beginning with a dependent clause linked to a sentence in the preceding stanza. In classical skaldic composition the stanzas are grammatically and thematically distinct. In poetry of the twelfth century and later we occasionally encounter stanzas linked by a conjunction, but it is always a conjunction between two independent clauses in the manner of *Geisli* 15–16 and 67–8.

2.1. *heims*. In *dróttkvætt* metre *aðalhending* is not considered desirable in an odd-numbered line, hence the emendation to *húms* by several editors. But exceptions were tolerated, and the rhyming pattern here is *iðurmælt*, one of the special effects explained in *Háttatal*: 'Her er þrimsinvm haft samhending tysvar ifysta ok iii. v(isv) o(rði), en iavoðrv ok hinv fiorþa er haldit afhending sem idvnhendvm hætti' (Here the *samhendingar* [coincident rhymes] continue throughout the half-stanza and link with the second full rhyme in the second and fourth lines) (*SnE 1931*, 236; *Edda*, trans. Faulkes, 195. See also *Háttalykill* 29 [*Skj* IA: 552]). The repetition of 'heims'/'heimi'/'heims' is also an echo of the prologue to the Gospel of John: 'That was the true light, which enlighteneth every man that cometh into this *world*. He was in the *world*: and the *world* was made by him: and the *world* knew him not' (John 1:9–10). The B version of line 5 ('biartr fra biartri') follows a similar pattern and echoes the *lumen de lumine* of the *Credo*; it is probably the better reading. See *NN* § 2051 for a discussion of the phenomenon in this stanza and elsewhere in skaldic poetry.

2.4. *vedr- ... -hallar*. The pattern of tmesis whereby the elements of a compound are separated and relegated to the initial and final syllables of a line with another word interposed is common in skaldic poetry. The compound 'vedr- hallar' occurs in *Harmsól* 4.6, 8 in the kenning 'fýlkir vedr hallar' (*Skj* IA: 562) and the *Lexicon Poeticum* records the analogous compounds *veðrheimr* and *veðrhiminn*. See Meissner, *Die Kenningar*, 105–6 for a discussion of heaven-kennings based on weather phenomena. The formula 'king of heaven,' the basis for 'visi vedr-hallar,' was widely used in Christian skaldic poetry (see Meissner, *Die Kenningar*, 370), and it appears in a variety of forms in *Geisli*: cf. 'konungr dagbols' 5.8; 'lofdungs himintunglá rannz' 46.6, 8; 'himna valldz' 63.6; 'lofdungs lioss hyriar vegs' 64.1, 2, 3, 4; 'iofur hreggsalar' 64.5, 6; 'siklings solar bæls' 67.5, 6; and 'veg hæs vagnræfrs' 71.7, 8. It is analogous to the *rex cælestis* of the liturgical *Gloria*, and Einarr would also have known the image from the hymn *Christe, cæli Domine* (*AH* 51:12) and the sequence *Regem celi cantico* (*ONid*, 399).

2.4. *kalladizst.* The middle verb form is reflexive: it alludes to the Gospel of John, where Christ repeatedly calls himself the light of the world (John 8:12, 9:5, 12:46).

2.5, 6. *Leet berazst madr.* In keeping with the traditional doctrine of the Incarnation, *láta* has an active sense: 'he caused himself to be born a man.' The Norwegian Nativity homily uses the same terminology: 'drotten var lete berafc i þenna hæim af Mariu møyiu' (Our Lord caused himself to be born in this world of the Virgin Mary) (*GNH*, 32).

2.6. *skyiadri.* The proper meaning of *jaðarr* is 'edge' or 'rim.' The word was used to denote the seacoast, and by metonymy came to mean 'land.' 'Cloud-land' is a kenning for heaven. The phrase 'vnd skyiadri' can be construed with both 'leet berazst madr' (that sun clearly caused himself to be born a man under heaven) and with 'frægr faurnudr stod af þui' (widely renowned prosperity under heaven proceeded from that). Its central position in the *helmingr* suggests that Einarr intended the dual meaning.

2.7, 8. *frægr faurnudr stod af þui.* Cf. John 1:14, 16: 'et Verbum caro factum est et habitavit in nobis et vidimus gloriam eius gloriam quasi unigeniti a Patre plenum gratiae et veritatis ... et de plenitudine eius nos omnes accepimus et gratiam pro gratia' (And the Word was made flesh, and dwelt among us, and we saw his glory, the glory as it were of the only begotten of the Father, full of grace and truth ... And of his fullness we all have received, and grace for grace).

2.7, 8. *flædar stiornu.* This widely used epithet for the Blessed Virgin Mary first appears in the ninth-century hymn *Ave, maris stella* (*AH* 51: 140; *ONid*, 326, 328; *HASC*, 271–4). It occurs in only one other skaldic poem, the fourteenth-century *Máríudrápa*, where Mary is called 'siofar stiarna' (star of the sea) in stanzas 3.4 and 30.2 (*Skj* IIA: 464, 469).

2.8. *raudull.* The idea of the Incarnation as an enlightenment is ancient and pervasive in Christian literature: it is rooted in the Old Testament (e.g., Psalm 111:4, Isaiah 9:2, Malachi 4:2), and was further developed by the Gospel writers (e.g., John 1:9: 'erat lux vera quae inluminat omnem hominem venientem in mundum' (that was the true light, which enlighteneth every man that cometh into this world) and the liturgical *Benedictus* and *Nunc dimittis* [Luke

1:78–9 and 2:32]). The image of Christ as sun abounds in the Advent and Christmas liturgies (see, e.g., *ONid*, 152–7), perhaps the most famous example being the antiphon *O oriens* for 21 December: 'O Oriens, splendor lucis aeternae, et sol justitiae: veni, et illumina sedentes in tenebris, et umbra mortis' (O rising sun, splendor of eternal light and sun of righteousness; come and illuminate those sitting in darkness and the shadow of death) (*CAO* 3, § 4050, *ONid*, 147). A Nativity homily in the *Icelandic Homily Book* explicates the symbol: 'sol *cr*istr sialfr sa er lys*er* allan hei*m*. af villo eilifs blindleix' (the sun is Christ himself, who enlightens the whole world from the error of eternal blindness) (ed. de Leeuw van Weenen, fol. 22v).

2.8. This line contains a rhyming effect which Einarr uses frequently, although it seldom occurs elsewhere in skaldic poetry. The *aðalhendingar* are in the first and fifth syllables, at the outside edges of the line, with a pair of *skothendingar* ('-nudr'/ 'raud-') between them. This *abba* pattern occurs in *Geisli* 3.2, 4.4, 12.4, 15.4, 16.6, 16.8, 25.2, 28.8, 39.4, 50.2, 57.4, 66.8. It also appears with two pairs of *skothendingar* in the odd-numbered lines 8.5 and 25.7. The manuscript spellings 'faurnudr' and 'stiornu' are curious: *au* and *o* were both used to designate *u*-umlaut of *a*, but we might expect the scribe to use consistent orthography when writing a pair of rhymes.

3.1–4. 'Sidar bra solar liosi, þat var audfinnendum fyrir betra [liosi] heilags setrs annars omiors roduls.' Construe 'liosi' with both 'solar' and 'betra': the key position of the word in the final trochee calls attention to its double function.

3.1. *Sidar.* Finnur Jónsson and Kock read this as the noun *siðr* and construe 'Ljósi sólar heilags siðar brá' (*Skj* IB: 427; *NN* § 2315). I prefer to read *síðar*, the comparative form of the adverb *síð*. The word is a reference to the preceding stanza; its initial position in stanza 3 suggests that it is meant as a transition between the two.

3.1. *heilags.* The metre of the line is defective: there are seven syllables where there should be six. The *B* scribe has written 'heilgs,' followed by an illegible ligature which appears to involve a larger form of 's.' Cederschiöld (*Geisli*, 1) suggests comparison with *Geisli*, 30.1, where the words *es* and *at* are combined in an odd ligature to indicate that the metre requires that they be heard as one syllable.

3.1, 4. *solar liosi.* The image has a double meaning. Its primary sense is a continuation of the symbolism of stanzas 1 and 2: the sun signifies Christ and 'bra solar liosi' expresses the fact of his death. But there is also a sense of the homiletic figure of God as the sun and Christ as its light. Just as the eclipse does not destroy the sun, although it prevents its rays from lightening the earth, God is unchanged by the Crucifixion, although it temporarily obscures the light of Christ which is the manifestation of God's presence in the world.

3.2. *betra.* The darkness of the Crucifixion paradoxically leads to the new and more powerful light of the risen Christ. Cf. the Lenten hymn *Ternis ter*:

Mors per crucem nunc interit
Et post tenebras lux redit;
Horror dehiscat criminum,
Splendor nitescat mentium.

[Now death is ruined by the cross, and after darkness light returns; the horror of sins falls away, the splendour of souls shines forth.] (*AH*: 51: 66–7)

3.3. *audfinnendum.* The kenning is a reminder of the benefits brought by the death of Christ. The spelling *-endum* rather than *-ondum* reflects the influence of *i*-umlaut (see Noreen, *Altnordische Grammatik*, § 422, Anm. 1).

3.4. *omiors.* The word is a compound of *mjór* and the negative prefix *ó-* (variant of *ú-*). The rhyme with 'liosi' indicates that Einarr pronounced it 'ómjós' (cf. 'huers'/'þessi' in the *F* text of 70.2 and see Kahle, *Die Sprache der Skalden*, 151–3). The *F* scribe misunderstood the cause of the apparent lack of rhyme and attempted to rectify it by emending *ljósi* to 'lorsi' or ('liorsi'). I have printed the standard form of the word in the normalized text. 'Annars omiors roduls' is a *heiti* for God, his 'holy abode' is heaven.

3.5, 6. *Æzstr þrifnudr reed efnázst oss.* This sentence expresses the theme of the stanza in simple prose order. *Þrifnuður* means 'salvation' or 'prosperity'; here it personifies God's providence.

3.6, 7, 8. *lif allre fyrda iardar.* A kenning for Christ, analogous to the Scriptural image of Christ as 'life' (cf. John 11:25, 14:6, and Colossions 3:4). The use of an abstract noun as the base word of a kenning is unusual and attests to Einarr's knowledge of Christian theology and fascination with continental diction. He may have been influenced by the popular Holy Names sequences *Deus Pater piissime* (*AH* 15:21), *Alma chorus Domini* (*AH* 53:152; *ONid*, 262, 263, 427, 431, 435), and *Christe Salvator* (*AH* 8:37; *ONid*, 431), which list 'vita' (life), 'vita omnium' (life of all), and 'vita sæculi' (life of the world) as names for Christ. For a discussion in the Holy Names in medieval Scandinavia see Peter Foote, '*Nafn guðs hit hæsta.*'

3.8. *onaudigr.* 'He was offered because it was his own will' (Isaiah 53:7). Cf. *Líknarbraut* 21.1–4:

Lýste miskun mesta
milldr þa er saklaus villde

einn firi ǫllum monnum
ey hialms konungr deyia.

['The gentle king of the land's helmet showed great mercy when he wished
to die innocently for all mankind.'] (*Skj* IIA: 154)

4.1, 4. *kunnr allrar skepnu.* 'Known to all creation': the genitive is objective.
According to Scripture (e.g., Romans 16:25–6), the Resurrection made the
hidden mystery of Christ's saving power known to all nations.
4.4. *rettlætis sunnu.* 'Iustitiæ sol oriens' (rising sun of justice) (cf. Malachi
4:2) is a name for Christ in the sequence *Deus Pater piissime* (*AH* 15:13), and
Jons Saga Postola IV spells out the metaphor when it speaks of 'sialf rettlætis
solin lukt i likam, drottinn vær Jesus Cristus' (the sun of righteousness itself,
our Lord Jesus Christ, enclosed in a human body) (Unger, ed., *Postola Sögur*,
466). In Old Norse prose the image is usually associated with the Incarnation
and Nativity, but the Norwegian homily 'Jn die ſancto paſce' links it to the
rising sun of Easter: 'At upp-runnínní ſolo ſáo þær ængil hia grof. þvi at þa
megom vér ſcilia himneſca luti ef ret-lætes ſol ſkin í hiortum vaorum' (At the
rising of the sun they saw an angel by the grave, from which we may under-
stand that a part of the sun of righteousness shines in our hearts) (*GNH*, 82).
4.5. *Veit ek at.* A skaldic formula which also occurs in 40.1. Cf. 'fra ek' 12.2,
17.1, 17.5, 43.1; 'fregit hef ek' 15.1, 38.1; 'fyrr var hitt' 19.5; 'satt var at'
22.5, 34.1; 'raun er at' 30.1; 'menn hafa sagt at' 35.1; and 'fregn ek at' 51.5.
4.6. *meginfioldi.* The prefix *megin-* denotes strength or greatness; *fjolði* means
'multitude' and in poetry is frequently modified by a partitive genitive (see
Lexicon Poeticum). The *helmingr* is an allusion to Matthew 27:52–3: 'And the
graves were opened: and many bodies of the saints that had slept arose, And
coming out of the tombs after his resurrection, came into the holy city and
appeared to many.'
5.1. *yndi.* The word has no synonym in English: it has connotations of success,
prosperity, happiness, comfort, and ease.
5.4. *allz ræðanda.* Cf. 1.2. the kenning for God can be construed with 'sonr'
or with 'æzstrar hallar,' but 'God's best hall' is unlikely, and 'æzstrar hallar'
can stand alone as a metaphor for heaven (cf. 'hæstri hall' 11.2, 4).
5.6, 7. *audlinga doglings.* Kennings of this type ('king of kings') signify
Viking kings in earlier skaldic poetry (see Meissner, *Die Kenningar*, 371).
Their use as God-kennings in *Geisli* (cf. 'drottinn harra' 25.7) and *Heilags
Anda Vísur* ('hesta konungr iofra' 12.3, 4 [*Skj* IIA: 162]) may be either a bor-
rowing from skaldic tradition or an imitation of the Biblical variations on the

theme (cf. Ezekiel 26:7; 2 Maccabees 13:4; 1 Timothy 6:15; Revelation 1:5, 17:14, 19:16). The figure appears frequently in Latin and Old English poetry.

5.6. *hnigr.* An allusion to the book of Revelation, where the twenty-four elders, the angels, and the blessed are said to fall down before the King of Kings (Revelation 4:10, 5:8, 7:11).

5.7. *dyrum.* The *F* reading, 'dyran,' is grammatically impossible. *B*'s reading ('dyrdar') is good: we can construe 'dyrdar stoli.' But given the likelihood that the *F* scribe simply wrote superscript *n* for *m*, I prefer to read 'dyrum,' which involves the emendation of an inflection rather than of a word. 'Hird'/ 'dyrum' is an acceptable rhyme: see Kahle, *Die Sprache der Skalden*, 136–41 for other examples of *r/r skothending*.

5.8. *dagbols.* *Dagr* (day) is a metonymy for 'sun'; the sun's home is heaven. The kenning 'konungr dagbols' is well chosen: it sustains the sun-metaphor for Christ, whose home after the Ascension is heaven. See also commentary on 2.4.

6.1. *dyrdar.* The word can be construed with either 'drottinn' or 'vætta.' 'Dyrdar drottinn' would be analogous to the Scriptural 'Lord of glory' (1 Corinthians 2:8) and 'king of glory' (Psalms 23:7–10). The syntax of the *helmingr* supports this interpretation, but *dýrðar váttr* as a kenning for martyr is attested later in *Geisli* (62.3) and in *Plácitus drápa* 26.3 (ed. Louis-Jensen, 105). 'Vætta,' whether construed with 'dyrdar' or standing alone, refers to the apostles, who witnessed the glory of the Holy Spirit at Pentecost, and who later earned the crown of martyrdom.

6.2. *dæduandr.* Cf. 'iduandr' 4.2. Both compounds refer to Divine Providence.

6.2. *giafir.* Here inflected as an *i*-stem. Many *o*-stems alternated between the two paradigms (Noreen, *Altnordische Grammatik*, § 375), and in 64.4 it follows the *o*-stem declension.

6.2, 4. *mattigs anda.* A translation of the 'mighty wind' (*spiritus vehementis*) of Pentecost (Acts 2:2).

6.3. *kynazst.* Used reflexively with an object in the accusative the verb means 'to study, to ponder, to make oneself familiar with.' The 'excellent men' are the exegetes who study and interpret the Scriptures, the testimony of the witnesses.

6.4. *framir.* Used substantively.

6.5, 6, 8. *alþyd kristnni su er einum gudi hlydir.* An echo of Peter's preaching on the day of Pentecost: 'And it shall come to pass that whosoever shall call upon the name of the Lord shall be saved' (Acts 2:21).

6.6. *alþyd.* Related to the noun *alþýða* and the adjectives *þýðr* and *alþýðuligr.* 'Alþyd kristni' means 'catholic Christianity' or 'universal church.' The cognate *alþýða* appears in both versions of the Old Norse Pentecost homily (*GNH*, 93; *Icelandic Homily Book*, fol. 10v).

6.7. *hæstr skiolldungr.* A *heiti* for God, cf. 'hilmis ens hæsta' 67.7.

6.7. *haulldum.* Both manuscripts give the Norwegian form of the word, which is necessary to maintain proper *skothending.* According to Noreen the change *o/au* before *l* + consonant did not occur in Iceland until around 1300 (*Altnordische Grammatik*, § 105 and Anm.). The syntax of the *helmingr* is good, making the possibility of scribal tampering unlikely. Einarr may have chosen the form to avoid *aðalhending* in an odd-numbered line. In 4.6 he uses the form 'holda' to rhyme with 'meginfioldi.'

6.8. *himinvistar.* The analogous *himna vist* occurs in *Guðmundar kvæði byskups* 5.6 (*Skj* IIA: 349) and *Pétersdrápa* 2.7 (IIA: 501) as well as in the Icelandic *Homily Book* (fols. 98v–99r). *Vist* means 'abode' or 'provisions,' and is often used in the context of a host offering hospitality. The image of Christ offering his followers a heavenly home parallels the Germanic tradition of the chieftain rewarding his retainers with hospitality and gifts of land, and is sustained by the man-*heiti* 'haulldum' (landed farmers).

7.1–4. Stanza 7 is embellished throughout with additional rhymes. Einarr makes the name Óláfr the focal point of the first *helmingr* by surrounding it with rhyming words: 'skulum,' 'hallar,' 'allir,' 'alstyrkann,' 'vel.'

7.1. *Nu skulum ... geisla.* The *skothending* depends on our hearing the *s* of 'skulum' together with 'nu' ('nus-') to rhyme with 'geis-,' a reminder that skaldic poetry was meant for the ear, not the eye. For a discussion of the phenomenon of an initial consonant being combined with the preceding word to form a rhyme, see Kahle, *Die Sprache der Skalden*, 20–1, and Kristján Árnason, *The Rhythms of Dróttkvætt*, 102–3. It is unusual to separate the cluster *sk*. Kristján Árnason discusses this example and suggests that the rules of the dróttkvætt which forbade the separation of the consonant clusters *sp-*, *st-*, and *sk-* may have been less stringent with respect to rhyme than they were concerning alliteration (*The Rhythms of Dróttkvætt*, 105–6).

7.1, 2. *gofgann geisla Guds hallar.* The kenning for Óláfr echoes 'geisli miskunar solar' in stanza 1.

7.4. *alstyrkann.* Like 'gunnoflugr' 1.6, the adjective emphasizes Óláfr's strength. The only other instance of it is in *Heilags anda vísur* 16.8 (*Skj* IIA: 163), where it refers to the Holy Spirit.

7.4. *dyrka.* An instance of vowel shortening (see Noreen, *Altnordische Grammatik*, § 127.5). Cf. 24.2 and 57.6.

7.5–6. *hridblasnum sal heida.* 'Storm-blown hall of the heath,' a kenning for heaven. Cf. 'valldr blasenna tiallda hreggs' (ruler of the wind-blown tents of the storm) in *Harmsól* 57.6, 7 (*Skj* IA: 570).

7.8. *skina.* The verb sustains the metaphor of the first *helmingr*: Óláfr, the sun-beam, 'shines' with miracles. This technique, which Snorri calls *nýgerving* (*SnE 1931*, 190–1), was used sparingly by early skalds but grew in popularity under the influence of Latin poetry.

8.1. *afreks orda.* The kenning for poetry has multiple meanings: 'afreks' refers to both Óláfr's miracles and Einarr's poetry. The rhyme in this line is between 'heyr du' and 'orda.' Wennberg, Cederschiöld, and Wisén construe 'afreks' with 'konungr.'

8.2. *Eysteinn.* Eysteinn Haraldsson was Einarr's principal patron and the commissioner of the poem (cf. stanza 71). He is mentioned first among the kings and he alone is designated by a royal epithet ('konungr').

8.4. *hue ek fer verka.* Such formulas, beginning with *hvé*, are common in skaldic poetry, and the phrase may be either a boast or a sincere request for appraisal. The adjective 'snoggum' in 8.3 suggests that it is a boast.

8.5. Einarr treats Ingi the hunchback, Eysteinn's rival half-brother who eventually killed him, with less respect. He grants him only one line of poetry, depriving him of the customary flattering epithet, and does not address him directly.

8.6. *styrkna.* F reads 'styrkua,' an unlikely form. The scribe may have made the common error of writing *u* for *n*. 'Styrkna' is feasible if we read the line as a parenthesis and construe 'mærd' as syntactically parallel with 'od,' but the lack of rhyme confirms that the text is corrupt. The B version, 'stydia,' improves the rhyme and metre, but makes the syntax more difficult. Finnur Jónsson emends B to

> yðvarrar biðk styðja
> mærð, þat's miklu varðar,
> máttigt hǫfuð áttar

[I ask the mighty head of your line to strengthen the poem ...] (*Skj* IB: 429)

and Kock conflates the two texts:

> yðvart biðk magn styðja
> mærð, þat's miklu varðar,
> máttig, hofuð attar!

[I ask that your strength, mighty heads of the nation, support this poem ...] (*NN* § 2052)

The plural form 'mattig hofud' in *F* makes better sense than *B*'s 'maktvgt hofud' in the context of an address to three joint monarchs, although in Finnur's reading 'mighty head of your line' could refer to Óláfr.

9.1, 2, 3, 4. *Yfirmanni allrar alþydu lærdra.* A kenning for Archbishop Jón, who as superior of the clergy in his see was the 'over-man of the whole multitude of learned men.'

9.5. *Hefium hendr.* The gesture was associated with prayer and would have been familiar from Scripture (Psalms 27:2, 43:21, 62:5, 87:10, 118:48, 133:2, 142:6; Lamentations 3:41; 1 Timothy 2:8). The psalmist's formula appears in a line from the widely used hymn *Rerum creator optime* (*AH* 51: 28; *ONid*, 185, 195, 198; *HASC*, 153–4): 'Mentes manusque tollimus' (we lift up our minds and our hands). Liturgical books commonly use the rubric *manus elevans* (with hands lifted).

9.6. *vin roduls tiggia.* The kenning for Óláfr has associations with both the skaldic and Latin traditions. The Scriptural *amicus Dei* (friend of God) (Judith 8:22, Wisdom 7:27, James 2:23), translated as *guðs vinr* in Old Norse, became a commonplace in hagiography. In skaldic poetry it was customary to praise a *jarl* or lesser chieftain by calling him the close friend or confidant of a more powerful man (see Meissner, *Die Kenningar*, 362); here Einarr emphasizes Óláfr's closeness to God. Cf. 'lausnara spialli' 30.2 and 'lausnara langvinr' 62.5, 7. The God-kenning 'roduls tiggia' echoes the sun-imagery of the preceding stanzas.

9.7. *stols vex hæd.* The spread of Óláfr's cult and the consequent influx of pilgrims meant rapid growth for the see of Trondheim, with respect to both ecclesiastical prestige and material wealth.

9.8. *heilagr.* *F* reads 'heilag' with *r* written above the *g*, but this appears to be a correction by the scribe rather than the *–ar* abbreviation.

9.8. *fagran.* Óláfr's body, faithful to the tradition of sanctity, remained beautiful and uncorrupt in his tomb.

10.1–4. There is a discrepancy between the two manuscript versions of the *helmingr. B* reads:

> Oss samir enn at þessv,
> orðgnottar bið ek drottinn
> alldar Olæfs gillða
> itrgeðs lofi kuedia.

There are no metrical or grammatical flaws, but the syntax is awkward: both 'gillða' and 'itrgeðs' must be construed with 'Olæfs.' In the *F* version, 'aulld' can be construed with 'gillda,' providing a link with the second *helmingr* that is schematic as well as thematic: lines 1 and 5 have the same triple-rhyme scheme ('aulld'/'Ol-'/'gilld-'; 'aulld'/'uál'/'villd-'). Line 2 is a complete parenthetic phrase, preferable to *B*'s 'ek bið alldar drottinn orðgnottar.' *F* probably represents the original text: at some point in the transmission of the *B* version lines 1 and 3 were transposed, and then later emended by a scribe attempting to make sense of the *helmingr*.

10.2. *ordgnottar bid ek drottinn.* This is the earliest instance of the formulaic prayer for 'word-wealth' which became a commonplace in Christian skaldic poetry. Cf. 1.1–4. Kristina Attwood ('Intertextual Aspects of the Twelfth-century Christian Drápur') points out that *Leiðarvísan* contains three instances of the word *orðgnótt* (1.8, 2.6, 4.8 = *Skj* IA: 618–19) as well as the analogous hapax legomenon *málsgnótt* (3.8 = *Skj* IA: 619), all in the context of a prayer for eloquence. The only other occurrences of *orðgnótt* are in Arnórr jarlaskáld's *Magnússdrápa* 5.2 (Whaley, ed., *The Poetry of Arnórr jarlaskald*, 119, 192–4) and a fragmentary verse attributed to Ormr Steinþórsson (*Skj* IA: 416). Attwood (227 and 235) suggests that this word belongs to a group of words particular to the Christian *drápur* and notes the similarity of 10.2, 'ordgnottar bid ek drottinn,' to *Leiðarvísan* 2.6, 'ord gnottar mer drottinn' (*Skj* IA: 619). Cf. also *Leiðarvísan* 3.8, 'máls gnott fae drottenn' (*Skj* IA: 619). She notes that 'these might be independent exploitations of a popular rhyming pair; of the two other occurrences of *orðgnótt* in *Leiðarvísan*, one (1.8) forms a *hending* with *dróttinn*, as does *málsgnótt* (3.8).' Arnórr jarlaskáld's *Magnússdrápa* 5.2 (Whaley, 119, 192–5) also contains the *orðgnótt/dróttinn* rhyme.

10.3. *odgerd.* Einarr probably created this compound, which chimes with 'ordgnottar' in the preceding line. It also occurs in *Líknarbraut* 49.3 (*Skj* IIA: 159) and in *Postula Sögur*, 510.

10.4. *itrgeds.* The meaning of the first element of the compound is clear, but there is no antecedent for an adjective *geðr*. *Geð*, a neuter noun, is well attested, and Kock proposes a nominal compound *ítrgeð* (high-minded one). In his interpretation the *helmingr* reads 'it is fitting for us to summon Óláfr's able men to this poetry-making, to the praise of the high-minded one' (*NN* § 929). But *ítrgeð* is unlikely as a noun, and the lexicographers allow an adjective *ítrgeðr*. I follow Finnur Jónsson's reading: 'it is fitting for us to summon able men to this poetry-making, to the praise of high-minded Óláfr' (*Skj* IB: 429).

10.6. *vallriodanda.* The elements of this *nomen agentis* kenning for 'warrior' are *vollr* and *rjóðandi*. The 'field-reddener' is the warrior who reddens the battlefield with the blood of his enemies. There may be a pun on *valrrjóðandi* (corpse-reddener).

11.2. *þegns prydibrag.* Previous editors have emended to *þegnprýðis brag* based on *B*. This interpretation assumes a hapax legomenon *prýðir* cognate with *prýða* (to ornament). *Þegn-prýðir* (people-ornamenter) becomes a kenning for Óláfr, and 'hæstri hall Kristz' a kenning for heaven. The *F* version is equally acceptable and may be preferable. The hapax legomenon 'prydibrag' is a more likely compound than *þegnprýðir* (the dictionaries list a variety of compounds with *prýði-*) and 'þegns Kristz' can be a kenning analogous to the *miles Christi* familiar from Scripture (2 Timothy 2:3) and hagiography (cf. 'Guds ridari' 18.6). The kenning for heaven, 'hæstri hall' (cf. 'æzstrar hallar' 5.3, 4) is better than 'hæstri hall Kristz,' where the superlative is redundant.

11.6–8. Construe 'Dyrd elianhress þiod-konungs er ordin ægæt i þessum, ne fædizst þuilikr þeingill i riki.' It is necessary to understand an object for 'þessum' ('the fame of the brave people-king has become renowned among these [men]), but the additional preposition 'i' and the plural form of 'þessum' suggest that at least the scribe (if not the skald) understood the phrase this way. For other interpretations see *Skj* IB: 429–30; *NN* § 931; and Wisén, ed., *Carmina Norrænæ*, 55. The theme of the *helmingr*, 'such a king will never again be born,' is a skaldic commonplace (cf. stanzas 13, 14, 21, and 51). The two couplets of the second *helmingr* are linked by secondary alliteration: the final word of line 6 ('þessum') alliterates with the *stuðlar* of the following couplet ('þiod'/'þeingill'/'þuilikr').

11.7–8. *þiod- ... -konungs.* The compound occurs again with tmesis in a similar context in 14.3–4.

12.2. *soknbrads.* I have emended to the *B* reading. The only possible objects for 'soknbradr' are 'Sigvatr' and 'Ottar.' 'Vehement in battle' is an unlikely epithet for a skald, and it would be a breach of protocol for the only epithet in the *helmingr* to refer to a poet rather than to the king.

12.5–8. Construe 'þeir, er hetu hofud skalld, hafa lystann frama þeingill Mæra, þvi er syst, ek lyt helgum iofri fira.' 'Hetu' must be understood as a passive verb, and 'fira iofri' as an epithet for Óláfr parallel with 'gram drottar' 12.4. For another reading see *Skj* IB: 430.

12.5. *þeingil Mæra.* Óláfr was king over a unified Norway, and throughout *Geisli* Einarr emphasizes the universality of his reign by naming him king of the individual districts.

13.1–4. The couplets of the first *helmingr*, paratactically juxtaposed, present the two aspects of Óláfr's character which Einarr wants both to acknowledge and to contrast: his public existence as a warrior king and his secret inner life of sanctity.

13.2. *munnriodr Hugins.* A typical warrior-kenning. Huginn was Óðinn's raven (by metonymy any raven), a traditional beast of battle or carrion-eater.

13.5–8. The envelope structure of the second *helmingr*, which deals with Óláfr's concealment of his holiness, reflects its meaning. The parenthesis 'fær gramr hefir frægri fæz' interrupts the main clause and obscures 'hæleitri gæzsku,' the object of 'Leyndi,' until it is revealed at the conclusion of the stanza.

13.7. The line lacks a rhyme: the *B* reading ('fremre' versus *F* 'frægri') is probably correct.

13.7–8. *fær gramr hefir frægri fæz.* A commonplace, cf. stanzas 11, 14, 21, and 51.

14.1–4. Construe 'sa tiirbradr, er trudi a Gud, red lædi þria vetr vm tolf; þegnar muna fæda betra þiod-konung' (he who believed in God, eager for praise, ruled the land for three winters beyond twelve; thanes will not engender a better people-king). This interpretation relies on assuming a pronoun (or pronoun plus adjective) subject, but it may be preferable to emendation. For readings based on emendation see *Skj* IB:430 and *NN* § 932.

14.3–4. *þegnar muna fæda betra þiod-konung.* The topic also occurs in stanzas 11, 13, 21, and 51. For a discussion of the compound 'þiod-konung' see commentary on 11.7-8.

14.5. *æðr.* Einarr was one of the first skalds to join the *helmingar* of a stanza with a subordinating conjunction. After the twelfth century the technique became increasingly common, and by the fourteenth century the *helmingr* was almost never an independent syntactic unit.

14.5. *fullhugadr.* The adjective echoes 'iduandr' and 'dæduandr,' which describe Christ in stanzas 4.2 and 6.2. It suggests that Óláfr, like Christ, was conscious of his participation in the divine economy. Snorri emphasizes this in his *Óláfs saga helga.*

14.5. *felli.* The use of the subjunctive is puzzling. It may suggest that Óláfr's death, like Christ's, was preordained.

14.8. *Aulfishaug.* Einarr doubtless knew that Óláfr fell at Stiklarstaðir (cf. stanzas 17 and 43). 'Aulfishaug' may be an allusion to a battle recorded in the sagas of St Óláfr (*Hkr*, 2: 178–81; and *Den store saga*, 261–9) as well as in the *Annales regii* (1021), *Gottskalks Annáll* (1021), and *Oddverja Annáll* (1020), all printed in Storm, *Islandske Annaler*. A powerful Trondheimer named Qlvir persisted in conducting pagan sacrifices on a grand scale long after Óláfr's imposition of Christianity, and Óláfr finally invaded the district with a large army. He interrupted the rites, killing Qlvir and sentencing others to imprisonment, mutilation, banishment, or execution. And thus, says Snorri, he returned all the people to the true faith, gave them teachers, and built and consecrated churches. References to these events reinforce the theme 'hann speni oss fra baulfi.' Just as at Qlvishaugr Óláfr protected his people from the evil of paganism, by his martyr's death at Stiklarstaðir (he was killed by Ǫlvir's son, according to the sagas) he gained the power to protect Norway supernaturally. Ǫlvishaugr was just a few miles from Stiklarstaðir, and Einarr's audience would have recognized the correspondence between the two places and events. The *Ǫlvir/bǫlvi* wordplay associates Ǫlvir with Óðinn (one of whose names was *Bǫlverkr*), and both with evil. Einarr uses *bǫl* again in reference to the killing of Óláfr in stanza 17.7.

15.2. *bardizst.* *F* reads 'berdizst,' an impossible form. The scribe probably emended to correct the faulty rhyme (*skothending* in place of *aðalhending*).

16.1. *Ok. Geisli* and *Plácitus drápa* (cf. stanzas 5, 7, 26, 30, 51, and 55) are the earliest skaldic poems in which a conjunction links two stanzas. This is the only instance in *Geisli*. Einarr probably imitated the technique from Latin hymn writing.

16.1. *hagliga.* The line lacks a rhyme in the *F* version, and *B*'s reading is probably correct. In the *F* reading, the adjective *hverlofaðr* can be construed with the kenning for Óláfr: 'hverlofaðr stríðandi látrs hins døkkva hrøkkviseiðs lyngs' (the praised-by-all enemy of the lair ...).

16.2, 3, 4. *stridandi lœtrs hins dockua lyngs hrockuiseids.* The kenning for Óláfr has multiple levels of meaning. On the surface it is a variation of the kenning-type 'dispenser of gold.' The dark, winding fish of the heather is a snake, and 'snake' is a metonymy for the dragon Fafnir of the Vǫlsung-Niflung legends. Fafnir's lair, a reference to the hoard he guards, is gold, and the enemy of gold is the generous lord who breaks his own treasure into pieces and distributes it to his *hirð*. Óláfr was a treasure-dispenser in this literal sense during his lifetime, and after his death he continues to reward his followers with miracles. A pun on the word *seiðr* gives the metaphor further significance. *Seiðr* was the name for a species of pollack (here it simply means 'fish'), but its more commonly used homonym was the word for the rites performed in pagan temples (cf. Modern Icelandic *seiður*, Danish and Norwegian *seid*). Thus there is also an allusion to Óláfr as the destroyer of temples, the lairs of the dark rites of heathendom.

16.5. *Leit.* The spelling ('ei' for *é*) reflects the fourteenth-century development of diphthongal allophones for long vowels (see Hreinn Benediktsson, 'The Vowel System of Icelandic,' 298 and Noreen, *Altnordische Grammatik*, § 103).

16.5. *landzfolk gætir.* This slight emendation, well supported by the evidence of other manuscripts, is necessary for the metre. The kenning 'landz folkgætir' not only spoils the trochaic rhythm, it violates Craigie's law, which states that 'no long nomen is permitted in positions 3 or 4 in even *dróttkvætt* lines if the first two positions are occupied by two long nominal syllables; in odd lines, no nomen is permitted in those positions if alliteration falls in positions 1 and 5 and positions 1–2 are occupied by two long nomina' (Gade, *The Structure of Old Norse* Dróttkvætt *Poetry*, xviii; see also 29).

16.7, 8. *vmgeypnandi allz heims.* Psalm 94:4 ('in his hands are all the ends of the earth') is probably the inspiration for this God-kenning. Cf. 'vm gavpnandi allr*ar* skepnv' (holding all creation in his hands), *Máríugrátr* 2.5 (*Skj* IIA: 472); 'u*m* geypna*n*di allrar skepnu,' *Kátrinar drápa* 36.3 (IIA: 523); 'skýstallz skr*í*ngeyp[na]nde skepnu' (holding the resting place of the cloud in his hands) *Harmsól* 29.7 (IA: 566); and 'hei*m* spen*n*e' (world-spanner), *Harmsól* 64.6 (IA: 571).

16.8. *sniallum.* The proper form is *snjǫllum*, showing the influence of *u*-umlaut. In Einarr's time *a* and *ǫ* constituted a full rhyme, but changes in pronunciation made the pair unacceptable as *aðalhendingar* by the end of the twelfth century (see Hreinn Benediktsson, 'Phonemic Neutralization and inaccurate Rhymes'). The fourteenth-century scribe of Flateyjarbók altered *snjǫllum* to 'sniallum' to make the rhyme appear correct according to the pronunciation of his own time.

17.1. *Vakit.* There is a play on the word, which refers both to the commencement of the battle and to Óláfr's awakening from his dream. Tradition held that the battle was beginning as the king awoke.

17.1, 2. *Stikla-* ... *-stodum.* The word occurs with tmesis every time it appears in poetry, probably due to the metrical difficulty of dealing with its four syllables.

17.4. *almreyrlitudr.* The kenning is consistent with the imagery of its context: Óláfr, who causes the wounds of his enemies to bleed, reddens his arrows with their blood.

17.6. *huatir.* The adjective suggests not only that Óláfr's adversaries were quick in battle, but also that they were hasty or rash in their opposition of him.

17.7. *brigdu.* The decidedly Christian reference to the 'transitory life of this world' contrasts sharply with the bloody battle imagery which predominates in the stanza.

17.8. *branddrif.* A typical warrior-kenning, but there is also a foreshadowing of the *Hneitir* miracle (stanzas 47–50), in which the supernatural Óláfr causes his sword to move under its own power.

17.8. *numin lifi.* Cf. 'numin alldri' 62.6 and 'hedann numin fra angri' 63.1, 4.

18.1. *er.* The use of the third person singular verb form for first person singular was common by the middle of the fourteenth century (Noreen, *Altnordische Grammatik*, § 531.1). The original text must have read *em*.

18.1. *vann visir.* The phrase reappears in 57.1 in a *helmingr* of similar style and content.

18.2. *flestra*. The word must be understood substantively: 'he was a great king over many.' The *B* reading, 'flestar,' improves the syntax. Finnur Jónsson emends and construes 'Emk fúss vanda stef, ef mættak, því vísi vann flestar mann-dýrðir; hann vas mestr konungr; drótt nemi mærð' (I am eager to make a *stef*, if I can, because the prince won the most man-ornaments; he was a great king; may the *drótt* accept praise) (*Skj* IB: 431).

18.6. *Guds ridari*. *F* reads 'ridadri,' showing confusion between the two spellings *ríðari* and *riddari*. The scribe may have intended *riddari* and simply transposed *d* and *a*, but I have emended to 'ridari,' the reading of 30.6 where he writes out the *stef* again. This is the earliest instance of the word in poetry. The kenning *Guðs ríðari* also occurs in Árni's *Guðmundardrápa* 32.1 (*Skj* IIA: 418), but more interestingly, it appears in the Old Norse translation of the Dialogues of Gregory the Great, which links St Paul's escape from prison and Benedict's abandonment of the unruly monks:

Gvþs riþari vildi eigi hondlaþr verþa i borginni, heldr gek hann ut a voll til orrosto. Sva gørþi oc sia helgi Benedictus, þa er hann fvrlet þessa munka, es hann mati eigi lera til lifs, þa reisti hann marga aþra up af andar davþa i avþrom stavþom.

[God's knight did not want to remain idle in the fortress; he preferred to go out onto the battlefield. The holy Benedict did likewise, when he abandoned these monks, whom he could not teach about life – he then raised up many others from spiritual death in other places.] (Unger, *Heilagra manna søgur*, 1:205)

Einarr may be suggesting a parallel with Ólafr, who escaped the prison of this transitory world in favour of a heavenly existence whereby his labours could prosper. See also commentary on 11.2.

18.8. *gram solar*. Einarr introduced this image (which has no precise analogues in Scripture or in Latin hymns) into skaldic poetry, and it was widely imitated. Cf. Eilífr *kúlnasveinn*, *Kristdrápa* 1.4: 'solkonvngr' (*Skj* IA: 572); Kolbeinn Tumason, *Jónsvisur* 2.2, 3: 'avðlings sunnu' (IIA: 37) and Lausavísur 9.5: 'roðla gramr' (IIA: 40); Arngrimr *ábóti*, *Guðmundar kvæði byskups* 4.2: 'solar þengils' (IIA: 349); and the anonymous *Máriugrátr* 3.2: 'audlingr biartra rodla' (IIA: 473).

19.1–4. The *helmingr* echoes stanza 15 of Sigvatr's *Erfidrápa Ólafs helga*, composed a century earlier. Note especially the words *náðit, máttit, rǫðull*:

Undr láta þat ytar
eigi smátt er máttið

scæniorðungu*m* scorðo
scylá*s* ra*/*ðull hlyia
driúg var*þ* a *þvi* dǫgri
dagr naðit lit fǫgro*m*
orʀosto f*ra* ec a*/*stan
atburð k*onung*s furða.

[Men grant that it was not a small miracle, when the cloud-free sun could not warm the *Njǫrðungs* of the horse of the prop (i.e., men of the ship, men); that miracle of the king took place on that day – the day could not show its fair face – I have heard of that happening during the battle in the east.] (*Skj* IA: 242)

Cf. also the Legendary Saga:

Nu let Olafr konongr þar lif sitt. Þar varð sva mikil ogn, at solen fal gæisla sinn oc gerði myrct, – en aðr var fagrt veðr – æftir þui sem þa var, er sialfr skaparenn for af verolldenne. Syndi Guð þa mikla ogn.

[Now king Óláfr gave up his life there. The terror was so great that the sun concealed its rays and it grew dark – it had been fine weather just before – just as it did when the Creator himself departed from the world. God showed dreadful signs.] (*OH.Leg*, 196)

Einarr's phrase 'Næðit biartr roðull skina' bears a close verbal resemblance to the saga's 'solen fal gæisla sinn,' and likewise his 'syndi saluorðr sin takn' corresponds to the saga's 'Synði guð þa mikla ogn.'

19.1. *Næðit.* F reads 'Næðiz.' The forms of *z* and *t* are similar in the manuscript, and the scribe has confused them. Cf. 'vandiz' for *vandit* 20.3 and 'fariz' for *farit* 26.4.

19.2. *baugskiallda.* Literally 'ring-shield,' it seems to refer to the shield's circular shape. In Snorri's discussion of weapon-kennings he explains, 'Afornvm skioldvm var titt at skrifa ravnd þa, er bavgr var kallaðr, ok er við þann bavg skilldir kendir' (On ancient shields it was customary to decorate the border which was called the circle, and shields are referred to by means of this circle) (*SnE 1931*, 150; *Edda*, trans. Faulkes, 118). 'Beiðir baugskiallda' is a kenning for Óláfr.

19.3. *saluorðr grundar.* 'Guardian of the hall of the earth,' a kenning for God. The image of God as guardian occurs frequently in Old English poetry, and after Arnórr Þórðarson introduced the God-kennings *skapvǫrðr himins* in

Magnússdrápa 10.6 (Whaley, ed., *The Poetry of Arnórr jarlaskáld*, 121, 201–3) and *Girkja vǫrð ok Garða* in *Haraldsdrápa* 17.3 (ibid., 132, 300–1) the formula became popular with Christian skalds (see Meissner, *Die Kenningar*, 376). Einarr may have chosen the base word to distinguish between Divine Providence (God the Father) and Christ as king of heaven ('harra haudrtiallda' 19.5, 6). Kristina Attwood points out that the kenning *salvǫrðr grundar* also appears in *Leiðarvísan* 6.5 (*Skj* IA: 619), and notes that the line is strikingly similar to *Geisli* 19.3: cf. 'syndi saluordr grundar' (*Geisli* 19.3) and 'sen*n*di salv*o*rdr gru*n*ndar' (*Leiðarvísan* 6.5). The first word of each line is the subjunctive form of the verb of which the kenning is the subject (Attwood, 'Intertextual Aspects of the Twelfth-Century Christian *Drápur*,' 227).

19.5–8. The text of the second *helmingr* is corrupt in *F*, and it is impossible to read it without emending. In line 6 the manuscript reads 'bar,' written with the *-ar* abbreviation, which seems to be an instance of careless copying. It is more difficult to understand why line 8 has 'skinu' rather than 'skini.' *B* reads 'skine,' and if 'happ' and 'mættu' are understood as the separated elements of a compound, a reasonable interpretation is possible: 'previously, the blessing-rich shining of the sun ceased at the death of the king of earth's roof; speech-tools are of use to me.' It is possible to retain the reading 'skinu' and make sense of the *helmingr*, but only if we assume that the manuscript reads *mætta*, and not *mættu*. The last letter of the word is smudged beyond certain recognition, and the possibility that it may be *a*, although unlikely, cannot be disallowed. Reading *mætta* and *skinu*, Lars Wennberg proposes: 'hitt var fyrr at dauða happ harra hauðrtjalda brá skinu sólar; mætta máltól nýast mér' (previously, the good fortune of the death of the prince of earth's roof stopped the shining of the sun. May my speech-tools be of use to me) (Wennberg, ed., *Geisli*, 55).

19.7. *happ-* ... *-mættu*. The compound means something like 'blessing-rich,' and refers to the blessings conveyed from God to the world by Christ (and likewise, Óláfr).

19.8. *maltol*. Kennings for the voice, tongue, and lips are common in skaldic poetry, but Einarr was the first to describe the organs of speech as the tools of his trade. Cf. 'bragar tolum' 50.4, 'mælsku töl' (*Guðmundardrápa* 23.3 [*Skj* IIA: 416]), and 'radd*ar* tolu*m*' (*Lilja* 3.3 [*Skj* IIA: 364]). Guðrún Nordal discusses tongue-kennings which regard the tongue as a tool of poetry in *Tools of Literacy*. She points out that these kennings are not accounted for in the poetic treatises and suggests that 'they were new in twelfth-century verse, and therefore not part of the skaldic poet's classical diction.' She notes the possible exception of Egill Skalla-Grímsson's *Arinbjarnarkviða*, which contains the tongue-kenning *ómunlokarr* (plane of sound), but reminds us that the dating of the poem has been questioned by scholars (Guðrún Nordal, *Tools of Literacy*, 252–3; see also Meissner, *Die Kenningar*, 133–4).

20.3. *vandit.* *F* reads 'vandiz,' an instance of scribal confusion between *t* and *z*; see commentary on 19.1. Note the similarity between 20.3, 'gramr <vandit> sæa syndum' and *Harmsól* 15.7, 'era van*n*de sa sýn[da]' (*Skj* IA: 564).

20.4. *miklar.* The *F* reading, 'milar,' is a scribal error.

20.6–7. *logskids sendiz.* The kenning ('sender of sea-skis') is perplexing in the context. It may be a subtle allusion to the traditional Viking funeral ritual in which the dead man journeyed to paradise in a burning ship. Cf. 'skidrennandi vnnar' 41.2, 3.

20.8. *samdægrs.* The line lacks a syllable, and Einarr probably intended the alternate spelling *samdægris.* The *B* reading, 'samdægurs,' is ungrammatical. The word appears in the Norwegian homilist's account of Óláfr's death: '*ok let ha*n*n lif ſitt þegar ſam-døgreſ*' (and he gave up his life at once that same day) (*GNH*, 111).

21.1. *drottins.* The emendation from manuscript 'drottin' is drastic, but it is impossible to construe the verse as it stands in *F*. The scribe may have confused the forms *dróttin/dróttins* here and in 22.5, which is written on the following line in the manuscript. The formula *dyrð* + genitive epithet is common in skaldic poetry.

21.2. The line is corrupt in both manuscripts: the original must have been lost fairly early in the history of the text. The *F* reading makes sense as it stands (*B*'s is garbled), but it cannot be said to represent the original. The form 'hrærða' would have been *hrœrða* in Einarr's time, and the spelling here reflects a mid-thirteenth-century change in the language: *œ* became *æ* (Alexander Jóhannesson, *Íslenzk Tunga*, § 104). It is unlikely that Einarr intended the faulty rhyme *mærð/hrærða*; the reading is probably the attempt to correct a corrupt version of the line by a scribe writing after the sound change had occurred, for whom 'mærd' and 'hrærda' would have been *aðalhendingar*.

21.3. *itr.* The word can be construed with both 'odlingr' and 'grædari.'

21.3, 4. *munat odlingr betri fædaz.* A commonplace, cf. stanzas 11, 13, 14, and 51.

21.4. *allz grædari.* Cf. 'heims læknis' 57.8. Einarr was the only skald to use this kenning for God or Christ. It may have a Scriptural base (cf. Exodus 15:26 and Psalm 102:3) or be related to hymns like *Rex æterne, Domine*

Tu vulnerum latentium
Bonus assistis medicus ...

[You are with us as a good physician for our hidden wounds ...] (*AH* 51:5; *HASC*, 175–81) and *Magnum salutis gaudium*

Iesus, redemptor gentium
sanavit orbem languidum ...

[Jesus, redeemer of the nations, you healed the languishing world ...] (*AH*
51: 73; *ONid*, 218, 221, 368–9, 428–30)

The kenning here suggests that God heals Óláfr's bodily suffering by granting
him a heavenly existence.

22.4. *hans batnadar*. *Batnaðr* (from *batna*) has the specific meaning
'improvement of morals' or 'improvement of behaviour' (cf. Modern English
betterment). The word occurs only in Christian literature, and always in the
context of an evil person amending his or her ways under Christian influence.
The precise meaning of 'hans batnadar' here is obscure. It may refer to
improvement of Óláfr himself, who abandons the life of a warlike (albeit
secretly holy) king to become a dispenser of mercy. This would be in harmony
with the imagery of healing in stanza 21, and the washing of his body can be
interpreted as a symbolic catharsis, a kind of second baptism. On the other
hand, we can understand 'vôn hans batnadar gledr hug' as an aside referring to
the reformation of society in general, by means of Óláfr's miracles and
patronage, with the genitive used in a causal sense to mean 'improvement
caused by him.' The *B* reading ('hars batnadar') supports this interpretation.

22.5. *drottins*. *B*'s reading is smoother and may represent the skald's intention
(it is possible that the scribe confused the forms *dróttin/dróttins* here and in
stanza 21.1, which is written on the preceding line on the manuscript). If the
reading 'drottins' is retained, the *helmingr* can be construed in two ways; both
depend on understanding 'Gudi kærann' as a substantive ('the one dear to
God'). 'Hrings særendr logdu Gudi kærann i grof Sygna drottins' is possible,
but perhaps it is better to read 'særendr hrings logdu kærann Gudi i grof –
megu dreingir Sygna drottins heyra hans brogd' (the wounders of the ring laid
God's dear one in the grave – may the men of the lord of Sogn hear his deeds).
Óláfr was regarded as *rex perpetuus* of Norway, and it would not have been out
of place for Einarr to refer to his audience as Óláfr's men. Nevertheless, the
sense of the *B* reading is superior to both of *F*'s possibilities: *særendr hrings
lǫgðu Sygna drottin, kæran guði, í grǫf – megu drengir heyra hans brǫgð.*

22.6, 7. *særendr hrings*. This kenning ('wounders of the ring,' i.e., generous
lords) is strange in this context. Einarr may have chosen it for sound rather
than sense, or perhaps he wished to emphasize that Óláfr's burial was carried
out by worthy, noble men.

23.2. *blid verk*. 'Verk' can refer either to Einarr's work of poetry or Óláfr's miraculous act of healing.

23.3. *audar niotr*. Einarr extends the sense of 'niotr' in this traditional formula to signify not so much the material gifts of a chief to his retainers as the divine mercies people receive from God by way of the saint. Einarr uses kennings of this type throughout the poem to indicate the beneficiaries of Óláfr's miracles.

23.5. *Sionbrautir*. A kenning for the eyes.

23.7, 8. *arr orms lands*. The kenning is parallel to 'audar niotr' 23.3. 'Arr' (servant or messenger) is unusual as a base word; it signifies that the cured man is the vehicle through which Óláfr's favor with God is made known in the world. The gold-kenning 'orms lands' (land of the dragon) is an allusion to the hoard of the dragon Fafnir of the Vǫlsung-Niflung legends.

24.1. *Sion feck seggr*. Cf. the parallel formula 'Mæl feck madr' 26.1. As in the Biblical miracles of the restoration of sight, bodily sight is associated with intellectual or spiritual insight.

24.2. *dyrd*. Vocalic length is not indicated in the manuscript, but the rhyme with *fyrðum* indicates that *dýrð* has been shortened to *dyrð*. Shortening of *ý* in *ðýrð* (and in the cognates *dýrka* and *dýrr*) was a linguistic phenomenon in Icelandic dialects (Noreen, *Altnordische Grammatik*, § 127.5), and Kahle cites several examples from skaldic poetry in which *dyrð* rhymes with forms of *fyrðar* and *yrðr* (Kahle, *Die Sprache der Skalden*, 58–9).

25.1, 2, 3, 4. *tynir tandrauds fasta vala strætis*. The 'street of the hawks' is the arm, its 'fire' is gold. The nominative form 'tandraudr' in *F* must be a scribal error: it is clear that the adjective modifies 'fasta.'

25.3. *fremdar lystr*. Óláfr's desire for recognition causes his coffin to rise to the surface. The epithet also occurs in *Plácitus drápa* 9.3 (ed. Louis-Jensen, 94).

25.6. *vlfs nistanda*. The kenning is jarring in this context: its only connotations are of fierceness in battle. Einarr may be attempting to distinguish between Óláfr the warrior king, who lies in the coffin, and the glorified saint living perpetually in heaven – it is even conceivable that the kenning *dróttinn harra* 'lord of princes' refers to Óláfr in his exalted state.

25.7. *lætr*. Use of the historical present tense, although widespread in the sagas, is rare in poetry. *B*'s reading, 'let,' is probably the original version.

26.1. *Mæl feck madr*. Cf. 'Sion feck seggr' 24.1.

26.2. *margfridr*. The only other occurrence of the word is in *Harmsól* 51.8 (*Skj* IA: 569). Kristina Attwood ('Intertextual Aspects of the Twelfth-Century Christian *Drápur*,' 226 and 235) suggests that this belongs to a group of words found only in the Christian *drápur* and notes the similarity of 26.2, 'margfridr iofurr sidan' to *Harmsól* 51.8, 'margfridr skǫrungr sidan' (*Skj* IA: 569).

26.3. *orda hlyru.* 'Ship-bow of words,' a kenning for 'tongue.' Einarr uses a similar kenning, 'ær odar,' in 40.7, 8. Finnur Jónsson emends 'hlyru to *hlýðu* on the basis of rhyme with 'adr,' but as Kristján Árnason and Kari Gade have demonstrated, it was not necessary for all the consonants following a vowel to participate in a rhyme, so that '*or*da' and 'hl*y*ru' are acceptable *skothendingar* and alteration is unnecessary (Gade, *The Structure of Old Norse* Dróttkvætt *Poetry*, 5–6; Kristján Árnason, *The Rhythms of Dróttkvætt*, 98–100). According to Guðrún Nordal, sailing imagery occurs only in late skaldic verse, and this stanza and stanza 40 contain the earliest known examples. She notes that the comparison of the tongue or poetry to a ship ('the poem sets sail like a ship on a voyage') is well known in classical Latin verse (see Guðrún Nordal, *Tools of Literacy*, 250–1, and her reference to Curtius, *European Literature and the Latin Middle Ages*, 128–30).

26.4. *afskurdi.* Some form of emendation is required in this *helmingr*; I have chosen that which does the least violence to the text. The participle *afskurðr* (from *skera af*) was used nominatively to refer to cut-off bits of cloth or meat, and here it refers to the man's tongue. *Fara*, used with a dative object, means 'to forfeit' or 'to pay in recompense for a crime,' and by changing manuscript 'afskurdr' to a dative form we can construe 'sidan madr, sa er adr hafdi farit afskurdi orda hlyru, feck mæl.' For another interpretation, see *Skj* IB: 433.

26.4. *farit.* The manuscript reading 'fariz' is another instance of scribal confusion between *t* and *z*, cf. 19.1 and 20.3.

26.6. *folksterks.* A hapax legomenon. The primary meaning of *folk*, 'people' or 'nation' is more relevant in this context: Óláfr is strong in his people and makes the nation strong. *Folk* can also mean 'army' or 'battle,' and the *Lexicon Poeticum* defines *folksterkr* as 'battle-strong.'

26.7. *iofrs.* A contraction of *jǫfurs*, analogous to the contracted forms of *faðir* and *bróðir* commonly used in poetry (Noreen, *Altnordische Grammatik*, § 420, Anm. 2; cf. 'faudr' 27.1). The repetition of a noun within a skaldic stanza was considered highly undesirable, and the double use of *jǫfurr*, as well as the unusual form of the word in this line, suggests textual corruption.

26.7. *fremz.* A contraction of *fremask*.

26.8. *danska.* The word was used for all the Scandinavian dialects; this is not a particular reference to the Danish language.

26.8. *tungu.* A grisly pun on the theme of the first *helmingr*.

27.1, 4. *Faudr Magnus.* The epithet for Óláfr anticipates the miracle described in stanzas 28–30. The form 'faudr' is a poetic contraction: see Noreen, *Altnordische Grammatik*, § 420, Anm. 2, and cf. 'iofrs' 26.7.

27.1. *fremdarþiod.* The dictionaries do not record the compound, but it is clearly written as one word in the manuscript and there is no reason to read *fremðar þjóð* instead. Compounds with *fremdar-* as the first element are common.

27.3. *mædir*. There may be an intentional pun with *móðir*, a play on words looking back to 'faudr' 27.1.

27.4. *Magnus*. The genitive form of the name was often written with one *s* (see Lind, *Norsk-isländska dopnamn*, cols. 754–6).

28.1, 2. *sueckuir solar straums*. A kenning for Óláfr: the 'sun of the stream' is gold, an allusion to the *Rheingold* of the Vǫlsung-Niflung legends. 'Sueckuir' is a diphthongal spelling of *søkkvir* (see Haugen, *The Scandinavian Languages*, 254–7). Einarr avoids confusion between Óláfr and Magnús by using kennings to designate the saint and one-word *heiti* for his son.

28.2. *i drauma*. 'In a dream:' the use of the plural is idiomatic.

28.3. *valld folldar*. The other manuscripts read *valdr foldar*, a typical kenning which may be the correct reading. But the *F* version ('strength of the land') is appropriate in this context. Abstract nouns were rarely used as base words in kennings (cf. 'lif' 3.6), but Einarr may be imitating Scripture, where God is repeatedly called *fortitudo* and *robur*. Cf. especially the circumlocutions in Psalm 27:8, *fortitudo plebis suae* (the strength of his people), and Joel 3:16, *fortitudo filiorum Israhel* (the strength of the children of Israel).

28.3. *fylgia*. There may be a suggestion that Óláfr will be his son's *fylgja*, or guardian spirit. In the entry for *fylgjur* in the *Cassell Dictionary of Norse Myth and Legend*, Andy Orchard notes that 'in *Njáls saga*, in the course of an account of the conversion of Iceland, Hall of Síða will consent to be baptized only if Saint Michael will be his *fylgjuengill* ("guardian angel"), a term that clearly owes something to the native conception of the *fylgja*.'

28.4. Line 4 is *minni alhent*: it contains a pair of words linked by *skothending* (*-lyndum/mundu*) in addition to the mandatory *aðalhending* (*fram-/gram*). The scribe may have written *mundu* as 'myndu' to give the appearance of a full rhyme (*aðalhenda*) with 'lyndum.'

29.1. *iarplidan*. Line 1 lacks a syllable and it is likely that the scribe wrote 'iarplidr' for 'iarplitan,' the reading in *B* and *Hr*. The word does not occur elsewhere, but it is a compound of *jarpr* (brown) and *litr* (coloured). If we take the word substantively as a *heiti* for raven, we can construe 'Magnus enn godi let iarplidan fagna Hugins ætu; mælmþings kennir raud munn arnar iods.' The skalds often used the characteristic epithets 'black' and 'dark-coloured' in reference to the raven (see Meissner, *Die Kenningar*, 117), and Einarr sustains the metaphor by using 'ætu Hugins' as a kenning for the slain. Stanza 29 thus contains references to the three traditional beasts of battle: the raven, the eagle, and the wolf.

29.1, 4. *ǫtu Hugins.* A kenning for carrion. Huginn, the name of Óðinn's raven, became a stock *heiti* for 'raven.'

29.3. *mǫlmþings kennir.* 'Prover of the weapon-meeting,' a kenning for Magnús.

29.6. *leggia.* There may be a pun intended here. The word is clearly meant to be the infinitive of the verb *leggja*: *leggja á flótta* was an idiomatic expression meaning 'to take flight,' and we should construe 'hrætt folk vard at leggia a flotta' (the frightened army fled). But it was also common in poetry to speak of weapons 'biting,' and in this line the position of 'leggia' calls to mind its homonym *leggr*, producing an image of the sharp blade biting at legs. Confusion between the words probably caused the *Hr* scribe to write 'leggi' (accusative plural of *leggr*) for 'leggia.'

29.8. *gindu.* An example of a weak preterit form of a strong verb (see Noreen, *Altnordische Grammatik*, § 482, Anm. 2). The vowel has been shortened to facilitate *aðalhending* with 'Vindversk.' Kahle discusses this phenomenon in *Die Sprache der Skalden*, 57–9.

30.2. *lausnara spialli.* 'Confidant of the saviour,' a kenning for Óláfr. Cf. commentary on 9.6, which contains the analogous 'vin roduls tiggia.'

30.5-8. The *stef* is written out in full: the *F* scribe abbreviates it everywhere but here and in stanza 18. The text differs slightly, suggesting that the scribe wrote it out from memory: this second version has 'þat er' (line 7) where the first reads 'sem.' The scribe's reason for writing the *stef* here has to do with the layout of the manuscript. When he finished copying the first *helmingr* of stanza 30 he found that one ruled line remained at the foot of the column, enough space for four lines of *dróttkvætt*. Rather than begin a new stanza and split the text between two columns of writing, he filled out the space with the *stef*.

31.1. Stanzas 31–3 are missing from the *F* text, probably due to the scribe's carelessness. Stanza 30 lies at the end of a column in the manuscript, and the following column begins with stanza 34. Both stanzas 30 and 33 have the *stef* as the second *helmingr*, and when the scribe shifted columns he mistook the conclusion of stanza 33 for stanza 30. The inclusion of stanza 34 proves that the scribe's exemplar contained the story of Gutthormr, and I have supplied the missing stanzas from the *B* text.

31.1-4. The syntax of the *helmingr* is slightly awkward. Finnur Jónsson construes 'Gutthormr reyndi við sléttan þrǫm grundar, hvat bænir alkæns Óláfs téðu við goð; hann gatt áðr rétt' (*Skj* IB: 435). Kock takes 'gat hann rett' as a parenthesis and reads 'adr hvat' as *hvat áðr*, arguing convincingly that such transposition in correlative constructions was an accepted technique

(*NN* §§ 937 and 246.D). His interpretation makes better sense: 'On the flat coast of the land Gutthormr proved how previously the prayers of much-skilled Óláfr prevailed with God; he knew well.'

31.7–8. *Avngvlseyiar- ... -svnde*. It would be nearly impossible to use a word this long (six syllables, the length of an entire line) in *dróttkvætt* without tmesis. Skalds often faced this problem when using proper names, cf. *Stiklarstaðir* in stanzas 17 and 43.

32.1, 2. *lid þrimr lvtum minna*. The early vernacular versions report that Margaðr had sixteen ships against Gutthormr's five (*Brudst*, 35; *OH.Leg*, 210, 212), while the Latin versions and the Norwegian Homily Book give the number as fifteen (*MHN*, 134; *Passio Olaui*, 76; *GNH*, 113).

32.1, 2, 4. *lestir linnz grundar*. This kenning for Gutthormr ('breaker of the land of the snake) may be an anticipatory reference to his gift of a silver cross to the Trondheim cathedral, but the epithet 'heiptar milldr' 32.3 suggests an allusion to the treasure he broke and took for himself after Margaðr's refusal to share it. The gold-kenning 'linnz grundar' is an allusion to the hoard of the dragon Fafnir of the Vǫlsung-Niflung legends.

32.5. *Þo red*. The rhyme of the line depends on hearing 'Þor-' as a rhyme with 'hvor.' See Kahle, *Die Sprache der Skalden*, 20–21, Kristján Árnason, *The Rhythms of Dróttkvætt*, 102–3, and commentary on 7.1.

32.5–8. The syntax of the *helmingr* is in an envelope pattern: line 5 and the last three words of line 8 form a sentence, with two phrases interposed. Construe 'Þo at hvorv red hann gagne or styr; af þvi fekst harr hagnadr; moðirhlyre tioði honom vel.'

32.6, 7. *moðir- ... -hlyre*. The compound is analogous to *móðirbróðir*, the usual term for maternal uncle.

33.1, 2, 4. *enn milldi litravðs aunnar bliks*. The definite article is a sign that 'milldi' is used substantively as the base word of the kenning. The meaning of the kenning is ambiguous: it clearly refers to Óláfr, but the light imagery also makes us think of Christ, 'the king of the sun,' whose radiance is associated with the saint. The 'king' in this multivalent metaphor can be the mortal Óláfr, generous with gold; the heavenly Óláfr, generous with miracles; or Christ, generous with the grace of his saints. This last meaning is suggested by the parenthesis 'Krist mære ek linan.' The gold-kenning 'aunnar bliks' (light of the waves) is an allusion to the *Rheingold* of the Vǫlsung-Niflung legends.

33.2. *aunnar*. The misspelling is mysterious. The skald clearly intended *unnar*, and there is no linguistic or metrical explanation for the form given in *B*.

33.2. *miclum*. The manuscript reads 'miclu,' the neuter dative singular form, which is grammatically impossible (there is no corresponding noun in the *helmingr*).

33.3. *Krist mære ek linan.* The previous editors have emended to *lim Krists*, creating a kenning for Óláfr (cf. 'lim konungs himna sals' 66.6), but I prefer to read 'linan,' which involves only one change. I suspect that the scribe simply neglected to copy a superscript *n*. The addition of a syllable does not stretch the line inordinately: the cliticized *mærik* ('mære ek') is neutralized into a single foot, resulting in a Sievers Type A line. Kari Gade discusses this phenomenon and gives examples of similar lines where there is neutralization in position 2 (Gade, *The Structure of Old Norse* Dróttkvætt *Poetry*, 60–2; see also Kristján Árnason, *The Rhythms of Dróttkvætt*, 126–8). Other possible emendations are to *linr* (modifying 'konungr') or to *lina* (modifying 'Avlld').

33.3. *leysta.* The form is accusative singular feminine, in agreement with 'Avlld,' rather than the usual singular neuter inflection. This was an accepted means of forming the perfect (Noreen, *Altnordische Grammatik*, § 541), and Einarr used it here to provide the requisite trochee at the end of the line.

34.1–8. The Norwegian Homily Book and the Legendary Saga use language strikingly similar to *Geisli* 34 in their accounts of Gutthormr's donation of the memorial cross:

> *ok* let gera þegar roðo ſva myccla ór ſilfri at allz coſtar er hon lengri *ok* mæri en manzvaxtar. *ok* pryddi þegar þeſ hælga manz húſ með þærri dyrð ſér til ſalo-bota. *ok* til minni *ok* fra-ſagnar iarteina þærra en hinn helgi Oláfr konungr gerði þa við hann.

> [and immediately after, he had a silver cross set up, which was larger than life size. And he ornamented at once the holy man's house with this splendor for the salvation of his soul and as a reminder and a witness of the miracles which the holy King Óláfr had done for him at that time.] (*GNH*, 113; cf. *OH.Leg*, 212)

34.2. *hollr.* Finnur Jónsson and Kock emend to 'hollz,' the *B* reading. Finnur construes 'Gutthormr lét her gerva róðu grams, seggjum holls, skreytta silfri ok golli; þat es hróðr' (*Skj* IB: 435). Kock's version is smoother: he construes *seggjum holls grams* with *hróðr*: 'that is praise of the king, friendly to men' (*NN* §§ 938 and 2247.D). As it stands in the manuscript, *hollr* can be construed with *seggjum* to form a flattering epithet for Gutthormr: 'Satt var at Guthorm, seggium hollr, let her gerfa rodu, skreytta silfri ok gulli. Þat var grams hrodr.'

34.4. *Guthorm.* All of the early editions of *Geisli* print *Guthormr*, but there is no evidence that this was based on the manuscript. The last letter of 'Guthorm' and the first letter of 'gerfa' are legible, with no space between for another character. There may have been a superscript *r* (cf. 'Olafr' 30.8) which can no longer be seen, but *Guthorm* was widely used as the nominative form of the name (Lind, *Norsk-isländska dopnamn*, cols. 395–400).

34.7, 8. *i Cristz kirkiu midri.* This can be understood as a simple reference to the position of Gutthormr's crucifix in the church (the Trondheim cathedral was dedicated to Christ), or as a more grandiose claim that the sign of Óláfr's honour holds a central place in Christendom. The Norwegians were proud of the popularity of Trondheim as a pilgrimage goal.

34.8. *nidr.* F reads 'vidr,' which makes no sense as the only possible subject of 'gaf.'

35.2. *sunnr.* An early form of *suðr* (Noreen, *Altnordische Grammatik*, § 261), used here for the sake of the *aðalhending* with 'kunnir' (and *liðhenda* with Skanungum).

35.4. *almilds.* Cf. 'a mildi kᴏnungr' (*GNH*, 115); 'sa milldr konongr' (*OH.Leg*, 214).

35.7, 8. *þa vard grion at granu grioti.* Cf. 'brauð þat allt varð at griote' (*GNH*, 115); 'brauð þat allt varð at griote' (*OH.Leg*, 214).

36.3. *sunnan.* Finnur Jónsson construes the adverb with the parenthesis in line 3 ('sannspurt es þat sunnan' [*Skj* IB: 436]), but Kock argues that it belongs with the main clause. He cites a number of examples of similar one-line parentheses in the poem where the final word of the line is clearly not to be construed with the preceding phrase (*NN* § 2791.B). I prefer Kock's version ('Since then the feast of the clever warrior has been observed in the south, throughout all Denmark; that is truly known'), but both readings are grammatically sound and the syntax of the *helmingr* may be intentionally ambiguous. The location of this miracle attests to the establishment of Óláfr's cult in Denmark.

37.1–4. There are close verbal parallels in the Legendary Saga:

Þora het kona, Guðþorms dotter, moðer Sigurðar, er skera let tungu or hofði manne, þæim er Kolbæinn het, firir æingi mæiri soc, en hann hafðe tækit af krasadisci hænnar nokcot.

[There was a woman named Þóra, the daughter of Gutthormr and the mother of Sigurðr, who had the tongue cut out of the head of the man who was called Kolbeinn for no greater reason than that he had taken something from her plate of delicacies.] (*OH.Leg*, 228; cf. *Brudst*, 36)

37.1. *Horn.* Hǫrn is a traditional name for a troll-wife, or possibly for Freyja (*Þul* IV), and came to be a *heiti* for 'woman.' There is a hidden pun in the kenning 'Horn huitings:' *hvítingr* means 'drinking horn,' synonymous with *horn*.

37.1. *hofdi.* F reads 'hofi,' which must be a scribal error.

37.3. *audar aumum beidi.* Just as Einarr often compares Óláfr the miracle dispenser to a chieftain generous with his gold, he likens the beneficiary of the miracle to a 'poor seeker of riches.' The dative is used in an ablative sense to signify deprivation (see Nygaard, *Norrøn Syntax*, § 113): 'audar aumum beidi' is appositive to 'or hofdi.'

37.7. *hodda niot.* This kenning echoes 'audar aumum beidi' in line 2.

37.8. *Hlid. Hlíð* was a popular farm name in medieval Norway (Rygh, *Norske Gaardnavne*, lists over sixty examples) and the reference here is not a clue to the location of the incident.

38.2. *mælma stridir.* The kenning formula 'enemy of weapons' was used in Viking poetry to designate warriors (who break weapons in battle). It is out of place here, and Einarr may be playing on the meaning of the words: 'mælma stridir' can be interpreted literally to signify an enemy of strife, a peaceful Christian man.

38.4. *harmskerdanda.* The B version of this hapax legomenon must be the correct reading. F reads 'harskerdanda,' which is nonsense. 'Harm-diminisher' emphasizes the image of Óláfr expressed by the *stef*, and is analogous to 'færskerdandi' (misfortune-diminisher) 63.7.

38.7. *snæka vangs slongui.* 'Distributor of the field of the snake.' The kenning for Óláfr is an allusion to Fafnir's hoard: cf. 'stridandi lætrs hins dockua lyngs hrockuiseids' in stanza 16.

38.8. *slungin.* B reads 'slvngins,' which must be construed with 'snæka' to mean 'twisted serpent.' The F reading is at least as good: *slyngva* normally means either 'to throw, throw away' or 'to provide, procure,' and both meanings are apt when 'slungin' is construed with 'mal.' The reference can be either to the man's lost speech (or even to the tongue itself being thrown away), or to his restored faculties.

39.1. *Dyrd er agæt ordin.* A formula, cf. 11.5.

39.2. *sliku.* To be understood substantively ('from such things').

40.1–8. The fragment AM 325 IVa, 4to has verbal echoes of this stanza: 'Vindr toko maN er haldoR het ... drogo ut tung kverkina scaro þar af' (the Wends took a man named Halldórr, drew his tongue out from his throat, and cut from it) (*Brudst*, 36). Einarr's repetition of *sk* sounds ('skauti'/'skerdu'/'skyfanda'/ 'skæru') calls to mind the sound of the knife and adds a grisly onomatopoetic effect.

40.1–4. Construe 'veit ek at Vindr meiddu fir nidranda skauti gialfrs grundar, enn þeir skerdu sarliga. Bragr verdr greiddur.' In Einarr's poetry, form and matter are related; here his tortuous syntax reflects the gruesome theme of the stanza.

40.1, 3. *skauti grundar gialfrs*. *Grund gjalfrs* (land of noise) is a kenning for 'mouth,' and the *skaut* (shoot, twig) of the mouth is the tongue. On the use of the dative see Nygaard, *Norrøn Syntax*, § 113; cf. *Geisli* 37.3.

40.3. *nidranda*. In skaldic poetry, *níð* can refer to any body of water, and *randi* is a poetic form of *rǫnd* (rim, edge). 'Fir nidranda' means 'beside the seacoast' or 'on the 'riverbank,' perhaps a pun on the name *Níðaróss*. This is the only account of the miracle that specifies a location.

40.4. *greiddur*. One of the few instances in *F* of the svarabhakti vowel. The word must be pronounced *greiddr* for the sake of the metre.

40.5. *endr fir*. 'A long time ago.'

40.5. *tru tyndir*. 'Men lost from the faith.' The emendation is necessary for the grammatical sense of the phrase. The story of their backsliding was presumably known to Einarr's audience.

40.7. *audskyfanda*. The victim may have been a nobleman, a distributor of material wealth, but more likely he was a cleric who dispensed spiritual treasure.

40.7, 8. *odar ær*. A clever kenning for 'tongue.' 'Aŕ' is a pun on *ár* (oar) and *ǫr* (rune stick). 'Oar of poetry' is the primary meaning: *ár* makes a better rhyme with *skáru*. The formula was imitated by later Christian skalds, cf. 'stirða hefir ek áŕ til orða' (*Guðmundar kvæði byskups* 2.5 [*Skj* IIA: 349]), 'taɼv ræþi' (*Háttatal* 81.4 [IIA: 73]), and 'mals stýri' (*Leiðarvísan* 37.3 [IA: 625]). The man may have been a sailor (cf. 'skidrennandi vnnar' 41.2, 3) or a poet. 'Rune stick of poetry' is also a potent metaphor, and the hearer's mind would have been quickly drawn to it by association with the everyday idiom *skera or* (see examples in Fritzner's *Ordbog*).

41.2, 3. *skidrennandi vnnar*. 'Ski-runner of the waves,' i.e., 'the one who runs on the skis of the waves.' The kenning may indicate that Halldórr was a sailor, or Einarr may have chosen the word simply for the alliteration's sake. Cf. 'logskids sendiz' 20.6, 7.

41.4. *dreka boli*. The gold-kenning (to be construed with 'skreytta') is another allusion to Fafnir and his hoard.

41.5–8. Cf. the verbal echoes in the prose accounts:

> hét á h*a*nn til hialpa. *ok* mifcu*n*nar. bað í guðſ nafne léá ſer mals *ok* hæilſo. Ðvi næſt fecc h*a*nn mal *ok* mifcu*n*n af þæi*m* góða k*o*nu*n*ge.

> [He called on him for help and mercy. He prayed in God's name for speech and healing. Immediately he received speech and mercy from the good king.] (*GNH*, 116, cf. *OH.Leg*, 226)

42.1–4. The themes of stanza 42 reflect the responsorium and antiphon from vespers in the earliest St Óláfr liturgy:

℟. O sancte olaue conciuis gloriose martyrum secretorumque scrutator celestium et qui altissimi iudicis ad tribunal assistis incoinquinatus releua nostram fragilitatem quesumus ab inmanium criminum squaloribus.
℣. Te martyr inclyte celum possidet. terra assumptum ueneratur angelorum exercitus exultans amplectitur. unde et sublimi uoce et supplici corde.
Ant. Exultemus omnes in deo salutari nostro qui recordatus misericordie sue suscepit sanctum regem olauum in collegio martyrum.

[℟. O holy Olaf, glorious fellow-citizen of the martyrs and investigator of heavenly secrets, you stand undefiled at the tribunal of the highest judge. We beseech you, free our weakness from the stain of great offences.
℣. Glorious martyr, taken up from earth, you possess heaven. The exulting army of angels venerates you and embraces you ...
Ant. Let us exult in God our salvation, who mindful of his mercy has taken up holy king Olaf into the company of martyrs ...]
(*The Leofric Collectar*, 1:210; *Breviarium Nidrosiense*, qq. vi; Østrem, *The Office of Saint Olav*, 282)

42.2. *heims domari.* The emendation is necessary if the sentence is to have a subject. The dittography indicates scribal carelessness, and 'domara' for 'domari' may be a simple error. Einarr may have chosen this kenning for God to suggest that the perpetrators of the crime will not go unpunished.

42.4. *ferd himneska.* The concept of heaven as a great mead hall in the sky was dear to the early Christians in Germanic lands, and Einarr's fondness for the image (cf. stanzas 2, 7, 11) may be due to a vernacular tradition as well as to ecclesiastical influence.

43.2, 3, 4. *hialldrs orra ilbleikum.* 'Pale-footed heathcock of battle,' a kenning for the carrion-eating raven.

43.2. *vopna galldri.* 'Song of weapons,' battle.

43.4. *steikar.* The *B* reading is required for the rhyme with 'ilbleikum.' *Stik* (stick, pole) makes no sense in this context. The *B* reading is a graphic image of butchery: *steik* (cf. Modern English *steak*) refers to a roasted piece of meat.

43.6. *þunn vaxinn sky gunnar.* 'Cloud of battle' is a shield-kenning. 'Þunn vaxinn' can mean either that the shields became thinner as they were hacked by swords, or that the array of men holding shields grew thin as the warriors fell. This is another example of the metaphor of the sun breaking through clouds: see commentary on 43.8.

43.7. *Stikla-.* Clearly the correct form. On the tmesis, see commentary on 17.1, 2.

43.8. *valbastar raudli.* A sword-kenning, but the meaning of *valbǫst* is unclear. Lexicographers have defined it as some part of the sword, perhaps the hilt, but Richard Schrodt argues that it is a sword-*heiti* meaning 'corpse-striker' (see 'Zwei altnordische Waffen(teil)namen und Egil Skallagrímsson, *Lv* 40'). *Rǫðull* here has its proper meaning 'light' or 'sun.' This kenning, along with 'sky gunnar' evokes the image of Óláfr's sword cleaving the shields of his enemies like the sun breaking through clouds, a variation of the light-versus-darkness symbolism which dominates the poem.

44.2. *fylkis kundr.* It is unclear which of Óláfr's royal predecessors is implied in this kenning. The reference is probably to either Haraldr *hárfagri* or Óláfr Tryggvason, both of whom he claimed as ancestors.

44.4. *gram þrænskum.* 'The Trondish king,' Óláfr.

44.6. *hrings stridanda.* A kenning for Óláfr, portraying him as a treasure-dispenser. Emendation is necessary for the syntax: the nominative form 'stridandi' is not grammatically feasible in the *helmingr*.

44.7. *gulli merktr.* The sword was damascened.

45.1. *sa.* In the *F* version, 'sa' must refer to Eindriði ('sa er gaf gumnum armglædr, Eindridi vngi, slaung rædu i brag'). This is grammatically correct, but the *B* reading is better: 'Nv gaufug dyrd fremr iofur fyrdá, þann er gaf gumnum armglædur' (Now excellent fame promotes the prince of men, the one who gave men the fire of the arm).

45.2. *Dýrð* is shortened to 'dyrd' for the *aðalhending* (see commentary on 24.2).

45.3. *Eindridi vngi.* Eindriði was a well-known Norwegian contemporary of Einarr Skúlason. He travelled extensively and spent many years as a mercenary in Constantinople (see *Orkneyinga Saga*, 193–224, 236–7; *Hkr*, 3:324, 370–2, 378, 381–3, 390; Benedikz, *The Varangians of Byzantium*, 148–55, 185–7, 217; and the biography in Schöning's *Heimskringla*, 3:488–90). The mention of his name is meant to enhance the story's authenticity.

46.1–4. The structure of the first *helmingr* is unusual. It consists of two independent clauses in an envelope pattern.

46.2. *þess er gaf ringa.* A prose kenning referring to Óláfr in his earthly life, parallel to 'þess er lid læknar' 46.5.

46.2, 3. *styriar sniallz milldings.* 'Clever-of-battle prince,' i.e., Óláfr. The *F* reading, 'snallz,' must be a scribal error.

46.4. *styrkann.* Styrkr is an alternative form of *sterkr* showing the effect of ablaut (Noreen, *Altnordische Grammatik*, § 167). It is presumably used here for the sake of the rhyme with *yrkja*. The ordinary masculine singular accusative form of the word is *styrkjan*, but *styrkan* occurs in later manuscripts (ibid. § 431).

46.5–8. The *helmingr* works at two levels. The primary meaning is that Óláfr's miracles are signs given by God as proof of the saint's holiness. 'þess er lid læknar' and 'lofdungs himintunglá rannz,' a variation on the 'king of heaven' formula (see commentary on 2.4), are clearly kennings for Christ. But they can also refer to Óláfr: although the miracles are ultimately God's, a point which Einarr emphasizes, they are also Óláfr's in the sense that he is their efficient cause. Likewise he claims the title 'prince of heaven' because he is a prince whose abode is now the 'house of stars.' The two *helmingar* of stanza 46 juxtapose not only Óláfr and Christ, but also the Óláfr who gave rings and the Óláfr who heals. These eight lines thus concisely express the theme of the *drápa*.

47.1. *Gerdiz*. The *B* reading ('Gyrdest') is better, but the *F* reading is not impossible. The sense is that the man prepared, or equipped himself with the sword.

47.1. *hæla herdum*. 'Highly hardened,' or 'well-tempered,' referring to 'vetþryma nadri.'

47.1. 'Rather late in the evening.' *Síðalla* occurs occasionally as a variant of *síðarla*.

47.3. *glaumkennandi gunnar*. 'Noise-experiencer of battle,' warrior.

47.4. *vetþryma nadri*. The meaning of *véttrim* is obscure: it seems to refer to a part of either the sword or the shield. For possible etymologies see Sijmons and Gering, eds., *Die Lieder der Edda*, 3(2): 210. 'Vetþryma nadri' is clearly a kenning for 'sword,' and Einarr's choice of *naðr* (snake) as the base word evokes the image of the sword creeping away from the man like a serpent.

47.7. *landreka*. According to Snorri (*Hkr*, 3:370), this man was the Byzantine king Kirjalax, who Metcalfe (*Passio Olaui*, 76 n. 6) identified as Alexios I Komnenos (the Old Norse name is derived from Κύριος 'Αλέξιος), who reigned 1081–1118. More recently, Benedikt S. Benedikz has suggested in his revision of Sigfús Blöndal's *Væringja saga* that the name Kirjalax here refers to Alexios's son, John II Komnenos (*The Varangians of Byzantium*, 122). Carl Phelpstead discusses the question in Kunin, trans., and Phelpstead, ed., *A History of Norway*, 111–12.

47.8 *ognfimr*. The *F* reading, *ormfimr*, is probably too unlikely, but it is tempting to read *ormr* as a *heiti* for 'sword' (cf. the sword-kennings *vígs ormr*, *ormr vals*, *ormr randar* listed in the *Lexicon Poeticum*) and retain the compound *ormfimr*, 'clever with the sword.' Schöning suggests as another alternative *armfimr*, 'having a good arm.'

48.2, 4. *borgar Regins væda*. A shield-kenning. According to the Vǫlsung legends, the dwarf Reginn made his foster son Sigurðr a powerful sword named Gramr, with which Sigurðr killed the dragon Fafnir and later Reginn himself. 'Reginn's peril' is a kenning for 'sword'; its 'fortress' is the shield.

48.3. *mundrida.* 'That which is quickly moved with the hand.' The word is etymologically related to *mund* (hand) and *riða* (to tremble). The *mundriði* of the shield is the sword.

48.3. *steindrar.* The form 'steindra,' the *F* reading, can be construed only with 'mundrida.' The image of a painted sword is odd: the implication could be that the sword is stained with blood (cf. 'marglitendr eggia' 59.2), but the *B* reading, 'steindrar,' which would modify 'borgar,' and refer to a painted shield, is much more likely.

48.6. *seimþiggiandi.* 'Gold-receiver,' a pun referring both to the spiritual grace the man obtains from Óláfr and the gold he receives from the Byzantine ruler in payment for the sword.

48.7, 8. *gylldis kindar gomsparra.* 'Gum-spar of the wolf's offspring.' An allusion to a story told in Gylfaginning: the Æsir wedged a sword between the gaping jaws of the Fenrisulfr to prevent him from swallowing them up (*SnE 1931*, 37). Gerd Wolfgang Weber suggests that in this kenning '"the jaws of the wolf" are associated with the "Jaws of Hell," which the Varangians with the help of St Óláf force open just as Christ did at his resurrection' ('Saint Óláfr's Sword,' 660). This is probably saying too much, but he is certainly right in seeing eschatological associations here: the sword of Óláfr kept the Byzantine empire from being subsumed by the ever-threatening barbarous hordes to the east just as the wolf's gum-spar kept the Æsir from being eaten by the wolf.

49.1. *grimur.* The *F* reading, 'grimar,' is grammatically impossible: *grima* belongs to the *on*-stem declension.

49.2. *Haralldz brodir.* The sense of the *helmingr* makes it clear that 'brodir' is the subject of the sentence, and the nominative form of the word in *B* must be the correct reading. The epithet for Óláfr refers to his half-brother Haraldr Sigurðarson (Haraldr *harðráði*), the son of Óláfr's mother and stepfather. Haraldr fought alongside Óláfr at Stiklarstaðir, and was king in Norway after Magnús the Good (1046–1066). He died in the battle of Stamford Bridge.

49.3. *rauckstefnanda Reifnis.* Reifnir is the name of a mythological sea king; 'horse of Reifnir' is a ship-kenning. 'Horse-driver of Reifnir' is a kenning for a sailor or a Viking.

49.5. *þrifhuassir.* A hapax legomenon, made of the elements *þrif* (luck, prosperity) and *hvass* (sharp), meaning 'lucky' or 'very prosperous.' 'Þrifhuassir firar' refers to the Varangian mercenary soldiers who told the Greek king of the miracle.

49.6. *þingdiarfs jnga.* The phrase can be construed with 'þrifhuassir firar,' in which case it could refer to Óláfr or Kirjalax (most likely the latter), or with 'iartegnir,' in which case it must refer to Óláfr. The *B* reading, 'þrekhva⁄ssum yngva,' makes for a smoother syntax ('the lucky men told the strong king of the miracles').

49.7. *bauga snyrtis.* The kenning for Óláfr literally means 'polisher of rings,' i.e., possessor of treasure.

50.1. *eisu mœs iardar.* The 'land of the gull' is the sea, and the 'fire of the sea,' by analogy with the *Rheingold*, is gold.

50.2. *allualldz.* The *B* reading, 'allzvalld,' is better, but the *F* reading is not impossible. We can construe 'let giallda eisu mœs iardar fir alualldz hior, þann er Olæafr ætti' ([he, Kirjalax,] had the sword of the all-ruler, the one which Óláfr owned, paid for with the fire of the gull's land). The syntax is much improved if we take 'allzvalld' as a *heiti* for Kirjalax and the subject of the sentence: 'the ruler of all paid for the sword, the one which Óláfr owned ...'

50.3. *slettig.* A contraction of *slétti ek.*

50.4. *bragar tolum.* The 'tools of poetry' can refer to artistic skills and talents as well as to the voice, lips, tongue, etc. Cf. 'mæltol' 19.8 and commentary.

50.5. *Yfirskiolldungr iofra.* Kirjalax.

50.6, 7, 8. *grand oddhridar gardz.* 'The harm of the yard of the point-shower.' The shower of points refers to arrows or spears launched in battle, and the 'yard' or 'garden' of arrows is the shield. 'Harm of the shield' is a kenning for 'sword.'

51.2. *Girklandi.* *F* reads 'ġkłdi.' The dot above the *g* is probably a careless slip for either 'gⁱ' (*gri*) or 'g'' (*gir*). I have expanded to 'Girklandi' on the basis of the analogous 'g'kia' ('girkia') 44.7.

51.3. *mœl.* Several meanings of the word are apt here. Óláfr's invervention is matter for colloquy or conversation, and Óláfr is held up as a measure or example for men. Finally, *mál* can refer to ornament (Óláfr is an ornament for his men), and specifically the inlaid ornamentation on a sword-hilt, which may be an allusion to the Hneitir miracle.

51.4. *margþarfr.* The *F* reading, 'margþæþr,' is unexplainable and may be a scribal error.

51.4. *Haralldz arfi.* A reference to Óláfr's father Haraldr *grenski* and probably also an allusion to his ancestor Haraldr *hárfagri*, with whom Óláfr liked to associate himself, claiming that the kingdom of Norway established by Haraldr *hárfagri* was his rightful paternal inheritance (*Hkr*, 2: 44).

51.5. *ognar.* 'aungir,' the *F* reading, must be a scribal error.

51.6. *megud.* The form is second person plural, a direct address to the audience. The topic of outdoing is already familiar from stanzas 11, 13, 14, and 21.

51.8. *dagræfrs.* On the poetic use of the genitive to designate place, see Nygaard, *Norrøn Syntax*, § 141.

52.3. *gunnar mær.* 'Gull of battle,' a raven-kenning.

52.3, 4. *geira gaull.* 'Noise of spears,' a kenning for battle.

52.4. *Pecinavǫllum.* The name the Norse writers use for the location of the battle has traditionally been thought to have been coined by the Varangians who fought in the battle (*vǫllr* means 'field' or 'plain,' and 'Pecina' may be an adaptation of Πετξινάκοι, the Greek name for the Petchenegs), but Odd Sandaaker, in a reexamination of all the literary sources of the story, argues convincingly that *Pecinavǫllr* refers to the area around the confluence of the Pčinja and Kriva Rivers near Skopje in Macedonia ('Mirakelet på Pezinavollane,' 92–3).

52.7. *hrid Hamdis kleda.* A battle-kenning. Hamðir was a mythological hero in the Vǫlsung legends, and his 'clothing' is armour or the accoutrements of battle.

53.3. *dugde lid.* 'The army was of avail.'

53.4. *lagar elldbrota.* 'Flame-breaker of the sea,' i.e., breaker (distributor) of gold (yet another allusion to the *Rheingold*), a kenning for the Byzantine king.

53.5. *byr brannda.* 'Fair breeze of swords,' battle.

53.6. *bardraugns.* 'Prow-ox,' a kenning for 'ship.' The *F* reading, 'fæit' (painted), demands a neuter singular object, and there is none. Construe 'fæir' with 'Verinngiar' (a few Varangians). The prose accounts emphasize that the Varangians had only a handful of men (*Brudst*, 35–6; *Hkr*, 3:373).

53.6–7. *bardraugns rauduls vedre.* A battle-kenning. The 'sun of the ship' is the shield, alluding to the custom of hanging the round shield along the gunwhales of Viking ships. The 'storm of the shield' is battle.

54.2. *af trausti.* Cf. *GNH*, 112: '... á hann hafa callat með traufti ...'

54.3. *svall.* *F*'s reading, 'stall,' could mean either 'steel' (i.e., weapons) or 'stole' (preterite of *stéla*); neither makes sense in the *helmingr*. It is also unlikely that the skald would have used the same word in two succeeding lines, and this may be an instance of scribal dittography. Emendation to *svall* (swelled, increased), leads to the unusual warrior-kenning *ógnar eyðir* (destroyer of fear), although the kenning could refer to Óláfr and be analogous to *málma stríðir* (destroyer of weapons) 38.2 (see commentary). The *B* version of the line is somewhat more coherent: 'strið svall ogn þa er oðuzt' (strife increased fear then when [they] were destroyed).

54.4. *Olæf.* The accusative form is necessary for the syntax: 'hraustir menn hetu hart a itran Olæf.' The form of the name in Einarr's original may have been *Áláf* or *Áleif* (see Kahle, *Die Sprache der Skalden*, 203–4), or *Óláf*:

Hreinn Benediktsson argues that historical nasalized /õ/ was indistinguishable from /a/ and hence *Óláf* would have rhymed with *stála* ('Phonemic Neutralization and Inaccurate Rhymes,' 8–9).

54.4. *gny staala*. 'Noise of steel,' battle.

54.5. *einum*. The *B* reading, 'einn,' is better. The dative form in *F* is syntactically awkward and it stretches the metre.

54.4, 6. *orfa flug*. 'Flight of arrows,' battle.

54.6. *vndbaarum*. 'Wound-waves,' blood.

54.7, 8. *Reifnis rann*. 'Reifnir's house,' a kenning for 'shield,' alluding to its protective qualities. *Reifnir* is a *heiti* for 'sea-king.' The spelling of 'rann' ('a' for ǫ) reflects the change in pronunciation of the two vowels, which were neutralized at the time of the composition of *Geisli*, but had become distinct when the text was recorded in *F* and *B* (see Benediktsson, 'Phonemic Neutralization and Inaccurate Rhymes'). The scribes therefore wrote 'rann' to ensure that there was at least eye rhyme with *manna*. Cf. the same phenomenon in *Geisli* 16.8, where *snjǫllum* is written 'sniallum.'

54.8. *sex tigir*. The Old Norse prose versions also mention the sixty-to-one advantage of the Petchenegs over the Varangians (*Brudst*, 35; *OH.Leg*, 214; *Hkr*, 3:372; *OH.St*, 636).

55.1–4. The syntax of the *helmingr* is awkward. A possible construction is 'Þa rauk, er lid heidingia gingi af riki; stæls regn dreif hialmniordungum harda æ þegna.' *Rauk* is used impersonally; the verb *drífa* can be used with a dative/accusative construction to indicate something being showered on someone. Here, the warriors themselves are the precipitation that batters the Varangians. *Harða* can be understood both as an adverb and as an adjective modifying *þegna*.

55.2. *regn stæls*. 'Rain of weapons,' battle.

55.3. *hialmniordungum*. *Njǫrðungr*, cognate with the name of the god Njǫrðr, is used in skaldic poetry as a *heiti* for 'man.' According to Snorri, Njǫrðr controls wind and fire (*SnE 1931*, 30), and Einarr may have used his name in this *hapax legomenon* kenning to emphasize the imagery of smoke and storm. *Hjalmnjǫrðungr* (helmet-men) means 'warriors,' here, the Petchenegs.

55.5, 6. *Haalft fimta hundrad*. 'Half of the fifth hundred,' i.e., four 'hundreds' and half of another. In the Norse system of reckoning, a *hundrað* was 120, so the reference is to 540 men. See Ulff-Møller, 'The Higher Numerals in Early Nordic Texts.'

55.6, 8. *val brimis sunda*. 'The falcon of the sound of the sword.' The 'sound of the sword' is a wound (or blood), in which the sword 'swims' as a fish in the sea (cf. 'hresiks' 69.6). The falcon of the wound is the carrion-eating raven. The *B* reading must be the correct version: the *F* reading, 'brimils' (seal's) makes no sense in the context.

55.7. *nærra.* Construe the infinitive with 'þordu.'

56.2. *gaufugr þeingill.* Óláfr.

56.3. *vagna borg.* Both Snorri (*Hkr*, 3:371) and John Kinnamos (*Deeds of John and Manuel Comnenus*, 16) describe the Petchenegs' tactic of drawing their wagons into a fortified circle.

56.5–8. The text of the second *helmingr* is corrupt, but it is possible to read it without emendation: 'vngr nennir at inna aulld verk dædsniallz doglings slungins brimloga, þau er dyrka alla verolld.'

56.6. *vngr.* The word must be understood as a substantive, referring to the skald (the young man strives to tell men ...).

56.6, 7. *slunginns brimloga doglings.* 'The prince of scattered river-fire,' i.e., gold (an allusion to the *Rheingold*), a kenning for Óláfr.

57.6. *dyrka.* The vowel has been shortened for the sake of the rhyme. Cf. 7.4 and 24.2, and see Noreen, *Altnordische Grammatik*, § 127.5.

57.8. *heims læknis.* Cf. 'allz grædari' 21.4 and commentary. The kenning anticipates the miracle of healing in the following stanzas.

58.1. *fylldra.* Emendation is necessary to make sense of the *helmingr*. Read 'angrs fylldra manna' (men full of sin).

58.1, 3. *alldar milldings þionn.* 'Servant of the king of mankind' (i.e., God) is a kenning for the priest Ríkarðr. The phrase *servus Dei* found its way from Scripture into liturgy and hagiography, where it became a commonplace (cf., e.g., archetypal texts like Bede's *Historia*, the poems of Fortunatus, and Gregory's *Dialogues*, where the terms *servus Dei* and *famulus Dei* appear throughout). The kenning associates Ríkarðr with the saints and emphasizes the seriousness of the crime against him. Cf. 'Guds þræl' 61.8.

58.4. *margfalldr.* 'Many-sided,' with connotations of deceit and duplicity.

58.8. *hialldrstrid.* The adjective emphasizes Einarr's point that lying can be as powerful a source of evil and destruction as battle.

59.2–4. The syntax is awkward and the meaning of 'rotum' is ambiguous: *rót* can mean both 'root, cause' or 'disturbance, disorder.' Possible readings are 'marglitendr eggia lustu sex fot i sundr i sande; fion greri hord med rotum alldrtrega fyrda' (the frequent-stainers of blades broke apart the man's leg in the sand; hatred grows hard with the disturbances of the unceasing strife of men), or alternatively, 'hord fion greri med rotum alldrtrega fyrda' (hard hatred grows with roots in the unceasing sorrows of men).

59.2. *marglitendr eggia.* A kenning for the evil-doing brothers and an appropriate image in the context. Cf. 'steindra mundrida' 48.3. *F*'s 'marglitudr,' a past participial form, is unlikely.

59.5–6. The manuscripts are hopelessly corrupt here. The *F* reading 'lim leystu,' which may be related to Modern Icelandic *limlesta* (mutilate) is logical in itself, but it is impossible to construe it with the remainder of the *helmingr*. *B* and *W* have instead the idiom *lǫg lestu* (broke the law). *F*'s 'feyfdar' is either a hapax legomenon with an obscure meaning or an error, and *W*'s 'leygðar' likewise is impossible. 'Krofd,' which is clearly related to the verb *krefja* (demand), could be either a participle or an early occurrence of the noun *krǫf* (demand, cf. *W*). If it is a participle, it must be construed with 'himintungl heila' (heavenly bodies of the brain [eyes]) to give the meaning that the priest's eyes were demanded of him. If the word is a noun, which seems more likely, the phrase *líknar krǫf* (demand of mercy) would be appositive to *lǫg*. The case of 'prest' is uncertain. As an accusative it would work well with the *F* reading 'Prest þeir er limleystu' (those who mutilated the priest), but if this reading is abandoned for the alternative, it can be construed only as a genitive. The genitive form of *prestr* occurs not infrequently without final *-s*, probably because of the difficulty of pronouncing the final consonant cluster in *prests* (see Noreen, *Altnordische Grammatik*, § 302). Its use here facilitates the rhyme with *leystu*.

59.7, 8. *heila himintungl.* 'Suns (or stars) of the sky of the brain,' 'heavenly bodies of the brain,' i.e., the eyes. Guðrún Nordal suggests that this kenning may be an allusion to the myth of the murdered giant Ymir, from whose skull the sky was made (see *SnE 1931*, 15). She notes that the juxtaposition of the inner parts of the body (e.g., the brain) with its external features or with the natural world was a distinct feature of later skaldic verse (Guðrún Nordal, *Tools of Literacy*, 286, 293).

60.1–4. In the first *helmingr* two verb clauses depend on a single subject. Construe 'tungan tirkunnz var lokin med tangar munni ok þrysuar skorin knifi' (the tongue of the man accustomed to praise was grasped by the mouth of tongs and cut with a knife three times).

60.2. *tirkunnz.* 'Accustomed to praise,' i.e., accustomed to praising God. This hapax legomenon is in adjectival form but must be understood as a substantive, referring to the priest Ríkarðr.

60.3. *þrysuar.* This is explained in the prose accounts:

sid*an* drogo þeir ut tvngo h*an*s oc sko:o af mikit oc sp*u*rdo ef h*ann* metti mela en h*ann* leitadi vid at m*ela* þa toko þeir i t*un*go stufiɴ oc sko:o af tysvar þadan af oc i tungo rot*om* it sidarsta siɴ.

[then they drew out his tongue and cut off much of it and asked him if he could speak. And he tried to speak. Then they got hold of the stump of his

tongue and cut from it twice, and finally from the root of the tongue.]
(*Brudst*, 37; cf. *Hkr*, 3: 336; *OH.St*, 652–3)

60.5. *Audskiptir.* A kenning for the priest, who as a missionary was a dis-
penser of spiritual riches. Cf. the kennings in stanza 40. The only other occur-
rence of the word is in *Plácitus drápa* 17.1 (ed. Louis-Jensen, 101). Kristina
Attwood ('Intertextual Aspects of the Twelfth-Century Christian *Drápur*,'
226 and 235) suggests that this belongs to a group of words found only in the
Christian *drápur* and notes the similarity of 60.5, 'Audskiptir læ eftir,' to
Plácitus drápa 17.1 'þá es auðskiptis eptir' (ed. Louis-Jensen, 101).
60.6. *a strondu.* The prose versions tell us that the incident took place on the
shore of a lake. Einarr specifies a similar location in his account of the man
mutilated by the Wends (stanza 49); he may have confused the circumstances
of the two miracles.
61.1–4. The language parallels the Norwegian homily: '... ſtyfðu af tungunni.
ok ſtungu bæði æugun or hæfði honu*m*' (... they cut off the tongue and stung
both eyes out of his head) (*GNH*, 117).
61.1. *styfdrar.* Although both manuscripts read 'styfdar,' the grammar of the
clause demands the past participle: 'of styfdrar tungu' is parallel to 'ut
stunginna augna.'
61.2. *gram.* According to Craigie's law (see Gade, *The Structure of Old Norse
Dróttkvætt Poetry*, 29–30, and commentary on 16.5 above), the word must be
in the accusative for the sake of the metre. It can be understood as a *heiti*,
albeit a strange one, for the recipient of the miracle, and as an appositive
to 'itran þegn.' Since this means that the sentence lacks a noun subject,
and given that this is not the only problem with the line's metre ('lamins' has
to be regarded as a single syllable), it is tempting to disregard Craigie's
law and emend to *B*'s 'gramr,' which would then function as a *heiti* for
Óláfr.
61.3. *sem.* The use of *sem* as a conjunction is awkward here, but emendation
may be preferable to the seemingly superfluous preposition *til*, the Flateyjar-
bók version. Possible readings which would avoid emendation, none of them
entirely satisfactory, include construing *til* with the infinitive ('til [at] njóta')
or with *láta* to form the idiom *láta til* (to grant [something] to [someone]). Or
if *njóta* is understood in a nominal sense, it could denote respect ('use of his
lame leg, cut-off tongue, and stung-out eyes').
61.7, 8. *ger munu guilld þeim er byriar ofugmæli.* Einarr expresses similar
sentiments in stanzas 17 and 37, but his tone here is uncharacteristically sharp.
The comment may have been *ad hominem*: Einarr does not use names, but his
audience must have known that the crime was linked to Sigurðr's family, and
the two brothers themselves may have been present.

61.8. *Guðs þræl.* See commentary on 58.1, 3.

62.2. *orugt.* The word ordinarily means 'certainly' or 'confidently,' but its literal meaning is 'without fear,' and here it may refer to Einarr's unrestrained comments on the crimes of Sigurðr's mother and brothers.

62.3. *dyrdar vottr.* The kenning for Óláfr translates *martyr*, cf. 6.1.

62.5, 6. *lausnara langvinr.* 'Friend of God' is one of Einarr's favourite metaphors for Óláfr. 'Lausnara langvinr' appears again in 68.1, 2; cf. also stanzas 9, 63, and 64.

62.6. *lids valldr.* A reference to Óláfr's earthly kingship.

62.6. *numin alldri.* Cf. 'numin lifi' 17.8 and 'hedann numin fra angri' 63.1, 4.

62.7. *firdi sik syndum.* An allusion to the theme of stanza 13.

62.8. Part of the saint's function as a witness is that by his miracles he manifests the glory of God in the world, even though he is no longer a part of it.

63.1, 4. *Hedann fra angri numin.* See commentary on 62.6.

63.2. *vini flesta.* Grammar requires the accusative forms: the words must be construed with 'sina' and 'reynir.'

63.6. *himna valldz.* A God-kenning, see commentary on 2.4. The kenning also occurs in *Plácitus drápa* 19.7 (ed. Louis-Jensen, 102).

63.7. *færskerdandi.* Cf. 'harmskerdanda' 38.4. The only other occurrence of the word is in *Leiðarvísan* 11.1 (*Skj* IA: 620). Kristina Attwood suggests that this belongs to a group of words found only in the Christian *drápur* ('Intertextual Aspects of the Twelfth-Century Christian *Drápur*,' 226).

63.8. *fridarsyn.* The compound is a direct translation of *visio pacis*, which was believed to be the meaning of the name Jerusalem (Augustine, *Enarrationes in Psalmos*, 50.22, *CCSL*, 38). This etymology was well known in the Middle Ages and appears frequently in theological writings and in hymns, the most famous being the hymn *Urbs beata Hierusalem, dicta pacis visio* (*AH* 51:119; *ONid*, 292–3, 335–6). The image of the martyrs and confessors living in endless heavenly bliss, ultimately derived from Scripture (Revelation 7:13–17, 21: 3–4, etc.), is a commonplace in hymns for the feasts of saints. Cf. also the Icelandic Christmas homily:

Méttem ver þa fæþor oc sun oc anda helgan i eino velde. oc fagrt eþle yver engla. þar monom ver siá helga friþar sýn þa er vár bíþr meþ sinom trúlegom borgmænnom.

[There we shall meet the Father and the son and the Holy Spirit ruling in one kingdom, and a beautiful homeland above the angels. There we shall see the holy vision of peace, where we shall abide with its faithful citizens.] (*Icelandic Homily Book*, fol. 23v)

64.1, 2, 3, 4. *lofdungs lioss hyriar vegs.* A 'king of heaven' kenning, see commentary on 2.4. Cf. 'hyriar heids' in *Harmsól* 14.7, 8 (*Skj* IA: 564). The adjective 'lioss' can be construed with any of the nouns in the kenning. At another level the metaphor evokes the image of Óláfr; the 'path of fire' calls to mind the martyrdom through which he confirmed his kingship.

64.5. *hyggium.* Verbs of saying or understanding are normally followed by an accusative-infinitive clause or by a noun clause introduced by the particle *at.* Here, as in the following stanza, the nominative subject and finite verb suggest that an omitted *at* is implied. This is common in modern Scandinavian languages, but the phenomenon has not been sufficiently studied in Old Norse to know whether it should be regarded as anachronistic and unlikely here. This reading was accepted by Schöning (*Heimstringla eðr Noregs Konunga Sögur,* 478) and Wennberg (*Geisli,* 71), but all the subsequent editors of *Geisli* have emended following Bergsbók.

64.5, 6. *hreggsalar iofur.* A kenning for God or Christ, see commentary on 2.4. Note the similarity between 64.6, 'heitfastr iofur veit[ir]' and *Harmsól* 45.4, 'heít fastr iðfurr [v]eite' (*Skj* IA: 568).

64.8. *dyrdar vin.* A reference to the fame and honour God gives his 'friend' Óláfr by working miracles through him.

65.1. *hygg ek.* See commentary on *hyggium* 64.5. Again, the noun clause following *hygg ek* implies an omitted *at.*

65.1, 2. *hofuds menn.* The defective *aðalhending* of the *F* reading (m*annz* / *þenn*a) suggests that the *B* version is to be preferred. Guðrún Nordal suggests that the kenning 'hǫfuðsmenn heims' (head-men of the world) may reflect the Neoplatonic macrocosm-microcosm cosmology which began to appear in skaldic poetry as the teachings of the twelfth-century platonists of France and England made their way to Iceland (Guðrún Nordal, *Tools of Literacy,* 276).

65.3, 4. *tiggi solar.* Cf. 'gram solar' 18.8.

65.4. *erchistoli.* The word is clearly the object of 'kuomu' and must be in the dative.

65.5. *himna geruis.* A kenning for Christ, the creative Word through whom God made the universe (Hebrews 1:1–2). The image of Christ as creator occurs frequently in hymns; Einarr would have known, e.g., *Conditor alme siderum* (*AH* 51:46; *ONid,* 131, 133, 135, 137–41, 144–5, 149–50; *HASC,* 181–4), *Regni cælestis conditor* (*AH* 51:3), and *Christe, cælorum conditor* (*AH* 51:41). Cf. also Markús Skeggjason's *Kristdrápa:*

Gramr skop grvnd *ok* hi*m*na
gly<small>G</small>ranz sem h*er* dy<small>G</small>ian

eɪn still*ir* ma a/llv
ald*ar* kr*i*str of valda.

['The king of the storm-house created the earth and the heavens as well as
the doughty army. Christ, who alone is king of mankind, can rule over
everything.'] (*Skj* IA: 452)

65.6, 8. *heilagr vidr piningarcrossi.* King Sigurðr *Jórsalafari* brought the relic
to Trondheim after receiving it as a gift from Baldwin I of Jerusalem during a
trip to Palestine in 1110 (*Ágrip*, 50–1; *MHN*, 66; *Hkr*, 3: 250).
65.7. *yfirskiolldungr alldar.* *Qld* has two meanings: it can refer to time (an
age, era, or epoch) or collectively to the human race. Finnur Jónsson assumed
that it had the latter meaning in this kenning for God (see *Lexicon Poeticum
Skj* IB: 444), but it almost certainly has the former. The epithet *rex saecu-
lorum* (king of the ages) occurs in Scripture (1 Timothy 1:17 and Revelation
15:3) and was widely used in liturgical texts of all sorts (cf., e.g., *ONid*, 184,
188, 325). Analogous kennings for God occur in Gísli Súrsson's Lausavísa 26
('allvalldr alldar,' *Skj* IA: 107), Markús Skeggjason's '*Kristdrápa*' ('still*ir*
ald*ar*,' *Skj* IA:452), and in *Plácitus drápa* 28 ('konungr aldar,' ed. Louis-
Jensen, 107).
66.1–4. The syntax is exceptionally difficult, but it is possible to read the
helmingr without emending: 'Aulld nytr hars Olafs milldi; hofum skyrda alla
dyrd þingsniallz iofurs; verolld þrotnar fra þessum.' The sense may be that the
world pales in the face of the glories of Óláfr which have been told in the
poem. Curtius gives examples of similar extravagant comparisons in contem-
porary Latin eulogies (*European Literature and the Latin Middle Ages*, 162–
6). Alternatively, the meaning could be that the golden age of Óláfr has passed
and that the world has been declining ever since. Bergsbók offers an entirely
different reading: 'þreksnioll avlld nytr milldi þrottar hvass Olafs af ollum
þessum frama; hofum skyrda dyrd iofurs' (the strong people enjoy the mild
powers of brave Óláfr with respect to all these instances of assistance; we
have made clear the fame of the king).
66.3 *hars.* The rhyme between 'hars' and 'þessum' (*-s/-rs*) is feasible, cf.
'omiors'/'liosi' 3.4, and see also Kahle, *Die Sprache der Skalden*, 151–3.
66.5. *luti.* Kristina Attwood ('Intertextual Aspects of the Twelfth-Century
Christian *Drápur*,' 232–3) points out the similarity between this *helmingr*, the
first *stef* of *Leiðarvísan*, and the *helmingr* that introduces the second *stef* of
Plácitus drápa:

Luta eíngl*ar* itr*u*m
ótt laust *ok* lid dr*o*tne

einn er siklingr sunnu
seturs huíuetna betri.

[Angels and people bow down to the glorious lord without fear; the one
king of the seat of the sun is better than everything else.] (*Leiðarvísan* 13.5–
8, *Skj* IA: 620)

Lýtr engla lið ítrum
angrhrjóðanda ok þjóðir
einn es ǫllu hreinni
alt gótt sá er skóp dróttinn.

[The company of angels and races of men bow down to the glorious
destroyer of sorrow; the one lord, who made all (that is) good, is purer than
everything else.] (*Plácitus drápa* 32.1–4, ed. Louis-Jensen, 108).

66.6. *lim konungs himna sals*. This kenning for Óláfr is analogous to the imag-
ery of stanza 2, where Óláfr is called the sunbeam and Christ the sun. The
image of the saint as the limb of Christ derives from St Paul (1 Corinthians
6:15). The reading 'salmls' is a careless error and suggests that 'konungi' is
likewise a simple mistake.

67.2. *fridgegns*. The epithet has decidedly Christian connotations: Óláfr now
dwells in peace in the heavenly Jerusalem (cf. *Geisli* 63). Einarr's imagery is
strikingly similar to a passage in Jerome's commentary on Titus:

Si enim sumus filii pacis et uolumus super nos pacem requiescere et
accessimus ad Hierusalem caelestem quae ex pace nomen accepit.

[For if we are sons of peace, and if we wish peace to rest upon us, then we
have drawn near to the heavenly Jerusalem, which takes its name from
peace.] (*CCSL* 77, C: 60)

67.4. *bragar stoli*. The kenning is multivalent. The *Lexicon Poeticum* identi-
fies it as a reference to the poet's breast or soul, but it could also refer to his
voice or mouth, or even (secondarily) to the seat from which he proclaimed
his poem to the audience.

67.5–8. *heidbiartr seggr*. The meaning could be that the man who praises God
and is in turn loved by him is especially blessed, but the *B* reading, 'heidbiar-
trar solar,' may be preferable.

67.5, 6. *solar bǫals siklings*. A God-kenning. See commentary on 2.4.

67.7. *hilmis ens hæsta*. Cf. 'hæstr skiolldungr' 6.7.

68.1. *Sua*. Stanza 68, joined to the preceding lines by this subordinating conjunction, continues the prayer begun in the second *helmingr* of stanza 67.

68.1, 2. *lausnara langvinr*. A kenning for Óláfr, cf. stanzas 9, 63, and 64. The form 'langvinn' in *F* is probably a variant nominative form: the syntax of the *helmingr* demands that the word be the subject of the clause.

68.4. *vid tru*. Construe with 'naudum' to mean 'need with respect to the faith,' i.e. imperfect faith.

68.5, 6. *velendr viga skys*. 'Choosers of the cloud of battle,' cf. 'sky gunnar' 43.6. 'Chooser of the shield' is a traditional formula for a warrior-kenning, but Einarr may have intended an additional meaning based on wordplay. The *Passio Olaui* (72; Kunin, and Phelpstead, trans. ed., *A History of Norway*, 30) and the liturgical texts for the celebration of Óláfr's feast refer to the 'shield or breastplate of faith' (*scutum* or *lorica fidei*), an image with roots in Scripture (Isaiah 59:17, Ephesians 6:14–17, 1 Thessalonians 5:8). The office of vespers for the feast of St Óláfr in the Leofric Collectar has the *capitulum*:

> Beatus vir cuius capiti dominus coronam imposuit muro salutis circumdedit. scuto fidei et gladio muniuit. ad expugnandas gentes et omnes inimicos.

> [Blessed is the man on whose head the Lord has placed a crown; whom he has surrounded with a wall of safety and armed with a sword and the shield of faith, so that he might overcome the heathens and all enemies.] (*The Leofric Collectar*, 210; Østrem, *The Office of Saint Olav*, 282)

And the later medieval office of St Óláfr contains the matins responsary:

> Itaque devotissime perficiens officium evangeliste indutus lorica fidei et galea salutis, Circuibat civitates, vicos et villas, salutarem doctrinam ubique disseminans.

> [And thus most devotedly fulfilling the office of an evangelist, girded with the corslet of faith and the helmet of salvation, he travelled among cities, villages, and farms, spreading everywhere the doctrine of salvation.] (Østrem, *The Office of Saint Olav*, 77–9; *Breviarium Nidrosiense*, qq.iii; *ONid*, 372)

The warriors in Einarr's twelfth-century audience were not Vikings but 'Óláfr's men,' who now were to follow him in spiritual, rather than material conquest.

69.1. *iofri*. Presumably King Eysteinn, who commissioned the poem. Einarr's announcement of the completion of his assignment is typically skaldic. The *B* reading, 'iofra,' is an acknowledgment of the three kings and may be preferable: 'We have told the family of kings ... the mind follows this counsel.'

69.2. *ordhags*. The epithet is puzzling in this context: it may refer to Óláfr's power as an intercessor.

69.2. *kyni*. The family of Eysteinn, Sigurðr, and Ingi. The 'counsel to the family' may be an allusion to Einarr's comments on the behaviour of Þóra and her brothers.

69.4. *hapsdœdir*. Cf. 'happ-mættu' 19.7.

69.5–8. The manuscript tradition is obviously corrupt here, and it is impossible to read without some emendation. Finnur Jónsson conflates the two manuscripts and changes the plural *gæðum* to singular *gæði* to arrive at the construction 'fǫm létt holl laun þessa gǫfugs óðar, goðs blessun, ef hreinum hræsíks þrimu gœði líkar lof' (We will easily obtain a good reward for this noble poem, God's blessing, if the pure increaser of the storm of the corpse-salmon likes the praise). Kock follows Bergsbók, emending *gæðir* to *F*'s *gæðum* and introducing *lát* as a substitute for 'let.' He sees a clearly formulated sentence in the opening and closing words of the *helmingr*: *Laun fǫm holl ... lofs þessa* (we will receive a friendly reward for this praise) and interprets *goðs blessun* as a reference to the reward (though it could also be an appositive reference to the poem itself). He construes the subordinate clause *ef gǫfugs óðar lát líkar hreinum gæðum hræsíks þrimu* (if the sound of the noble poem is pleasing to the pure increasers of the storm of the corpse-salmon) (*NN* § 953). By emending *F*'s 'af' to *ef* and 'gædum' to *gæðir* it is possible to read 'fæum holl laun þessa lofs, ef hanum likar; Guds blezon gofugs odar hialp hræsiks þrimu gædi' (we will receive a friendly reward for this poem, if it pleases him; may God's blessing of the noble poem help the increaser of the storm of the corpse-salmon). The phrase 'ef hanum likar' could refer both to King Eysteinn and to God, and the warrior-kenning could refer either to Eysteinn or the skald. It would also be possible to retain the plural form of *F*, which would invoke God's blessing on all present, but this seems improbable. Cf. 'ef ... lifði' in the following stanza: Einarr has a tendency to repeat syntactic constructions, e.g., 'lofs þessa' in this stanza and 'brag þenna' in the previous, or the repetition of *hyggja* in stanzas 8.3/9.6 and 64.5/65.1. It is possible that the original version of the text had another kenning base word, later replaced by 'hanum,' which had 'hresiks þrimu' as the defining elements. 'Gofugs odar' would then have been free to link with the base word 'gædi.'

69.6, 7. *hresiks þrimu gædi*. A warrior-kenning. *Hræsíkr* is a *heiti* for 'sword,' cf. 'val brimis sunda' in stanza 55.

70.1, 2. The text of these lines is corrupt in both manuscripts. All the editors since Cederschiöld have without further ado (or a convincing explanation) emended *F* 'brennda' and *B* 'grondv' to *brǫndum* and replaced *F* 'huers' with *B* 'ness.' This makes possible the somewhat redundant gold-kenning *brandar baugnes* (flames of the ness of the bracelet = flames of the arm). It is tempting to retain the Flateyjarbók text, which yields the gold-kenning *brenda baug ens huers* (refined treasure of the cauldron). The problem with this reading is the nearly impossible syntax, the separation of the article and the noun it modifies. For examples of other kennings based on the refining process, see Meissner, *Die Kenningar*, 223. The rhyme between *huers* and *þessi* (-*s*/-*rs*) is feasible, cf. 'omiors'/ 'liosi' 3.4 and 'hars' / 'þessum' 66.3, and see Kahle, *Die Sprache der Skalden*, 151–3.

70.3. *rausnarskap.* The compound denotes a disposition to generosity. It is made up of the elements *rausn* (munifence) and *skap* (condition, state of mind).

70.4. *raundyrliga.* 'Magnificently.' The proper meaning of *raun* is 'trial' or 'test,' but in compounds it often means 'very' or 'truly.'

70.4–5. The *helmingar* are linked by a subordinating conjunction ('ef'), and the bond between the two is reinforced by the alliteration of the last word in line 4 with the *stuðlar* in line 5. The entire stanza is a single sentence with two parentheses interposed.

70.6. *Sigurðr.* Sigurðr *Jórsalafari*, who was renowned for his generosity.

71.1. *Bæn.* The word appears in key position in the first line of the poem, and it is with a sense of symmetry that Einarr uses it here.

71.2. *stodat framla.* The boasting is typically skaldic.

71.3. *iofri.* Óláfr.

71.5, 6. *æzstann Eysteinn.* The rhyming epithet is clever, and may be what caused the *F* scribe to omit the name 'Eysteinn' in line 6: a kind of haplography by aural association. But the rhyme of line 5 is imperfect and the *B* reading, 'jtrann,' may be correct.

71.7, 8. *veg hæs vagnræfrs visa.* The compound *vagnræfrs* (wagon-roof's) is a kenning for heaven: *Karlsvagn* was the Norse name for the constellation Ursa Major, the Big Dipper. The adjective 'hæs' can be construed with either 'visa' or 'vagnræfrs,' and perhaps should be read with both. *Vegr* has two meanings: 'path' and 'honour.' Both are apt here and Einarr may have chosen the word with the intention of conveying two ideas. The kenning 'visa vagnræfrs' signifies Christ, but it can also refer to Óláfr, and the ambiguity is a way of expressing the identity of Christ and the saint. See also commentary on 2.4.

71.7. *elskig.* The *B* reading, 'elskit,' appeals more to modern sensibilities (it makes the phrase an exhortation rather than a pious exclamation), but 'elskig' may have been the self-conscious skald's intent.

71.8. *en ek þagna*. The abrupt conclusion is typical of medieval European poetry (see Curtius, *European Literature and the Latin Middle Ages*, 89–91), and although the small number of complete *drápur* makes it impossible to generalize, it is probably typical of skaldic poetry as well. The phrase appears again at the conclusion of *Rekstefja* (*Skj* IA: 552).

Glossary

All words that appear in the text are fully indexed. Headwords are the standard dictionary forms (infinitives of verbs, nominative singular of nouns, nominative singular masculine of adjectives), even when these forms do not occur in the text, and most headwords appear in classical, standardized spellings. This convention is not altogether satisfactory, but it is traditional in ON lexicography and its use here should facilitate consultation of the available dictionaries and word lists. Following the headwords are the forms found in the text, identified by verse and line numbers. Every form and every spelling is recorded, including those identical with the headwords. When irregular forms and spellings differ from the headwords to the extent that they may cause confusion, they are entered separately with cross-references. Cross-references are also provided for forms of strong verbs and other words conforming to phonological laws. Spellings involving the orthographic variants *ǫ/á*, *i/j*, *u/v*, *œ/æ*, and *d/ð* are not cross-indexed, but separate entries with cross-references are given for variant spellings involving *u*-umlaut of *a*, which can be more confusing.

Definitions are brief and give only those meanings of a word which are applicable to the text; it should be noted that these definitions do not always represent primary or well-known meanings of words. They are intended as suggestions rather than pronouncements, and the reader is urged to consult dictionaries with fuller entries to supplement the glosses given here.

Nouns are identified by gender, case, and number following citations of forms in the text. One-letter abbreviations mark case and number: ns. would indicate nominative singular. Participles used as substantives are ordinarily treated as nouns, without cross-references to verb infinitives.

Adjectives are identified by case, number, and gender (e.g., npn. for nominative plural neuter). The declension of most adjectives is strong; declension is indicated only in the instance of weak forms. Where comparative and super-lative forms differ significantly from the positive forms which serve as head-words, they are listed separately with cross-references. Participles used adjectivally are recorded only under verb infinitives.

Pronouns are identified by case, and, where applicable, number and gender; all forms are listed only under the nominative headword. Treatment of prepo-sitions is varied. If the meaning of a preposition is clear and consistent in every instance in the text, only references to occurrences are recorded. But where a word occurs with less uniformity, fuller glosses are provided.

Following the headwords, Arabic numerals mark the ablaut classes of strong verbs, and Roman numerals mark the conjugations of weak verbs. Reduplicating verbs and preterite-present verbs are indicated by the abbrevia-tions red. and pret.-pres., followed by Arabic numerals designating ablaut class. Verb forms are parsed according to voice, tense, person, number, and mood (e.g., pass. pret. ex. subj. for passive preterite third person subjunctive), but the voice and mood of a form are specified only where the voice is other than active or the mood other than indicative. Tense is not given for present infinitives and present imperatives. Middle verb forms are designated as hav-ing passive, reflexive, or reciprocal sense, although distinctions between pas-sive and reflexive meanings are not always precise.

Words and compounds not attested elsewhere are preceded by a dagger (†). In the ordering of the alphabet *ð* is together with *d*, *þ* follows *t*, and *æ*, *ø*, *œ*, and *ǫ* follow *y*. The following abbreviations are used:

a, acc.	accusative
adj.	adjective
adv.	adverb
art.	article
aux.	auxiliary
comp.	comparative
conj.	conjunction
contr.	contraction
d, dat.	dative
def.	definition
dem.	demonstrative
f.	feminine
fut.	future
g, gen.	genitive
imp.	imperative
impers.	impersonal

indecl.	indeclinable
inf.	infinitive
irr.	irregular
m.	masculine
md.	middle
mon.	monosyllabic
n.	neuter
neg.	negative
nom.	nominative
num.	numeral
ON	Old Norse
p, pl.	plural
pass.	passive
p.n.	proper name
poss.	possessive
pp.	past participle
prep.	preposition
pres.	present
pres. part.	present participle
pret.	preterite
pret. pres.	preterite-present
pron.	pronoun
recip.	reciprocal
red.	reduplicating
reflex.	reflexive
rel.	relative
s, sg.	singular
subj.	subjunctive
sup.	superlative
w.	with
wk.	weak

-**a**, -**at**, neg. suffix used w. verbs. muna, 14.3; nædid, 19.1; vandit, 20.3; munat, 21.4, 24,3; ridrat, 57.4; vara, 60.3.

á, prep. (1) w. dat. *on, in, at, etc.*: a krossi, *on the cross*, 3.6; a dag þridia, *on the third day*, 4.2; a dyrum stoli, *on the precious throne*, 5.7; a Stiklastodum, 17.1; a Hlyrskogsheidi, 28.5; æ lædi, *in the land*, 27.3; a flotta, *in flight*, 29.5; a þvi deili, *proof in that matter, proof of that*, 41.8; a Stiklastaudum, 43.7; a kuelldi, *in the evening*, 47.2; a vangi, *on the plain*, 47.5; a slettri grundu, *on the flat ground*, 48.5; a Girklandi, 51.2; æ Pecinavǫllum, 52.1; a strondu, *on the coast*, 60.6; a iardriki, *in the earthly kingdom*, 62.8. (2) w. acc. *on, in*: trudi a Gud, *believed in God*, 14.2; a danska tungu, *in the Norse language*, 26.8; huert a annat, *one on the other, one after another*, 46.8; hetu a Olæf, *called on Olaf*, 54.1; gingi æ þegna, *went at the thanes, went against the thanes*.

aar, see **ǫr**.

ætti, see **eiga**.

áðr, adv. *before, previously*: ædr, 14.5, 15.2, 25.5, 49.5; adr, 26.3, 28.5, 31.3.

af, prep. w. dat. *from, over, in, etc.*: af þui, *from that, because of that*, 2.7, 32.7; af iordu til himna, *from earth to heaven*, 15.8; af gram, *from the king*, 18.8, 21.8, 24.8, 27.8, 30.8, 33.8, 36.8, 39.8, 42.8, 44.4, 45.8; þo sueita af liki, *washed blood from the body*, 22.2; af blodi, *from the blood*, 24.1; af þvi verki, *because of that deed*, 26.6; af sliku, *because of such things*, 39.2; af gulli vordu, *covered with gold*, 50.7; af trausti, *in faith, in confidence*, 54.2; af riki, *with strength, powerfully*, 55.1; af villu, *from delusion*, 58.2; af hæstri fridarsyn, *in the highest vision of peace*, 63.5; af pingarcrossi, *from the cross of suffering*, 65.5; i fiolda af iartegnum, *in the multitude of miracles*, 67.2; af bragar stoli, *from the seat of poetry*, 67.3; brag af astum Cristz, *poem about the love of Christ*, 68.7; af hanum, *from him*, 69.5.

afrek, n. *extraordinary achievement*: gs. afreks, 8.1.

afskurðr, m. *a cut-off piece*: ds. afskurdi, 26.4.

ágætr, adj. *renowned, excellent*: nsm. agætr, 71.5; nsf. ægæt, 11.5, agæt, 39.1; asm. agætan, 1.7.

aldr, m. *life*: ds. alldri, 19.2, 62.6.

aldri, adv. *never*: alldri, 10.5, 63.6.

aldrtregi, m. *life-sorrows, unceasing grief*: gs. alldrtrega, 59.4.

†alkœnn, adj. *much-skilled*: gsm. alkæns, 31.4.

alldar, see **ǫld**.

alldri (10.5), see **aldri**.

alldri (19.2), see **aldr**.

alldrtrega, see **aldrtregi**.

allr, adj. *all*: npm. allir, 7.2, 11.4; nsn. allt (used adverbially), 51.5; gsm. allz, 16.8; gpm. allra, 3.7, 10.6; allrar, 4.1, 9.3; gsn. allz, 1.2, 5.4, 21.4; allz mest, *as a rule, generally*, 63.2; asf. alla, 26.7, 36.4, 56.8, 66.4; asn. allt, 18.7, 21.7, 24.7, 27.7, 30.7, 33.7, 36.7, 39.7, 42.7, 45.7.

allskonar, indecl. adj. *every kind*: allzkonar sælu, *every kind of blessedness*, 62.1.

allvaldr, m. *all-ruler*: gs. allualldz, 50.2.

alnenninn, adj. *extremely effective, competent, capable*: gsm. alnenins, 68.8.

almildr, adj. *all-mild, generous, peaceful*: gsm. *almilldz*, 35.4.

†**almreyrlituðr**, m. *arrow-reddener*: ns. almreyrlitudr, 17.4.

alstyrkr, adj. *all-strong*: asm. alstyrkann, 17.4.

altári, n. *altar*: ds. alltari, 50.8.

alþýða, f. *all people, a great crowd of people*: gs. alþydu 9.4.

alþýðr, adj. *common to all people*: nsf. alþyd, 6.6.

andi, m. *spirit*: gs. anda, 6.2.

angr, n. *sorrow, sin*: gs. angrs, 58.1; ds. angri, 63.1.

annarr, adj. *another*: gsm. annars, 3.3; asn. annat, 46.8.

ár, f. *oar*: as. ær, 40.8 (?).

arfi, m. *heir, offspring*: ns. arfi, 51.4; ds. arfa, 30.4.

armglóð, f. *arm-fire, gold*: ap. armglædur, 45.4.

armglædur, see **armglóð**.

arnar, see **ǫrn**.

árr, m. *servant, messenger*: ns. arr, 23.7.

ast, f. *love*: dp. astum, 68.7; as. æst 67.7.

at, prep. w. dat. *to, at, etc.*: at odgerd þessi, *to this recitation of poetry*, 10.3; at hialldri, *at the battle*, 32.3; at hvorv, *at whichever, nevertheless*, 32.5; hafa at minnum, *remember, have in memory*, 34.5; vard at grioti, *turned to stone*, 35.7; at vopna galldri, *at the song of weapons, at the battle*, 43.2.

at, conj. introduces indirect discourse after verbs of saying or knowing, *that*: 4.5, 8.3, 12.1, 12.3, 13.3, 15.1, 19.5, 22.5, 30.1, 34.1, 35.1, 38.1, 40.1, 43.1, 46.5, 51.5, 64.1; þvi at, *because*, 18.1, 62.5; sva at, *so that*, 52.5, 68.1.

at, particle. marks inf.: 15.7, 29.6, 35.5, 46.4, 56.5, 57.2.

áta, f. *food*: ds. ætu, 29.1.

att, f. *family, race*: gs. attar, 8.8.

†**auðfinnandi**, m. *finder of riches*: dp. audfinnendum, 3.3.

audlinga, audlings, see **ǫðlingr**.

auðr, m. *riches, wealth*: gs. audar, 5.2, 23.3, 37.3.

†**auðskýfandi**, m. *wealth distributor, generous man*: gs. audskyfanda, 40.7.

auflugs, see **ǫflugr**.

auga, n. *eye*: gp. augna, 61.3.

Aulfishaug, see **Ǫlvishaugr**.

aulld, see **ǫld**.

aumr, adj. *poor, wretched*: dsm. aumum, 37.3; dpf. aumum, 38.3.

aund, see **ǫnd**.

Avngvlseyiar, see **Ǫngulsey**.

bæls, see **ból**.

baka, I. *bake*: inf. baka villdi, *wanted to bake*, 35.4.

bardiz, bardizst, see **berja**.
barðraukn, n. *prow-ox, ship*: gs. bardraugns, 53.6.
barg, see **bjarga**.
batnaðr, m. *improvement*: gs. batnadar, 22.4.
†**baugnes**, n. *ness of the bracelet, arm*: 70.2.
baugr, m. *ring, bracelet, treasure*: gp. bauga, 49.7.
†**baugskjǫldr**, m. *shield ornamented with ring-design*: gp. baugskiallda, 19.2.
baulfi, see **bǫl**.
beiðir, m. *desirer*: ns. beidir, 19.1; ds. beidi, 37.3.
bein, n. *bone*: ap. bein, 23.4.
beinn, adj. *even, smooth*: gp. beinna, 8.2.
beit, see **bíta**.
bending, f. *sign, portent*: ap. bendingar, 49.4.
bera, 4. *bear, bring*: pres. 3s. berr, 8.5; pret. 3p. subj. bęre, 53.8; pass. pres. 3s. er borin, 9.2; md. (pass.) inf. leet berazst, *was born, caused himself to be born*, 2.6.
bergr, see **bjarga**.
berja, II. *slay*; (md.) *fight*: md. (recip.) pret. 3s. bardiz, 20.1, 28.6; md. (recip.) pret. 3p. subj. bardizst, 15.2.
berr, adj. *certain, clear, bare*: nsn. (used adverbially) bert, 2.5; npn. ber, 67.3; dsm. berum, 47.8.
betra, betri, see **góðr**.
beztr, see **góðr**.
bíða, 1. *suffer from; obtain, get* (w. gen.); *ask someone to do something* (w. inf.): pres. 1s. bid styrkna, 8.6; byd hlyda, 9.1; bid ordgnottar, 10.2; pres. 1p. sem bidium, *as we ask, as we pray*, 65.6; inf. skulum bidia fulltings, 27.1.
birta, III. *show, make clear, illuminate*: md. (refl.) pres. 3p. birtazst, 51.1.
bíta, 1. *bite*: pret. 3s. beit, 29.6; pret. 3p.bitv, 31.8, 43.7.
bjarga, 3. *save, rescue, deliver* (w. dat.): pres. 3s. bergr, 65.3; pret. 3s. barg, 56.2; sg. imp. biarg, 65.7.
bjartr, adj. *bright*: nsm. biartr, 19.1; dsf. biartri, 2.5; apn. biort, 49.7, 51.1.
bjóða, 2. *offer*: pres. 1s. byd, 1.7; pres. 3s. bydr, 6.7.
blanda, red. 3. *blend*: pass. pret. 3s. var blandinn, 23.8.
blezan, f. *blessing*: as. blezon, 69.8.
blíðr, adj. *happy*: dsn. blidu, 58.8; asn. blid, 23.2.
blik, n. *light*: gs. bliks, 33.2.
blíkja, 1. *gleam, shine*: pret. 3p. bliku, 53.7.

blindr, adj. *blind*: nsm. blindr, 23.1.

blóð, n. *blood*: ds. blodi, 24.4.

boða, I. *proclaim, announce*: pres. 3s. bodar, 1.5.

ból, n. *dwelling place*: gs. bæls, 67.5; ds. boli, 41.4.

bol, see **bǫl**.

borg, f. *fortress*: gs. borgar, 48.2; as. borg, 56.3.

borin, see **bera**.

bra, see **bregða**.

bráðr, adj. *quick*: nsm. bradr, 48.4; (nsn. used adverbially) bratt, 20.1.

bragð, n. *deed*: np. brogd, 49.8; ap. brogd, 22.8.

bragnar, m. (pl. only) *men*: np. bragnar, 27.4; gp. bragna, 58.5.

bragr, m. *poetry*: ns. bragr, 40.2, 70.1; gs. bragar, 50.4, 67.4; ds. brag, 9.4; as. brag, 1.8, 45.4, 68.6, 71.6.

bran, see **brenna**.

†**branddrífr**, m. *sword-driver*: as. branddrif, 17.8.

brandél, n. *sword-shower, battle*: as. brandel, 51.2.

brandr, m. *flame, fire*: dp. brondum, 70.1

brandr, m. *sword*: gp. brannda, 53.5.

brauð, n. *bread*: ds. braudi, 35.5.

bregða, 3. *change, bring an end to* (w. dat.): pret. 3s. bra, 2.2, 3.1 (impers.), 19.6 (impers.); perf. 3s. hefir brugdit, 58.5.

brenna, 3. *burn, smelt, refine, purify*: pret. 3s bran, 20.5; pp. wk. gsm. brenda, 70.1.

brennheitr, adj. *burning hot*: dsn. brennheitu, 35.6.

brigðr, adj. *transitory, uncertain*: dsn. bridgu, 17.7.

brimir, m. *sword*: gs. brimis, 55.6.

brimlogi, m. *sea-fire, gold*: gs. brimloga, 56.6.

brjóta, 2. *break, destroy*: pres. 3s. brytr, 58.6.

†**broddrjóðr**, m. *point-reddener*: ns. broddriodr, 20.2.

bróðir, m. *brother*: ns. brodir, 49.2.

brogd, see **bragð**.

brúðr, f. *bride, woman*: ns. brudr, 35.5.

brugdit, see **bregða**.

brunnr, m. *liquid*: ds. brunni, 23.6.

brytr, see **brjóta**.

burr, m. *son*: ds. bur, 28.1.

byd (1.7), **bydr**, see **bjóða**.

byd (9.1), see **biðja**.

bygð, f. *dwelling*: as. bygd, 39.4.

byrja, II. *put into motion*: pres. 1s. byria, 23.1; pres. 3s. byriar, 61.7; inf. skal byria, 38.5.

byrr, m. *fair wind*: as. byr, 53.5.

bæði, adv. *both*: bædi, 38.6.

bœn, f. *prayer, request*: np. bænir, 31.4; as. bæn, 71.1; ap. bænir, 1.1.

bœta, III. *atone for* (w. acc.): pret. 3s. bætti, 13.3.

bǫl, n. *harm, evil, wickedness*: ds. baulfi, 14.8; as. bol, 17.7.

Cristr, see **Kristr**.

dáð, f. *deed*: ap. dædir, 12.2, 13.1.

dáðmildr, adj. *good-doing*: gsm. dædmilldz, 25.8.

dáðsnjallr, adj. *quickly acting*: gsm. dædsniallz, 56.8.

†**dáðvandr**, adj. *carefully acting*: nsm. dæduandr, 6.2.

dagból, m. *day's (sun's) dwelling, heaven*: gs. dagbols, 5.8.

dagr, m. *day*: ns. dagr, 47.6; ds. dag, 4.2; as. dag, 31.5.

†**dagræfr**, n. day's *roof, sky*: gs. dagræfrs, 51.8.

dála, adv. *completely, entirely*: dælá, 51.7.

Danmǫrk, f. *Denmark*, p.n.: as. Danmork, 36.4.

danskr, adj. *Norse, Danish*: gsf. danskrar, 35.8; asf. danska, 26.8.

dauði, m. *death*: ds. dauda, 19.6; as. dauda, 3.8.

deili, n. (pl. only). *proof*: ap. deili, 41.8.

dockua, see **døkkr**.

doglings, dǫglings, see **dǫglingr**.

dómari, m. *judge*: ns. domari, 42.2.

draga, 6. *move, draw*: md. (reflex.) pres. 3s. dragizst, 21.2.

draumr, m. *dream*: as. draum, 15.4; ap. drauma, 28.2.

dreif, see **drífa**.

dreingr, dreingir, dreingr, dreingum, see **drengr**.

dreki, m. *serpent, dragon*: gs. dreka, 41.4.

drengr, m. *man*: ns. dreingr, 8.5, 47.5; np. dreingir, 22.7; dp. dreingium, 56.2.

dreyra, III. *bleed*: inf. leet dreyra vndir, *caused wounds to bleed, wounded*, 17.4.

drífa, 1. *go, drive; splash or splatter something (dat.) on something or someone (acc.)*: pret. 3s. dreif, 55.2.

drótt, f. *band of retainers, people*: ns. drott, 15.3, 18.3, 22.1; gs. drottar, 12.4; ap. drottir, 28.8.

dróttinn, m. *lord*: ns. drottinn, 6.1, 25.7; drottins, 21.2, 22.5; ds. drottni, 62.3; as. drottinn, 10.2.

drýgja, II. *commit, perpetrate*: pret. 3p. drygdu, 17.7.

du, see **þú**.

duga, IV. *avail*; *befit*; *show prowess*, *do one's best*: pres. 3s. dugir, 15.7 (impers.); pret. 3s. dugde, 53.3.

dyggr, adj. *valiant*, *doughty*: comp. nsm. dyggri, 62.4.

dynr, m. *din*, *noise*: as. dyn, 14.6.

dýrð, f. *majesty*, *honour*, *fame*: ns. dyrd, 11.5, 24.2, 39.1, 45.2, 51.7; gs. dyr-dar, 6.1, 62.3; as. dyrd, 21.1, 66.2; ap. dyrdar, 64.8.

dýrka, I. *honour*, *praise*: pres. 3p. dyrka, 56.7; inf. skulum dyrka, 7.4, 57.6.

dýrr, adj. *costly*, *dear*, *precious*: nsm. dyrr, 25.7, 47.5; dsm. dyrum, 5.7; asm. dyrann, 22.1.

døkkr, adj. *dark*, *black*: wk. gsm. dockua, 16.2.

dǫglingr, m. *prince*: gs. dǫglings, 5.7; doglings, 15.3, 22.2, 56.7.

ef, conj. *if*: ef, 18.3, 70.5.

efla, III. *strengthen*, *fulfil*: inf. ma efla, 4.7.

efna, I. *carry out*, *bring into effect*: md. (reflex.) inf. reed efnázst os, *decided to make itself efficacious on our behalf*, 3.5.

efri, comp. adj. (lacks positive). *higher*: nsm. efri, 5.5.

eftir, see **eptir**.

Egðir, m. (pl. only) p.n., *inhabitants of Agder*: gp. Egda, 26.5.

egg, f. *blade*, *sword*: ns. egg, 29.6; gp. eggia, 59.2.

eiga, pret. pres. 1. *own*: pret. 3s. ætti, 50.3.

Eindriði, m. p.n.; ns. Eindridi, 45.3.

einn, pron. adj. *one*; *a*; *alone*, *only*: gsm. eins, 1.1; dsm. einum, 6.5, 13.4, 54.5; dsn. einu, 10.7.

eisa, f. *fire*: ds. eisu, 50.1.

ek, pron. *I*, *we*, *etc.*: ns. ek, 1.7, 4.5, 7.7, 8.4, 8.6, 9.1, 9.6, 10.2, 10.5, 12.1, 12.7, 15.1, 17.1, 17.5, 18.1, 18.3, 23.1, 30.3, 33.3, 38.1, 38.6, 40.1, 41.6, 43.1, 51.5, 62.2, 65.1, 70.3, 71.1, 71.6, 71.8; np. ver, 7.2, 37.5; ds. mer, 1.4, 19.7, 41.3, 46.1; dp. oss, 3.6, 10.3, 35.3; ap. oss, 14.7, 65.8.

eldbroti, m. *fire-breaker*: gs. elldbrota, 53.4.

eldi, n. *food*, *nourishment*: gs. eldis, 28.7.

†**eljanhress**, adj. *mentally robust, brave*: gsm. elianhress, 11.6.

ellri, see **gamall**.

elska, I. *love*: pres. 1s. subj. (w. suffixed pron.) elskig, *may I love*, 71.7.

endr, adv. *previously*: endr fyrir, *a long time ago*, 40.5.

engill, m. *angel*: dp. englum, 5.5.

en, **enn**, conj. *also*, *and*, *but*, *moreover*; *than* (w. comp.): enn, 9.5, 23.1, 25.5, 29.7, 35.5, 38.5, 40.2, 62.4; en, 71.8.

enn, **ens**, see **inn**.

eptir, adv. *after*: eftir, 60.5.

er, rel. pron. *who, which*: er, 1.3, 2.1, 6.5, 7.3, 12.7, 14.1, 16.5, 23.7, 26.3, 30.7, 38.3, 41.5, 43.3, 45.1, 46.2, 46.5, 50.3, 51.1, 56.7, 57.1, 57.5, 59.5, 61.1, 61.7, 66.7, 67.5, 67.8, 68.5.

erchistoli, see **erkistóll**.

erkistóll, m. *archbishopric*. ds. erchistoli, 65.4.

et, see **inn**.

eyðir, m. *destroyer, eliminator*: gs. eydis, 54.3.

Eysteinn, m. p.n. (Eysteinn Haraldsson gilla): ns. Eysteinn, 8.2, 71.6.

fæir, fæm, fæt, see **fár**.

fæum, see **fá**.

fá, red. 3. *get, receive*: pres. 1p. fæum, 69.5; pres. 3s. subj. fai, 67.5; pret. 3s. feck, 24.1, 26.1, 38.5, 41.7; md. (reflex.) pret. 3s. fekst, 32.7.

faðir, m. *father*: dsm. (contr.) faudr, 27.1.

fagna, I. *be glad, rejoice*: inf. let fagna, *caused to rejoice*, 29.4.

fagr, adj. *beautiful*: asm. fagran, 9.8, 15.5.

falla, red. 3 *fall*: pret. 3s. fell, 44.1, 52.6; pret. 3s. subj. felli, 14.5.

fann, see **finna**.

fár, adj. *few*: nsm. fær, 13.7; npm. fæir, 53.6; dpf. fæm, 37.8; asn. fætt, 67.1.

fara, 6. *go, fare; deal with, handle; forfeit, pay in punishment for a crime* (w. dat.): pres. 1s. fer, 8.4; ferr, 46.8; past perf. 3s. hafdi farit afskurdi, *had forfeited a cut-off piece (of his tongue)*, 26.4.

†**fárskerðandi**, m. *misfortune-diminisher*: ns. færskerdandi, 63.7.

fasti, m. *fire*: gs. fasta, 25.3.

faudr, see **faðir**.

faurnudr, see **fǫrnuðr**.

feck, fekst, see **fá**.

fella, III. *fell, cause to fall*: pret. 3p. felldu, 17.6.

fell, felli, see **falla**.

fer, ferr, see **fara**.

ferð, f. *band of retainers, men*: ds. ferd, 15.2; dp. ferdum, 38.4; as. ferd, 42.4.

fimm, num. *five*: fimm, 25.4.

fimr, adj. *accustomed; clever*: nsm. stiornar fimr, *accustomed to leadership, clever in leadership*, 15.6.

fimti, num. *fifth*: nsn. fimta, 55.5.

finna, 3. *find*: inf. megud finna, 51.6; pret. 1s. fánn, 10.5, pret. 3p. fundu, 56.4; md. (pass.) pres. 3s. (contr.) finnz, 51.3; md. (reflex.) pres. 3p. finnaz, 41.3; md. (pass.) perf. 3s. hefir fundiz, *has been found*, 44.8.

fiolda, see **fjǫlð**.

fiolgodr, see **fjǫlgóðr**.
fir, see **fyr**.
firar, m. (pl. only). *men*: np. firar, 49.6, 59.8; gp. fira, 12.8.
firra, III. *remove, withdraw*: pret. 3s. firdi, 62.7.
fiǫnndum, see **fjandi**.
fjandi, m. *enemy*: dp. fiǫnndum, 53.1.
fjarri, adv. *far*: fiarri, 48.8.
fjón, f. *hatred*: ns. fion, 59.3.
fjǫlði, m. (sg. only). *great quantity*: as. fiolda, 67.1.
fjǫlgóðr, adj. *very good*: nsm. fiolgodr, 24.4
flesta, flestra, see **margr**.
flótti, m. *flight*: ds. vard a flotta, *were in flight, were fleeing*, 29.7.
flugr, m. *flight*: ds. flug, 54.6.
flœðr, f. *sea, flood*: gs. flædar, 2.7
flœja, II. *flee*: pret. 3p. flędu, 52.8.
fold, f. *land*: gs. folldar, 28.3.
folk, n. *army*; *people*: ns. folk, 29.5.
†**folksterkr**, adj. *battle-strong*: gsm. folksterks, 26.6.
†**folkvaldr**, m. *ruler of men, army leader*: ns. folkualldr, 14.6.
fòrnudr, see **fǫrnuðr**.
fótr, m. *foot*: gs. fotar, 61.2; as. fot, 59.4.
frá, prep. w. dat. *from*: fra biartri stiornu flædar, 2.5; fra molldu, 4.5; fra
   haudri, 5.2; fra baulfi, 14.8; fra miclum navdum, 33.2; fra miklu angri, 63.1;
   fra þessum, 66.3; fra strangri kuol, 68.2.
fra (12.1, 17.1, 17.5), see **fregna**.
fram, adv. *forward*: fram, 53.8.
framan, adv. *forward, forth*: framan, 68.6.
framdi, see **fremja**.
frami, m. *urging onward, help to move on*; *praise, honour*: dp. frama, 66.4
   (*B*).
framla, adv. *excellently*: framla, 71.2.
framlyndr, adj. *forward-striving*: nsm. framlyndr, 42.3; dsm. framlyndum,
   28.4.
framr, adj. *brave, excellent*: npm. framir, 6.4; dsm. fromum, 30.4; asm.
   frama, 12.6.
fránn, adj. *sharp*: nsf. fran, 29.6.
fregna, 5. *learn by asking, hear*: pres. 1s. fregn, 51.5; pret. 1s. fra, 12.1, 17.1,
   17.5, 43.1; perf. 1s. hef fregit, 15.1; (contr.) hef frett, 38.1.
fremd, f. *accomplishment, fame*: gs. fremdar, 10.8, 25.3.
†**fremdarþjóð**, f. *valiant people*: as. fremdarþiod, 27.2.

fremja, II. *promote, further, advance*: pres. 3s. fremr, 45.1; pret. 3s. framdi, 20.8; md. (pass.) pres. 3s. fremz, 26.7.

frett, see **fregna**.

friðarsýn, f. *vision of peace*: ds. hæstri fridarsyn, *highest vision of peace*; *the heavenly Jerusalem*, 63.8.

†friðgegn, adj. *peaceful*: gsm. fridgegns, 67.2.

friðr, m. *peace*: as. frid, 58.6.

fróðr, adj. *wise*: nsm. frodr, 1.3.

fromum, see **framr**.

frægð, f. *fame*: ns. frægd, 26.5.

frægr, adj. *widely renowned*: nsm. frægr, 2.7; comp. nsm. frægri, 13.7.

frœkn, adj. *brave, sharp*: wk. nsm. frækni, 44.1.

fullhugaðr, adj. *very wise*: nsm. fullhugadr, 14.5.

fullting, n. *help*: gs. fulltings, 27.1.

fundiz, see **finna**.

fundr, m. *meeting, battle*: ns. fvndr, 32.4.

fundu, see **finna**.

fúss, adj. *eager*: nsm. fuss, 18.1.

fylgja, II. *follow, accompany*; *help* (w. dat.): pres. 3s. fylgir, 69.3; past fut. inf. letz myndu fylgia, *said that he would help*, 28.3.

fylkir, m. *leader*: gs. fylkis, 26.5, 44.2.

fylla, III. *fill*: pres. 3s. fyllir, 42.3; pp. gpm. angrs fylldra manna, *men filled with sin*, 58.1.

fyr (**fyrir**, **fir**), prep. (1) w. dat. *before, in front of, in the face of*: fir Inga, 8.5; fir gram, 16.8; fir nidranda, 40.1; fyrir hiorfue, 52.5; fir þiod, 57.2; fir kalldri ofund, 58.3; fir innan, *within, inside*, 14.7. (2) w. acc. *before in time*: fyrir betra, 3.2; fyrr var hitt, 19.5; endr fir, *a long time ago*, 40.5. (3) gjalda fyr (w. acc.) *pay for*: giallda fir hior, 50.2.

fyrðar, m. (pl. only). *men*: gp. fyrda, 3.7, 45.2, 59.3, 63,7; dp. fyrdum, 24.2.

fyrir, see **fyr**.

fyrnask, III (mid. only). *grow old, be forgotten*: me. (pass.) fut. 3s. (w. neg. suffix) munat fyrnaz, *will not be forgotten*, 24.3.

fæda, fædizst, fædaz, fæz, see **fœða**.

fœða, III. *give birth to*; *rear, bring up*: fut. 3s. (w. neg. suffix) mun fæda, *will not produce*, 14.3; md. (pass.) pres. 3s. fædizst, 11.7; md. (pass.) fut. 3s. (w. neg. suffix) munat fædaz, *will not be born*, 21.4; pass. perf. 3s. hefir fæz, 13.8.

fǫrnuðr, m. *prosperity, good fortune*: ns. faurnudr, 2.8; fôrnudr, 24.3.

gaf, see **gefa**.

gagn, n. *advantage, gain, victory in battle*: ds. gagne, 32.8.

galdr, m. *song*: ds. galldri, 43.2.

gamall, adj. *old*: comp. nsm. ellri, 70.8.

ganga, red. 3. *go*: inf. hugdiz vpp ganga, *thought he went up*, 16.3; pret. 3s. geck, 28.1; pret. 3s. subj. gingi, 55.4.

garðr, m. *yard*, *courtyard*, *garden*, *etc.*: gs. gardz, 50.7.

gat, see **geta**.

gaufug, **gaufugr**, see **gǫfugr**.

gaull, see **gǫll**.

geck, see **ganga**.

gefa, 5. *give*: pres. 3s. gefr, 38.3; pret. 3s. gaf, 30.1, 34.8, 43.4, 45.1, 46.2.

geirr, m. *spear*: gp. geira, 52.3.

geisli, m. *ray*, *beam*: ns. geisli, 1.5; as. geisla, 7.1.

gera, IV. *make*, *do*, *prepare*: pres. 3s. gerir, 66.8; inf. let gerfa, 34.3; md. (pass.) pres. 3s. illr geriz hugr, 58.2; md. (pass.) pret. 3p. gerdiz iarteignir miklar, 20.1; gerdiz vetþryma nadri, 47.1; pass. fut. 3p. (w. *vera* understood) ger munu giolld, *punishments will be prepared*, 61.7.

gerfa, see **gera**.

gervir, m. *maker*: gs. geruis, 65.5.

geta, 5. *get*; *understand*, *perceive*: pres. 3s. getr, 1.3; pret. 3s. gat hann rett, *he understood well*, 31.2; gat sed, *got seen*, *saw*, 48.5.

giafar, **giafir**, see **gjǫf**.

gildr, adj. *valid*, *excellent*, *first-rate*: asf. gillda, 10.1.

gína, 1. *yawn*, *gape*: pret. 3p. gindu, 29.8.

gingi, see **ganga**.

giolld, see **gjald**.

giorfallra, see **gjǫrvallr**.

gipta, f. *luck*, *gift*, *endowment*: gs. giptu, 57.5.

Girkland, n. p.n. (Greece): ds. Girklandi, 51.2.

girkr (grikr), m. p.n. (*a Greek*): np. Grikkir, 52.8; gp. Girkia, 44.7.

gjald, n. *payment*, *punishment*, *penalty*: np. giolld, 61.7.

gjalda, 3. *pay*: inf. giallda fir, *pay for*, 50.2.

gjalfr, n. *noise*: gs. gialfrs, 40.3.

gjǫf, f. *gift*: ap. giafir, 6.2; giafar, 64.4.

gjǫrvallr, adj. *all*: gpn. giorfallra, 61.6.

gladdir, see **gleðja**.

glaðr, adj. *happy*: nsm. gladr, 47.4.

†**glaumkennandi**, m. *noise-experiencer*: ns. glaumkennandi, 47.3.

gleði, f. *joy*: ns. gledi, 63.8.

gleðja, II. *gladden*: pres. 3s. gledr, 22.3; pp. npm. gladdir, 56.1.

gnótt, f. *enough*, *plenty*, *abundance*: as. gnott, 28.8.

gnýr, m. *noise, din*: ds. gny, 54.4.

góði, m. *good thing*; *goodwill, friendship*: as. goda, 1.3.

góðr, adj. *good*: wk. nsm. godi, 29.2; wk. gsm. goda, 27.2; gsn. gods, 28.7; comp. nsm. betri, 21.3; comp. dsn. betra, 3.2; comp. asm. betra, 14.4; sup. nsm. bezstr, 5.3.

gofgann, gofugs, gofugt, see **gǫfugr**.

gómsparri, m. *gum-pole, gum-spar*: as. gomsparra, 48.8.

gramr, m. *king*: ns. gramr, 13.7, 15.8, 20.3, 70.5; gs. grams, 34.4; ds. gram, 16.8, 18.8, 21.8, 24.8, 27.8, 28.4, 30.8, 33.8, 36.8, 39.8, 42.8, 44.4, 45.8, 57.8; as. gram, 12.4, 17.6, 61.2 [as a *heiti* for *man*].

grand, n. *harm*: as. grand, 50.8.

gránn, adj. *grey*: dsn. granu, 35.7.

greiða, III. *bring into words*: pp. nsm. bragr verdr greiddur, *poetry is made*, 40.4.

greiðr, adj. *ready, free, easy*: nsn. (used adverbially) greitt, 18.5, 21.5, 24.5, 27.5, 30.5, 33.5, 36.5, 39.5, 42.5, 45.5.

greri, see **gróa**.

grikkir, see **girkr**.

gríma, f. *night*: np. grimur, 49.1.

grimmliga, adv. *horribly*: grimliga, 40.8.

grimr, adj. *grim*: nsm. grimr, 70.8.

grjón, n. *grain, meal*: ns. grion, 35.7.

grjót, n. *stone*: ds. grioti, 35.8.

gróa, red. 5. *grow, increase*: pret. 3s. or pres. 3s. subj. greri, 59.3.

grof, see **grǫf**.

grund, f. *land, earth*: gs. grundar, 19.3, 31.1, 32.4, 40.3, 44.2; ds. grundu, 48.7.

grœðari, m. *healer*: ns. grædari, 21.4.

grǫf, f. *grave*: as. grof, 22.8.

Guð, m. *God*: ns. Gud, 20.8, 63.3; gs. Guds, 1.4, 7.2, 18.6, 21.6, 24.6, 27.6, 30.6, 33.6, 36.6, 39.6, 42.6, 45.6, 57.5, 61.8, 69.8; ds. Gudi, 6.6, 13.4, 22.6; as. Gud, 14.2, 31.4.

gull, n. *gold*: ds. gulli, 34.2, 44.7, 50.7.

gumi, m. *man*: np. gumnar, 56.1; dp. gumnum, 18.5, 21.5, 24.5, 27.5, 30.5, 33.5, 36.5, 39.5, 42.5, 45.1, 45.5.

gunndjarfr, adj. *battle-eager*: gsm. gunndiárfs, 44.8.

gunnr, f. *battle*: gs. gunnar, 43.6, 47.3, 52,3; gp. gunna, 13.2.

gunnstyrkr, adj. *battle-strong*: gsm. gunnstyrks, 57.6.

†**gunnǫflugr**, adj. *battle-strong*: nsm. gunnoflugr, 1.6.

Gutthormr, m. p.n. (Guthormr Gunnhildarson): ns. Gutthormr, 31.1; Guthorm, 34.3.

gylðir, m. *wolf*: ns. gyldir, 28.7; gs. gylldis, 48.7.

gæta, III. *watch over, tend, care for*: pres. 3s. gætir, 16.5.

gœðir, m. *strengthener, increaser, improver, ornamenter*: dp. gædum, 69.7.

gœzka, f. *goodness, strength, virtue*: ds. gæzsku, 13.8.

gǫfugr, adj. *stately, solemn*; *splendid, magnificent*; *noble*: nsm. gaufugr, 56.2; nsf. gaufug, 37.1, 45.2; gsm. gofugs, 69.7; asm. gofgann, 7.1; asn. gofugt, 1.5.

gǫll, f. *noise*: ds. gaull, 52.4.

hæleitri, see **háleitr**.

hadiz, see **heyja**.

hafa, IV. (1) *have*; *wield, influence*: pres. 3s. hefir mikla, *influences much, has much influence over many events*, 67.6; pres. 3p. hafa, 34.5; pret. 3s. hafdi, 32.1. (2) used as aux.: pres. 1s. hef fregit, 15.1; hef frett, 38.1; hef stodat, 71.1; pres. 1p. hofum skyrda, 66.2; hofum sagdar, 69.1; hafum vnnit, 71.3; pres. 3s. hefir spurt, 12.3; hefir fæz, 13.7; hefir leysta, 33.1; hefir verit halldin, 36.1; hefir fundiz, 44.5; hefir brugdit, 58.5; pres. 3p. hafa lystann, 12.5; hafa sagt, 35.1; pret. 2s. hafdi farit, 26.4; pret. 3p. hofdu þuegit, 23.4.

hafa (44.5), see **hár**.

hagliga, adv. *easily, comfortably*, 16.1.

hagnaðr, m. *luck, advantage*: ns. hagnadr, 32.8.

hála, adv. *to a high degree, highly*: hæla, 47.1.

halda, red. 3. *hold, keep*: pass. perf. 3s. hefir verit halldin, *has been observed*, 36.1.

†**haldframr**, adj. *excellently strong*: dsm. halldfromum, 57.7.

háleitr, adj. *high-looking, sublime, lofty*: dsf. hæleitri, 13.8.

halfr, adj. *half*: nsn. hælft, 55.5.

hall (**hǫll**), f. *hall*: gs. hallar, 5.4, 7.2; ds. hall, 11.4.

Hamðir, m. p.n. (*mythological hero*): gs. Hamdis, 52.7.

hamla, I. *mangle*: pp. nsm. hamladr, 60.8.

hann, pron. m. *he, etc.*: ns. hann, 11.3, 14.7, 18.2, 31.2, 32.5, 38.5; np. þeir, 12.5; gs. hans, 15.7, 22.4, 22.8, 64.2; ds. hænum, 4.8; honum, 32.6; hanum, 69.5; as. hann, 7.5, 66.8.

†**happmætr**, adj. *blessing-rich*: dsn. (w. tmesis) happ-mættu, 19.7.

happsdǫð, f. *blessed deed, miracle*: ap. hapsdædir, 69.4.

hapsdædir, see **happsdǫð**.

hár, adj. *high, in a high degree*: nsm. harr, 32.7; gsm. hæars, 42.1; hars, 66.3; wk. gsm. hafá, 44.5; gsf. harar, 57.7; gsn. hæas, 71.7; asn. hætt, 38.6; sup. nsm. hæstr, 6.7; sup. wk. gsm. hæsta, 67.7; sup. dsm. hæstum, 4.3; sup. dsf. hæstri, 11.3, 63.5.

Haraldr, m. p.n.: gs. Haralldz, (Haraldr Sigurðarson) 49.2; (Haraldr in gren-ski Guðrøðarson) 51.4.

harða, adv. *very*; *greatly*: harda, 53.6.

harðgeðr, adj. *hard-minded*: nsm. hardgedr, 28.6.

harðr, adj. *hard*: nsm. hardr, 32.4; nsf. hord, 59.3; nsn. (used adverbially) hart, 54.1; apm. harda, 55.3.

†**harmskerðandi**, m. *harm-diminisher*: gs. harmskerdanda, 38.4.

harri, m. *prince, king*: gs. harra, 19.5; gp. harra, 25.7.

hátíð, f. *feast day*: ns. hætid, 36.2.

hauðr, n. *earth, ground*: ds. haudri, 5.2.

†**hauðrtjald**, n. *earth-roof, heaven*: gp. haudrtiallda, 19.6.

haulldum, see **hǫlðr**.

Haurda, see **Hǫrðar**.

heðan, adv. *hence, from here*: hedann, 63.1.

hef, **hefir**, see **hafa**.

hefja, 6. *lift up*; *begin (recitation of a poem)*: pres. 1p. hefium, 9.5.

†**heiðbjartr**, adj. *heaven-bright*: nsm. heidbiartr, 67.8.

heiðingi, m. *heathen*: gp. heidingia, 55.4.

heiðinn, adj. *heathen*: apf. heidnar, 28.8.

heiðr, f. *heath*: gp. heida, 7.5.

heilagr, adj. *holy*: nsm. heilagr, 9.8, 41.8, 65.6; gsm. heilags, 3.1; wk. gsm. helga, 69.3; dsm. helgum, 12.7; asm. helgann, 42.1.

heili, m. *brain*: gs. heila, 59.7.

heill, adj. *healthy, whole*: asm. vann heilann, *healed*, 61.5.

heilsa, f. *health*: as. heilsu, 41.7.

heimr, m. *world*; *land*; *abode*: gs. heims, 2.1, 2.2, 16.8, 17.5, 39.4, 42.2, 57.8, 65.1; ds. heimi, 2.1; as. heim, 38.3.

heimta, III. *bring home*: pp. asm. vann heimtann, *took home*, 55.5.

heipt, f. *hatred*: gs. heiptar, 32.3, 58.7.

heita, red. 1. *name, call*; *be named*: pres. 3s. heitir, 7.3; (impers.) 37.7; pret. 3s. heti, 43.1; pret. 3p. hetu, 12.7, 54.1.

heitfastr, adj. *promise-keeping*: nsm. heitfastr, 64.6.

heldr, adv. *more, rather*: helldr, 47.2.

helgann, **helgum**, see **heilagr**.

hendr, see **hǫnd**.

hér, adv. *here*: her, 34.3, 38.5, 65.5.

herða, III. *make hard, harden*: pp. dsm. herdum, 47.1.

hermð, f. *anger, indignation*: gs. hermdar, 58.7.

heti, **hetu**, see **heita**.

heyja, II. *hold a battle or meeting*: md. (pass.) pret. 3s. hadiz, 52.1.

heyra, III. *hear, listen*: sg. imp. heyr, 8.1; inf. megu heyra, 22.7.

hialp, see **hjǫlp**.

hialpa, see **hjalpa**.

hildingr, m. *warrior*: gs. hilldings, 36.1.

hildr, f. *battle*: gs. hilldar, 70.6.

hilmir, m. *prince*: ns. hilmir, 41.7; gs. hilmis, 67.7.

himinn, m. *heaven*: gp. himna, 15.6, 63.6, 65.6, 66.6; ds. himni, 47.8.

himinríki, n. *heavenly kingdom*: as. himinriki, 16.6.

himintungl, n. *heavenly body, star*: gp. himintunglá, 46.6; ap. himintungl, 59.8.

†himinvist, f. *hospitality in heaven*: gs. himinvistar, 6.8.

himneskr, adj. *heavenly*: asf. himneska, 42.4.

hingat, adv. *hither*: hingat, 65.1.

hins, **hit**, see **inn**.

hiorr, see **hjǫrr**.

hirð, f. *band of retainers*: ns. hird, 5.7.

hjaldr, m. *din, battle*: ns. hialldr, 52.1; gs. hialldrs, 43.2; ds. hialldri, 32.3.

†hjaldrstríðr, adj. *battle-strong, battle-hard*: nsf. hialldrstrid, 58.8.

†hjalmnjǫrðungar, m. (pl. only). *helmet-men, warriors*: dp. hialmniordungum, 55.3.

hjalmskœðr, adj. *dangerous to helmets*: dsm. hialmskęd, 52.8.

hjalpa, 3. *help*: sg. imp. hialp, 69.7.

hjǫlp, f. *help*: as. hialp, 38.3.

hjǫrr, m. *sword*: ns. hiorr, 43.4, 44.5; ds. hiorfue, 52.5; as. hior, 50.2.

Hlíð, f. p.n. *gateway, wide gap*: ns. Hlid, 37.8.

hlutr, m. *part*: dp. lid minna þrimr lvtum, *an army fewer by three parts, three times smaller*, 32.2.

hlýra, f. *ship's bow (?)*: gs. hlyru, 26.3.

hlýða, III. *obey, listen to* (w. dat.): pres. 3s. hlydir, 6.6; inf. byd hlyda, 9.4; skulu hlyda, 11.2.

Hlýrskógsheiðr, f. p.n.: ds. Hlyrskogsheidi, 28.5.

Hneitir, m. p.n. '*Stinger*' (Olaf's sword): nsm. Hneitir, 43.1.

hníga, 1. *bow down*: pres. 3s. hnigr, 5.6.

hodd, f. *treasure, gold*: gp. hodda, 37.7.

hofdu, see **hafa**.

hofdi, **hofud**, see **hǫfuð**.

hofudskæld, see **hǫfuðskald**.

holda, see **hǫlðr**.

hollr, adj. *friendly; true, constant*: nsm. hollr, 34.2; asm. hollann, 66.7; apn. holl, 69.5.

hond, see **hǫnd**.

Horda, see **Hǫrðar**.

horn, see **hǫrn**.

hoskr, adj. *wise*: nsm. hoskr, 64.1.

hraustr, adj. *vigorous, strong*: nsm. hraustr, 63.5; npm. hraustir, 52.4.

†**hreggsalr**, m. *storm-hall*: gs. hreggsalar, 64.5.

hreinn, adj. *pure*: gsm. hreins, 61.6; dsn. hreinu, 22.3, 24.1.

hresiks, see **hræsiks**.

hríð, f. *storm*: ns. hrid, 52.7.

†**hríðblásinn**, adj. *storm-blown*: dsm. hridblæsnum, 7.6.

hringr, m. *ring*: gs. hrings, 22.7, 44.6; ap. ringa, 46.2.

hrockviseids, see **hrøkkviseiðr**.

hróðr, m. *fame*; *praise*; *poem*: ns. hrodr, 34.4.

hrósa, I. *praise* (w. da.): pres. 1s. hrosa, 30.3; inf. hrosa, 15.7.

hryggr, adj. *sorrowful*: gsm. hryggs, 53.3.

hræ, n. *corpse*: as. hræ, 56.4; ap. hræ, 29.8.

hræða, III. *frighten*: pp. nsn. hrætt, 29.5.

hrærda, see **hrœra**.

hræsíkr, m. *corpse-salmon, sword*: gs. hresiks, 69.6.

†**hrøkkviseiðr**, m. *coiling fish*: gs. hrockviseids, 16.2.

hrœra, III. *set in motion*: pp. asf. lætr dyrd hrærda, *causes (his) fame to have been disseminated*, 21.2.

hugdiz, see **hyggja**.

Huginn, m. p.n. (Odin's raven): gs. Hugins, 13.2, 29.4, 41.6.

hugr, m. *mind*: ns. hugr, 58.2, 69.3; as. hug, 22.3.

hulidr, see **hylja**.

hungr, m. *hunger*: as. hunngr, 52.2.

hvárr, pron. *which of two*: dsn. at hvorv, *nevertheless, all the same*, 32.5.

hvass, adj. *sharp, brave, keen*: npm. huatir, 27.4; gsm. hvass, 66.3 (*B*); asm. huassann, 17.5.

hvat, pron. *what; how, in what way*: nsn. (used adverbially) hvat, 31.3.

hvatr, adj. *hasty, rash, quick*: npm. huatir, 17.6, 27.4.

hvé, adv. *how, why*: hue, 8.4, 71.6.

†**hverlofaðr**, adj. *praised by all*: nsm. huerlofadr, 16.1.

hverr, m. *kettle, cauldron*: gs. huers, 70.2.

hverr, pron. *each; who*: nsm. huer, 64.1; huerr, 66.7, 67.5; nsn. huert a annat, *one after another*, 46.8.

hvíla, III. *rest, repose*: pres. 3s. huilir, 9.7, 26.1.

hvítingr, m. *drinking-horn*: gs. huitings, 37.2.

hvoru, see **hvárr**.

hingat, adv. *here, to this place*: hingat, 65.1.

hyggja, II. *think, consider, believe; intend, purpose*: pres. 1s. hygg, 9.6; pres. 1p. hyggium, 64.5; pres. 3s. subj. hyggi, 62.4; sg. imp. hygg, 8.3, 65.1; md. (reflex.) pret. 3s. hugdiz, 16.1.

hylja, II. *hide, cover*: pass. pret. 3s. var hulidr, 25.2.

hyrr, m. *fire*: gs. hyriar, 64.1.

hæð, f. *height; value*: ns. hæd, 9.7.

hæstr, hæstri, hæstum, see **hár**.

hættr, adj. *dangerous, unlawful*: nsn. hætt, 59.7.

hǫfuð, n. *head*: np. hofud, 8.8; ds. hofdi, 37.1, 59.6.

hǫfuðskald, n. *head-skald, principal skald*: ap. hofud-skælld, 12.8.

hǫfuðsmaðr, m. *'head man,' chieftain, ruler*: np. 65.2

hǫlðr, hauldr, m. *man*: gs. holda, 4.6; dp. haulldum, 6.7.

hǫnd, f. *hand*: ns. hond, 61.5; ap. hendr, 9.5.

Hǫrðar, m. (pl. only). p.n. (inhabitants of Hordaland): gp. Haurda, 15.8; Horda, 21.1, 39.3.

Hǫrn, f. p.n. a name for a troll-wife, or possibly for Freyja (*heiti for* woman): ns. Horn, 37.1.

i, prep. (1) w. dat. *in, within*: i heimi, 2.1; i einu ranni, 10.7; i hæstri hall, 11.3; i þessum, 11.6; i riki, 11.8; i dyn skiallda, 14.6; i brunni, 23.6; i stridum, 30.6; j svnde, 31.7; i kirkiu, 34.7; i lidi, 44.7; j geira gaull, 52.3; j bardraugns raduls vedre, 53.7; i gny stæla, 54.4; i orfa flug, 54.5; i nyium odi, 57.3; i sande, 59.1; i lifi þessu, 64.3. (2) w. acc. *in, into*: i lopt, 16.3; i grof, 22.8; i drauma, 28.2; i brag, 45.4; j byr brannda, 53.5; i sundr, 59.1; i stad, 65.2; i fiolda, 67.1.

iardar, see **jǫrð**.

íðvandr, adj. *carefully acting*: nsm. iduandr, 4.2.

iflauss, adj. *doubtless*: nsn. (used adverbially) ifláust, 4.7, 71.3.

ilbleikr, adj. *pale-footed*: dsm. ilbleikum, 43.4.

illr, adj. *wicked*: nsm. illr, 58.2.

Ingi, m. p.n. (Ingi Haraldsson gilla): ds. Ingá, 8.5.

ingi, m. *king*: gs. jnga, 49.6.

inn, def. art. *the*: nsm. enn, 29.2, 33.1, 44.1, 70.8; nsn. hitt, 19.5; gsm. hins, 1.2, 16.2; ens, 27.2, 44.5, 67.7, 69.3, 70.1; asn. it, 8.6; et, 41.1.

inna, III. *tell, report; do, perform*: pres. 1s. inni, 7.7; inf. nennir at inna, 56.5; pres. part. npm. innenndr ognar, *doers of battle*, 51.6.

Innþrœndir, m. (pl. only). p.n. (*inhabitants of Trondheim*): dp. innþrændum, 17.3.

iordu, see **jǫrð**.

ítr, adj. *excellent, glorious, bright*: nsm. itr, 7.3, 21.3; gsm. itrs, 47.7; dsm. itrum, 1.7, 66.5; asm. itran, 54.1, 61.3.
ítrgeðr, adj. *high-minded*: gsm. itrgeds, 10.4.

jafnan, adv. *immediately*: iafnan, 68.4.
jarðríki, n. *earthly kingdom*: as. iardriki, 62.8.
†**jarplitr**, adj. *brown-coloured*: asm. (used substantively) iarplidan, 29.1.
jarteign, f. *miracle*: np. iarteignir, 20.4; gp. iarteigna, 34.6; dp. iarteignum, 7.8; iartegnum, 67.2; ap. iárteignir, 49.8.
jóð, n. *child, offspring*: gs. iods, 29.2.
Jón, m. p.n. (Jón Birgisson): as. Jon, 9.3.
jǫfurr, m. *prince*: ns. iofurr, 26.2; jofur, 31.6; iofur, 64.6; gs. iofurs, 23.4, 66.2; (contr.) iofrs, 26.7; gp. iofra, 5.3, 50.5; ds. iofri, 12.8, 69.1, 71.3; as. iofur, 45.2.
jǫrð, f. *earth*: np. iardir, 53.2; gs. iardar, 3.7, 50.1; ds. iordu, 15.8.

kaldr, adj. *cold, disagreeable, hostile*: dsf. kalldri, 58.4.
kalla, I. *call*: pres. 1p. kollum, 9.3; md. (reflex.) pret. 3s. kalladizst, 2.4.
kann, see **kunna**.
kemr, see **koma**.
kenna, III. *teach*: inf. ma kenna, 1.4.
kennir, m. *prover, tester*: ns. kennir, 29.3.
kind, f. *race, kind, family*: gs. kindar, 48.7.
kirkja, f. *church*: ds. i kirkiu midri, *in the middle of the church*, 34.7.
kista, f. *box, coffin*: as. kistu, 25.6.
klauf, see **kljúfa**.
kljúfa, 2. *cleave*: pret. 3s. klauf, 43.5.
klofna, I. *be cloven*: pret. 3p. klofnudu, 54.7.
klæði, n. *clothing*: gp. klęda, 52.7.
knífr, m. *knife*: ds. knifi, 60.4.
kollum, see **kalla**.
koma, 4. *come*; *bring* (w. dat.): pres. 3s. kemr, 46.7; pres. 3p. koma, 67.3; inf. lætr koma, 25.8; pret. 3s. kom, 23.1; pret. 3p. kuomu, 65.1.
konungr, m. *king*: ns. konungr, 5.8, 8.2, 9.8, 15.4, 18.2, 28.6, 33.4; gs. konungs, 12.2, 24.4, 34.8, 66.6; as. konung, 51.8.
kraptr, m. *strength*: ns. kraptr, 58.7; ds. krapti, 4.3; as. krapt, 57.5.
krefja, II. *demand* (w. gen.): pp. apn. krofd 59.6 [?].
Kristni, f. *Christianity, Christendom*: ns. kristni, 6.8.
Kristr, m. p.n.: ns. Cristr, 4.3; gs. Kristz, 11.3; Cristz, 34.7, 68.7; as. Krist, 33.3.

krofd, see **krefja**.
kross, m. *cross*: ds. krossi, 3.6.
krǫf, f. *demand*, 59.6 [?].
kundr, m. *descendant*: ns. kundr, 44.2.
kunna, pret. pres. 3. *know*: pres. 1s. kann, 70.3; pres. 1p. kunnum, 71.4.
kunnr, adj. *known, renowned*: nsm. kunnr, 4.4; npm. kunnir, 35.2; gsm. kunnz, 23.6.
kuol, see **kvǫl**.
kveðja, II. *address, summon*: inf. samir kuedia, 10.4.
kveld, n. *evening*: ds. kuelldi, 47.2.
kverk, f. *throat*: dp. kuerkum, 40.6.
kvæði, n. *poem*: ds. kvædi, 38.6.
kvǫl, f. *torment*: ds. kuol, 68.2.
kyn, n. *race, kind, family*: ds. kyni, 69.2; as. kyn, 20.2.
kynna, III. *make known*: md. (reflex.) prex. 3p. kynazst, *become acquainted with, study*, 6.3.
kærr, adj. *dear*: asm. kærann, 22.6.

læa, see **liggja**.
láð, n. *land*: ds. lædi, 14.2, 25.8, 27.3.
lagar, see **lǫgr**.
laminn, adj. *lame*: gsm. lamins, 61.2.
land, n. *land, country*: gp. landa, 23.8.
landreki, m. *king, prince*: gs. landreka, 47.7.
landsfolk, n. *lands people, inhabitants*: ns. landzfolk, 66.5; as. 16.5.
langvinr, m. *long-time friend*: ns. langvinr, 62.7, 68.2.
láta, red. 4. *let, allow, cause* (w. inf.): pres. 3s. lætr dyrd hrærda, *causes (his) fame to be dissemminated*, 21.1; lætr koma, 25.7; lætr verdan, *causes to be worthy*, 42.1; lætr aund, *gives up the ghost*, 60.6; pret. 3s. leet berazst, 2.5; leit opnaz, 16.5; leetdreyra, 17.3; let fagna, 29.1; let gerfa, 34.3; let prydazt, 31.5; let giallda, 50.1; let standa, 50.5; let niota, 61.1; md. (reflex.) pret. 3s. letz myndu fylgia, *said that he would help*, 28.3.
látr, n. *lair*: gs. lætrs, 16.4.
lauk, see **lúka**.
laun, n. (pl. only). *payment, reward*: ap. laun, 69.5.
launa, I. *reward*: past fut. 3s. subj. mundi vera launadr, *would be rewarded*, 70.4.
lausnari, m. *saviour*: gs. lausnára, 30.2, 62.5, 68.1.
léa, IV. *lend, give* (w. gen.): pres. 3s. let, 57.7.
leet, **let**, see **láta**.

leggja, II. *lay, place*: inf. vard at leggia a flotta, *took flight, fled*, 29.6; pret. 3p. logdu, 22.8.

leikmildr, adj. *eager for play*: nsm. leikmilldr, 70.6.

leit, see **láta**.

leita, I. *look for, search for*: inf. tok leita, *went to look for*, 35.6.

lestir, m. *breaker*: ns. lestir, 32.1.

letz, see **láta**.

létta, III. *relieve, alleviate*: inf. mæa letta, 18.5, 21.5, 24.5, 27.5, 30.5, 33.5, 36.5, 39.5, 42.5, 45.5.

leyfa, III. *praise*: inf. hygg leyfá, 9.5; pass. pres. 3s. er leyfdr, 61.1.

leyna, III. *hide, conceal* (w. dat. of the thing; acc. of the person): pret. 3s. leyndi, 13.5.

leysa, III. *release, free; dissolve, loosen; solve; fulfil; determine, decide*: pres. 3s. subj. leysi, 62.5, 68.1; pret. 1s. leysta, 71.6; pret. 3p. leystu, 59.5; perf. 3s. hefir leysta, 33.3.

lið, n. *men, army*: ns. lid, 53.3, 55.4; gs. lids, 62.6; ds. lidi, 44.8; as. lid, 32.1, 46.5.

†**liðgegn**, adj. *fair with men*: nsm. lidgegn, 13.6.

líf, n. *life*: ns. lif, 3.6; ds. lifi, 17.8, 64.3.

lifa, IV. *live*: pres. 3s. lifir, 11.3, 63.5; pret. 3s. subj. lifdi, 70.5.

liggja, 5. *lie*: inf. gat sed liggia, *saw it lie, saw it lying*, 48.6; pret. 3s. læa, 60.5; past fut. 3s. subj. munndi liggia, *would lie*, 53.3.

líka, III. *please* (impers.): pres. 3s. likar, 69.6.

líki, n. *body*: ds. liki, 20.5, 22.2.

líkn, f. *mercy*: gs. liknar, 59.6.

†**líknframr**, adj. *outstandingly merciful*: nsm. liknframr, 16.6.

limr, m. *limb*: ds. lim, 66.6.

linnr, m. *snake*: gs. linnz, 32.2.

linr, adj. *gentil, mild, merciful*: asm. linan, 33.3.

líta, 1. *see*: inf. megu lita, 64.7.

lítill, adj. *little, small*: asf. litla, 37.2; comp. apf. minni, 60.7, comp. asn. minna, 32.2.

†**litrauðr**, adj. *red-coloured*: gsn. litravŏs, 33.4.

ljós, n. *light*: ns. lios, 20.5; ds. liosi, 3.4; as. lios, 1.5, 2.3.

ljóss, adj. *bright, shining, clear, evident*: nsf. lios, 46.7; gsm. lioss, 64.3.

ljósta, 2. *strike, smite*: pret. 3p. lustu, 59.1.

lof, n. *praise*: gs. lofs, 69.8; ds. lofi, 10.4, 57.6; as. lof, 67.8.

lofa, I. *praise*: pp. nsm. lofadr, 5.5.

lofðar, m. (pl. only). *men*: gp. lofda, 70.5.

lofðungr, m. *prince*: ns. lofdungr, 13.5; gs. lofdungs, 46.6, 64.4.

log, see lǫg.
logdu, see leggja.
logskids, see lǫgskíð.
lokin, see lúka.
lopt, n. *air*, *sky*, *upper region*: as. lopt, 16.3.
lúka, 2. *close*; *enclose*: pret. 3s. lauk, 19.2; pass. pret. 3s. var lokin, 60.2.
lustu, see ljósta.
lúta, 2. *bow down*, *do homage*: pres. 1s. lyt, 12.7; pres. 3s. subj. luti, 66.5.
lvtum, see hlutr.
lygi, f. *lie*, *falsehood*: ns. lygi, 58.5.
lyng, n. *heather*: gs. lyngs, 16.3.
lýsa, III. *illuminate*; *become light*; *explain*; *proclaim*: pres. 1s. (w. suffixed pron.) lysek, 70.7; pret. 3s. (impers.) lysti, 48.1; perf. 3p. hafa lystánn, *have proclaimed*, 12.6.
lysta, III. *like*, *desire* (impers. w. gen.): pp. nsm. fremdar lystr, *desirous of fame*, 25.3.
lyt, see lúta.
lækna, I. *heal*: pres. 3s. læknar, 46.5.
læknir, m. *healer*: gs. læknis, 57.8.
læra, III. *learn*, *teach*: pp. gpm. lærdra, 92.
lætr, see láta.
lǫg, n. (pl. only). *law*, *laws*: ap. log, 59.5.
lǫgr, m. *sea*, *water*: gs. lagar, 53.4.
lǫgskíð, n. *sea-ski*, *ship*: gs. logskids, 20.6.

ma, mæa, see mega.
mænudr, see mánuðr.
maar, mæas, see már.
maðr, m. *man*, *human being*, : ns. madr, 2.6, 26.1, 44.4, 48.1, 60.6; np. menn, 7.7, 34.5, 35.1, 54.2; gs. mannz, 37.4; gp. manna, 10.8, 54.8, 58.3, 66.8; dp. monnum, 6.3, 51.3.
magn, n. *strength*, *might*: as. (w. suffixed art.) magnit, 8.6.
Magnús, m. p.n. (Magnus the Good): ns. Magnus, 29.4; gs. Magnus, 27.4.
mál, n. *speech*, *saying*, *report*; *matter*, *undertaking*; *measure*; *ornament*: ns. 51.3; np. mæl, 6.3, 59.7; gs. mæls, 41.7; ds. numin mæli, *bereaved of speech*, 37.6; as. mæl, 7.7, 26.1; mal, 38.8.
malmr, m. *weapon*: gp. mælma, 38.2.
malmþing, n. *weapon-meeting*, *battle*: gs. mælmþings, 29.3.
†máltól, n. *speech-tool*: np. mæltol, 19.8.
manna, mannz, see maðr.

manndýrð, f. *man-ornament, that which brings a man honour*: ap. manndyrdir, 18.4.

mánuðr, m. *month*: ap. mænudr, 25.1.

már, m. *gull*: ns. mær, 52.3; gs. mæs, 50.1.

margfaldr, adj. *many-sided, false*: nsm. margfalldr hugr, 58.4.

margfríðr, adj. *very beautiful*: nsm. margfridr, 26.2.

†**marglitendr**, m. (pl. only). *frequent-colourers, frequent-stainers*: np. marglitendr, 59.2.

margr, adj. *many*: nsm. margr madr, *many a man*, 60.7; nsn. (used substantively) mart, 27.3; apf. margar, 13.1; sup. gpm. flestra, 18.2; sup. apm. flesta vini sina, *most of his friends*, 63.2; sup. asf. flesta, 39.4.

†**margþarfr**, adj. *very useful*: nsm. margþarfr, 51.4.

mark, n. *mark, sign*: ns. mark, 34.7.

mart, see **margr**.

máttigr, adj. *mighty*: npn. mætig, 8.8; gsm. mattigs, 6.4.

máttr, m. *might, strength*: gs. mættar, 15.3.

með, prep. w. dat. *with*: med, 4.3, 4.8, 5.1, 20.7, 22.3, 31.5, 59.3, 60.1, 62.3.

meðan, adv. *while*: medan, 2.3.

mega, pret. pres. 5 (aux. only). *may*: pres. 2p. megud finna, 51.6; pres. 3s. ma kenna, 1.1; ma efla, 4.7; mæ letta, 18.5, 21.5, 24.5, 27.5, 30.5, 33.5, 36.5, 39.5, 42.5, 45.5; pres. 3p. megu heyra, 22.7; megu lita, 64.7; pres. 3s. subj. megi segia, 64.2; pret. 1s. subj. mætta stef vanda, 18.3.

†**meginfjǫlði**, m. *a great assembly of men*: ns. megin fioldi, 4.6.

meiða, III. *mutilate*: pret. 3p. meiddu, 40.4.

mein, n. *wrongdoing, injury*: gp. meina, 61.6; ap. mein, 13.4.

mensamliga, adv. *harmfully, dangerously*: meinsamliga, 60.8.

meir, adv. *more; still*: meirr, 34.6.

menn, see **maðr**.

mer, see **ek**.

merkja, II. *mark, notice*: inf. naudr at merkia, *need to notice*, 57.2; pp. nsm. merktr, 44.7.

messa, f. *mass, feast day*: as. messo, 35.3.

mest, mestr, see **mikill**.

miclum, see **mikill**.

miðr, adj. *middle*: dsf. i kirkiu midri, *in the middle of the church*, 34.8.

mikill, adj. *much, great*: npm. (used substantively) mikla, 67.6; npf. miklar, 20.4; dpt. miclum, 33.2; dsn. miklu, 63.4; asf. mykly, 8.7; sup. nsm. mestr, 18.2; sup. nsf. mest, 39.4; sup. nsn. mest, 53.1; allz mest, *as a rule, usually*, 63.2.

miklagarðr, m. p.n. (ON name for Constantinople): ns. Miklagarðr, 53.2.

mildi, f. *generosity, mercy, grace*: gs. milldi, 66.1.

mildingr, m. *generous man, king*: gs. milldings, 39.3, 46.2, 58.3.

mildr, adj. *generous, merciful, kind*; *generous with* (w. gen.): nsm. milldr, 4.5, 5.2, 32.3; wk. nsm. milldi, 33.1.

minn, poss. pron. *my, our*: asn. min, 7.8; dpm. orum, 67.3; apf. ossa, 4.8.

minni, n. *memory*: dp. minnum, 34.5.

minna, **minnni**, see **lítill**.

miskunn, f. *mercy*: gs. miskunar, 1.6.

missa, III. *miss, lose* (w. gen.): pret. 3s. misti, 48.1.

†moðirhlýri, m. *maternal uncle*: ns. (w. tmesis) moðirhlyre, 32.6–7.

móðr, adj. *brave*: nsm. modr, 13.1.

mold, f. *earth, dust*: ds. molldu, 4.5.

monnum, see **maðr**.

morginn, m. *morning*: ns. morginn, 48.2.

mundriði, m. *that which is quickly moved with the hand*: gs. mundrida, 48.3.

munnr, m. *mouth*: ds. munni, 60.2; as. munn, 29.3.

munnrjóðr, m. *mouth-reddener*: ns. munnriodr, 13.2.

munr, m. *difference, distinction*: ds. muné sidar, *later*, 23.2.

munu, pret. pres. 4 (aux. only). *will, shall*: pres. 3s. (w. neg. suffix) muna fæda, *will not produce*, 14.3; munat fædaz, *will not be born*, 21.3; munat fyrnaz, *will not be forgotten*, 24.2; (w. *vera* understood) fôrnudr mun þat, *that will be good fortune*, 24.3; pres. 3p. ger munu giolld, *punishments will be prepared*, 61.7; pret. 3s. munndi liggia, *would lie*, 53.1; mundi vera launadr, *would be rewarded*, 70.1; pret. inf. letz myndu fylgia, *said that he would help*, 28.4.

mykill, **myklu**, see **mikill**.

myndu, see **munu**.

myrkr, n. *darkness*: dp. myrkrum, 2.2.

mæla, III. *speak*: pres. 1s. (contr.) mæl, 62.2.

mæra, III. *praise*: pres. 3s. mære, 33.3.

mærð, f. *poem, praise*: ns. mærd, 9.2, 21.2, 39.3; as. mærd, 8.7.

mætta, see **mega**.

mœða, III. *plague*; *affect*: pres. 3s. mædir, 27.3.

Mœrir, m. (pl. only). p.n. (inhabitants of Møre): gp. Mæra, 12.5.

ná, IV. *be able to, manage to*; *be allowed to*: pret. 3s. (w. suffixed neg.) nædit, 19.1

naðr, m. *snake, serpent*: ds. nadri, 47.4.

nafnkuðr, adj. *famous*: nsm. nafnkudr, 68.4.

nátt, f. *night*: ap. nætr, 25.4.

nauðr, f. *need*: ns. naudr, 57.3; dp. navdum, 33.4, 68.3.

naut, see **njóta**.

né, adv. *not*: ne, 11.7, 51.5.

nema, 4. *take, accept*: pres. 3s. subj. nemi, 18.3; pres. 3p. subj. nemi, 7.7; pp. nsm. numin alldri, 62.6; pp. asm. numin, 17.8; numin mæli, *bereaved of speech*, 37.6; pass. pret. 3s. var numin, 63.4.

nenna, III. conj. *unless, except that*: nema, 53.5.

niðr, m. *relative, descendant*: ns. nidr, 34.8.

†**níðrandi**, m. *river bank, seacoast*: ds. nidranda, 40.3.

nista, III. *feed, nourish*: pres. part. gsm. nistanda, 25.6.

njóta, 2. *use, enjoy* (w. gen.): pres. 3s. nytr, 15.3, 66.1; inf. let niota, 61.2; pret. 3s. naut, 28.7.

njótr, m. *user*: ns. niotr, 23.3; as. niot, 37.7.

Norðmaðr, m. *Norseman*: np. nordmenn, 11.4; gp. nordmanna, 55.8.

nú, adv. *now*: nu, 7.1, 45.1, 57.1, 63.5.

numin, see **nema**.

nýr, adj. *new*: dsm. nyium, 57.3.

nýta, III. *make use of*: md. (pass.) pres. 3p. nytaz, 19.7.

nýtr, adj. *useful*: nsm. nytr, 48.5; gsm. nytra, 58.6; asf. nyta, 68.3; sup. asm. nyzstann, 55.7.

nytr, see **njóta**.

næra, III. *nourish, feed*: inf. þordu nærra, *dared to feed*, 55.7.

nærr, adj. *next*: sup. nsn. (used adverbially) næst, *next*, 57.4.

næst, see **nærr**.

nætr, see **nátt**.

oddhrið, f. *point-shower, battle*: gs. oddhridar, 50.6.

óðgerð, f. *poetry-making, recitation of poetry*: ds. odgerd, 10.3.

odlingr, see **ǫðlingr**.

óðr, m. *poetry*: gs. odar, 40.7, 69.7; ds. odi, 57.3; as. od, 8.5, 50.3.

of, prep. (1) w. dat. *over, against*: lx manna of einum, *sixty men against one*, 54.5. (2) w. acc. *over, about, because of*: vargar gindu of hræ, *wolves gaped over the corpses*, 29.8; yrkia of stilli, *make poetry about the king*, 46.3; of minni sorgir, *because of fewer sorrows*, 60.7; enn þiod of hyggi, *than people can think about*, 62.4; megi segia of giafar, *can tell about the gifts*, 64.2. (3) = af (*off, from*): of slongui snæka vangs, *from the dispenser of the serpent's field*, 38.7; of styfdrar tungu, *cut-off tongue*, 61.1.

ofugmæli, see **ǫfugmæli**.

ofund, see **ǫfunð**.

ógn, f. *battle, fear, threat*: gs. ognar, 51.5; ap. ognar, 54.3.

†**ógnfimr**, adj. *battle-clever, quick in battle*: nsm. ognfimr, 47.8.

ok, conj. *and*: ok, 1.1, 2.3, 11.4, 16.1, 25.3, 34.2, 38.8, 40.5, 41.5, 53.2, 59.5, 60.3, 61.4.

Óláfr, m. p.n. (Olaf Haraldsson, St Olaf): ns. Olafr, 7.3, 18.8, 21.8, 24.8, 27.8, 30.8, 33.8, 36.8, 39.8, 42.8, 45.8; Olæfr, 50.4; gs. Olafs, 10.1, 23.7, 31.3, 35.3, 43.3, 51.7, 61.5, 66.1, 69.1; Olæfs, 41.4, 67.4; ds. Olæfi, 1.8; as. Olæf, 54.4.

†**ómjór**, adj. *not-small*: gsm. omiors, 3.4.

onaudigr, see **unauðigr**.

opna, I. *open*: md. (pass.) inf. leit opnaz, *caused to be opened*, 16.7.

opt, adv. *often*: opt, 33.1.

ór, prep. w. dat. *out of, from*: or, 25.5, 32.8, 37.1, 40.6, 59.6, 68.3.

orð, n. *word*: np. ord, 41.3, 67.3; gp. orda, 8.1, 26.3; ap. ord, 1.1.

orðgnótt, f. *word-wealth, eloquence*: gs. ordgnottar, 10.2

orðhagr, adj. *eloquent*: gsm. ordhags, 69.2.

ordin, see **verða**.

ormr, m. *serpent*: gs. orms, 23.8.

orri, m. *heathcock*: ds. orra, 43.3.

orti, see **yrkja**.

orugt, see **ǫruggr**.

orum, see, **minn**.

oss, see **ek**.

ossa, see **minn**.

óttarr, m. p.n. (Ottar the Black): ns. Ottar, 12.4.

ox, see **vaxa**.

†**Pézínavellir**, m. (pl. only). p.n.: dp. Pecinavǫllum, 52.4.

†**píningarkross**, m. *torture-cross*: ds. piningarcrossi, 65.8.

prestr, m. *priest*: gs. prest, 59.5.

prýða, III. *adorn, ornament*: md. (pass.) inf. let prydazt, 31.6.

†**prýðibragr**, m. *splendid, cleverly wrought poem*: ds. prydibrag, 11.2.

ráð, n. *counsel*: ds. rædi, 69.4.

ráða, red. 4. *rule, control; decide* (w. inf.): pret. 3s. red, 14.1; reed efnazst oss, *decided to make itself efficacious for us*, 3.5; red gagne, *controlled the victory, won*, 32.5; red skera, *decided to cut*, 37.1; red sofna, *decided to sleep*, 47.5.

ráðandi, m. *ruler*: gs. rædanda, 1.2, 5.4.

rann, n. *house*: np. rann, 54.8.

rann, see **rinna**.

raud, see **rjóða**.

raudli, raudull, rauduls, see **rǫðull**.

rauk, see **rjúka**.

rauknstefnandi, m. *horse-driver*: ds. rauckstefnanda, 49.3.

raumar, m. (pl. only). p.n. (*inhabitants of Romerike*): gp. Rauma, 15.4, 43.5.

raun, f. *experience, test, proof*: ns. raun, 30.1, 46.7; as. ráun, 10.7.

†**raundýrliga**, adv. *magnificently*: raundyrliga, 70.4.

raunnd, see **rǫnd**.

rauskr, see **rǫskr**.

rausn, f. *greatness*: ds. rausn, 15.7.

†**rausnarskap**, n. *great generosity*: as. rausnarskap, 70.3.

red, reed, see **ráða**.

Regin, m. p.n. (*legendary smith*): gs. Regins, 48.4.

regn, n. *rain*: ns. regn, 55.2.

reiða, III. *cause to ride, spread talk*: pres. 3s. reidir, 67. 8.

Reifnir, m. p.n. (*mythological sea-king*): gs. Reifnis, 49.3, 54.7.

reis, see **rísa**.

rekja, II. *drive, pursue, advance*: pp. npn. rekin, 43.7.

réttlæti, n. *righteousness*: gs. rettlætis, 4.4.

réttr, adj. *right, just, correct*: nsn. (used adverbially) rett, 10.7, 31.2.

reyna, III. *try, prove, test*: pres. 3s. reynir, 63.3; pret. 3s. reynði, 31.1.

ríða, 1. *ride, travel*: pres. 3s. ridr, 26.5, 39.3, 51.7; w. suffixed neg. ridrat, 57.4.

ríðari, m. *knight, rider*: ns. ridari, 18.6, 21.6, 24.6, 27.6, 30.6, 33.6, 36.6, 39.6, 42.6, 45.6.

ríki, n. *power, strength; realm, kingdom*: ds. riki, 11.8, 55.1.

ríkr, adj. *powerful*: nsm. rikr, 49.4; gsm. riks, 22.2, 39.2.

ringa, see **hringr**.

rinna, 3. *run*: pret. 3s. rann upp, *ascended*, 4.1.

rísa, 1. *rise*: pret. 3s. reis, 4.6, 6.5.

rjóða, 2. *redden, make red*: pret. 3s. raud, 29.3; pp. npn. rodin, 54.7.

rjúka, 2. *smoke, fly about, rise up* (*like smoke or dust*); *drive*: pret. 3s. rauk, 55.1 (impers.).

róða, f. *rood, crucifix*: as. rodu, 34.4.

rodin, see **rjóða**.

rodull, roduls, see **rǫðull**.

rofna, I. *break; lose power*: md. (pass.) pret. 3s. rofnadiz, 47.6.

rót, n. *root; cause*: dp. rotum, 59.4.

rót, n. *disturbance, strife*: dp. rotum, 59.4.

ryðja, II. *clear, make empty*: pret. 3p. ruddu, 56.1.

ræsir, m. *king*: gs. ræsis, 70.3; as. ræsi, 42.1, 46.7.

rœða, f. *speech*: as. rædu, 45.4.

rǫðull, m. *sun*: ns. raudull, 2.8; rodull, 19.4; gs. roduls, 3.4, 9.6; rauduls, 53.7; ds. raudli, 43.8.

rǫnd, f. *shield*: as. raunnd, 53.5.

rǫskr, adj. *brave*: nsm. rauskr, 18.7, 21.7, 24.7, 30.7, 33.7, 36.7, 39.7, 42.7, 45.7.

sá, dem. pron. *that*: nsm. sa, 1.3, 2.5, 14.1, 16.5, 26.3, 44.5, 45.1, 61.1; sæa, 20.3, 32.4, 38.1; npm. þeir, 12.5, 17.7, 40.2, 59.5, 68.5; nsf. su, 6.5, 24.2; nsn. þat, 3.2, 4.7, 24.3, 30.7, 34.4, 34.5, 36.3, 57.4, 59.7; npn. þau, 6.3, 51.1, 56.7; gsm. þess, 43.3, 46.2, 46.5, 57.5, 70.7; gsf. þeirrar, 2.1; gpn. þeira, 34.6; dsm. þeim, 23.7, 41.5, 43.5, 61.7; dsn. þui, 2.7, 8.3; þvi, 12.6, 26.6, 32.7, 41.8, 46.1, 69.4; þvi at, *because*, 18.1, 46.5, 62.5; asm. þann, 7.3, 37.5, 38.3, 50.3; asf. þa, 8.7; asn. þat, 34.8, 51.3, 62.2; apn. þau, 57.1.

sæm, see **sjá**.

sagdar, sagdi, sagt, see **segja**.

salr, m. *hall*: gs. sals, 66.6; ds. sal, 7.6.

salvǫrðr, m. *hall-guardian*: ns. saluordr, 19.3.

sama, IV. *befit, beseem, become*: pres. 3s. samir kuedia, 10.1; raun samir, 10.7.

samdægris, adv. *the same day*: samdægrs, 20.8.

sandr, m. *sand*: ds. sandi, 25.2, 59.1.

sannr, adj. *true*: nsn. satt, 13.3, 15.1 (used adverbially), 22.5, 34.1; apn. saunn, 41.6.

†**sannspurðr**, adj. *truly experienced, truly said*: nsn. sannspurt, 36.3.

sárliga, adv. *painfully, grievously*: sarliga, 40.4.

saunn, see **sannr**.

sed, see **sjá**.

seggr, m. *man*: ns. seggr, 24.1, 67.5; gs. (contr.) sex, 59.2; dp. seggium, 23.6, 34.2, 65.3.

segja, IV. *say, tell*: pres. 3s. segir, 71.5; inf. megi segia, 64.2; pret. 3s. sagdi, 15.1; pret. 3p. sogdu, 49.8; pret. 3s. sugj. segdi, 12.1; perf. 1p. hofum sagdar, 69.2; perf. 3p. hafa sagt, 35.1.

seimþiggjandi, m. *one who asks for gold, gold-receiver*: ns. seimþiggiandi, 48.6.

sem, conj. *as, as well as, likewise, which*: sem, 7.7, 18.7, 21.7, 24.7, 27.7, 33.7, 36.7, 39.7, 42.7, 45.7, 60.3, 61.3, 65.6, 71.4.

sendir, m. *sender*, *commander*: gs. sendiz, 20.7.

ser, see **sín**.

setr, n. *seat*, *abode*: gs. setrs, 3.2.

síð, adv. *late*: sidallá, 47.2.

síðan, adv. *then*, *since*: siþan, 16.4, 17.2, 20.6, 36.2, 41.2, 44.6, 50.6; sidan, 26.2, 37.8, 38.2.

Sighvatr, m. p.n. (Sighvatr Þórðarson): ns. Sighuatr, 12.1.

sigr, m. *victory*: ds. sigri, 31.5; as. sigr, 30.1.

Sigurðr, m. p.n. (Sigurðr *munnr* Haraldsson): ns. Sigurdr, 8.3, 70.6.

sik, see **sín**.

siklingr, m. *king*, *prince*: ns. siklingr, 13.3, 63.4; gs. siklings, 67.6.

silfr, n. *silver*: ds. silfri, 34.1.

sín, refl. pron. *himself*, *etc*.: ds. ser, 20.7, 48.8, 66.8; as. sik, 20.4, 62.7.

sinn, poss. pron. *his*: dsm. sinum, 28.1, 30.1, 64.8; asm. sinn, 15.4, 31.5; apm. vini flesta sina, *most of his friends*, 63.3; apf. sinar, 23.5; apn. sin, 13.4, 19.4.

sitja, 5. *sit*: pres. 3s. sitr, 5.5.

siþan, see **síðan**.

sjá, 5. *see*: pret. 3s. sa, 15.5; pret. 1p. sæm, 37.5; pp. gat sed liggia, *saw it lying*, 48.5.

sjá, dem. pron. *this*: npm. þessir, 49.5; þessi, 70.2; gsm. þessa, 17.5; gsn. þessa, 69.8; dsm. þeima, 2.2, 49.1, 57.8; dpm. þessum, 11.6; dsf. þessi, 10.3; dsn. þessu, 64.3; dpn. þessum, 66.3; asm. þenna, 65.2, 68.8.

sjón, f. *sight*: as. sion, 24.1.

†**sjónbraut**, f. *sight-path*, *eye*: ap. sionbrautir, 23.5.

skæru, see skera.

skal, see **skulu**.

Skánungar, m. (pl. only). p.n. (*inhabitants of Skåne*): dp. Skanungum, 35.2.

skap, n. *mind*: ds. skapi, 58.8.

skati, m. *man*, *warrior*: np. skatnar, 17.6, 64.7.

skaut, n. *sprig*, *shoot*, *twig*: ds. skauti, 40.1.

skepna, f. *created thing*, *creation*: gs. skepnu, 4.1.

skera, 4. *cut*: inf. red skera, 37.4; pret, 3p. skæru, 40.8; pass. pret. 3s. var skorin, 60.4.

skerða, III. *cut a notch*; *diminish*: pret. 3p. skerdu, 40.2.

skiallda, see **skjǫldr**.

skíðrennandi, m. *ski-runner*: ns. skidrennandi, 41.2.

skin, n. *light*, *shining*: ds. skini, 19.8.

skína, 1. *shine*: inf. veit skina, 7.8; nædit skina, 19.4.

skiolldungr, see **skjǫldungr**.

skjǫldr, m. *shield*: gp. skiallda, 14.6.

skjǫldungr, m. *prince*, *king*: ns. skiolldungr, 6.7.

skorin, see **skera**.

skreyta, III. *ornament*: pp. asf. skreytta, 34.1; pp. asn. skreytt, 64.7; pp. wk. asn. skreytta, 41.1.

skrín, n. *shrine*: as. skrin, 41.1, 64.8.

skulu, pret. pres. 4 (aux. only). *shall*, *must*: pres. 1s. skal byria, 38.6; skal skyra, 46.1; pres. 1p. skulum dyrka, 7.1, 57.5; skulum bidia, 27.1; pres. 3p. skulu hlyda, 11.1.

ský, n. *cloud*: gs. skys, 68.5; ap. sky, 43.6.

†**skýjaðarr**, m. *cloud-rim*, *cloud-coast*, = *cloud-land*, *heaven*: ds. skyiadri, 2.6.

skýra, III. *explain*, *make clear*: inf. skal skyrá, 46.1; perf. 3p. hofum skyrda, 66.2.

skyrda, see **skýra**.

slaung, see **slyngva**.

slétta, III. *make smooth*: pres. 1s. (w. suffixed pron.) slettig, 50.3.

sléttr, adj. *smooth*, *flat*: dsf. slettri, 48.5; asm. slettan, 31.2.

slíkr, adj. *such*: dsn. (used substantively) sliku, 39.2; asf. slikár, 49.4; apn. slik, 62.8.

slongui, see **slǫngvir**.

slungin, **slunginns**, see **slyngva**.

slyngva, 3. *throw*, *cast*; *provide*, *procure*: pret. 3s. slaung, 45.3; pp. gsm. slunginns, 56.6; pp. asn. slungin, 38.8.

sløkkva, III. *slake* (*hunger or thirst*): pret. 3s. slǫkte, 52.2.

slǫngvir, m. *distributor*, *dispenser*: ds. slongui, 38.7.

slǫkte, see **sløkva**.

smár, adj. *small*: sup. dsn. ridrat þat smæstu, *that is not of small significance*, 57.4.

smæstu, see **smár**.

snákr, m. *snake*, *serpent*: gp. snæka, 38.7.

snarr, adj. *doughty*, *able*: nsm. snarr, 65.3; apm. snara, 13.6.

snilli, f. *honour*: ns. snilli, 26.7.

snjallr, adj. *clever*, *eloquent*: nsm. sniallr, 30.2; gsm. sniallz, 36.4, 46.3; wk. gsm. snialla, 1.2; dsm. sniallum, 16.8; dsf. sniallri, 15.2.

snoggum, see **snøggr**.

snót, f. *woman*: gs. snotar, 35.8.

snyrtir, m. *polisher*, *ornamenter*: gs. snyrtis, 49.7.

snøggr, adj. *quick*: dsm. snoggum, 8.3.

sofna, I. *sleep*: inf. red sofna, 47.6.

sogdu, see **segja**.

sok, see **sǫk**.

sókn, f. *meeting, battle*: ns. sokn, 44.3.

sóknbráðr, adj. *vehement in battle*: gsm. soknbrads, 12.2.

sóknsterkr, adj. *battle-strong*: nsm. soknsterkr, 8.4.

†sóknþýðr, adj. *battle-mild*: nsm. soknþydr, 31.6.

sól, f. *sun*: gs. solar, 1.8, 3.1, 18.8, 19.8, 21.8, 24.8, 27.8, 28.2, 30.8, 33.8, 36.8, 39.8, 42.8, 45.8, 65.4.

sómi, m. *honour*: gs. soma, 42.2.

sonr, m. *son*: ns. sonr, 5.1.

sorg, f. *sorrow*: as. sorg, 29.7; ap. sorgir, 60.7.

sotti, see **sœkja**.

spenja, II. *guide, persuade*: pres. 3s. hefir spurt, 12.3.

spjalli, m. *friend, confidant*: ns. spialli, 30.2.

spurt, see **spyrja**.

spyrja, II. *hear, learn*: perf. 3s. hefir spurt, 12.3.

staðr, m. *place*: as. stad, 65.2.

stál, n. *steel, weapon*: np. stæl, 43.7; gs. stæls, 55.2; gp. stæla, 54.4.

standa, 6. *stand*: pres. 3s. stendr, 34.7; inf. sa standa, 15.5; let standa, 50.8; pret. 3s. stod af, *proceeded from*, 2.7.

ste, see **stíga**.

stef, n. *refrain*: as. stef, 18.4.

steik, f. *roasted meat*: ap. steikár, 43.4.

steina, III. *color, stain*: pp. gpf. steindra, 48.3.

stendr, see **standa**.

sterkr, adj. *strong*: gsm. sterks, 40.6; (w. ablaut) styrks, 48.3; as. (w. ablaut) styrkann, 46.4.

stíga, 1. *step*: pret. 3s. ste, 5.1.

stigi, m. *ladder*: as. stiga, 15.5.

Stiklarstaðir, f. (pl. only). p.n.: dp. (w. tmesis) Stikla-stodum, 17.1–2; Stikla-staudum, 43.7–8.

stillir, m. *king, ruler*: ns. stilir, 42.3; as. stilli, 46.3.

stinga, 3. *sting*: pret. 3p. stungu, 59.8; pp. gpn. stunginna, 61.4.

stiornu, see **stjarna**.

stjarna, f. *star*: ds. stiornu, 2.8.

stjórn, f. *rule, leadership*: gs. stiornar fimr, *accustomed to leadership*, 15.6.

stod, see **standa**.

stoða, I. *fulfil*: perf. 1s. hef stodat, 71.2.

stóll, m. *seat, throne*: gs. stols, 9.7; ds. stoli, 5.8, 67.4.

strangr, adj. *great, strong, powerful*: dsf. strangri, 68.2.

straumr, m. *stream*: gs. straums, 28.2.

stríð, n. *affliction; strife, battle*: ns. strid, 54.3; dp. stridum, 18.6.

stríðandi, m. *enemy*: ns. stridir, 38.2.

stríðir, m. *enemy*: ns. stridir, 38.2.

strondu, see **strǫnd**.

stræti, n. *street*: gs. strætis, 25.4.

strǫnd, f. *strand, coast*: ds. strondu, 60.6.

stund, f. *while, time*: dp. stundum, *at times, sometimes*, 58.6.

stunginna, stungu, see **stinga**.

stýfa, III. *cut-off*: pp. gsf. styfdrar, 61.1.

styrkann, styrks, see **sterkr**.

styrkna, I. *become strong*: inf. bid styrkna, 8.6.

styrr, m. *battle*: gs. styriar, 46.3; styrs, 48.4; ds. styr, 32.8.

su, see **sá**.

sueckuir, see **søkkvir**.

sund, n. *sea, sound*: gp. sunda, 55.6; ds. svnde, 31.8.

sundr, adv. *apart, in pieces*: lustu i sundr, *broke into pieces*, 59.1.

sunna, f. *sun*: gs. sunnu, 4.4.

sunnan, adv. *in the south*: sunnan, 36.3.

sunnr, adv. *in the south*: sunnr, 35.2.

svá, adv. *so, thus, such, also*: sva, 9.3, 63.3, 64.1, 68.1; svo, 52.5.

svall, see **svella**.

svanni, m. *woman*: ns. suanni, 35.1.

sveiti, m. *blood*: as. sueita, 22.1.

svella, 3. *cause to increase, swell*: pret. 3s. svall, 54.3.

sverð, n. *sword*: as. suerd, 44.3.

svænskr, adj. *Swedish*: nsm. suænskr, 44.4.

Sygnir, m. (pl. only). p.n. *(inhabitants of Sogn)*: gp. Sygna, 22.5.

sýna, III. *show*: pret. 3s. syndi, 19.3.

synd, f. *sin*: dp. syndum, 20.3, 62.7.

sýsla, III. *act, do, deal with*: pass. 3s. er syst, 12.6.

sæla, f. *luck, blessedness*: gs. sælu, 62.2.

sæll, adj. *blessed*: nsm. sæll, 66.7.

særa, III. *wound*: pres. part. npm. særendr, 22.6.

søkkvir, m. *enemy*: ns. sueckuir, 28.1.

sœkja, III. *seek*: pret. 3s. sotti, 38.1, 41.1.

sǫk, f. *guilt, fault*: as. sok, 37.2.

táka, 6. *take, accept*: pret. 3s. tok, 44.1; tok dauda, *accepted death*, 3.8; tok leita, *went to look for*, 35.6.

tákn, n. *sign*: np. takn, 46.5; ap. takn, 19.4; tækn, 51.1.

tandrauðr, adj. *flame-red*: gsm. tandrauds, 25.2.

tangar, see **tǫng**.

téa, IV. *help, avail*: pret. 3p. tedu, 31.3.

teiti, f. *gladness*: as. teiti, 41.6.

telja, II. *tell*: pres. 3p. telia, 68.6; pret. 1s. talda, 67.1.

tiggi, **tiggia**, see **tyggi**.

til, prep. w. gen. *to*: til, 5.3, 6.8, 8.1, 15.6, 44.2, 58.7.

†**tírbráðr**, adj. *eager for fame*: nsm. tiirbrædr, 14.2.

†**tírkunnr**, adj. *accustomed to praise*: gsm. (used substantively) tirkunnz, 60.2.

tírr, m. *fame, honour*: gs. tirar, 40.6; as tir, 55.7.

tjóa, 3. (w. wk. pret.). *help*: pret. 3s. tioði, 32.6.

tok, see **taka**.

tól, n. *tool*: dp. tolum, 50.4.

tolf, num. *twelve*: tolf, 14.1, 25.1.

traust, n. *trust, confidence*: ds. trausti, 54.2.

trú, f. *faith, the Christian religion*: ds. tru, 40.5, 68.4.

trúa, IV. *believe*: pret. 3s. trudi, 14.1.

tunga, f. *tongue; language*: ns. tunga, 64.4; (w. suffixed art.) tungan, 60.1; gs. tungu, 61.4; as. tungu, 26.8, 37.4, 38.8.

tyggi, m. *king*: ns. tiggi, 65.3; gs. tiggia, 9.6.

týna, III. *lose, forget, deny*: pp. npm. tyndir, 40.5; md. (pass.) pres. 3s. tyniz, 63.8.

týnir, m. *destroyer*: ns. tynir, 25.1.

tǫng, f. *pair of tongs*: gs. tangar, 60.1.

þá, adv. *then, when*: þa, 3.6, 6.5, 19.1, 20.1, 20.7, 31.7, 35.5, 35.7, 44.1, 48.2, 55.1.

þagna, I. *become silent*: pres. 1s. þagna, 71.8.

þannig, adv. *thither*: þannig, 21.2.

þar, adv. *there*: þar, 9.7, 23.1, 26.1, 37.7, 50.6, 52.5, 54.5, 55.7, 56.3, 63.6, 64.5.

þegn, m. *thane, man*: np. þegnar, 14.3; gs. þegns, 11.2; gp. þegna, 13.6; as. þegn, 61.3; ap. þegna, 55.2.

þeim, se **sá**.

þeingill, see **þengill**.

þengill, m. *prince, king*: ns. þeingill, 11.7, 56.2; þengill, 43.5, 71.1; as. þeingill, 12.5.

þiggja, II. *take, get, receive*: pres. 3s. þiggr, 18.7, 21.7, 24.7, 27.7, 30.7, 33.7, 36.7, 39.7, 42.7, 45.7.

þingat, adv. *there*: þingat, 5.6.

þingdjarfr, adj. *battle-brave*: gsm. þingdiarfs, 49.6.

†**þingsnjallr**, adj. *battle-quick, brave*: gsm. þingsniallz, 66.4.

þinn, poss. pron. *your*: asf. þina, 71.1.

þjóð, f. *people, nation*: ns. þiod, 7.5, 52.5, 62.4; gs. þiodar, 20.2; ds. þiod, 57.2; as. þiod, 68.3.

þjóðkonungr, m. *king of the people*: gs. (w. tmesis) þiod-konungs, 11.7–8; as. (w. tmesis) þiod-konung, 14.3–4.

þjóðnýtr, adj. *useful to people*: nsm. þiodnytr, 49.2.

þjónn, m. *servant, slave*: ns. þionn, 58.3.

þó, conj. *nevertheless*: þo, 32.5.

þo, þð, see **þvá**.

þora, IV. *dare*: pret. 3p. þordu nærra, *dared to feed*, 55.8.

þravm, see **þrǫmr**.

þreklyndr, adj. *strong-minded*: gsm. þreklyndz, 11.1.

þrekrammr, adj. *very strong*: nsm. þrekrammr, 71.2.

þreksnjallr, adj. *strong and brave*: nsf. þreksnioll 66.4 (*B*).

þrenning, f. *trinity*: ns. þrenning, 1.4.

þriði, num. *third*: dsm. þridia, 4.2.

†**þrifhvass**, adj. *luck-sharp, lucky*: nsm. þrifhuassir, 49.5.

þrifnuðr, m. *prosperity, luck, success*: ns. þrifnudr, 3.5.

þrima, f. *noise*: gs. þrimu, 69.6.

þrimr, see **þrír**.

þrír, num. *three*: nf. þriar, 49.1; dm. þrimr, 32.2; am. þria, 14.4.

þrotna, I. *decline, dwindle, diminish*: pres. 3s. þrotnar, 66.3.

þróttr, m. *power, strength, fortitude*: np. þrottar, 66.3 (*B*).

þrysvar, adv. *thrice*: þrysuar, 60.3.

þræll, m. *slave, thrall*: as. þræl, 61.8.

þrænzkr, adj. *Trondish, from Trondheim*: dsm. þrænskum, 44.4.

Þrœndir, m. (pl. only). p.n. (*inhabitants of Trondheim*): np. Þrændir, 11.1; gp. Þrænda, 13.5.

þrǫmr, m. *rim, edge, coast*: as. þravm, 31.2.

þú, pron. *you*: ns. du, 8.1; þu, 65.7.

þungr, adj. *heavy*: apm. þunngan, 52.2.

þunnr, adj. *thin*: apn. þunn, 43.6.

þúsund, f. *a thousand*: dp. þushunndum, 52.6.

þvá, 6. *wash*: pret. 3s. þo, 22.1; þð, 23.5; past perf. 3p. hofdu þuegit, 23.4.

þuegit, see **þvá**.

þvílíkr, adj. *like, similar*: þuilikr, 11.8.

ulfr, m. *wolf*: gs. vlfs, 25.6.
um, prep. w. acc. *about, concerning; during; beyond; around*: um, 12.4, 14.1, 35.5, 36.4, 37.2, 39.4, 46.7, 51.3.
umgeypnandi, m. *one who holds (something) in his or her hands*: ns. vmgeypnandi, 16.7.
†unauðigr, adj. *willingly, voluntarily*: nsm. (w. adverbial sense) onaudigr, 3.8.
und, f. *wound*: ap. vndir, 17.3.
und, prep. w. dat. *under*: vnd, 2.6, 7.5; vnnd, 53.1.
undan, adv. *away*: flẹdu vnndan, *fled away, fled*, 52.6.
†undbára, f. *wound-wave, blood*: dp. vndbærum, 54.6.
undir, prep. w. dat. *under, below*: vndir, 47.7.
†undreyr, n. *wound-reed, arrow*: np. vnðreyr, 31.8.
ungr, adj. *young*: nsm. vngr, 56.6, 63.1; wk. nsm. vngi, 45.3; gsm. vngs, 26.8, 37.4.
unnin, see **vinna**.
unnr, f. *wave*: gs. unnar, 33.2; 41.3.
upp, adv. *up*: 4.1, 5.1, 6.5, 9.2, 16.3, 25.5.
út, adv. *out*: ut, 61.4.

vaði, m. *danger, peril; dangerous object*: gs. væda, 48.4.
vagn, m. *wagon*: gp. vagna, 56.3.
†vagnræfr, n. *wagon's roof, heaven* (Karlsvagn *was the ON name for the Big Dipper*): gs. vagnræfrs, 71.8.
vakit, **vakti**, see **vekja**.
val, n. *choice, selection*: as. uál, 10.5.
válaust, adv. *without a doubt*: vælaust, 37.6.
valbastar, see **valbọst**.
valbọst, f. *sword-hilt (?)*: gs. valbastar, 43.8.
vald, n. *guardian, ruling authority, strength*: ns. valld, 28.3.
valdr, m. *ruler*: ns. valldr, 62.6; gs. valldz, 63.6.
valr, m. (and ma. in pl.). *falcon*: gp. fala, 25.4; as. val, 55.8.
†vallrjóðandi, m. *field-reddener, warrior*: gp. vallriodanda, 10.6.
ván, vón, f. *hope, expectation*: ns. vọn, 22.3; as. væn, 4.8.
vanda, I. *make (something) with great skill and precision*: inf. mætta vanda, 18.4.
vandit, see **venja**.
vandr, adj. *difficult*: nsn. vant, 46.4.

vangr, m. *field*: gs. vangs, 38.7; ds. vangi, 47.5.

vann, see **vinna**.

vápn, n. *weapon*: np. vopn, 53.7; gp. vopna, 43.2.

†**vápnsundraðr**, adj. *weapon-sundered, torn by weapons*: asn. vopnsundrat, 56.4.

vard, see **verða**.

varða, I. *be of value*: pres. 3s. vardar, 8.7.

vargr, m. *wolf*: np. vargar, 29.7, 56.3.

vatn, n. *water*: ds. vatni, 22.4.

váttr, m. *witness, martyr*: ns. vottr, 62.3; gp. vætta, 6.4.

vaxa, 6. *grow*: pres. 3s. vex, 9.7; pret. 3s. ox, 52.7; pp. apn. vaxinn, 43.6.

veðr, n. *storm*: ds. vedre, 53.7.

veðrhǫll, f. *hall of the storm, heaven*: gs. (w. tmesis) vedr-hallar, 2.4.

vegr, m. *way, path; honour, glory*: gs. vegs, 64.2; as. veg, 70.7, 71.7.

veit, see **vita**.

veita, III. *give (to), help, assist* : pres. 3s. veitir, 64.6; pret. 3s. veitti, 6.1.

vekja, II. *waken, arise, cause*: pret. 3s. vakti, 41.5; pass. pret. 3s. (w. *vera* understood) vakit, 17.1.

vel, adv. *well, easily*: vel, 1.3, 7.4, 32.6, 41.5, 52.2.

veldi, n. *kingdom*: ns. vellde, 53.4.

velja, II. *choose*: pres. part. (used substantively) npm. velendr, 68.6.

vell, n. *gold*: dp. vellum, 70.8.

venja, II. *accustom*: pret. 3s. (w. suffixed neg.) vandit, 20.3.

vera, 5. (1) *be*: pres. 1s. er, 18.1; pres. 3s. er, 1.3, 8.7, 30.1, 36.3, 46.1, 57.1, 61.1, 64.1, 66.7; pres. 3p. eru, 49.7, 51.1; pret. 1p. uorum, 37.5; pret. 3s. var, 2.3, 3.2, 13.3, 18.2, 19.5, 22.5, 32.4, 34.1, 34.4, 48.2, 59.7; (w. suffixed neg.) vara, 60.3; pret. 3p. væru, 54.6. (2) used as aux.: pres. 3s. er borin, 9.2; er syst, 12.6; er ordin, 11.5, 39.1; inf. mundi vera launadr, 70.2; pret. 3s. var blandinn, 23.8; var hulidr, 25.1; var ordin, 44.3; var lokin, 60.1; var skorin, 60.4; var numin, 63.1; pp. hefir verit halldin, 36.2.

verða, 3. *become*: pres. 1s. verdr, 40.2; pret. 3s. vard, 29.5, 35.7, 58.1; perf. 3s. er ordin, 11.5, 39.1; pass. pret. 3s. var ordin, 44.3.

verðr, adj. *worthy, worthy of* (w. gen.): asm. verdan, 42.4.

verja, II. *cover, surround*: pp. dsn. vordu, 50.7.

verk, n. *work*: ds. verki, 26.6; dp. verkum, 30.3; as. verk, 23.2; ap. verk, 56.7, 57.2, 62.8.

verki, m. *work, composition*: ds. verka, 8.4.

verolld, see **verold**.

verold, f. *world*: ns. verolld, 66.4; as. verolld, 56.8.

vetr, m. *winter*: ap. vetr, 14.4.

véttrim, f. *a part of the sword (?) or a part of the shield (?)*: gp. vetþryma, 47.4.

vex, see **vaxa**.

við, prep. w. acc. *with*; *against*: vid, 20.2, 28.8, 31.2, 31.4, 68.4.

vída, adv. *widely*: vida, 7.6.

víðlendr, adj. *widely landed, possessing many lands*: nsm. vidlendr, 17.2.

viðr, m. *wood*: ns. vidr, 65.6.

víðr, adj. *wide*: dpm. vidum, 52.1; dsn. vidu, 25.5.

†**viðrlíf**, n. *treatment, maintenance*: ns. vidrlif, 60.4.

víf, n. *woman*: np. vif, 29.7.

víg, n. *battle*: gp. viga, 68.5; as. vig, 17.1.

vígdjarfr, adj. *battle-bold*: gsm. vigdiarfs, 30.4.

vika, f. *week*: dp. vikum, 37.8.

vildr, adj. *agreeable, pleasing*: comp. asn. villdra, 10.5.

vilja, II. *wish, will*: pret. 3s. baka villdi, *wanted to bake*, 35.4.

villa, f. *error, delusion*: ds. villu, 58.2.

Vinðr, m. (pl. only). p.n. (*Wends*): np. Vindr, 40.1.

vinðverskr, adj. *Wendish*: npn. vindversk, 29.8.

vinna, 3. *perform, carry out*: pret. 3s. vann, 13.1, 18.1, 49.1, 57.1; vann heimtann, *took home*, 55.5; vann heilann, *healed*, 61.5; pp. nsf. vnnin, 9.1; perf. 3p. hafum vnnit, *have performed*, 71.4.

vinr, m. *friend*: ds. vin, 64.8; as. vin, 9.6; ap. vini flesta sina, *most of his friends*, 63.2.

vísi, m. *leader, prince*: ns. visi, 2.3; gs. visa, 20.5, 30.3, 68.5, 70.7, 71.7.

vísir, m. *prince*: ns. visir, 18.1, 57.1.

víss, adj. *certain, clear*: nsn. (used adverbially) vist, 32.1.

vita, pret. pres. 1. *know*: pres. 1s. veit, 4.5, 40.1, 41.6; pres. 3s. veit, 7.5.

vǫn, see **ván**.

vordu, see **verja**.

vottr, see **váttr**.

vænn, adj. *hopeful, promising, likely*: sup. nsn. vænst, 60.3.

Væringjar, m. (pl. only). p.n. (*Norse mercenary soldiers*): np. Vęrinngiar, 53.8.

yðvarr, poss. pron. *your* (pl.): asn. yduart, 8.6.

yfir, prep. w. dat. *over*: yfir, 20.6.

yfir, prep. w. dat. *over*: yfir, 20.6.

yfirmaðr, m. *over-man, one who wields authority*: ds. yfirmanni, 9.1.

yfirskjǫldungr, m. *over-king*: ns. yfirskiolldungr, 50.5, 65.7.

yndi, n. *luck, success, contentment, joy*: ds. yndi, 5.1.

yrkja, III. *compose poetry*: inf. mer er vant at yrkia, *there is need for me to compose*, 46.4; pret. 3s. orti, 12.3.

ýtar, m. (pl. only). *men*: np. 23.3.

æzstann, æzstr, æzstrar, see **œðri**

œðri, œztr, comp. adj. (lacks positive). *higher, highest*: comp. gsf. ædri, 62.1; sup. nsm. æzstr, 3.5; sup. gsf. æzstrar, 5.3; sup. asm. æzstann, 71.5.

œskja, III. *desire*: pres. 3s. æskir, 18.7, 21.7, 24.7, 27.7, 30.7, 33.7, 36.7, 39.7, 42.7, 45.7.

ǫðlingr, m. *prince, nobleman*: ns. odlingr, 21.3; gs. audlings, 39.2; gp. audlinga, 5.6.

ǫflugr, adj. *full of strength*: gsm. auflugs, 68.7.

ǫfugmæli, n. *slander*: as. ofugmæli, 61.8.

ǫfunð, f. *hatred*: ds. ofund, 58.4.

ǫld, f. *age, epoch, era*; *man, mankind*: ns. aulld, 12.3, 66.1; gs. alldar, 58.1, 65.7; ds. ofund, 58.4.

Ǫlvishaugr, m. p.n.: as. Aulfishaug, 14.8.

ǫnd, f. *soul, spirit*: as. aund, 20.7, 60.6.

Ǫngulsey, f. p.n. (*Angelsey*): gs. Avngvlseyiar, 31.7.

ǫr, f. *arrow*: gp. orfa, 54.5; *message stick, rune stick*: ær, 40.8 (?).

ǫrn, m. *eagle*: gp. arnar, 29.2.

Abbreviations and Short Titles

AASS: *Acta Sanctorum quotquot toto orbe coluntur*
Ágrip: *Ágrip af Nóregs konunga sögum*
AH: Dreves, Guido Maria S.J., and Clemens Blume, S.J., ed. *Analecta Hymnica Medii Ævi*
ANF: *Arkiv för nordisk filologi*
APS: *Acta Philologica Scandinavica*
Brudst: Louis-Jensen, Jonna, ed. '"Syvende og ottende brudstykke." Fragmentet AM 325 IV 4to'
CAO: Hesbert, Renato-Joanne, ed., *Corpus Antiphonalium Officii*
CCCM: Corpus Christianorum Continuatio Mediaevalis
CCSL: Corpus Christianorum Series Latina
CN: Wisén, Theodor, ed., *Carmina Norrœnæ*
CPB: Vigfússon, G., and F. York Powell, eds., *Corpus Poeticum Boreale*
EAK: Kock, E.A., ed. *Den norsk isländska skaldediktningen*
EETS: Early English Text Society
EHR: *English Historical Review*
GNH: *Gamal norsk homiliebok*
HASC: Milfull, Inge B. *The Hymns of the Anglo-Saxon Church*
Hkr: Snorri Sturluson, *Heimskringla*
ÍF: Íslenzk Fornrit
JEGP: *Journal of English and Germanic Philology*
KLNM: *Kulturhistorisk Lexicon for Nordisk Middelalder*
LMA: Lexikon des Mittelalters
MGH: Monumenta Germaniae Historica
MHN: *Monumenta Historica Norvegiæ*
NN: Kock, Ernst Albin, *Notationes Norrœnae*
OH.Leg: *Olafs Saga hins Helga* [the 'Legendary Saga']

OH.St: *Den store saga om Olav den Hellige*
ONid: *Ordo Nidrosiensis Ecclesiae*
Passio Olaui: *Passio et Miracula Beati Olaui*
PL: Patrologia Latina
Skj: Finnur Jónsson, ed., *Den norsk-islandske skjaldedigtning*
SnE 1931: Snorri Sturluson, *Edda Snorra Sturlusonar*
SRD: *Scriptores Rerum Danicarum Medii Aevi*
SRS: *Scriptores Rerum Suecicarum*
VSD: Gertz, M. Cl., ed., *Vitae Sanctorum Danorum*

Notes

Introduction

1 Hans Kuhn, *Das Dróttkvætt* (Heidelberg, 1983), 316.
2 Palaeographical and codicological studies of *Flateyjarbók* include: O.A. Johnsen and Jón Helgason, eds., *Den store saga om Olav den hellige* (Oslo, 1941), 1026–30; Finnur Jónsson, ed., *Flateyjarbók (Codex Flateyensis): Ms. no. 1005, fol. in the Old Royal Collection in the Royal Library of Copenhagen*, Corpus codicum islandicorum medii ævi, 1 (Copenhagen, 1930), 1–7; Finnur Jónsson, 'Flateyjarbók,' *Aarbøger for Nordisk Oldkyndighed og Historie*, 1927, 139–90; Kristian Kålund, *Katalog over de oldnorsk-islandske håndskrifter i det store kongelige bibliotek* (Copenhagen, 1900), 10–16; Jonna Louis-Jensen, 'Den yngre del af Flateyjarbók,' in *Afmælisrit Jóns Helgasonar. 30 júní 1969*, ed. Jakob Benediktsson, Jón Samsonarson, Jónas Kristjánsson, Ólafur Halldórsson, and Stefán Karlsson (Reykjavík, 1969), 235–50; Harry Törnquist, 'Olika Händer i Flatöboken,' *Aarbøger for Nordisk Oldkyndighed og Historie*, 1938, 91–8; G. Vigfússon and C.R. Unger, eds., *Flateyjarbók* (Christiania, 1868), 3: I–XXIV; and Christian Westergård-Nielsen, 'Nogle Bemærkninger til Flatøbogens Historie,' in *Nordisk Studier i Filologi och Lingvistik. Festskrift Tillägnad Gösta Holm på 60-Årsdagen den 8 Juli 1976*, ed. Lars Svensson, Anne Marie Wieselgren, and Åke Hansson, 432–44 (Lund, 1976).
3 Palaeographical and codicological studies of Bergsbók include: Vilhelm Gödel, *Katalog öfver Kungliga Bibliotekets fornisländska och fornnorska handskrifter* (Stockholm, 1897–1900), 1–5; *Bergsbók. Perg. Fol. Nr. 1, Royal Library, Stockholm*, ed. G. Lindblad, Early Icelandic Manuscripts in Facsimile, 5 (Copenhagen, 1963); *Den store saga om Olav den hellige*, ed. O.A. Johnson and Jón Helgason, 1005–25; Stefán Karlsson, 'Perg. Fol. Nr. 1 (Bergsbók) og Perg. 4to Nr. 6 í Stokkhólmi,' *Opuscula*, 3, Bibliotheca Arnamagnæana, 29 (Copenhagen, 1967),

74–82; Jakob Benediktsson, 'Nogle Bemærkninger om Bergsbók,' *Acta Philologica Scandinavica* 16 (1942–3): 121–8; Asgaut Steinnes, 'Om Bergsbók i 1500 åri,' *Maal og Minne* (1962): 9–30; D. Slay, ed., *Romances. Perg. 4:o NR 6, Royal Library, Stockholm*, Early Icelandic Manuscripts in Facsimile, 10 (Copenhagen, 1972).

4 See, e.g., Vemund Skard, 'Harmsól, Plácítúsdrápa og Leiðarvísan,'*ANF* 69 (1953): 97–108 and Katrina Attwood, 'Intertextual Aspects of the Twelfth-Century Christian *Drápur*,' *Saga Book* 24 (1996): 221–39. F. York Powell, no fan of Einarr, harboured a 'grave suspicion' that 'Einar was the person who re-edited and polished and veneered many of the poems we find in the Kings' Lives and Snorri's Edda' (*CPB*, 2: 258–9). Another explanation for the similarity might be that Einarr's poetry represents a style that was both admired and imitated.

5 Einarr is not listed among Skalla-Grímr's descendants in *Landnámabók*, but a fourteenth-century MS of *Gunnlaugs saga* (Stockholm, Holm perg. 4to, nr. 18) names him as a member of the distinguished family: 'Svá segja fróðir menn, at margir í ætt Mýrmanna, þeir sem frá Agli eru komnir, hafi verit menn vænstir, en þat sé þó mjok sundrgreiniligt, því at sumir í þeiri ætt hafa ok verit margir atforvismenn um marga hluti, sem var Kjartan Óláfsson pá ok Víga-Barði ok Skúli Þorsteinsson. Sumir váru ok skáldmenn miklir í þeiri ætt: Bjorn Hítadœlakappi, Einarr prestr Skúlason, Snorri Sturluson ok margir aðrir.' *Borgfirðinga Sǫgur*, ed. Sigurður Nordal and Guðni Jónsson (Reykjavík, 1938), 51 n.3.

6 See Gustav Storm, *Sigurd Ranessöns Proces* (Kristiana, 1877), 16.

7 *Morkinskinna*, ed. Finnur Jónsson (Copenhagen, 1932), 390–1.

8 Ibid., xxxi.

9 *Skj* IA: 456–8.

10 *Edda Snorra Sturlusonar* (Copenhagen, 1887), 3: 251–69.

11 *Diplomatarium Islandicum*, ed. Jón Sigurðsson and Jón Þorkelsson (Copenhagen, 1857), 1: 186.

12 See Martin Chase, 'Framir kynnask vátta mál: The Christian Background of Einnar Skúlason's *Geisli*,' in *Til Heiðurs og Hugbótar: Greinar um Trúarkveðskap Fyrri Alda*, ed. Svanhildur Óskarsdóttir and Anna Guðmundsdottir (Reykholt, 2003), 11–32, and 'The Refracted Beam: Einnar Skúlason's Liturgical Theology,' in *Verbal Encounters: Anglo-Saxon and Old Norse Studies for Roberta Frank*, ed. Antonina Harbus and Russell Poole (Toronto, 2005), 203–21.

13 *Skj* IA: 458 (*Haraldssonakvæði* and *Sigurðardrápa*), 473–5 (*Runhenda* and *Eysteinsdrápa*), and 476 (*Ingadrápa*).

14 *Morkinskinna*, 446.

15 'Einarr S[kúlason] was with the brothers S[igurðr] and Eysteinn, and Eysteinn was his great friend. Eysteinn asked him to compose Óláfsdrápa, and he did. He himself went north to Christ Church in Trondheim, and that was accompanied by

a great miracle: a wonderful odor came into the church, and men say that that was a sign from the king himself that he valued the poem highly' (*Morkinskinna*, 446).

16 Arne Odd Johnsen, *Studier vedrørende Kardinal Nicolaus Brekespears Legasjon til Norden* (Oslo, 1945), 104.

17 See Lars Boje Mortensen, 'The Nordic Archbishoprics as Literary Centres around 1200,' in *Archbishop Absalon of Lund and His World*, ed. Karsten Friis-Jensen and Inge Skovgaard-Peterson, 133–57 (Roskilde, 2000), esp. 154. On the theme of nationalism, see also Gerd Wolfgang Weber, 'Saint Óláfr's Sword: Einarr Skúlason's Geisli and its Trondheim Performance AD 1153 – A Turning Point in Norwego-Icelandic Scaldic Poetry,' *The Sagas and The Norwegian Experience / Sagaene og Noreg: Proceedings of the 10th International Saga Conference* (Trondheim, 1997), 655–61.

18 *Skj* IA: 477.

19 *Glælognskviða av Toraren Lovtunge*, ed. Hallvard Magerøy (Oslo, 1948).

20 Ca. 1043, according to G. Turville-Petre, *Origins of Icelandic Literature* (Oxford, 1953), 145.

21 *Skj* IA: 257–65.

22 'Quomodo vero mox omnipotens Deus merita martyris sui Olavi declaraverit cæcis visum reddendo et multa commoda ægris mortalibus impendendo, et qualiter episcopus Grimkel – qui fuit filius fratris Sigwardi episcopi, quem Olavus filius Tryggva secum adduxerat de Anglia – post annum et quinque dies beatum corpus e terra levaverit et in loco decenter ornato reposuerit in Nidrosiensi metropoli, quo statim peracta pugna transvectum fuerat, quia hæc omnia a nonnullis memoriæ tradita sunt, nos notis immorari superfluum duximus' (*MHN*, 43–4; English translation, David McDougall and Ian McDougall, *Theodoricus Monachus* [London, 1998], 33).

23 *MHN*, xxxiv and n. to 44.3; Sigurður Nordal, *Om Olaf den helliges saga* (Copenhagen, 1914), 10–12; E. Skard, 'Kirchliche Olavus tradition bei Theodoricus monachus,' *Symbolae Osloenses* 14 (1935): 119–25 at 125; Turville-Petre, *Origins of Icelandic Literature*, 171; Bjarni Guðnason, 'Theodoricus og íslenskir sagnaritarar,' in *Sjötiu ritgerðir helgaðar Jakobi Benediktssyni*, ed. Einar G. Pétursson and Jónas Kristjansson (Reykjavik, 1977), 108; Erik Gunnes, *Erkebiskop Eystein, statsmann og kirkebygger* (Oslo, 1996), 207.

24 See Inger Ekrem, Lars Boje Mortensen, and Karen Skovgaard-Petersen, eds., *Olavslegenden og den latinske historieskrivning i 1100-tallets Norge* (Copenhagen, 2000) (see esp. Mortensen, 'Olav den helliges mirakler'; Inger Ekrem, 'Om Passio Olavis tilblivelse'; Jon Gunnar Jørgensen, 'Passio Olavi og Snorre'; Østrem, 'Om en nyoppdaget Olavslegende'); Mortensen, 'The Anchin Manuscript of *Passio Olavi* (Douai 295), William of Jumièges, and Theodoricus Monachus:

New Evidence for Intellectual Relations Between Norway and France in the 12th Century,' *Symbolae Osloenses* 75 (2000): 165–89; Mortensen, 'The Nórdic Archbishoprics as Literary Centres'; and Eyolf Østrem, *The Office of Saint Olav: A Study in Chant Transmission* (Uppsala, 2001).

25 Østrem, *The Office of Saint Olav*, 29–33; Mortensen, 'The Anchin Manuscript,' 170.

26 Østrem, *The Office of Saint Olav*, 33–40.

27 Matthew 11:27, Mark 7:4, Luke 4:6 and 10:22.

28 Østrem, *The Office of Saint Olav*, 35. See also G. Lange, *Die anfängeder isländisch-norwegischen Geschichtsschreibung* (Reykjavík, 1989), 52–3.

29 Østrem, *The Office of Saint Olav*, 30; see also Bruce Dickins, 'The Cult of Saint Olave in the British Isles,' *Saga Book* 12 (1940): 53–80.

30 Østrem, *The Office of Saint Olav*, 31.

31 *The Leofric Missal*, ed. Frederick Warren (Oxford, 1883), 274.

32 Ibid., 210–14.

33 Edited in *Brudst*.

34 *Brudst*, 36.

35 Ibid., 59.

36 Ibid., 58–9.

37 *OH.Leg.*

38 *Passio Olaui*; English translation by Devra Kunin and Carl Phelpstead, *A History of Norway and The Passion and Miracles of the Blessed Óláfr* (London, 2001).

39 *MHN*, 125–44; on the date see Erik Gunnes, 'Om hvordan Passio Olavi ble til,' *Maal og Minne* (1973): 1–11 at 4.

40 Ekrem, 'Om *Passio Olavis* tilblivelse,' 108–56.

41 Mortensen, 'Olav den helliges mirakler,' 89–107; Mortensen, 'The Anchin Manuscript.'

42 Mortensen, 'Olav den Helliges mirakler,' 97; Mortensen, 'The Anchin Manuscript,' 186.

43 See, e.g., Else Mundal, 'Den latinspråklege historieskrivinga og den norrøne tradisjonen,' *Olavslegendum og den latinske historieskrivning*, ed. Ekrem, Mortensen, and Skovgaard-Peterson, 9–25.

44 Mortensen, 'The Nordic Archbishoprics as Literary Centres,' 150.

45 *GNH*, 108–29.

46 *Ágrip af Nóregs konunga sögum*, ed. Finnur Jónsson (Haille, 1929).

47 *Brudst*, 59.

48 Gustav Storm, ed., *Otte Brudstykker af den Ældste Saga om Olav den Hellige* (Christiania, 1888).

49 *Brudst*, passim.

50 Sigurður Nordal, *Om Olav den helliges saga* (Copenhagen, 1914), 69–133.

51 *Hkr*, vol. 2 (ÍF, 27).

52 *Hkr*, vol. 3 (ÍF, 28).

53 *OH.St.*

54 Adam of Bremen, *Gesta Hammaburgensis ecclesiae*, ed. Bernhard Schmeidler, MGH, Scriptores rerum Germanicarum in usum scholarum separatim editi, 2, 3rd ed. (Hannover, 1917).

55 Ed. Gustav Storm, *MHN*, 1–68.

56 Saxo, *Saxonis Gesta Danorum*, ed. J. Olrik and H. Raeder (Copenhagen, 1931), 302–3.

57 John Kinnamos, *Deeds of John and Manuel Comnenus*, trans. Charles M. Brand (New York, 1976), 4.

58 See Susan Boynton, 'Training for the Liturgy as a Form of Monastic Education,' in *Medieval Monastic Education*, ed. George Ferzoco and Carolyn Muessig, 7–20 (London, 2000). As Boynton notes (16), 'The liturgy was in many ways a school within the monastery, and its incessant rhythm made liturgical training a constant preoccupation – the central focus of monastic education and formation.'

59 See Chase, 'Framir kynnask vátta mál' and 'The Refracted Beam.'

60 On the *drápa* form see Eduard Sievers, *Altgermanische Metrik* (Halle, 1893), 95–8; Finnur Jónsson, *Den oldnorske og oldislandske litteraturs historie* (Copenhagen, 1894), 1: 409–16; Sigurður Nordal, 'Icelandic Notes 1: Drápa,' *APS* 6 (1931–2): 144–9; Jón Helgason, 'Norges og Islands digtning,' 101–11; Hallvard Lie, 'Dråpa,' *KLNM* 3: 351–2; Hans Schottmann, *Die isländische Mariendichtung*, Münchner Germanistische Beiträge, 9 (Munich, 1973), 204–13; Bjarni Fidjestøl, *Det Norrøne Fyrstediktet* (Øvre Ervik, 1982), 182–90; Kuhn, *Das Dróttkvætt*, 209–14; Hans Schottmann, 'Drápa,' *LMA* 3: 1367–8.

61 Sigurður Nordal, 'Icelandic Notes,' 148.

62 See Schottmann, *Die isländischen Mariendichtung*, 205 and 208. Wolfgang Lange states without further comment that the disposition of *Geisli* is 18 // 27 (9   3) // 26 (*Studien zur Christlichen Dichtung der Nordgermanen 1000–1200*, Palaestra, 222 [Göttingen, 1958], 121).

63 See below, 44.

64 See, e.g., Schottmann, *Die isländische Mariendichtung*, 207.

65 Martin Chase, '*Concatenatio* as a Structural Element in the Christian *Drápur*,' in *The Sixth International Saga Conference: Workshop Papers* (Copenhagen, 1985), 1: 115–29.

66 Kuhn, *Das Dróttkvætt*; Kristján Árnason, *The Rhythms of Dróttkvætt and Other Old Icelandic Metres* (Reykjavík, 1991); Kari Ellen Gade, *The Structure of Old Norse* Dróttvkætt *Poetry*, Islandica, 49 (Ithaca, NY, 1995).

67 Diana Whaley, *The Poetry of Arnórr jarlaskáld: An Edition and Study*, Westfield Publications in Medieval Studies, 8 (London, 1998), 85–92.

68 Sievers, *Altgermanische Metrik*, 31–6.

69 My scansion of *Geisli* is by no means definitive and can only serve as a rough
   guideline. It is good to keep in mind Gade's example of the same line scanned dif-
   ferently by six different scholars (*The Structure of Old Norse* Dróttkvætt *Poetry*,
   42).

70 Lines 1.1, 2.1, 2.5, 3.6, 3.7, 4.1, 4.3, 4.5, 4.6, 4.7, 4.8, 5.1, 5.2, 5.3, 5.5, 6.1, 6.8,
   7.3, 7.5, 7.7, 8.1, 8.3, 8.5, 8.7, 8.8, 9.2, 9.5, 9.7, 10.3, 10.7, 10.8, 11.3, 11.4, 11.5,
   11.6, 11.7, 12.1, 12.3, 12.5, 12.7, 13.1, 13.3, 13.5, 14.1, 14.3, 14.7, 14.8, 15.1, 15.2,
   15.3, 15.5, 15.6, 15.7, 15.8, 16.2, 16.3, 16.5, 17.1, 18.3, 18.5, 18.7, 19.3, 19.5, 20.1,
   20.5, 21.1, 21.3, 22.1, 22.2, 22.5, 22.7, 23.1, 23.3, 23.6, 23.7, 24.1, 25.3, 25.7, 26.1,
   26.3, 26.4, 26.5, 26.8, 27.1, 27.2, 27.3, 28.2, 28.5, 28.8, 29.2, 29.3, 29.5, 29.6, 29.7,
   30.1, 30.3, 31.1, 31.7, 32.3, 33.1, 33.2, 34.1, 34.2, 34.5, 34.7, 35.1, 35.8, 35.4, 37.3,
   37.5, 37.7, 38.2, 38.3, 38.5, 38.7, 38.8, 39.1, 39.2, 39.4, 40.1, 41.1, 41.7, 42.1, 42.3,
   43.1, 43.2, 43.3, 43.5, 43.7, 44.1, 44.2, 44.3, 44.7, 46.1, 46.2, 46.3, 46.4, 46.7, 46.8,
   47.1, 47.5, 47.8, 48.1, 48.5, 48.7, 49.7, 50.1, 50.3, 50.7, 51.5, 52.1, 52.3, 52.5, 52.7,
   53.1, 53.2, 53.7, 54.1, 54.2, 54.3, 54.5, 55.1, 55.2, 55.7, 56.1, 56.3, 56.5, 56.7, 57.2,
   57.3, 57.5, 58.3, 58.5, 58.7, 59.1, 59.3, 59.6, 60.3, 60.6, 60.7, 61.3, 61.7, 62.3, 62.4,
   63.1, 63.5, 63.6, 64.1, 64.3, 64.7, 65.4, 65.5, 65.6, 66.1, 66.3, 66.5, 66.7, 67.1, 67.3,
   67.7, 68.3, 68.5, 68.7, 68.3, 68.5, 70.1, 70.8, 71.1, 71.4.

71 Lines 3.1, 10.1, 19.1, 25.5, 31.3, 35.3, 37.1, 39.3, 40.6, 51.1, 52.8, 53.6, 58.2, 61.1,
   65.1, 67.5.

72 Lines 2.8, 3.2, 3.4, 5.8, 6.2, 6.4, 6.6, 7.1, 8.2, 9.6, 9.8, 10.4, 11.1, 11.8, 12.2, 13.4,
   13.6, 15.4, 16.6, 17.2, 17.4, 18.8, 19.4, 19.8, 20.6, 22.6, 24.3, 24.4, 25.2, 25.4, 25.8,
   26.2, 27.4, 28.6, 29.4, 30.4, 31.6, 32.2, 33.4, 35.4, 36.1, 36.2, 37.6, 37.8, 41.4, 41.6,
   44.8, 46.6, 48.4, 49.2, 49.6, 50.4, 51.3, 51.6, 51.8, 55.6, 56.8, 57.6, 58.4, 59.8, 60.1,
   60.2, 63.4, 54.4, 64.6, 66.4, 66.6, 67.4, 67.6, 68.6, 69.1, 69.2, 69.6, 70.2, 70.6, 71.2,
   71.3, 71.5.

73 Lines 1.3, 2.3, 40.5, 41.5, 46.5, 53.5, 59.5, 70.5.

74 Lines 6.5, 14.5, 31.5, 32.5, 35.5, 35.7, 44.5, 49.5.

75 Lines 14.5, 16.1, 62.5, 64.5.

76 Lines 1.2, 1.4, 3.3, 3.5, 4.4, 5.4, 6.3, 6.6, 7.8, 8.4, 10.6, 13.8, 16.4, 16.6, 19.7, 20.4,
   21.2, 25.1, 25.6, 28.3, 34.3, 34.6, 35.2, 38.4, 40.3, 40.7, 41.2, 42.4, 43.8, 44.6, 47.2,
   47.3, 48.6, 49.3, 49.4, 49.8, 50.5, 50.8, 51.6, 52.4, 55.3, 55.4, 55.5, 55.6, 63.7, 63.8,
   65.8.

77 Lines 1.5, 2.2, 2.4, 7.4, 10.5, 12.6, 12.8, 13.2, 13.7, 14.4, 18.2, 18.6, 21.4, 22.3,
   22.4, 23.2, 23.4, 24.2, 29.1, 30.2, 34.8, 37.4, 40.4, 40.8, 42.2, 45.2, 45.3, 47.4, 47.6,
   47.7, 48.3, 53.4, 54.7, 54.8, 56.6, 57.4, 57.7, 58.8, 59.2, 59.4, 59.7, 60.4, 60.8, 61.8,
   62.2, 62.6, 63.2, 64.2, 66.2, 68.1, 70.3, 70.4, 71.8.

78 Lines 2.6, 7.2, 7.4, 9.3, 11.2, 16.8, 17.6, 18.1, 20.4, 22.8, 23.8, 26.7, 28.1, 28.7,

31.2, 32.6, 32.7, 33.3, 34.4, 36.3, 38.1, 38.6, 40.2, 41.3, 44.4, 48.8, 49.1, 50.6, 51.3, 52.2, 53.3, 55.5, 56.2, 58.1, 58.6, 62.2, 64.8, 65.3, 66.8, 69.7, 69.8, 71.7.

79 Lines 1.6, 1.7, 1.8, 3.8, 4.2, 5.6, 7.6, 8.6, 9.1, 9.4, 10.2, 12.4, 14.2, 14.6, 17.3, 17.5, 17.7, 18.4, 18.8, 19.2, 19.6, 20.2, 20.7, 20.8, 23.5, 26.6, 28.4, 29.8, 31.4, 32.1, 32.4, 32.8, 35.6, 37.2, 41.8, 43.4, 43.6, 45.1, 45.4, 48.2, 50.2, 51.2, 52.6, 53.8, 54.4, 54.6, 55.4, 55.8, 56.4, 57.1, 57.8, 60.5, 61.2, 62.7, 62.8, 63.3, 65.2, 65.7, 67.2, 67.8, 68.2, 68.4, 68.8, 69.4, 70.7, 71.6.

80 Whaley, *The Poetry of Arnórr jarlaskáld*, 89.

81 Gade (*The Structure of Old Norse* Dróttkvætt *Poetry*, 117–23) comments on this phenomenon, as does Kuhn (*Das Dróttkvætt*, 140), who says that there are just forty instances of A2k lines in the odd-numbered position in skaldic poetry before 1200.

82 Gade, *The Structure of Old Norse* Dróttkvætt *Poetry*, 118. She in turn refers to Kuhn, *Das Dróttkvætt*, 166, 174–5.

83 Whaley, *The Poetry of Arnórr jarlaskáld*, 86.

84 Lines 4.5–5.3, 11.2–12.3, 15.1–8, 26.1–5, 27.1–4, 29.2–7, 31.6–8, 39.1–4, 43.1–3, 44.1–3, 46.1–4, 58.2–5, 63.4–6, 65.4–6, 66.3–7, 71.1–5.

85 Lines 1.2–8, 2.2–4, 20.2–4, 32.4–8, 40.2–5, 45.2–4, 47.2–4, 53.3–5, 54.6–8, 55.3–5, 61.4–6, 62.5–8.

86 Two recent theoretical studies of the kenning are Edith Marold, *Kenningkunst: Ein Beitrag zu einer Poetik der Skaldendichtung* (Berlin, 1983), and Rolf Stavnem, 'Hør Kvasirs blod! Kenning og metafor i den norsk-islandske skjaldedigtning' (PhD dissertation, Københavns Universitet, 2002). Guðrún Nordal discusses Einarr's use of kennings (with a focus on his secular poetry) in Part Three of *Tools of Literacy: The Role of Skaldic Verse in Icelandic Textual Culture of the Twelfth and Thirteenth Centuries* (Toronto, 2001) ('Theory and Practice in Skaldic Poetics,' 197–338). The most detailed study of the diction of *Geisli* remains Lange, *Studien zur Christlichen Dichtung der Nordgermanen 1000–1200*, 120–6.

87 Guðrún Nordal, *Tools of Literacy*, 237–308.

Appreciation

1 English Bible translations are from the Douay-Rheims version, the emphasis here is mine.

2 'Pater est gloria. filius idem cum eo: et eum notificans homo factus, ut radius solem' (*Glossa Ordinaria*, ed. Nicholas of Lyra [Paris, 1590], 6: 795).

3 'Et mihi querenti nil probabilius occurrit ad credendum et intelligendum quam Dei Patris Verbum quod, instar radii ab inaccessibili et inuisibili sole, id est Patre, in universitatem sensibilis et intelligibilis creature, et maxime ac principaliter in angelicos et humanos creature, et maxime ac principaliter in angelicos et humanos

intellectus, diffunditur, implens omnia, perficiens imperfecta, penetrans obstrusa, illuminans mysteria, fomans uisiones in interioribus sensibus theologorum, aperiens intellectus eas uisiones querere et intelligere uolentium, et seipsum secundum analogiam uniuscuiusque omnibus in se intuentibus manifestans' (John Scotus Eriugena, *Expositiones in Ierarchiam Coelestem*, ed. J. Barbet, CCCM, 31 [Turnholt, 1975], 1.314–23).

4 'Ac de his efficit diuina agalmata, hoc est diuinas imagines, et specula clarissima et munda in quibus species diuine glorie resultat; et recipiunt principale lumen quod est Pater, diuinumque eius radium qui est eius Filius, Spiritumque amborum recipiunt' (John Scotus Eriugena, *Expositiones in Ierarchiam Coelestem*, 3.124–26).

5 *AH* 50: 11–12; *ONid*, 184, 194, 197; *HASC*, 142–4.

6 Bede, *Homelia in Nativitate Domini (Luc. ii, 15–20)*, ed. D. Hurst, *Bedae Venerabilis: Opera homiletica; Opera rythmica* (Turnhout, 1955), CCSL, 122 45–51.

7 Ælfric, *De Fide Catholica*, in *Ælfric's Catholic Homilies. The First Series*, ed. Peter Clemoes, EETS Supplemental Series, 17 (Oxford, 1997), 235–44, esp. 338. See also notes in Malcolm Godden's *Ælfric's Catholic Homilies. Introduction, Commentary, and Glossary*, EETS Supplemental Series, 18 (Oxford, 2000), 162.

8 *The Icelandic Homily Book: Perg. 150 in the Royal Library, Stockholm*, ed. Andrea de Leeuw van Weenen, Íslenzk handrit, Series in quarto, 3 (Reykjavík, 1993), fol. 102v; *GNH, Ómelia Gregorij*, 39–43 and *Sermo de sancta Maria*, 129–34.

9 '*Lux*, proprie, Christus; unde: *Ego sum lux mundi* ... Dicuntur praedicatores sancti, ut apostoli, unde in Evangelio: *Vos estis lux hujus mundi* ... Dicitur divina natura, unde in Apoc. de Deo dicitur: *Qui habitat lucem inaccessibilem*' (Alan of Lille, *Distinctiones*, PL 210: 844–5).

10 '*Lumen*, proprie. Dicitur Christi praedicatio, et Patris et Spiritus sancti cognitio; unde: Quoniam apud te est fons vitae et in lumine tuo videbimus lumen ... Dicitur sanctus, qui a Christo illuminatur, unde Jacobus: *Omne datum optimum descendens a Patre luminum*' (Ibid., 841–2).

11 '*Sol* proprie. Dicitur Christus ... Dicitur sanctus, unde in lib. Sapientiae: *Fulgebunt justi sicut sol* ... Dicitur divina Christi natura, quae illuminat humanam Christi naturam*' (Ibid., 947–8).

12 'In ipso vero orientii loco erat splendor mirablilis, lux inaccessibilis nimiae atque immensae claritatis ... ipsum tamen inibi [some manuscripts have 'tamen Iesum credebam'] esse credebam, de quo Petrus ait: *In quem desiderant angeli prospicere*. Ab ipso namque claritas immensa procedebat, ex qua omnis longitudo et latitudo sanctorum illustrabatur. Ipse quoque quodammodo erat in omnibus, et omnes in eo; ipse omnia exterius circumdabat, ipse omnes interius satiando regebat; ipse superius protegebat, ipse inferius sustinebat' (Rimbert, *Vita Anskarii* ed. G. Waitz, MGH, Scriptores rerum Germanicarum in usum scholarum, 55 [Hannover, 1884), 22–3].

13 'Sed cum Deum videre non possumus, habemus aliquid quod agamus, unde iter fiat

quo ad eum nostræ intelligentiæ oculus veniat. Certe quem in se videre nullo modo valemus, hunc in servis suis videre jam possumus. Quos dum mira conspicimus agere, certum nobis fit in eorum mentibus Deum habitare. In re autem incorporea a rebus corporalibus usum trahamus. Nemo etenim nostrum orientem clare solem, in sphæram illius intendendo, valet conspicere, quia tensi in ejus radiis oculi reverberantur; sed sole illustratos montes aspicimus, et quia jam sol ortus est videmus. Quia ergo solem justitiæ in seipso videre non possumus, illustratos montes claritate illius videamus, sanctos videlicet apostolos, qui virtutibus emicant, miraculis coruscant, quos nati solis claritas perfudit, et cum in seipso sit invisiblilis, per eos nobis quasi per illustratos montes se visibilem præbuit. Virtus enim divinitatis in se quasi sol in cælo est; virtus divinitatis in hominibus, sol in terra' (Gregory the Great, *XL Homiliarum in Evangelia*, 2.30.10, PL 76: 1226–7). This homily also survives in an Old Norse translation: see *Leifar fornra kristinna fræða íslenzkra*, ed. Þorvaldur Bjarnarson (Copenhagen, 1878), 35–6.

14 *CAO* 3: § 2908; *ONid*, 179, 284, 350, 371, 378, 393, 395, 406, 413.

15 Frederik Paasche, *Kristendom og Kvad* (Kristiania, 1914), 79, n.1.

16 Radbod of Utrecht, *Carmen Allegoricum de Sancto Switberto*, ed. Paulus de Winterfeld, MGH, Poetarum Latinorum Medii Aevi, 4 (Berlin, 1899), 166–7.

17 The image recurs (almost certainly inspired by *Geisli*) in the later *Jóns saga helga* and *Guðmundar saga Arasonar*, in *Byskupa Sögur*, ed. Guðni Jónsson (Reykjavík, 1948), 2: 1 and 243; see also *Biskupa Sögur I*, ed. Sigurgeir Steingrímsson et al., ÍF, 15 (Reykjavík, 2003), 1: CCXX-II.

18 Gregory of Tours, *Vitae Patrum*, ed. W. Arndt and B. Krusch, MGH, Scriptores rerum Merovingicarum (Hannover, 1884), 1: 662.

19 See, e.g., Erich Hoffmann, *Die heiligen Könige bei den Angelsachsen und den Skandinavischen Völkern: Konigsheiliger und Konigshaus* (Neumünster, 1975); Andrew Hughes, 'The Monarch as the Object of Liturgical Veneration,' in *Kings and Kingship in Medieval Europe*, ed. Anne Duggen (London, 1993); and Gerd Wolfgang Weber, 'Intellegere historiam: Typological Perspectives of Nordic Prehistory,' in *Tradition og historieskrivning: Kilderne Til Nordens ældste historie*, ed. Kirsten Hastrup and Preben Meulengracht Sørenson (Århus, 1987).

20 Cf. *Passio Olaui*, 72: 'hostes ... convenerunt in unum adversus dominum et adversus christum eius [the enemies came together as one against the Lord and against his christ]' (quoting Psalm 2:2: *adstiterunt reges terrae / et principes convenerunt in unum / adversus Dominum et adversus christum eius*). While texts like *Konungs skuggsjá* use the epithet *kristr dróttins* in reference to anointed kings and kings who rule as representatives of God, it is clear that in the typological saints' Lives there is also an allusion to Christ (see Sverre Bagge, *The Political Thought of the King's Mirror* [Odense, 1987], 43–9).

21 *Passio Olaui*; Kunin, trans. and Phelpstead, ed., *A History of Norway and The Passion and Miracles of the Blessed Óláfr*.

22 *MHN*, 1–68; *Theodoricus Monachus: Historia de Antiquitate Regum Norwagiensium*, trans. David and Ian McDougall (London, 1998); Else Mundal, 'Helgenkult og norske helgenar,' *Collegium Medievale* 8 (1995–6), 105–30.

23 *VSD*, 62–71.

24 *VSD*, 77–136.

25 *VSD*, 60–2.

26 *VSD*, 76.

27 Thomas Arnold, ed., *Memorials of St Edmund's Abbey*, Rerum Brittanicarum medii aevi scriptores, 96 (London, 1890–6), 1: 3–25.

28 Ibid., 1: 26–92.

29 James Raine, ed., *The Historians of the Church of York and Its Archbishops*, Rerum Brittanicarum medii ævi scriptores, 71 (London, 1879–94, repr., Wiesbaden, 1965), 1: 399–475.

30 M.R. James, 'Two Lives of St Ethelbert, King and Martyr,' *EHR* 32 (1917): 214–44.

31 J.A. Giles, ed., *Joannis Saresberiensis Opera Omnia Postea Episcopi Carnotensis* (London, 1848, repr. Leipzig, 1969), 5: 359–80.

32 *SRS*, 2: 270–317.

33 Bernt C. Lange, 'Olav den hellige: *Ikon.*,' *KLNM* 12: 568–77; Anne Lidén, *Olav den helige i medeltida bildkonst: Legendmotiv oc attribut* (Stockholm, 1999), 33. For discussions of a particular example, the Andenes altarpiece, see Lidén, 181–2.

34 *Skj* IIA: 218–19.

35 *Skj* IIA: 167.

36 Jacobus de Voragine, *De sancto Olauo rege norwegie ac dacie martire* (Leuven, 1485, 101–3; repr., *MHN*, 277–82).

37 Lidén, *Olav den helige i medeltida bildkonst*, 180–1. See also Gunnar Danbolt, 'Bilde som tale: St. Olavs-antemensalet i Nidarsdomen,' *Kunst og Kultur* 71 (1988): 138–58.

38 See, e.g., Gervais of Melkley, *Ars Poetica*, ed. Hans-Jürgen Gräbner (Munster, 1965), 153.

39 *Rhetorica ad Herennium*, in *M. Tulli Ciceronis Scripta quae Manserunt Omnia, Fasc. 1, Incerti Aucteris de Ratione Dicendi Ad C. Herennium Lils. IV*, ed. Friedrich Marx (Leipzig, 1923), 1.4, 6–7.

40 See Alexander M. Bruce, *Scyld and Scef: Expanding the Analogues* (New York, 2002), 5, and his references to Fred C. Robinson, *Beowulf and the Appositive Style* (Knoxville, 1985), 23–4 and J.R.R. Tolkein, '*Beowulf:* The Monsters and the Critics,' *Proceedings of the British Academy* 22 (1936): 245–95 at 271.

41 Joseph Braun, *Der Christliche Altar* (Munich, 1924), 1: 109–25. See especially the descriptions of the St Óláfr altar at Kaupanger (113) and the St Martin altar at Vich (110 and pl. 140); Kristian Bonnevie Bjerknes and Hans-Emil Lidén, *The Stave*

Churches of Kaupanger: The Present Church and its Predecessors (Oslo, 1975), 127.

42 'Principium est, cum statim auditoris animum nobis idoneum reddimus ad audiendum. Id ita sumitur, ut attentos, ut dociles, ut benivolos auditores habere possimus ... Attentos habebimus, si pollicebimur nos de rebus magnis, novis, inusitatis verba facturos aut de iis, auqe ad rem pertineant, aut ad eos ipsos, qui audient, aut ad deorum inmortalium religionem; et si rogabimus, ut attente audiant' (*Rhetorica ad Herennium*, 1.4, 6–7).

43 See Cecil Wood, 'The Skald's Bid for a Hearing,' *JEGP* 59 (1960): 240–54, and Gert Kreutzer, *Die Dichtungslehre der Skalden*, Hochschulschriften: Literaturwissenschaft, 1 (Meisenheim am Glan, 1977), 264–71.

44 Bjarne Fidjestøl, 'Sogekvæde,' in *Deutsch-nordische Begegnungen: 9. Arbeitstagung der Skandinavisten des deutschen Sprachgebiets 1989 in Svendborg*, ed. Kurt Braunmüller and Mogens Brøndsted (Odense, 1991), 67–9.

45 *OH.Leg*, 184, 186. The authorship and date of the Legendary Saga are uncertain – it is difficult to say more than that it dates from the twelfth century. For a survey of current ideas about the complicated textual history of the saga, see Theodore M. Andersson, 'Kings' Sagas (*Konungasögur*),' in *Old Norse-Icelandic Literature*, ed. Carol J. Clover and John Lindow, Islandica, 45 (Ithaca, NY, 1985), 197–238.

46 'Olaph ... fertur in papilione dormiens sompnium vidisse. Cumque supervenirent hostes adhuc illo quiescente, dux sui exercitus, Phin nomine, accedens regem suscitavit. Tunc ille suspirans: "O! quid fecisti?" inquit; "videbam me per scalam, cuius vertex sidera tangeret, ascendisse. Heu! iam perveni ad summum illius scalae celumque mihi apertum est ingredienti, nisi tu me suscitando revocasses." Postquem visionem vidit rex, circumventus a suis, cum non repugnaret, occiditur et martyrio coronatur' (Adam of Bremen, *Gesta*, 2.61.schol.41, p. 120).

47 Adam of Bremen, *Gesta*, XLII.

48 Mircea Eliade, *Patterns in Comparative Religion*, trans. Rosemary Sheed (London, 1958), 108.

49 'Et retuli statim fratri meo; et intelleximus passionem esse futuram, et coepimus nullam iam spem in saeculo habere' (*Passio Sanctarum Perpetuae et Felicitatis*, ed. Cornelius Ionnes Maria Joseph von Beek [Nijmegen, 1936], 14).

50 'Hanc ergo scalam / ita Christi amor / feminis fecit perviam, / ut dracone conculcato / et Aethiopis gladio / transito // Per omne genus / tormentorum caeli / apicem queant capere / et de manu confortantis / regis auream lauream / sumere (*AH* 53: 393–4, verses 6–7).

51 'Ecce dominum Deum tuum, quem diligis, stantem ad summitatem scale, tenentem coronam in manibus, quam in capite tuo ponere velit, et baculum ad regendum populum eius, ut sectatorem bonorum operum viam salutis doceas!' (*Vita Pardulfi*

Abbatis Waractensis, ed. B. Krusch and W. Levison, *Passiones Vitaeque Sanctorum Aevi Merovingici*, MGH, Scriptores rerum Merovingicarum, 7 [Hannover and Leipzig, 1920], 29.

52 'Ecce scala, quam, dum viveret, erexit ad caelum! Ecce sotii angeli, quos bonis operibus inherendo adquisivit in terra amicos! ... Ex hac ergo revelatione papenter datur intellegi, quod ... virtutes eam ad celsitudinem aeterni Regis et ad praemii coronam citius remunerandam perducturae erant. Qua ipsa sancta mater comperta visione cognovit, se quantotius e corpore esse migraturam ...' (*Vita Sanctae Balthildis*, ed. B. Krusch, *Fredegarii et Aliorum Chronica. Vitae Sanctorum*, MGH, Scriptores rerum Merovingicarum, 2 [Hannover, 1888], 489).

53 See Eliade, *Patterns in Comparative Religion*, 382.

54 See George S. Tate, 'The Cross as Ladder: *Geisli* 15–16 and *Líknarbrant* 34,' *Medieval Scandinavia* 11 (1978): 258–64.

55 Tate gives numerous references; cf. also the *Glossa Ordinaria*, 1: 324; Alan of Lille's *Distinctiones* (s.v. 'scala,' PL 210: 935); and the hymn *Triumphalis gloriae* (*AH* 51: 85).

56 *Stjórn*, ed. C.R. Unger (Oslo, 1862), 170; cf. Peter Comestor, *Historia Scholastica*, 73, PL 198: 1114.

57 *Laudes crucis attollamus, AH* 54: 188.

58 *Si vis vera frui luce, AH* 50: 534.

59 See *Glossa Ordinaria*, 1: 324, the hymn *Laudis crucis attollamus* (*AH* 54: 188), and the scriptural reference in John 12:32.

60 Arbeo of Freising, *Vita vel passio Haimhrammi episcopi et martyris Ratisbonensis*, ed. E. Dümmler, *Passiones Vitaeque Sanctorum Aevi Merovingici*, MGH, Scriptores rerum Merovingicarum, 4 (Hannover, 1892), 488.

61 Iohannis de Caulibus, *Meditaciones Vite Christi, olim S. Bonaventuro attributae*, ed. M. Stalling-Taney, CCCM, 153 (Turnholt, 1997), 271.

62 'Precedente die martirii sui dominus Ihesus ei in nocte apparuit. dicens. O olaue. aperi oculos tuos. et respice superius. Qui sursum respiciens uidit scalam pulcherrimam de celo depositam usque ad terram et descendentes angelos cum dulcissimo cantico. portantes coronas rubeas de rosis dicentes. Hiis rosis coronabitur rex et conciuis noster Olauus. Et christus ayt. Hanc scalam carissime Olaue cum cantico angelorum rosis martirii coronatus. matre mea dilectissima te cum omnibus electis meis expectante. cras hora nona ascendes' (*MHN*, 280). See also Tate, 'The Cross as Ladder,' 261.

63 *Breviarium Nidrosiense*, qq.iiii.; Østrem, *The Office of Saint Olav*, 81; *ONid*, 372. The response *Felix commercium*, based on a responsory verse from the Office of St Vincentius, echoes (and represents an inversion of) the traditional antiphon for the octave day of Christmas: 'O admirabile commercium: Creator generis humani, animatum corpus sumens, de Virgine nasci dignatus est: et procedens homo sine semine, largitus est nobis suam deitatem' (O marvellous exchange, the creator of the

human race, taking a living body, deigns to be born of a virgin. And proceeding as a human, though not of human seed, he has given us his godliness) (*CAO*, 3985; *ONid*, 167).

64 Isaiah 13:10, 24:23; Jeremiah 15:9; Ezekiel 32:7; Joel 2:10, 3:15; Amos 8:9.

65 Matthew 27:45; Mark 15:33; Luke 23:44–5.

66 James, 'Two Lives of St Ethelbert.'

67 'Nec mirum si signa que in morte Christi apparuerunt et ante mortem huius membri Christi eiusque dilecti eandem presagiencia contiguerunt. Sol autem obscuratus tanquam ne uideret faciem auertit' (James, 'Two Lives of St Ethelbert,' 225).

68 *OH.Leg*, 196.

69 'Regem sane gloriosum pro Ihesu Christi nomine martyrizandum, presentarium luci subtrahendum, celestique gloria coronandum' (James, 'Two Lives of St Ethelbert,' 238).

70 *Skj* IA: 261.

71 *OH.Leg*, 196.

72 *Hkr*, 2: 378.

73 *OH.St*, 586.

74 E.g., The Leofric Collectar (ca. 1050–60) and the Red Book of Darley (ca. 1060). See *ONid*, 124–5.

75 Knut Liestøl, 'Når Stod Slaget på Stiklarstaðir?' *Maal og Minne* (1932): 1–28.

76 Simeon of Durham, *Historia Regum*, ed. Thomas Arnold, Rerum Brittanicarum medii aevi scriptores, 75 (London, 1885), 2: 8; D.W. Rollason, 'The Cults of Murdered Royal Saints in Anglo-Saxon England.' *Anglo-Saxon England* 11 (1983): 1–22 at 5, 13.

77 *AASS* July, 4: 300; Rollason, 'The Cults of Murdered Royal Saints,' 9–10, 13 .

78 *AASS* June, 1: 86; Rollason, 'The Cults of Murdered Royal Saints,' 5–9, 13.

79 Raine, ed., *The Historians of the Church of York*, 2: 39; *Aelfric's Lives of Saints*, ed. Walter W. Skeat, EETS Original Series, 94 (Oxford, 1890, repr. 1966), 2: 136–7; Bede, *Bede's Ecclesiastical History of the English People*, ed. Bertram Colgrave and R.A.B. Mynors (Oxford, 1969), III.11, 246–7. Rollason, 'The Cults of Murdered Royal Saints,' 13. It is noteworthy that Ælfric refers to the light as a sun-beam: 'Hwæt þa god geswutelode þæt he halig sanct wæs. / swa þæt heofonlic leoht ofer þæt geteld astreht / stód up to heofonum swilce healic sunnbeam / ofer elle ða niht' (Behold then God showed that he was a holy Saint, so that a heavenly light, being extended over the tent, stood up to heaven like a lofty sunbeam all the night long).

80 James, 'Two Lives of St Ethelbert,' 229–30; Rollason, 'The Cults of Murdered Royal Saints,' 9, 13.

81 Christine Fell, ed., *Edward King and Martyr* (Leeds, 1971), 7. Rollason, 'The Cults of Murdered Royal Saints,' 2, 13.

82 Arnold, ed., *Memorials of St Edmund's Abbey*, 1: 27–8.

83 *The Anglo-Saxon Chronicle: A Collaborative Edition*, vol. 8: *MS F*, ed. Peter S. Baker (Cambridge, 2000), 54 (entry for 789); Rollason, 'The Cults of Murdered Royal Saints,' 3–5, 13.

84 William Dugdale, *Monasticon Anglicanum* (London, 1830; repr., Westmead, Hants., 1970), 6: 229–30; Rollason, 'The Cults of Murdered Royal Saints,' 11, 13.

85 *OH.Leg*, 196.

86 'Lucernæ lumen magis in edito proferri, qvam in abscondito debeat occultari; fama virtutum & constantiæ, prudentia nobilissimi Principis latius diffunditur' (*SRD*, 3:346).

87 'Hæc videntes ammirati sunt cuncti, gaudentes tripudio in Domino, Qui solus facit mirabilia in sæcula' (*Vita Oswaldi*, in Raine, ed., *The Historians of the Church of York*, 1:450), cf. Psalm 71:18.

88 PL 198: 1633–4. See Rose Jeffries Peebles, *The Legend of Longinus in Ecclesiastical Tradition and in English Literature*, Bryn Mawr College Monographs, 9 (Baltimore, 1911), 12–26.

89 *OH.Leg*, 206, 210.

90 *MHN*, 133.

91 *Passio Olaui*, 74–5; Kunin and Phelpstead, *A History of Norway and The Passion and Miracles of the Blessed Óláfr*, 32–3.

92 *GNH*, 112. Cf. *Hkr*, 2: 394–6 and *OH.St*, 587–9.

93 James, 'Two Lives of Ethelbert,' 243.

94 *Miracula Sancti Oswaldi*, in Raine, ed., *The History of the Church of York*, 2: 49.

95 *AASS*, 6: 589.

96 Cf., e.g., the stories about St Julian (Krusch, ed., MGH, Scriptores rerum Merovingicarum, 1: 565–6) and St Martin (ibid., 626).

97 *OH.Leg*, 206; *OH.St*, 598–601.

98 *Hkr*, 3: 208–9, *OH.St*, 640–1.

99 *VSD*, 273–4, 354, 401, 403.

100 *MHN*, 48–50; David and Ian McDougall, trans., *Theodoricus Monarchus: Historia de Antiquitate Regum Norwagiensium*, 37–8.

101 *Saxonis Gesta Danorum*, ed. J. Olvik and H. Ræder (Copenhagen, 1931), 1: 302–3. Saxo's account does not mention Óláfr – it reports that Magnús had a marvellous dream advising him of his victory.

102 *Ágrip*, 37–8. The story is also found in *Hkr*, 3: 43–5 and in *OH.St*, 628–30.

103 Adam of Bremen, *Gesta*, ch. 79 and schol. 56(57), 136–8.

104 *Henrik Høyers Annaler* (1042), *Annales Reseniani* (1043), *Annales Regii* (1043), *Gottskalks Annáll* (1043), and *Oddverja Annáll* (1043). See Gustav Storm, ed., *Islandske Annaler indtil 1578* (Christiania, 1888).

105 Paulus of Milan, *Vita di S. Ambrogio* Verba Seniorum. Collana di testi e studi patristici, n.s., 1 (Rome, 1961), 123–4.

106 Bjarni Guðnason, ed., *Danakonunga sǫgur: Skjǫldunga saga, Knýtlinga saga, Ágrip af Sǫgu danakonunga*, ÍF, 35 (Reykjavík, 1982), 292.

107 The earliest prose account is found in a fragment of a twelfth-century saga related to the lost *First Saga and OH.Leg*. See *Brudst*, 35. There are also versions in *OH.Leg* (210, 212); the *Acta Sancti Olavi* (*MHN*, 133–4); *Passio Olaui* (75–8); *GNH* (112–13); *Hkr*, 3: 135–7; and *OH.St* (631–3).

108 See Kunin, trans., and Phelpstead, ed., *A History of Norway and The Passion and Miracles of the Blessed Óláfr*, 109–10, for a discussion of Gutthormr's identity.

109 See ibid., 110, for a discussion of Margaðr's identity.

110 Lidén, *Olav den helige i medeltida bildkonst*, 201. Carl Phelpstead notes that 'Icelandic churches dedicated to Óláfr had stones carved from lava as reminders of this miracle' (Kunin, trans., and Phelpstead, ed., *A History of Norway and The Passion and Miracles of the Blessed Óláfr*, 114), and an informative note in *Diplomatarium Islandicum* reports that 'Óláfssteinar' could be seen in the churchyard at Þingvellir as late as 1873 (1: 1264–5).

111 *OH.Leg*, 214; *Acta Sancti Olavi* (*MHN*), 136–7; *Passio Olaui*, 78–9; *GNH*, 115; *Hkr*, 3: 137–8; *OH.St*, 636–7.

112 See C. Grant Loomis, *White Magic* (Cambridge, MA, 1948), 99–100 for numerous examples.

113 *Norges gamle love*, 1: 349.

114 The author of the Norwegian Homily comments, 'Nu mego þér høyra maclegaʀ repſſíngar ok fatiðlegar iartegnir' (Now you will hear of worthy discoveries and seldom miracles) (*GNH*, 115); and the *Acta* and the *Passio Olaui* exclaim 'O recens et ante tempus illud inauditum miraculum!' (O recent miracle, unheard before this time) (*Acta* [*MHN*], 137; *Passio Olaui*, 79).

115 E.g., the legends of St Pharahildis (*AASS* January, 1: 170–3) and Paulinus of Nola, *Georgii Florentii Gregorii Turonensis Libri Octo Miraculorum*, ed. B. Krusch, MGH, Scriptores rerum Merovingicarum 1 (Hannover, 1885), 818–19.

116 Henrique Florez, ed., *España Sagrada* (Madrid, 1753), 10: 507.

117 See the Martyrologies of Jerome (*AASS* November, 2, pt. 2:337) and Usuard (*AASS* June, 6: 328–9) and the twelfth-century calendar of the Abbey of St Mary and St Werburgh in Chester (Francis Wormald, ed., *English Benedictine Kalendars* after A.D. 400 [London, 1939], 1: 98, 105).

118 Cf. Matthew 4:3–4 and Luke 4:1–4.

119 *Brudst*, 36; *OH.Leg*, 214, 216, and 228; *MHN*, 137; *Passio Olaui*, 79–80; *GNH*, 115–16; *Hkr*, 3: 271–2; *OH.St*, 648–9. *Brudst*, *OH.Leg*, and *OH.St* identify the woman as Þóra Gutthormsdóttir, while Snorri mistakenly says she was the mother of Sigurðr *Jórsalafari*. The other versions do not mention the woman by name.

120 *Brudst*, 36; *OH.Leg*, 228; *MHN*, 137–8; *Passio Olaui*, 80; *GHN*, 116; *Hkr*, 3: 334; *OH.St*, 649.

121 *Hkr*, 3: 369–71.

122 *OH.St*, 605–7.

123 *Hkr*, 3: 370–1.

124 *Orkneyinga Saga*, ed. Finnbogi Guðmundsson, ÍF, 34 (Reykjavík, 1965), 193–224, 236–7; *Hkr*, 3: 324, 370–2, 378, 381–3, 390; and Benedikt S. Benedikz, *The Varangians of Byzantium* (Cambridge, 1978), 217, to which I am indebted for the following account.

125 *OH.St*, 834; Benedikz, *The Varangians of Byzantium*, 152–3.

126 Benedikz, *The Varangians of Byzantium*, 186.

127 *Brudst*, 35–6; *OH.Leg*, 212, 214; *MHN*, 135–6; *Passio Olaui*, 76–8; *GNH*, 114; *Hkr*, 3: 371–2; *OH.St*, 633–7.

128 The Petchenegs (*Πετζινάκοι*) were a Turkic people who had occupied much of the Ukraine, Moldavia, and Wallachia since the tenth century.

129 '... the emperor desired to dismount from his horse and continue the struggle on foot with the soldiers. When the Romans did not agree to this, he ordered the axe-bearers around him (this is the British nation [actually the Varangians], which has been in service to the Romans' emperors from a long time back) to cut apart with their axes the opposing [wagons]. Since they at once entered the conflict, the emperor thus became master of the Petchenegs' camp' (Joannes Cinnamus, *Ionnis Cinnami Epitome, rerum ab Ioanne et Alexio Comnenis gestarum*, ed. August Meineke, Corpus Scriptorum Historiae Byzantinae, 1 [Bonn, 1836], 7–8; John Kinnamos, *Deeds of John and Manuel Comnenus by John Kinnamos*, trans. Charles M. Brand [New York, 1976], 16).

130 Benedikz, *The Varangians of Byzantium*, 151; *Nicetae Choniatae Historia*, ed. Jan Louis van Dieten, Corpus Fontium Historiae Byzantinae, 11 (2 vols.) (Berlin, 1975), 1: 14–16.

131 Odd Sandaaker, 'Mirakelet på Pezina-vollane,' *Collegium Medievale* 4 (1991): 85–97.

132 *Brudst*, 36–7; *OH.Leg*, 216, 218; *MHN*, 138–9; *Passio Olaui*, 80–2; *GNH*, 117–18; *Hkr*, 3: 334–7; *OH.St*, 650–4.

133 *Hkr*, 3: 336.

134 Romans 8:28–30. Cf. James 1:12: 'Blessed is the man that endureth temptation: for when he hath been proved, he shall receive the crown of life which God hath promised to them that love him.'

135 *Geisli*, 62.5, 7.

136 *Geisli*, 63.2–3.

137 Raine, ed., *The Historians of the Church of York*, 1: 449.

138 *SRD*, 3: 343.

139 *Joannis Saresberiensis ... Opera Omnia*, 5: 364.

140 John 21:25.

Bibliography

Primary Sources

Acta Sanctorum quotquot toto orbe coluntur. Edited by Johannes Bollandus et al. 64 vols. Paris, 1863–75 [*AASS*].

Adam of Bremen. *Gesta Hammaburgensis ecclesiae pontificum*. In *Hamburgische Kirchengeschichte*, edited by Bernhard Schmeidler. MGH, Scriptores rerum Germanicarum in usum scholarum separatim editi, 2. 3rd ed. Hannover, 1917.

Ælfric's Catholic Homilies. The First Series. Text. Edited by Peter Clemoes. EETS Supplemental Series, 17. Oxford, 1997.

Ælfric's Catholic Homilies. Introduction, Commentary, and Glossary. Edited by Malcolm Godden. EETS Supplemental Series, 18. Oxford, 2000.

Aelfric's Lives of Saints. Edited by Walter W. Skeat. EETS Original Series, 76 and 82 (vol. 1), 94 and 114 (vol. 2). Oxford, 1881–1900. Reprint as 2 vols, 1966.

Ágrip af Nóregs konunga sögum. Edited by Finnur Jónsson. Halle, 1929 [*Ágrip*].

The Anglo-Saxon Chronicle: A Collaborative Edition. Vol. 8: *MS F: A semi-diplomatic edition with introduction and indices*. Edited by Peter S. Baker. Cambridge, 2000.

Arbeo of Freising. *Vita vel passio Haimhrammi episcopi et martyris* Ratisbonensis. Edited by E. Dümmler. *Passiones Vitaeque Sanctorum Aevi Merovingici*. MGH, Scriptorum rerum Merovingicarum, 4. Hannover, 1892.

Arnold, Thomas, ed. *Memorials of St Edmund's Abbey*. Rerum Britannicarum medii aevi scriptores, 96. 3 vols. London, 1890–6.

Augustine. *Enarrationes in Psalmos*. CCSL, 38–40. Turnhout, 1956.

Bede. *Bedae Venerabilis: Opera homiletica; Opera rythmica*. Edited by D. Hurst. CCSL, 122. Turnhout, 1955.

– *Bede's Ecclesiastical History of the English People*. Edited by Bertram Colgrave and R.A.B. Mynors. Oxford, 1969.

230   Bibliography

Bergsbók. Perg. Fol. Nr. 1, Royal Library, Stockholm. Edited by Gustaf Lindblad. Early Icelandic Manuscripts in Facsimile, 5. Copenhagen, 1963.

Biskupa Sögur I. Edited by Sigurgeir Steingrímsson, Ólafur Halldórson, and Peter Foote. ÍF, 15. 2 vols. Reykjavík, 2003.

Bjarni Guðnason, ed. *Danakonunga sǫgur: Skjǫldunga saga, Knýtlinga saga, Ágrip af sǫgu danakonunga.* ÍF, 35. Reykjavík, 1982.

Borgfirðinga Sǫgur. Edited by Sigurður Nordal and Guðni Jónsson. ÍF, 3. Reykjavík, 1938.

Breviarium Nidrosiense. Paris, 1519. Reprint, Oslo, 1964.

Byskupa Sögur. Edited by Guðni Jónsson. 2 vols. Reykjavík, 1948.

Cederschiöld, G., ed. *Geisli eða Óláfs Drápa ens Helga er Einarr orti Skúlason. Eftir 'Bergsboken' Utgifven.* Lunds Universitets Årsskrift, 10. Lund, 1873 [C].

Codex Regius to the Younger Edda. Ms. no. 2367 in the Old Royal Collection in the Royal Library of Copenhagen. Edited by Elias Wessén. Corpus codicum islandicorum medii aevi, 14 [facsimile ed.]. Copenhagen, 1940.

Codex Trajectinus: The Utrecht Manuscript of the Prose Edda. Edited by Anthony Faulkes. Early Icelandic Manuscripts in Facsimile, 15 [facsimile ed.]. Copenhagen, 1985.

Codex Wormianus (The Younger Edda). Ms. no. 242 fol. in the Arnemagnean Collection in the University Library of Copenhagen. Edited by Sigurður Nordal. Corpus codicum islandicorum medii aevi, 2 [facsimile ed.]. Copenhagen, 1931.

Diplomatarium Islandicum. Edited by Jón Sigurðsson and Jón Þorkelsson. 5 vols. Copenhagen, 1857–99.

Dreves, Guido Maria, S.J., and Clemens Blume, S.J., eds. *Analecta Hymnica Medii Ævi.* 55 vols. Leipzig, 1886–1922 [AH].

Edda. Translated by Anthony Faulkes. London, 1987.

Edda Snorra Sturlusonar. 3 vols. Copenhagen, 1848–87.

Faulkes, Anthony, ed. *Snorri Sturluson Edda: Skáldskaparmál.* 2 vols. London, 1998 [AF].

Fell, Christine, ed. *Edward King and Martyr.* Leeds, 1971.

Finnur Jónsson, ed. *Den norsk-islandske skjaldedigtning. A: Tekst efter håndskrifterne.* I–II. *B: Rettet Tekst.* I–II. Copenhagen, 1912–15 [Skj].

Flateyjarbók (Codex flateyensis). Ms. no. 1005 fol. in the Old Royal Collection in the Royal Library of Copenhagen. Edited by Finnur Jónsson. Corpus codicum islandicorum medii aevi, 1 [facsimile ed.]. Copenhaen, 1930.

Florez, Henrique, ed. *España Sagrada.* 51 vols. Madrid, 1747–1879.

Gamal norsk homiliebok. Edited by Gustav Indrebø. Oslo, 1931 [GNH].

Gertz, M. Cl., ed. *Vitae Sanctorum Danorum.* Novam Editionem Criticam. Selskabet for Udgivelse of Kilder til Dansk Historie. Copenhagen, 1908–1912 [VSD].

Gervais of Melkley. *Ars Poetica.* Edited by Hans-Jürgen Gräbner. Münster, 1965.

Glælognskviða av Toraren Lovtunge. Edited by Hallvard Magerøy. Oslo, 1948.

Glossa Ordinaria. Edited by Nicholas of Lyra. 7 vols. Paris, 1590.

Gregory of Tours. *Opera Omnia*. Edited by W. Arndt and B. Krusch. MGH, Scriptores rerum Merovingicarum, 1. Hannover, 1884–5.

Hesbert, Renato-Joanne, ed. *Corpus Antiphonalium Officii*. 6 vols. Rome, 1963–79 [*CAO*].

The Icelandic Homily Book: Perg. 150 in the Royal Library, Stockholm. Edited by Andrea de Leeuw van Weenen. Íslenzk handrit, Series in quarto, 3. Reykjavík, 1993.

Iohannis de Caulibus. *Meditaciones Vite Christi, olim S. Bonaventuro attributae*. Edited by M. Stallings-Taney. CCCM, 153. Turnholt, 1997.

Jacobus de Voragine. *De sancto Olauo rege norwegie ac dacie martire*. In *Historiae plurimorum sanctorum nouiter et laboriose ex diversis libris in unum collecte*. Leuven, 1485, 101–3. Reprint. *MHN*, 277–82.

James, M.R., ed. 'Two Lives of St Ethelbert, King and Martyr.' *EHR* 32 (1917): 214–44.

Jerome [Hieronymus]. *Comentarii in Epistulas Pauli Apostoli ad Titum et ad Philemonem*. Edited by Federica Bucchi. CCSL, 77 C. Turnhout, 2003.

Joannes Cinnamus. *Ioannis Cinnami Epitome rerum ab Ioanne et Alexio Comnenis gestarum*. Edited by August Meineke. Corpus Scriptorum Historiae Byzantinae, 25. Bonn, 1836.

Joannis Saresberiensis Postea Episcopi Carnotensis Opera Omnia. Edited by J.A. Giles. 5 vols. London, 1848; repr. Leipzig, 1969.

John Scotus Eriugena. *Expositiones in Ierarchiam Coelestem*. Edited by J. Barbet. CCCM, 31. Turnholt, 1975.

Kinnamos, John. *Deeds of John and Manuel Comnenus by John Kinnamos*. Translated by Charles M. Brand. New York, 1976.

Kock, Ernst A., ed. *Den norsk isländska skaldediktningen*. 2 vols. Lund, 1946–9 [*EAK*].

Kuhn, Hans. *Das Dróttkvætt*. Heidelberg, 1983.

Kunin, Devra, trans., and Carl Phelpstead, ed. *A History of Norway and The Passion and Miracles of the Blessed Óláfr*. Viking Society for Northern Research Text Series, 13. London, 2001.

Leifar fornra kristinna fræða íslenzkra. Edited by Þorvaldur Bjarnarson. Copenhagen, 1878.

The Leofric Collectar (Harl. ms. 2961). With an appendix containing a litany and prayers from Harl. ms. 863. Edited by E.S. Dewick and Walter Frere. 2 vols. Henry Bradshaw Society, 45, 56. London, 1914–21.

The Leofric Missal as Used in the Cathedral of Exeter during the Episcopate of its First Bishop A.D. 1050–1072, together with Some Account of the Red Book of Derby, the Missal of Robert of Jumièges, and a Few Other Early Manuscript Service

Books of the English Church. Edited by Frederick Edward Warren. Oxford, 1883.

Louis-Jensen, Jonna, ed. "'Syvende og ottende brudstykke." Fragmentet AM 325 IV 4to,' *Opuscula*, 4, 31–60. Copenhagen, 1970 [*Brudst*].

Milfull, Inge B. *The Hymns of the Anglo-Saxon Church*. Cambridge Studies in Anglo-Saxon England, 17. Cambridge, 1996 [*HASC*].

Monumenta Historica Norvegiæ. Edited by Gustav Storm. Kristiania, 1880 [*MHN*].

Morkinskinna. Edited by Finnur Jónsson. Samfund til udgivelse af gammel nordisk Litteratur, 53. Copenhagen, 1932.

Nicetae Choniatae Historia. Edited by Jan Louis van Dieten. Corpus Fontium Historiae Byzantinae, 11.1–2. 2 vols. Berlin, 1975.

Norges gamle love indtil 1387. 5 vols. Christiania, 1846–95.

Olafs Saga hins Helga: Die 'Legendarische Saga' über Olaf den Heiligen (Hs. Delagard. saml. nr. 8^II). Edited and translated by Anne Heinrichs, Doris Janshen, Elke Radicke, and Hartmut Röhn. Germanische Bibliothek. Reihe 4. Texte. Heidelberg, 1982 [*OH.Leg*].

Ordo Nidrosiensis Ecclesiae (Orðubók). Edited by Lilli Gjerløw. Oslo, 1968 [*ONid*].

Orkneyinga Saga. Edited by Finnbogi Guðmundsson. ÍF, 34. Reykjavík, 1965.

Passio Olaui: Passio et Miracula Beati Olaui. Edited by Frederick Metcalfe. Oxford, 1881 [Passio Olaui].

Passio Sanctarum Perpetuae et Felicitatis. Edited by Cornelius Ioannes Maria Ioseph von Beek. Nijmegen, 1936.

Paulus of Milan. *Vita di S. Ambrogio*. Edited by Michele Pellegrino. Verba Seniorum. Collana di testi e studi patristici, n.s., 1. Rome, 1961.

Plácitus drápa. Edited by Jonna Louis-Jensen. In *Plácidus Saga: with an Edition of Plácitus drápa by Jonna Louis-Jensen*, edited by John Tucker. Editiones Arnamagnæanæ, series B, vol. 31. Copenhagen, 1998.

[Rafn, C.C., et al., eds.] *Fornmannasögur eptir gömlum handritum*. 12 vols. Copenhagen, 1825–378 [*FMS*].

Raine, James, ed. *The Historians of the Church of York and Its Archbishops*. Rerum Britannicarum medii aevi scriptores, 71. 3 vols. London, 1879–94. Reprint, Wiesbaden, 1965.

Rhetorica ad Herennium. In *M. Tulli Ciceronis Scripta quæ Manserunt Omnnia. Fasc. 1. Incerti Auctoris de Ratione Dicendi ad C. Herennium Lib. IV*, edited by Friedrich Marx. Leipzig, 1923.

Rimbert. *Vita Anskarii*. Edited by G. Waitz. MGH, Scriptores rerum Germanicarum in usum scholarum, 55. Hannover, 1884.

Saxo. *Saxonis Gesta Danorum*. Edited by J. Olrik and H. Ræder. Copenhagen, 1931.

Schöning, Gerhardus, ed. *Heimskringla eðr Noregs Konunga Sögur*. 3 vols. Copenhagen, 1777–1826 [S].

Scriptores Rerum Danicarum Medii Aevi. Edited by Jacobus Langebek. 9 vols. Copenhagen, 1772–1878. Reprint, Nendeln, 1969 [*SRD*].

Scriptores Rerum Suecicarum. Edited by Eric Michael Fant. 3 vols. Uppsala, 1818–76. Reprint, Graz, 1966 [*SRS*].

Sievers, Eduard. *Altgermanische Metrik.* Sammlung Kurzer Grammatiken Germanischer Dialekte, Ergänzungsreihe, 2. Halle, 1893.

– *Zur Rhythmik des germanischen Alliterationsverses.* Beiträge zur Geschichte der deutschen Sprache und literatur, 10. Tübingen, 1885. Reprint, New York, 1909.

Sijmons, B., and H. Gering, eds. *Die Lieder der Edda.* 3 vols. Halle, 1903–31.

Simeon of Durham. *Symeonis Monachi Opera Omnia.* Edited by Thomas Arnold. Rerum Britannicarum medii aevi scriptores, 75. 2 vols. London, 1882–5.

Slay, D., ed. *Romances. Perg. 4:o NR 6, Royal Library, Stockholm.* Early Icelandic Manuscripts in Facsimile, 10. Copenhagen, 1972.

Snorre Sturlasons Edda: Uppsala – Handskriften DG 11. Facsimileedition i ljustryck på uppdrag av Sveriges Riksdag. Ed. Anders Grape [facsimile ed.]. 2 vols. Uppsala, 1962–77.

Snorri Sturluson. *Edda Snorra Sturlusonar.* Edited by Finnur Jónsson. Copenhagen, 1931 [*SnE 1931*].

– *Heimskringla.* Edited by Bjarni Aðalbjarnarson. ÍF, 26–8. Reykjavík, 1941–51, 2nd ed. 1979 [*Hkr*].

Stjórn. Edited by C.R. Unger. Oslo, 1862.

Den store saga om Olav den Hellige. Edited by Oscar Albert Johnsen and Jón Helgason. Norske historiske kildeskriftfond. Skrifter, 53. 2 vols. Oslo, 1930 [*OH.St*].

Storm, Gustav, ed. *Islandske Annaler indtil 1578.* Christiania, 1888.

– ed. *Otte Brudstykker af den Ældste Saga om Olav den Hellige.* Christiania, 1893.

Theodoricus Monachus Historia de Antiquitate Regum Norwagiensium: An Account of the Ancient History of the Norwegian Kings. Translated by David and Ian McDougall. Viking Society for Northern Research Text Series, 11. London, 1998.

Thomas Aquinas. *Summa theologiae: Latin Text and English Translation, Introductions, Notes, Appendices and Glossaries.* Edited by Thomas Gilby et al. 61 vols. London, 1964–81.

Unger, C.R., ed. *Heilagra manna søgur: Fortællinger og Legender om hellige Mænd og Kvinder.* 2 vols. Christiania, 1877.

– ed. *Postola Sögur: Legendariske Fortællinger om Apostlernes Liv. Deres Kamp for Kristendommens Udbredelse samt deres Martyrdød.* Christiania, 1874.

Vigfússon, G., and C.R. Unger, eds. *Flateyjarbók.* 3 vols. Christiania, 1860–8.

Vigfússon, G., and F. York Powell, eds. *Corpus Poeticum Boreale.* 2 vols. Oxford, 1883 [*CPB*].

Vita Pardulfi Abbatis Waractensis. Edited by B. Krusch and W. Levison. *Passiones Vitaeque Sanctorum Aevi Merovingici.* MGH, Scriptores rerum Merovingicarum, 7. Hannover and Leipzig, 1920.

Vita Sanctae Balthildis. Edited by B. Krusch. *Fredegarii et Aliorum Chronica. Vitae Sanctorum.* MGH, Scriptores rerum Merovingicarum, 2. Hannover, 1888.

Weber, Gerd Wolfgang. 'Saint Óláfr's Sword: Einarr Skúlason's *Geisli* and its Trondheim Performance AD 1153 – A Turning Point in Norwego-Icelandic Scaldic Poetry.' *The Sagas and the Norwegian Experience / Sagaene og Noreg: Proceedings of the 10th International Saga Conference.* Trondheim, 1997, 655–61.

Wennberg, Lars, ed. *Geisli. Einarr Skúlason orti. Öfversätning med Anmärkningar.* Diss. Lund, 1874 [*W*].

Wessén, Elias, ed. *Fragments of the Elder and the Younger Edda, AM 748 I and II 4:o.* Corpus codicum islandicorum medii aevi, 17 [facsimile ed.]. Copenhagen, 1945.

Whaley, Diana, ed. *The Poetry of Arnórr jarlaskáld: An Edition and Study.* Westfield Publications in Medieval Studies, 8. London, 1998.

de Winterfeld, Paulus, ed. *Poetae Latini Aevi Carolini.* MGH, Poetarum Latinorum Medii Aevi, 4. Berlin, 1899.

Wisén, Theodor, ed. *Carmina Norrœnæ. Ex Reliquiis Vetustioris Norrœnæ Poesis. Selecta, Regognita, Commentariis et Glossario Instructa* 1 [texts and commentary] – 2 [glossary]. Lund, 1886–9 [*CN*].

Secondary Studies

Alexander Johannesson. *Íslenzk Tunga í Fornöld.* Reykjavík, 1923–4.

Asgaut Steinnes, 'Om Bergsbók i 1500 åri.' *Maal og Minne* (1962): 9–30.

Attwood, Katrina. 'Intertextual Aspects of the Twelfth-Century Christian *Drápur*.' *Saga Book* 24 (1996): 221–39.

Bagge, Sverre. *The Political Thought of The King's Mirror.* Mediaeval Scandinavia Supplements, 3. Odense, 1987.

Benedikt S. Benedikz. *The Varangians of Byzantium: An Aspect of Byzantine Military History.* Cambridge, 1978 [= Sigfús Blöndal, *Væringja saga.* Reykjavík, 1954, 'translated, revised, and rewritten'].

Bjarni Guðnason, 'Theodoricus og íslenskir sagnaritarar.' In *Sjötíu ritgerðir helgaðar Jakobi Benediktssyni,* edited by Einar G. Pétursson and Jónas Kristjánsson, 107–20. Reykjavík ,1977.

Bjerknes, Kristian Bonnevie, and Hans-Emil Lidén. *The Stave Churches of Kaupanger: The Present Church and its Predecessors.* Norwegian Antiquarian Bulletin, 1. Oslo, 1975.

Boynton, Susan. 'Training for the Liturgy as a Form of Monastic Education.' In *Medieval Monastic Education,* edited by George Ferzoco and Carolyn Muessig, 7–20. London, 2000.

Braun, Joseph, S.J. *Der Christliche Altar*. 2 vols. Munich, 1924.

Bruce, Alexander M. *Scyld and Scef: Expanding the Analogues*. New York, 2002.

Chase, Martin. '*Concatenatio* as a Structural Element in the Christian *Drápur*.' In *The Sixth International Saga Conference: Workshop Papers*. 2 vols. Copenhagen, 1985, 1:115–29.

– 'Framir kynnask vátta mál: The Christian Background of Einarr Skúlason's *Geisli*.' In *Til Heiðurs og Hugbótar: Greinar um Trúarkveðskap Fyrri Alda*, edited by Svanhildur Óskarsdóttir and Anna Guðmundsdóttir, 11–32. Snorrastofa, Rit 1. Reykholt, 2003.

– 'The Refracted Beam: Einarr Skúlason's Liturgical Theology.' In *Verbal Encounters: Anglo-Saxon and Old Norse Studies for Roberta Frank*, edited by Antonina Harbus and Russell Poole, 203–21. Toronto, 2005.

Clover, Carol J., and John Lindow, eds. *Old Norse-Icelandic Literature: A Critical Guide*. Islandica, 45. Ithaca, NY, 1985.

Curtius, Ernst Robert. *European Literature and the Latin Middle Ages*. Translated by Willard R. Trask. Bollingen Series, 36. New York, 1953.

Danbolt, Gunnar. 'Bilde som tale: St Olavs-antemensalet i Nidarosdomen.' *Kunst og Kultur* 71 (1988): 138–58.

Dickins, Bruce. 'The Cult of Saint Olave in the British Isles.' *Saga Book* 12 (1940): 53–80.

Dugdale, William. *Monasticon Anglicanum: A History of the Abbies and Other Monasteries, Hospitals, Frieries, and Cathedral and Collegiate Churches, with their Dependencies, in England and Wales*. 6 vols. London, 1819–30. Reprint, Westmead, Hants, 1970.

Ekrem, Inger. 'Om *Passio Olavis* tilblivelse og eventuelle forbindelse med *Historia Norwegie*.' In *Olavslegenden og den latinske historieskrivning i 1100-tallets Norge*, edited by Inger Ekrem, Lars Boje Mortensen, and Karen Skovgaard-Petersen, 108–56. Copenhagen, 2000.

Ekrem, Inger, Lars Boje Mortensen, and Karen Skovgaard-Petersen, eds. *Olavslegenden og den latinske historieskrivning i 1100-tallets Norge*. Copenhagen, 2000.

Eliade, Mircea. *Patterns in Comparative Religion*. Translated by Rosemary Sheed. London, 1958.

Fidjestøl, Bjarni. *Det Norrøne Fyrstediktet*. Universitetet i Bergen. Nordisk institutts skriftserie, 11. Øvre Ervik, 1982.

– 'Sogekvæde.' *Deutsch-nordische Begegnungen: 9. Arbeitstagung der Skandinavisten des deutschen Sprachgebiets 1989 in Svendborg*. Edited by Kurt Braunmüller and Mogens Brøndsted, 57–76. Odense, 1991.

Finnur Jónsson. *Den oldnorske og oldislandske litteraturs historie*. 3 vols. Copenhagen, 1894–1902.

– 'Flateyjarbók.' *Aarbøger for Nordisk Oldkyndighed og Historie* (1927): 140.

Foote, Peter. '*Nafn guðs hit hæsta*.' In *Speculum Norrænum*, edited by Ursula Dronke, 139–54. Odense, 1981.

Gade, Kari Ellen. *The Structure of Old Norse* Dróttvkætt *Poetry*. Islandica, 49. Ithaca, NY, 1995.

Guðrún Nordal. *Tools of Literacy: The Role of Skaldic Verse in Icelandic Textual Culture of the Twelfth and Thirteenth Centuries*. Toronto, 2001.

Gunnes, Erik. *Erkebiskop Eystein, statsmann og kirkebygger*. Oslo, 1996.

– 'Om hvordan Passio Olavi ble til.' *Maal og Minne* (1973): 1–11.

Hallvard Lie. 'Dråpa.' *KLNM* 3:351–2.

Haugen, Einar. *The Scandinavian Languages: An Introduction to their History*. London, 1976.

Hoffmann, Erich. *Die heiligen Könige bei den Angelsachsen und den skandinavischen Völkern: Königsheiliger und Königshaus*. Quellen und Forschungen zur Geschichte Schleswig-Holsteins, 69. Neumünster, 1975.

Hreinn Benediktsson. 'Phonemic Neutralization and Inaccurate Rhymes.' *APS* 26 (1964): 9–11.

– 'The Vowel System of Icelandic: A Survery of Its History.' *Word* 15 (1959): 282–312.

Hughes, Andrew. 'The Monarch as the Object of Liturgical Veneration.' In *Kings and Kingship in Medieval Europe*, edited by Anne Duggan, 375–424. King's College London Medieval Studies, 10. London, 1993.

Jakob Benediktsson. 'Nogle Bemaerkninger om Bergsbók.' *APS* 16 (1942–3): 121–8.

Johnsen, Arne Odd. *Studier vedrørende Kardinal Nicolaus Brekespears Legasjon til Norden*. Oslo, 1945.

Jón Helgason. 'Norges og Islands digtning' (*Litteraturhistoria B*). *Nordisk Kultur*, 8B. Stockholm, 1944–53.

Jørgensen, Jon Gunnar. 'Passio Olavi og Snorre.' In *Olavslegenden og den latinske historieskrivning i 1100-tallets Norge*, edited by Inger Ekrem, 157–69. Lars Boje Mortensen, and Karen Skovgaard-Petersen. Copenhagen, 2000.

Kahle, Bernhard. *Die Sprache der Skalden auf Grund der Binnen- und Endreime. Verbunden mit einem Rimarium*. Strassburg, 1892.

Kock, Ernst Albin. *Notationes Norrænae: anteckningar till Edda och skaldediktning*. 27 vols. Lund, 1923–44 [*NN*].

Kreutzer, Gert. *Die Dichtungslehre der Skalden*. Hochschulschriften: Literaturwissenschaft, 1. 2nd rev. ed. Meisenheim am Glan, 1977.

Kristján Árnason. *The Rhythms of Dróttkvætt and Other Old Icelandic Metres*. Reykjavík, 1991.

Kuhn, Hans. *Das Dróttkvætt*. Heidelberg, 1983.

Lange, Bernt C. 'Olav den hellige: *Ikon.*' KLNM 12:568–77.

Lange, G. *Die anfängeder isländisch-norwegischen Geschichtsschreibung*. Studia Islandica, 46. Reykjavík, 1989.

Lange, Wolfgang. *Studien zur Christlichen Dichtung der Nordgermanen 1000–1200*. Palaestra, 222. Göttingen, 1958.

Lexicon Poeticum Antiquæ Linguæ Septentrionalis. Ordbog over det norsk-islandske skjaldesprog. Oprindelig forfattet af Sveinbjörn Egilsson. 2nd ed. Edited by Finnur Jónsson. Copenhagen, 1931.

Lidén, Anne. *Olav den helige i medeltida bildkonst: Legendmotiv oc attribut*. Stockholm, 1999.

Liestøl, Knut. 'Når Stod Slaget på Stiklestad?' *Maal og Minne* (1932): 1–28.

Lind, Erik Henrik. *Norsk-isländska dopnamn och fingerade namn från medeltiden*. Uppsala, 1905–15.

Loomis, C. Grant. *White Magic*. Cambridge, MA, 1948.

Louis-Jensen, Jonna. 'Den yngre del af Flateyjarbók.' In *Afmælisrit Jóns Helgasonar. 30. júní 1969*, edited by Jakob Benediktsson, Jón Samsonarson, Jónas Kristjánsson, Ólafur Halldórsson, and Stefán Karlsson, 235–50. Reykjavík, 1969.

Marold, Edith. *Kenningkunst: Ein Beitrag zu einer Poetik der Skaldendichtung*. Berlin, 1983.

Meissner, Rudolf. *Die Kenningar der Skalden: Ein Beitrag zur skaldischen Poetik*. Bonn/Leipzig, 1921.

Mortensen, Lars Boje. 'The Anchin Manuscript of *Passio Olaui* (Douai 295), William of Jumiæges, and Theodoricus Monachus: New Evidence for Intellectual Relations between Norway and France in the 12th Century.' *Symbolae Osloenses* 75 (2000): 165–89.

– 'The Nordic Archbishoprics as Literary Centres around 1200.' In *Archbishop Absalon of Lund and His World*, edited by Karsten Friis-Jensen and Inge Skovgaard-Petersen, 133–57. Roskilde, 2000.

– 'Olav den helliges mirakler i det 12. årh.: streng tekstkontrol eller fri fabuleren?' In *Olavslegenden og den latinske historieskrivning i 1100-tallets Norge*, edited by Inger Ekrem, Lars Boje Mortensen, and Karen Skovgaard-Petersen, 89–107. Copenhagen, 2000.

Mundal, Else. 'Den latinspråklege historieskrivinga og den norrøne tradisjonen: ulike teknikkar og ulike krav.' In *Olavslegenden og den latinske historieskrivning i 1100-tallets Norge*, edited by Inger Ekrem, Lars Boje Mortensen, and Karen Skovgaard-Petersen, 9–25. Copenhagen, 2000.

Noreen, Adolf. *Altnordische Grammatik, 1. Altisländische und altnorwegische Grammatik (Laut- und Flexionslehre) under Berücksichtigung des Urnordischen*. 4th ed. Halle, 1923.

Nygaard, Marius. *Norrøn Syntax.* Kristiania, 1905.

Orchard, Andy. *Cassell Dictionary of Norse Myth and Legend.* London, 1998.

Østrem, Eyolf. *The Office of Saint Olav: A Study in Chant Transmission.* Acta Universitatis Upsaliensis. Studia Musicologica Upsaliensia. Nova Series, 18. Uppsala, 2001.

– 'Om en nyoppdaget Olavslegende.' In *Olavslegenden og den latinske historieskrivning i 1100-tallets Norge,* edited by Inger Ekrem, Lars Boje Mortensen, and Karen Skovgaard-Petersen, 186–224. Copenhagen, 2000.

Paasche, Fredrik. *Kristendom og Kvad.* Kristiania, 1914.

Peebles, Rose Jeffries. *The Legend of Longinus in Ecclesiastical Tradition and in English Literature.* Bryn Mawr College Monographs, 9. Baltimore, 1911.

Robinson, Fred C. *Beowulf and the Appositive Style.* Knoxville, 1985.

Rollason, D.W. 'The Cults of Murdered Royal Saints in Anglo-Saxon England.' *Anglo-Saxon England* 11 (1983): 1–22.

Rygh, Oluf. *Norske Gaardnavne.* 18 vols. Kristiania, 1897–1915.

Sandaaker, Odd. 'Mirakelet på Pezina-vollane.' *Collegium Medievale* 4 (1991): 85–97.

Schottmann, Hans. 'Drápa.' *LMA* 3: 1367–8.

– *Die isländische Mariendichtung.* Münchner Germanistische Beiträge, 9. Munich, 1973.

Schrodt, Richard. 'Zwei altnordische Waffen(teil)namen und Egil Skallagrímsson, *Lv* 40.' *ANF* 90 (1975): 151–5.

Sievers, Eduard. *Altgermanische Metrik.* Halle, 1893.

– *Zur Rhythmik des germanischen Alliterationsverses.* Beiträge zur Geschichte der deutschen Sprache und Literatur, 10. Halle, 1885. Reprint, New York, 1909.

Sigurður Nordal. 'Icelandic Notes 1: Drápa.' *APS* 6 (1931–2): 144–9.

– *Om Olav den helliges saga.* Copenhagen, 1914.

Skard, E. 'Kirchliche Olavus tradition bei Theodoricus monachus.' *Symbolae Osloenses* 14 (1935): 119–25.

Skard, Vemund. 'Harmsól, Plácítúsdrápa og Leiðarvísan.' *ANF* 69 (1953): 97–108.

Stavnem, Rolf. 'Hør Kvasirs blod! Kenning og metafor i den norsk-islandske skjaldedigtning.' PhD diss., Københavns Universitet, 2002.

Stefán, Karlsson. 'NKS 1824b, 4to.' *Opuscula* 4: 368–9. Copenhagen, 1970.

– 'Perg. Fol. Nr. 1 (Bergsbók) og Perg. 4to Nr. 6 í Stokkhólmi.' *Opuscula* 3: 74–82. Copenhagen, 1967.

Steinnes, Asgaut. 'Om Bergsbók i 1500-åri.' *Maal og Minne,* 1962, 9–30.

Storm, Gustav. *Sigurd Ranessöns Proces.* Kristiania, 1877.

Tate, George Sheldon. 'The Cross as Ladder: *Geisli* 15–16 and *Líknarbraut* 34.' *Medieval Scandinavia* 11 (1978): 258–64.

– '*Líknarbraut*: A Skaldic *Drápa* on the Cross.' PhD diss., Cornell University, 1974.

Tolkien, J.R.R. '*Beowulf*: The Monsters and the Critics.' *Proceedings of the British Academy* 22 (1936): 245–95.

Turville-Petre, G. *Origins of Icelandic Literature*. Oxford, 1953.

Ulff-Møller, Jens. 'The Higher Numerals in Early Nordic Texts and the Duodecimal System of Calculation.' *The Audience of the Sagas: The Eighth International Saga Conference*. 2 vols. Göteborg, 1991, 2: 323–30.

Vilhelm Gödel. Katalog öfver Kungliga Bibliotekets fornisländska och fornnorska handskrifter. Stockholm, 1897–1900.

Weber, Gerd Wolfgang. 'Intellegere historiam: Typological Perspectives of Nordic Prehistory.' In *Tradition og historieskrivning: Kilderne til Nordens ældste historie*, edited by Kirsten Hastrup and Preben Meulengracht Sørensen. Acta Jutlandica 63: 3, Humanistisk Serie 61. Århus, 1987.

Westergård-Nielsen, Christian. 'Nogle Bemærkningar til Flatøbogens Historie.' In *Nordiska Studier i Filologi och Lingvistik. Festschrift Tillägnad Gösta Holm på 60-Årsgaden den 8 Juli 1976*, edited by Lars Svensson, Anne Marie Wieselgren, and Åke Hansson, 432–44. Lund, 1976.

Wood, Cecil. 'The Skald's Bid for a Hearing.' *JEGP* 59 (1960): 240–54.

Wormald, Francis, ed. *English Benedictine Kalendars after A.D. 400*. 2 vols. London, 1939.

Index

As in the glossary, ð is together with d, þ follows t, and æ, ø, œ, and ǫ follow z.

Toronto Old Norse–Icelandic Series